D1597588

Life Writing in Reformation Europe

Life Writing in Reformation Europe

Lives of Reformers by Friends, Disciples and Foes

IRENA BACKUS

ASHGATE

© Irena Backus 2008

Published by
Ashgate Publishing Limited
Gower House
Croft Road
Aldershot
Hampshire GU11 3HR
England

Ashgate Publishing Company
Suite 420
101 Cherry Street
Burlington, VT 05401–4405
USA

Ashgate website: http://www.ashgate.com

British Library Cataloguing in Publication Data
Backus, Irena Dorota, 1950–
    Life writing in Reformation Europe: lives of reformers by friends, disciples and foes. – (St Andrews studies in Reformation history) 1. Calvin, Jean, 1509–1564 2. Calvinists – Biography – History and criticism 3. Protestants – Biography – History and criticism 4. Biography – 16th century 5. Biography – 17th century 6. Christian biography – Europe
    I. Title
    284.2'0922

Library of Congress Cataloging-in-Publication Data
Backus, Irena Dorota, 1950–
    Life writing in Reformation Europe: lives of reformers by friends, disciples and foes / By Irena Backus.
        p. cm.—(St Andrews studies in Reformation history)
    Includes bibliographical references and index.
    ISBN-13: 978-0-7546-6055-2 (alk. paper)
    1. Reformation—Biography. 2. Europe—Church history—16th century. 3. Europe—Church history—17th century. I. Title.
    BR307.B33 2007
    274'.060922—dc22

                                                                    2007035129

ISBN 978-0-7546-6055-2

Printed and bound in Great Britain by MPG Books Ltd, Bodmin, Cornwall.

Contents

Introduction
Biography and Religious Biography: Pagan and Christian Models, and What Happened to Them in the Reformation Period

Sixteenth-century *Lives* of the Continental reformers have not been the object of any serious general study so far.[1] Although emanating from a wide variety of pens, the *Lives* written between 1533 and the mid-seventeenth century comprise a coherent and identifiable genre which falls into two subgenres: *Lives* of the reformers as restorers of true faith, and *Lives* of them as heretics. The latter subgenre was practically unknown in Antiquity and in the Middle Ages, and constitutes a specific feature of literary production of the Reformation period. One of my aims will be to isolate it and consider its place in religious biographical literature. The authors of *Lives* portraying the reformers as restorers of true faith, who were naturally favourable to the Reformation, could look to ancient Greek and Roman *Lives*, such as those written in the imperial era by Plutarch or Suetonius, and to *Lives* of the saints. For obvious reasons, they could not exploit either model to the full. The present work is not intended to be a general survey, but rather a study of specific issues to do with *Life*-writing and more specifically the writing of *Lives* of reformers in sixteenth- and seventeenth-century Europe. After a brief introduction to the concepts of biography and religious biography, and a reminder of

---

[1]   Swiss and Genevan reformers have been particularly neglected. For modern studies of Luther's *Lives* by Herte and others, see Chapter 1 below. For Genevan reformers, cf. article by Marianne Carbonnier-Burkard, 'Une *Histoire d'excellens personnages*', in Ilona Zinguer and Myriam Yardeni (eds), *Les deux Réformes chrétiennes. Propagande et diffusion* (Leiden: Brill, 2004), pp. 43–59. See also Daniel Ménager, 'Théodore de Bèze, biographe de Calvin', *Bibliothèque d'Humanisme et Renaissance*, 45 (1983): 231–55, and Jean-Robert Armogathe, 'Les vies de Calvin aux XVIe et XVIIe siècles', in Philippe Joutard (ed.), *Historiographie de la Réforme* (Paris: Delachaux & Niestlé, 1977), pp. 45–59. Armogathe briefly examines hostile *Lives* of Calvin, esp. Florimond de Raemond, Bolsec, Papire Masson (the author of the *Vita Calvini* later attributed by Maimbourg and others to Jacques Gillot), Richelieu. He is interested, as he points out, not so much in biography as genre as in religious controversy carried over to the biographical terrain. He concludes that Calvin's Catholic adversaries intended their biographies of him as counter-examples to the *Lives* of the saints. As for the *Lives* of Swiss reformers, we might mention Christian Moser's critical edition (in progress) of the *Lives* of Bullinger by Simler, Lavater and Stucki. I shall be discussing these among other Swiss *Lives* in Chapter 2 below.

the genesis of both these genres, I shall examine in the chapters to follow a representative sample of *Lives* depicting the reformers as saints and as heretics, outlining the dependence of these accounts on classical models, but also stressing their original features that mark them out as product of their age and circumstances. I shall be interested in the way certain biographies or biographical details crossed national boundaries and assumed a European dimension thus generating a lasting image or images of certain reformers, Luther and Calvin in particular. I shall treat the Reformation in chronological order, beginning with a selection of *Lives* of Luther, then going on to examine the *Lives* of the major Swiss reformers, and finally ending with those of the Genevan reformation leaders, Calvin and Beza. The present work does not claim to exhaust the genre or the topic of *Life*-writing in Reformation Europe. Concentrating on selected *Lives* of the chief reformers, I shall sketch out their genesis, method and aims as well as showing context and likely readership where possible. Focusing on the influence of contemporary or near-contemporary *Lives* (both favourable and hostile) on the reception of Reformation, I hope to demonstrate that the portrayal of an individual was emphatically not the prime object of most *Lives* of the reformers, and contemporary historians should be careful before they treat any of these writings as documentary evidence about Luther, Calvin or Beza. In this instance, chronological proximity does not mean greater accuracy, and we should beware of making statements such as 'Beza, Calvin's biographer says ...'.

Greek and Roman Biography

The paragraphs that follow do not set out to add anything new to what we know already about antique biography writing, but are intended to serve as a general reminder of the nature of the biographical genre and its evolution in history.[2] It is important to remember that biography in Antiquity, and especially in Greece, was not a clearly defined genre, and that the term covered types of writing as different from one another as an *encomium*, a detailed account of a person's life or simply a catalogue of deeds of a great man. Truthfulness did not apply as a criterion, and some antique biography is frankly fanciful. The impulse to celebrate individuals finds its earliest expression in the dirge and the funeral oration. Organisation of literary works around the experiences of an individual goes all the way back to Homer. Moreover, from the fifth century BC onwards, all Greek historians tended to insert biographical sketches into accounts of

---

[2]   For an excellent succinct account, see C. B. R. Pelling, 'Biography, Greek and Roman', in Simon Hornblower and Anthony Spawforth (eds), *The Oxford Companion to Classical Civilization* (Oxford and New York: Oxford University Press, 2004), pp. 116–18.

wars, and so on. Thus Thucydides included selective sketches of several figures, notably Pausanias and Themistocles. Biography was not always serious and not always an expression of respect or reverence, Ion of Chios' *Epidemiai*, a book of anecdotes about contemporary figures, being a case in point. In the fourth century BC, Isocrates published *Evagoras*, which was no more than an enumeration of the king of Salamis' virtues in a loose chronological framework. In a similar style, Xenophon in his *Agesilaus* gave first a catalogue of his hero's achievements followed by an account of his virtues. He also developed the personality of Socrates in his *Socratic Memoirs*. According to Pelling,[3] Aristotle gave biographical writing a new impetus by awakening interest in social and ethical history. This furthered a more critical approach to subjects of biographical accounts, and also the writing of more generalised *Lives*. Thus a fashion developed for collections of *Lives* in series or identifiable socio-cultural groups – for example *Lives* of the poets, *Lives* of philosophers, *Lives* of military leaders, a completely separate genre from the *encomium*. This became the standard way of presenting intellectual history. It also influenced the presentation of political history, although the latter had other forms of expression such as universal history, local chronicles, and so on, which also increasingly accommodated sketches of individual figures. In about 240 BC, Antigonus of Carystus displayed a far greater accuracy than had been the practice hitherto in his *Lives* of contemporary philosophers. Christian Gospels have points of contact with the earlier Greek tradition, with their charismatic hero and their anecdotal structure. A far greater seriousness was to be displayed by Plutarch's *Parallel Lives* and the later Greek and Roman biographical writings.

Before addressing the later Roman Empire period, a few words need to be said about early Roman biography and its specific features. Roman biography was not wholly derived from the Greek. Romans had their own political and family customs which meant that they found it important to record the deeds of the great via *encomia*, funeral laudations, dirges and sepulchral inscriptions, and to keep the *imagines* or likenesses of deceased ancestors. Their competitive quest for glory also led to the cultivation of self-justificatory and apologetic accounts either in the form of autobiography or in the form of biography. These accounts benefited from the development of forensic rhetoric in the late republic period. Thus the death of Cato the Younger inspired works by Cicero and Brutus which were answered first by Aulus Hirtius and then by Caesar in his *Anticato*, which was refuted in turn by Munatius Rufus. Pelling notes rightly[4] that these works represent the beginning of an important literature, a blend of martyrology and ideological propaganda, which came to cluster round the Stoic opposition to the first-

---

[3] Ibid., p. 116.
[4] Ibid., pp. 117–18.

century Principate. The *Deaths of famous men* genre, such as Gaius Fannius'
three books on Nero's victims, dwelt especially on martyrdoms, setting the
tone for Christian accounts of saints and martyrs.

Significantly, Jerome names a canon of Roman biographers in the preface
to his *De viris illustribus*, where he singles out Varro, Cornelius Nepos,
Hyginus, Santra and Suetonius. Although this is how the church father
creates a literary lineage for his own collection of biographical sketches,
his list shows that the *Life* form could accommodate a vast range of genres.
Varro could be named for his *Imagines* or for his biographies of poets.
Cornelius Nepos wrote long biographies of Cato the Elder and Cicero, as
well as a series of 18 books containing some 400 short *Lives* of which only
a fragment (*On foreign generals*) survives today. Suetonius' *Caesars* reduces
the element of historical narrative and concentrates on the emperors'
behaviour and character under a series of headings or common places.

In his *Development of Greek Biography*, Arnaldo Momigliano makes
the point that the only period of ancient biography which we know from
direct acquaintance with the original works is the Roman Empire.[5] He
considered this period as especially important in biographical writing.
There were various reasons for this, the chief of them being the international
outlook of the imperial age, which expressed itself in the need for a
gallery of common illustrious ancestors, Greek and Roman. Indeed, it is
common knowledge that Trajan and Nerva particularly aimed to make
provincial citizens take a more active part in the Roman Empire rather
than have them merely obey orders coming down from Rome. Trajan
also wanted to ensure the moral unity of the empire. Propaganda was one
way of achieving these goals, and that meant having recourse to writers,
sophists and philosophers. In this context, Plutarch's *Parallel Lives* were
simply meant to show the cohesion of Greek and Roman civilisations by
revealing the parallels between their heroes. Plutarch's near contemporary
Suetonius, whom I mentioned above, produced a different type of work
with his *Lives* of the twelve Caesars, although he shared Plutarch's goal of
cementing the different regions of the empire by giving them one common
illustrious lineage. Whereas Plutarch ordered his *Lives* chronologically
without any subject divisions, Suetonius tended to impose a systematic
ordering. Thus, to take a random example, his *Life of Augustus* was
divided up into sections on Augustus' ancestry, his boyhood, civil wars,
foreign wars, the constitution, and social and religious affairs; political
reforms to the senate, the equestrian order and the people; policy on public
spectacles, Italian and Imperial policy, Augustus' public virtues, his family
and household, personal habits and private life, writings and personal
religion; death, burial and deification. We can thus speak of the Plutarchan

---

[5]   Arnaldo Momigliano, *The Development of Greek Biography* (Cambridge, MA:
Harvard University Press, 1971), p. 9.

and Suetonian biographical models at least for the later period, although this does not alter the heterogeneous nature of the biographical form in Greco-Roman intellectual tradition in general.[6]

More aware of his method than Suetonius, Plutarch considered his *Lives* as portraits and thereby introduced a psychological element into his biographies. His prime object, as he put it, was to seize a man's character by concentrating on those actions which were most revealing of it. This way of going about things often entailed omitting the hero's most illustrious actions, the very ones which guaranteed him a place in history. Plutarch thus consciously introduced a distinction between biography and history, which, coupled with his concern for morality, made his *Lives* both edifying and entertaining, guaranteeing them popularity not only as reading matter through the ages but also as source material for writers of fiction including Shakespeare.[7] However, as I have already pointed out, the portrait method, although consecrated by Plutarch, was operative in Rome long before his time. The most interesting example here is the lost *Imagines* or *Hebdomades* of Varro, which date from *c.* 39 BC. Judging by the testimony of Cicero (*Ad Atticum* 16, 11.3) and especially Aulus Gellius (*Noctes atticae* 3.11) and Pliny (*Nat. Hist.* 35, 11), they were planned as a selection of 700 portraits (in the literal sense of the term) of famous men from all walks of life, from kings to dancers. Each portrait was accompanied by an epigram characterising the individual in question, with learned remarks, a sort of footnotes, accompanying the poetic text. Two points should be made here. Varro placed himself in the Roman aristocratic tradition of *imagines* of ancestors.[8] At the same time, however, he went beyond the tradition by including Greeks as well as Romans, and by making their *imagines* available not just to the select few, but to educated readers throughout

---

[6]   Ibid., p. 86, considers that both types already existed in the Hellenistic period.

[7]   This is the famous passage in the preface to his *Lives* of Alexander and Caesar which establishes a distinction between biography and history: 'For they must remember that my intent is not to write histories but only lives. For the noblest deeds do not always show men's virtues and vices, but oftentimes a light occasion, a word, or some sport makes men's natural dispositions and manners appear more plain than the famous battles won, wherein are slain ten thousand men or the great armies or cities won by siege or assault. For like as painters or drawers of pictures, which make no account of other parts of the body do take the resemblances of the face and favour of the countenance in the which consisteth the judgement of their manners and disposition, even so they must give us leave to seek out the signs and tokens of the mind only and thereby show the life of either of them, referring you unto others to write the wars, battles and other great things they did.' Cf. Plutarch, *Selected Lives*, trans. Thomas North, selected and with an introduction by Judith Mossman (Ware: Wordsworth Editions, 1998), p. 385 (para. 1.1–3). For Plutarch's interest in morality, see especially J. Duff, *Plutarch's Lives. Exploring Virtues and Vice* (Oxford: Clarendon Press, 1999).

[8]   *Imago* in Rome was an image of a distinguished ancestor who had been consul, praetor, and so on, usually made of wax and placed in the atrium of a Roman house, and carried in a funeral procession. Cf. Momigliano, *Greek Biography*, p. 96.

the empire. This was thoroughly in keeping with the imperial principle of making all its provinces participate in its spirit and outlook.

Before going on to discuss some of the *Lives* of the reformers in the light of these models, it is important to weigh up the earlier Christian variants on the Greco-Roman paradigm, if it can be called that. The most important variants are the introduction of the miraculous and the replacement of pagan by Christian piety and moral values. In *Lives* of the saints, the saint most worthy of imitation was not the most illustrious and heroic individual, but the one who served God and the church with the most ardour, preferably suffering martyrdom at the end. This meant altering the Greek and Roman concept of fame and distinction. Christian saints and martyrs were often of obscure origin and some of them were women. Because of the modest social status of some of the heroes and heroines and because of the *Lives*' strong emphasis on the miraculous, it was important to guarantee the truth of the account by an appeal to first-hand witness. This could be done in two ways. The saint was acknowledged as genuine if he (or, more rarely, she) was canonised either by the bishop or, from the thirteenth century onwards, by the pope. This entailed a formal recognition by the ecclesiastical authorities of the saint's feast day, marking his or her entrance into the kingdom of heaven. These saints could be prayed to as intercessors, and their *Lives* were a source of edification and inspiration, their canonisation serving as sufficient guarantee of their truthfulness, however much legendary material they contained. In the case of holy individuals, such as monks, who were not canonised, the author of the *Life* had to attest to having witnessed the events described in their biographies. In the *Vitaspatrum*, for example, the reader is continually told that the author is no more than repeating what he had been told by a holy man who was present when the events in question took place. Quite often, as is shown again by the *Vitaspatrum*, *Lives* of the saints were not *Lives* in any strict sense at all, but simply descriptions of one particularly edifying episode in a holy man's life. Now, as we shall see, these traditional saints' *Lives* obviously could not and did not provide a direct model for the *Lives* of the reformers, although these could not escape the hagiographical elements altogether. There existed also more structured and sober funeral orations, such as those of Gregory of Nazianzus as well as *Lives* of eminent churchmen. These too belonged to Christian biographical production, as witnessed by the fourth- and fifth-century funeral orations on Athanasius and Basil of Caesarea, and by the *Lives* of Cyprian, Ambrose and Augustine. These could and did serve the sixteenth-century religious biographers, but again only up to a point. Possidius' *Life* of Augustine, which I shall now briefly examine as one prototype of Christian biography, was a priori very likely to influence the writers of favourable *Lives* of the reformers. Whether it did in fact is another matter, as the subsequent chapters will try to show.

Possidius' *Life* of Augustine

As Christine Mohrmann[9] points out, Possidius' *Life* of Augustine differs
from most saints' *Lives* in that it contains barely any mention of miracles
and has no recourse to legend. It follows closely, but not slavishly, the
pattern set by Suetonius while showing an awareness of Plutarch's method.
It falls into either three or four parts. According to the tripartite distinction,
it is composed of a chronological account of Augustine's life partly based
on the *Confessions* (chaps 1–18), an account of his *mores* (chaps 19–27.5)
and an account of his last days and death (chaps 27.6–31). If we adopt the
fourfold division, the first part is the account of Augustine's life prior to his
ordination as bishop (chaps 1–5) and part two an account of his activities in
the North African Church (chaps 6–18), with the latter two parts remaining
the same. Possidius stresses his personal knowledge of Augustine as
guaranteeing the truthfulness of his account. He punctuates his work with
frequent references to the intervention of divine grace[10] and concentrates on
facts related to his subject's life. There is very little psychological analysis.
Possidius constantly stresses Augustine's achievements for the unity of
the North African Church, achievements obtained with the help of other
bishops, all aided by Christ. Another related *leitmotif* is Augustine's fight
against all heretics, conducted orally and in writing. Interestingly enough,
however, despite his awareness of the Suetonian tradition, Possidius
does not devote a separate section to Augustine's literary production. By
contrast, he remains fully in keeping with Suetonius by including a section
on Augustine's public and private morals and conduct. So far as public
morals are concerned, he makes it clear that he considers Augustine a
model bishop because of his tireless preaching and his teaching activities:
he taught orthodox Christianity to those who were most apt to receive it
so that they would then pass the message on to others. Augustine's private
morals take up chapters 22–27. Moderate in his eating habits and dress,
Augustine also imposed a moderate ascetic discipline which deviated
neither into extreme asceticism, nor into luxury. He had no interest in the
financial aspect of running a monastery, and his contacts with the opposite
sex were very strictly regulated. He only ever visited widows and orphans
in cases of manifest hardship, never entered nunneries except in cases of
urgent need, and never became involved in anything to do with marriage,
including mediation and attending weddings. The account of Augustine's
last days is largely taken up with barbaric invasions and the Siege of Hippo,
during which Augustine finally fell ill. Describing this illness, Possidius

---

[9]   See *Vite dei Santi*, ed. Christine Mohrmann, vol. 3: *Vita di Cipriano, Vita
di Ambrogio, Vita di Agostino*, ed. A. A. R. Bastiaensen, trans. into Italian by
L. Canali and C. Catena (Milan: Mondadori, 1997).
[10]   Ibid., p. XLVII.

makes his sole reference to miracles he performed, which were of two
types: exorcism, and miraculous healing. Both serve as an illustration of
the power of prayer.[11] A letter by Augustine to Bishop Honoratus on how
bishops should behave in the face of barbaric invasion precedes the sober
lines on the last stages of Augustine's illness when, according to Possidius,
he finally found the solitude for meditation which had been denied him in
his life. Convinced of the necessity of doing penance, he had the text of the
penitential Psalms posted up in his cell. This detail suggests that Augustine,
in contrast with Egyptian monks, did not know the Psalms off by heart.
His death, as he did not suffer martyrdom, was portrayed by Possidius as
a model of a good Christian death. He died peacefully, surrounded by the
prayers of friends and colleagues (*dormiuit cum patribus suis, enutritus in
bona senectute* [cf. 3 Reg 2, 10]). He was buried by his friends after they
had celebrated the Eucharist. Possidius contrasts the material poverty in
which he died with the riches he left behind in the shape of monasteries for
men and women with libraries containing his own and other works. He
concludes that they who were most enriched by him were those who had
occasion to hear him preach.

The *Vita* contains several characteristics of pagan and Christian
biography. Augustine is separated from history, and, although the level
of psychological analysis is not very high and no physical description
whatsoever is given, the reader is left with a sort of exemplary portrait of
a moderate, zealous, chaste bishop constantly at work for the good of his
church. Needless to say, no mention is made of Augustine's illegitimate
son, fruit of a longstanding concubinage. His morals are depicted as the
quintessence of what Christian morals should be, especially with regard
to sexuality and attitude to women. The miraculous element, although
kept down to a minimum, is not altogether absent. Finally, Augustine dies
a good death, as befits an exemplary Christian churchman. Augustine's
Confessions were available to Possidius' readers, and any of them could
have learnt about his hero's dissolute youth. The fact that Possidius,
although he does allude to them, chooses to pass over their value as
documentary evidence tells something of the chasm between biography
and history. Although Possidius is generally considered as the most factual

---

[11]   See ibid., pp. 21–212. See especially pp. 210–213 (paras 29, 4–5): '... noui quoque
eumdem et presbyterum et episcopum pro quibusdam energumenis patientibus vt oraret
rogatum, eumque in oratione lacrimas fundentem Deum rogasse et daemones ab hominibus
recessisse. Itemque ad aegrotantem et lecto vacantem quemdam cum suo aegroto venisse et
rogauisse vt eidem manum imponeret quo sanus esse posset respondisse si aliquid esse posset,
sibi hoc vtique primitus praestitisset. Et illum dixisse visitatum se fuisse sibique per somnium
dictum esse: vade ad Augustinum episcopum vt eidem manum imponat et saluus erit. Quod
dum comperisset, facere non distulit et illum infirmum continuo Dominus sanum ab eodem
discedere fecit.'

of early Christian biographers, evaluation of evidence is just as irrelevant to him as giving a balanced picture of his hero's life.

What ancient biography did not practise were accounts of lives of villains or, in the case of Christian biographers, heretics. Any information on the life of Arius, for example, had to be pieced together from the works of Athanasius, the *Panarion* of Epiphanius, and other sources. There are certainly no ancient or medieval collections of *Vitae impiorum virorum* or *Vitae haereticorum*.

Medieval Hagiography and the Renaissance

Before beginning to speak of Reformation hagiography, it is vital to clarify what is meant by medieval hagiography. The term, which goes back to the second century AD, covers a very wide spectrum of writings, ranging from lives of the saints and accounts of findings of relics, through to papal canonisation bulls, accounts of visions, collections of stories of miracles and so on. These writings exist in Greek and Latin, and also in vernacular languages. Hagiography was practised particularly intensely throughout the Middle Ages, when it was closely linked to the medieval concept of sainthood and to the ritual of the cult of the saints. For medieval Christians, especially from the thirteenth century onwards, the saints were the dead who had received special recognition and who had entered the kingdom of God. Unlike the reformers who considered all believers dead or alive as saints without paying them any particular homage, except as members of the true church, the medieval church honoured particularly a limited number of the deceased, to whom it accorded the title of saint. In order to merit the title, the deceased had to satisfy a certain number of conditions, the most important of which was the celebration of the day of the saint's death which was coterminous with his or her entry into the kingdom of heaven – for example, the feast of St John, the feast of St Catherine, and so on. Although frequently in the later Middle Ages, recognition of a saint by the church was due to popular pressure, no one could as a rule become a saint without official ecclesiastical recognition, or canonisation which could be granted either by the bishop or by the pope. The latter practice was to become dominant in the West from the thirteenth century onwards, which did not stop a certain number of local cults of the saints. At the same time, the Eastern Church continued to canonise its saints by episcopal authority. This meant a proliferation of lists of saints and of calendars. All the saints, local, national or canonised by Rome, continued to be venerated for hundreds of years after their death, as is the case to this day. The most common form of hagiography was thus the *Lives* of the saints, which commemorated their particular merits and holiness. Their *Lives* could be divided into two closely related subgenres: biographical accounts and sermons. The purpose of these writings was to depict the saints as models of how Christians should live, and not to give an historical account of their origins, social context or personalities. Thus Gregory of Tours entitled his collection of *Lives* of twenty-three Gallic saints *De vita patrum* or *Life of the fathers* in the singular, because he wanted to stress the merits and virtues which made up the one ideal of sainthood. Differences of the number and quality of miracles, or the different types of abnegation practised by each were not important. Given this underlying aim and scope, it is inevitable that *Lives* of the saints should obey very strict rules of composition and that the saints should be depicted as followers and imitators of Christ *par excellence*. Certain motifs and certain expressions became their hallmarks, and were generally applicable regardless of the particular saint's origins, gender or identity.[12]

In the Renaissance, biographies became more extensive and there was greater tendency to publish them as single works, as witnessed by Erasmus' *Life* of Jerome. However, the tradition of collections remained strong, especially as many ancient biographical collections such as those of Plutarch and Diogenes Laertius, not to mention Suetonius, were rediscovered and given a new lease of life. A similar phenomenon can be observed with regard to early and medieval *Lives* of the saints, which still maintained their corporate nature. The most interesting examples of this are Georg Major's expurgated and abridged version of Jacobus de Voragine's *Legenda aurea*, and pseudo-Jerome's *Vitaspatrum* for use by Lutherans and with prefaces by Luther himself.[13] On the Roman Catholic side, there are a large number of editions of the Pseudo-Abdias collection of the *Lives* of the Apostles.[14] At the same time, it cannot be stressed enough that the biographical genre as resuscitated by humanists retained

---

[12]   The literature on medieval *Lives* of the saints is very abundant, but there is no adequate general work in English. By way of a general introduction, see René Aigrain, *Hagiographie, ses sources, ses méthodes, son histoire* (Brussels: Société des Bollandistes, 2000), reprint of the original 1953 edition with new bibliography by Robert Godding. See also Jacques Dubois and Jean-Loup Lemaître, *Sources et méthodes de l'hagiographie médiévale* (Paris: Cerf, 1993).

[13]   See Georg Meier, *Vitae patrum in vsum ministrorum Verbi quo ad eius fieri potuit repurgatae. Per Georgium Maiorem cum praefatione D. Martini Lutheri* (Wittembergae, apud Seitzium, 1544).

In fact, Meier published just the first book containing accounts of 'respectable saints' and a certain number of *Apophtegmata*. He omitted the other parts; cf. J.-P. Migne (ed.), *Patrologiae cursus completus*, 217 vols (Paris, Migne, 1844–55), PL 73–74, and esp. Migne, PL 21= *Vitae patrum. Historiae eremiticae libri decem*, ed. H. Rosweyde (Antwerp, 1615).

[14]   Luther thought that the Bible contained everything the faithful needed to know about the Apostles' lives, which is why he admitted the *Vitaspatrum* and the *Golden Legend* while excising the saints of the apostolic era from the latter. For sixteenth-century Roman Catholic editions of Pseudo-Abdias, see I. Backus, *Historical Method and Confessional Identity in the Era of the Reformation (1378–ca. 1615)* (Leiden: Brill, 2003), pp. 292–321.

all of its polymorphous character. Some biographies were accurate, others anecdotal, some were an attempt to identify a group, others were works of justification. In most cases, at least until the 1560s, they tended to be published without much attention to chronology or dates. Some combined this with a self-justificatory or justificatory element, an aspect particularly present in biographies of Calvin. Others, such as Luther's early biographers, inserted their hero into the woof and warp of Reformation history while maintaining the sermon model of saints' *Lives*. As for collective biographies, these seem to have found a very strong following in Zurich. Moreover, portraits of religious groups began to flourish towards the end of the sixteenth century, as instanced particularly by Theodore Beza's *Icones* of 1580.

Religious Biography and the Reformation

Luther's *Lives*, as we shall see, were by and large not *Lives* at all, but either sermons or funeral orations. Moreover, his first biographers, Melanchthon in the Lutheran camp, and Cochlaeus in the Catholic, both showed a tendency to insert the reformer into the texture of sacred history, which meant very early on that he became either the embodiment of the Reformation, a sort of God's *Werkzeug* used by the Almighty to implement His eschatological design, or conversely a tool of the devil, complete with historical proof of his demonic association. For later pro-Luther biographers such as Selnecker or Mathesius, the reformer was thus fully identifiable with the unity of the Lutheran Church and therefore with the *Formula of Concord*. Disagreements between the various factions of the Lutheran Church were passed over in silence as if they had never existed. The *Augsburg Confession* was viewed as the Creed equal in importance to the early Ecumenical Creeds, such as Nicaea or Constantinople. In other words, most of the biographical activity favourable to Luther was vernacular and first and foremost of national interest, Melanchthon's *Vita* constituting the main exception. Written in Latin and placing Luther very firmly at the centre of God's eschatological design, it found a market outside Germany and was translated into French in the second half of the sixteenth century to become something of the received *Life* of Luther among European Protestants of every colouring.

Hostile biographies of the Wittenberg reformer tended to take a different shape, starting with Cochlaeus, who inserted the reformer not into God's eschatological design, but into the history of his time while stressing his links with the devil. He was copied and imitated by a large number of Roman Catholic writers, who created a fixed image of Luther which far transcended national boundaries.

In general, *Lives* which were favourable to the reformers were by and large not published in series, with the notable exception of Theodore Beza's *Icones*,[15] which first came out in 1580 and which can legitimately be considered as a Reformation version of Varro's *Imagines*. Otherwise, biographical literature concerning reformers tended to come out separately, sometimes in the form of prefaces to other works. Their *Lives* were most often published in Latin first, Luther's later *Lives* constituting a notable exception in this respect. They tended to be first written shortly after the subject's death by authors who had personally known him or someone connected with him, so as to guarantee the truthfulness of their account. Again with the exception of favourable *Lives* of Luther, which were very frequently first delivered in sermon form, the genre because of its mixed origins had difficulties in making an impact on religious literature of the period. Geneva constitutes a good example here. In 1555, the *Lives* of Zwingli, Oecolampadius and Luther were translated into French and published under the title *Histoire des vies et faits de trois excellens personnages, premiers restaurateurs de l'Évangile en ces derniers tems*. In 1564, Beza published a Latin *Life* of Calvin as a preface to the reformer's commentary on Joshua. In the same year, Beza translated the *Life* into French and published it separately under the title *Discours de M. Théodore de Besze, contenant en bref l'histoire de la vie et mort de Maistre Iean Caluin avec le Testament et derniere volonté dudict Calvin. Et le catalogue des liures par luy composez*.[16] This was immediately added to the *Histoire des trois excellens personnages*, which accordingly altered its title to *Histoire des vies et faits de quatre excellens personnages*.[17] As regards the Latin versions of the *Lives* of Zwingli, Oecolampadius and Luther, they were naturally not published together initially. Luther's *Life* by

---

[15]   Theodore Beza, *Icones id est verae imagines virorum doctrina simul et pietate illustrium, quorum praecipue ministerio partim bonarum litterarum studia sunt restituta, partim vera religio in variis orbis Christiani regionibus nostra patrumque memoria fuit instaurata, additis eorundem vitae et operae descriptionibus, quibus adiectae sunt nonnullae picturae quas Emblemata vocant* (Geneva, Jean de Laon, 1580). A year later, Simon Goulart produced a rather expanded and 'improved' French version with epigrams added to the prose text and one or two portraits that had not figured in the 1580 edition. The title of the French version is: *Les vrais pourtraits des hommes illustres en piete et doctrine, du travail desquels Dieu s'est servi en ces derniers temps pour remettre sus la vraye Religion en divers pays de la Chrestienté. Avec les descriptions de leur vie et de leurs faits plus memorables. Plus quarante quatre emblemes chrestiens* (Geneva, Jean de Laon, 1581). A reprint with an introduction by Alain Dufour came out in Geneva in 1986. On the work, see Christophe Chazalon, 'Les *Icones* de Théodore de Bèze (1580) entre mémoire et propagande', *Bibliothèque d'Humanisme et Renaissance*, 66 (2004): 359–76.

[16]   This *Life* was augmented and reworked by Nicolas Colladon, and appeared in his preface to the 1565 French translation of Calvin's *Commentary on Joshua*, published in Geneva by François Perrin.

[17]   See Carbonnier-Burkard, 'Une *Histoire d'excellens personnages*', pp. 43–59.

Philip Melanchthon (*De vita et actis Lutheri*) was published after Luther's death in 1549, and in contrast with the other *Lives* of the reformers was the object of a large number of subsequent editions, as I have already said. It seems likely, as Marianne Carbonnier-Burkard points out, that the Genevan editor of the *Histoire de quatre excellens personnages*, Jacques Poullain, wanted to gather up as many reformers' *Lives* as possible in order to make up a collection in French reminiscent of both Plutarch and collections of *Saints' Lives*. The ambivalent title of the volume, a priori acceptable to both moderate Catholics and to Protestants, would make it ideal conversion literature for the French situation. This is probably why Poullain added the *Life* of Calvin by Beza. However, the overall result was not convincing. Four *Lives* could hardly compare to a collection of *Lives* of the saints, or for that matter to the efforts of a Plutarch or a Suetonius. Carbonnier-Burkard thinks that no further *Lives* were added after that of Calvin because Beza, Calvin's biographer, considered him to be the last and the greatest of the reformers in the true sense of the word.[18] However, it is far more likely that the collection was not expanded simply because the genre had some difficulty in establishing itself. It is significant that if we take all the *Lives* published in the *Histoire*, only Luther's *Life* was intended for publication. The others were all initially intended either for private use or as prefaces to works. Thus Myconius' account of Zwingli was initially a letter to a friend, as was *De obitu Oecolampadii*, Capito's biography of the Basel reformer. Beza's *Life* of Calvin initially served as a preface to Calvin's Commentary on Joshua. Nothing could be further from the bold intentions of Plutarch or the authors of *Lives* of the saints. Indeed, apart from the *Histoire*, the only other 'collection' of *Lives* intended for French-speaking Protestants appeared late and hardly merited that appellation. It was in fact a French adaptation (by Antoine Teissier) of Beza's 1575 *Life* of Calvin and of Antoine de la Faye's 1606 *Life* of Beza.[19] It came out in 1681. Another point worth making is that these *Lives* were generally brief, quite unlike some luxuriant humanist biographies such as Erasmus' *Life* of Jerome or Camerarius' *Life* of Melanchthon.[20] With the exception of

---

[18]   See ibid., p 58.

[19]   De La Faye's *Life* of Beza first appeared in Latin in 1606: *De vita et obitu clariss. viri, D. Theodori Bezae Vezelii, Ecclesiastae et Sacrarum literarum Professoris, Genevae, 'hypomnêmation' / autore Antonio Fayo* (Geneuae, apud Jacobum Chouet, 1606). Teissier's French version of De La Faye's *Life* of Beza was in fact an edited account of La Faye, omitting all the contentious passages. See below, Chapter 4, pp. 138–53.

[20]   Joachim Camerarius the Elder, *De Philippi Melanchthonis ortu, totius vitae curriculo et morte, implicata rerum memorabilium temporis illius hominumque mentione atque indicio cum expositionis serie cohaerentium narratio diligens et accurata Joachimi Camerarii Pabergensis* (Leipzig, E. Voegelin, 1566). See on this, Timothy Wengert, 'With Friends Like This ... The Biography of Philip Melanchthon by Joachim Camerarius', in Thomas F. Mayer and D. R. Woolf (eds), *The Rhetorics of Life-Writing in Early Modern Europe: Forms of*

Zurich, where the *Lives* of Zurich reformers seem to have been planned as a collection, although they were never published as one, there was no concerted attempt at a group presentation. Theodore Beza's *Icones* of 1580, which consciously set out to present the *respublica christiana* by recourse to engraved portraits and short poems, were extremely stylised and made an impact mainly because of their emblematic value, rather like Varro's lost *Imagines*.

Why write *Lives* of Reformers?

So what exactly was the purpose of reformers' *Lives* such as those that made up the *Histoire des quatre excellens personnage*s? Daniel Ménager sees a strong apologetic element not just in the account of the Genevan reformer's life, but also in all the *Lives* that make up the *Histoire*.[21] Absurd rumours about the death of Luther, and Oecolampadius did indeed circulate. These accounts emanated from the Catholic camp and were intended to show that the reformers had died badly and that therefore no credence could be placed in their teaching. As Ménager notes, Calvin's case was further complicated by François Bauduin's accusations of 1558 of a Calvin personality cult with his disciples worshipping his portraits.[22] Later, rumours of false miracles performed by the reformer were propagated.[23] As regards all three versions of the *Life* of Calvin, Ménager claims that Beza could not in the face of spreading calumnies do anything other than write a eulogy of Calvin rather than a true biography in the modern sense of the term. Essentially, to Ménager the appearance on the market of the *Lives* of various reformers is motivated primarily by their biographers' desire to clear their reputation.[24] This, implicitly, is also the view of Jean-Robert Armogathe, who, confining his study to Calvin's *Lives*, points out that they

---

Biography from Cassandra Fedele to Louis XIV (Ann Arbor, MI: University of Michigan Press, 1995), pp. 115–31. There was also an anonymous (considerably shorter) account of Melanchthon's last days published by a group of Wittenberg professors who witnessed his end (*Breuis narratio exponens quo fine vitam in terris suam clauserit reuerendus vir D. Philippus Melanchthon vna cum praecedentium proxime dierum et totius morbi, quo confectus est breui descriptione. Conscripta a professoribus Academiae Witebergensis qui omnibus quae exponuntur interfuerunt* [Wittebergae, n.p., 1560]), not to mention numerous poems celebrating him. Cf. note 30 below.

21   See especially Ménager, 'Théodore de Bèze, biographe de Calvin', p. 233.

22   See ibid., pp. 235–6.

23   Ibid., p 244, and Armogathe, 'Les vies de Calvin', p. 46.

24   Ménager, 'Théodore de Bèze, biographe de Calvin', pp. 233–4: 'Les bruits les plus absurdes ou les plus scandaleux ont couru quant aux circonstances de la mort de Luther, ce qui oblige très vite Mélanchthon à donner la version véritable de la mort du réformateur … La même scène avait déjà eu lieu lors de la mort d'Oecolampade: on avait raconté, comme Grynée s'en plaint dans une lettre à W. Capiton, qu'il avait été tué par des proches ou qu'il avait mis fin à ses jours.'

arose in a polemical context.[25] Concentrating on accounts hostile to Calvin – not all of them *Lives*, but rather short one-paragraph sketches inserted into longer *Histories* of Dupréau, Florimond de Raemond and others –, he concludes that their aim was to create an image of the reformer as an example not to follow, or a sort of upside-down saint. This hypothesis, if found acceptable, would put these biographies on the same level as the Cato polemic between Cicero and Caesar, which was also fought out on the biographical battlefield.

I contend, however, that the claim that Calvin's and other reformers' *Lives* are to be seen as polemic, or as apologetics, ignores several factors and takes an unnecessarily reductive view. While there is no denying that *Lives* and short sketches of heretics emanating from the Roman Catholic camp were an attempt to discredit the Reformation through its main protagonists, it certainly cannot be said that *Lives* favourable to reformers invariably constituted an attempt to clear the deceased's reputation. Luther's *Lives*, as explained above, were for the most part not *Lives* at all. As for Calvin, why did Beza write two or three different *Lives* of his mentor with no new attacks to counter? Why did Antoine de la Faye write the *Life* of Beza, or a group of Strasbourg ministers the *Life* of Fagius? Indeed, of the *Lives* that make up the *Histoire des quatre excellens personnages*, only Capito makes an explicit claim about wanting to clear his subject's name. Melanchthon's *Life* of Luther only barely adverts to fictitious rumours about Luther, and considers they would have been refuted much better by an autobiography:

> Profitable indeed, would have been the narrative of his private life, clearly set forth, for it was full of examples calculated to confirm in after times the piety of the wise-hearted; and such an account would also have been profitable for informing posterity. Such a work would also have refuted the calumnies of those who profess that Luther, incited by the principal men of the day, or possibly by others, to seek the downfall of episcopal power and dignity, or inflamed by personal ambition, had become the instrument in loosing the bands of monastic thraldom. Much advantage would have been derived from a copious and complete notice of these incidents, illustrated and recorded by himself; and although malevolent persons may object that self-praise is an unworthy theme for a man to choose, yet we well know the character of Luther to have been of such solidity, that he would have written, even his own history, with the utmost good faith. We may also assert that many excellent and intelligent men are still alive who knew these events well. It would then have been great folly if, as it is sometimes done in works of imagination, he had fabricated any other narrative; but since his lamented death has deprived the world of his autobiography, we shall now, with accuracy relate those things connected with

---

[25] Armogathe, 'Les vies de Calvin', p. 45: 'Le développement des biographies de Calvin est essentiellement polémique, la controverse créant dès l'origine, l'objet à débattre au lieu d'analyser.'

his life which we have heard from his own lips, and those to which we have ourselves been eyewitnesses.[26]

As for the *Lives* of the Swiss reformers (Oecolampadius excepted), they certainly did not need their reputation clearing as they were never the object of concerted attacks of the type that the Genevans were subjected to in the last years of the sixteenth century. However, this is not how Beza saw either version of his *Life* of Calvin. Moreover, of the three versions of the *Life*, only the second, authored by Colladon, contains apologetic elements. As for Beza, if he tries to clear anything, it is Calvin's teaching and not his reputation. Finally, neither Armogathe nor Ménager considered situating the *Lives* of the reformers in a biographical tradition reaching back to Classical Antiquity. In fact, if we consider the *Lives* of the reformers in that context, it is easy to see that they are first and foremost intended to edify, each in a different way. In other words, their authors are more concerned to set up a Protestant model of piety, which is not a saint's *Life*, than to clear their subjects of calumnies. Given the tradition they work in and the models available, it is inevitable that the result should be uneven and unspectacular. With these provisos in mind, it makes no sense to look on any of the biographies we shall consider in the light of modern biographical writing any more than it does to see them as pure polemic or as pure apologetics.

This includes the *Lives* of Bullinger. However, in Zurich in the second half of the sixteenth century, the genre of reformers' and more generally 'pious Protestant' *Lives* seems to have gained rather more of a foothold than in Geneva, and in a way which made these accounts into a genre very distinct from either Geneva or Wittenberg *Life*-writing. To take but one example, Josiah Simler's *Life* of Peter Martyr Vermigli first appeared in 1563, a year after the reformer's death, and was a revised version of Simler's funeral oration.[27] It was reprinted six years later as part of a preface to Vermigli's commentary on *Genesis*, which was completed posthumously by Ludwig Lavater (Vermigli's work finished at Gen. 42, 45). It reappeared in subsequent editions of Vermigli's commentary on Genesis, and in his *Loci communes* from the 1582 Basel edition onwards. Some features are to be noted which provide an interesting point of comparison with Calvin's *Lives* by Beza and Colladon. Firstly, the biography, apart from the first imprint, was transmitted as a preface and did not alternate between preface and book in its own right, as Calvin's *Lives* did. Secondly,

---

[26]   *Vitae quatuor Reformatorum. Lutheri a Melanchthone, Melanchthonis a Camerario, Zwinglii a Myconio, Caluini a Theod. Beza conscriptae. Nunc iunctim editae*, ed. A. F. Neander (Berlin: G. Eichler, 1841), p. 1.

[27]   It was entitled *Oratio de vita et obitu viri optimi, praestantissimi theologi D. Petri Martyris Vermilii, Sacrarum litterarum in Schola Tigurina professoris* (Zurich, Froschouer, 1563).

again, unlike Calvin's *Lives*, it retained the form of a funeral panegyric. Thirdly, it was not initially produced against the background of personal attacks on Vermigli. Indeed, its content and the way it was transmitted would suggest that its prime object was to reassure the readers of the *Genesis* commentary and those of the *Loci communes* about the theology and moral attitude of the author of these works. It was not conceived as bilingual and was never translated, which suggests that it was primarily aimed at a learned public.[28] This affected not so much its content as its presentation of Vermigli, which, as I shall show, is much more personal than, say, Beza's presentation of Calvin. Now, Heinrich Bullinger, like Calvin, was the object of three *Lives* within one year of his death. However, the comparison stops there. The first of these, written by the same Simler, is also the best known. It was published in 1575 by Froschouer under the title, *Narratio de ortu, vita et obitu Reuerendi viri, d. Henrici Bullingeri, Tigurinae ecclesiae pastoris, inserta mentione praecipuarum rerum quae in ecclesiis Heluetiae contigerunt et appendice addita qua postrema responsio Iacobi Andreae confutatur auctore Iosia Simlero Tigurino.* Simler had been married to Bullinger's daughter Elisabeth. The second *Life* was added to it as an appendix. It was in fact Johann Wilhelm Stucki's funeral panegyric, which presumably would have been pronounced in a less polished form.[29] (The same Stucki then wrote the *Life* of Simler in 1577, also in the form of a funeral oration.) The third *Life*, based very largely on Simler's *Narratio*, was the work of Bullinger's other son-in-law, Ludwig Lavater (the husband of Margareta Bullinger, who, like her sister, died during the plague epidemic of 1564/65), who wrote it in German. Entitled *Vom läben und tod Heinrychen Bullingers*, it was published in 1576. The author's intention was very obviously to make his father-in-law's life known to a non-Latin-speaking public. Thus, unlike Calvin's three biographies which represent three attempts at *Life*-writing by the same team, Bullinger received three distinct biographies destined at making him known to all classes of the reformed community. Simler's *Narratio* was destined primarily for theological and pastoral circles, and contained not only a precise chronology, but also a defence of Bullinger's teaching; Stucki's *Oratio funebris* was an elegant piece in very much a

---

[28] Peter Martyr Vermigli, *Petri Martyris Vermilii Florentini, praestantissimi nostra aetate theologi Loci communes, ex variis ipsius authoris scriptis in vnum librum collecti et in quator Classes distributi* (Londinii, ex typographia Ioannis Kyngstoni, 1576). It appeared in the vernacular only in the English translation by Anthony Marten, under the title of *The Common Places of the most famous and renowned Divine Doctor Peter Martyr, diuided into four principall parts, with a large addition of manie theologicall and necessarie discourses, some neuer extant before. Translated and partlie gathered by Anthonie Marten one of the Sewers of hir Maiesties most honourable Chamber* (London, Henry Denham, 1583).

[29] *Item Oratio funebris auctore D. Ioanne Gulielmo Stukio Sacrarum litterarum professore in Schola Tigurina*. Both were published by Froschouer in 1575.

humanist spirit, containing the very minimum of theological or polemical references. Although ending with a prayer for all the Zurich ministers, it was obviously also addressed to wider, non-clerical circles favourable to the Reformation in Switzerland. As for Lavater's work, which appeared separately a year later, it was simply an adaptation and an abridgement of Simler's *Narratio* for the wider public. We must single out two features of the Zurich biographies of the latter sixteenth century: they are not defensive in the way that Genevan biographies are, but neither are they to be viewed primarily in an ecclesiastical context like the later *Lives* of Luther. There were no sermons preached on Bullinger's life as symbolic of such-and-such ecclesiastical document. Moreover, the authors distinguished carefully between Latin *Lives*, intended for the learned market, and vernacular *Lives*. Independently of that, all the Zurich *Lives* were overtly pedagogical and, as I shall show, several were intended to be used as school manuals. Simler was the only one to take up and develop doctrinal issues in his *Narratio*. Interestingly, unlike Myconius' *Life* of Zwingli, none of Bullinger's *Lives* came to be included in the *Histoire d'excellens personnages*. However, the existence in the Geneva Library of an artificial collection of Zurich and other *Lives* shows that Zurich had its own *excellens personnages*, and that its conception of religious biography had far more to do with a funeral *encomium* on the one hand, and with a school text book on the other hand, than with any other genre.[30]

I shall now examine a collection of Humanist *Lives* put together by the Lutheran lawyer Johannes Fichard and published in 1536. The interesting features of Fichard's collection from our point of view are its perspective, which spans all confessions, and its obvious interest in what constitutes a *Life* in view of antique models. Secondly, I shall examine one atypical reformer's *Life* emanating, as it happens, from Strasbourg. It is anonymous,

---

[30]   A sixteenth-century volume of artificially collected *Lives* of representatives of the German-speaking Reformation is held by the Geneva Bibliothèque publique et universitaire (shelfmark: Gk 31*). Apart from the Zurich *Lives* of Bullinger and Conrad Gesner, it contains the anonymous *Breuis narratio exponens quo fine vitam suam claruerit Philippus Melanchthon* by a collective of Wittenberg professors, published in 1560; Johannes Major's description of Melanchthon's funeral; Jacob Heerbrand's *Oratio funebris Philippi Melanchthonis*; Edon Hilderic's *Carmen de Philippo Melanchthone*; two hymns on angels by Philip Melanchthon and Johannes Strigel; 32 epitaphs of illustrious men who died of the plague emanating from the pens of anonymous members of the Basel Church and Academy, during the second half of the sixteenth century; *Epicedia*, or funeral dirges on the death of John Parkhurst, bishop of Norwich, by Rudolf Gwalther the Elder and the Younger (Zurich, Froschouer, 1576); two letters by Johann Sturm on the death of Erasmus of Limburg, bishop of Strasbourg (Strasbourg, Rihel, 1569); and an *Encomium* on the death of Martin Peyer, a lawyer from Schaffhausen, by Johannes Jezler and Johannes Ulmer (Basel, Episcopius, 1583). The volume also contains a piece by Rudolf Gwalther the Younger unconnected with biography and funeral orations, and entitled *Argo Tigurina. Elegia de naui qua delecti ciues Tigurini vnius diei spatio ex Tiguri spatio Argentinam vecti sunt.*

deals with a second-order theologian, and contains a theoretical justification of the sort that is either minimal or missing altogether in the *Lives* of the first-order reformers such as Luther, Calvin, or the Zurich reformers. These two cases, the *Life* of Fagius and Fichard's anthology, show, as we shall see, that biographers of first-order reformers did have models available that would have enabled them to cast the subjects in a more formal mode and to anthologise them while justifying their undertaking in far clearer terms than they sometimes did. Furthermore, there was nothing stopping them from remaining anonymous and presenting their work as a group effort. The fact that they did none of this, opting for other models, would suggest a deliberate religious strategy.

Johannes Fichard, or One Way of Resuscitating a Group Biography

Johannes Fichardus or Fichard (1512–81) was one of the most eminent jurists and diplomats of his era, as well as a syndic in Frankfurt am Main. After studying law at Freiburg im Breisgau and Speyer and obtaining his doctorate in 1531, he travelled to Italy and taught at Padua and Bologna. Among his main works are *Vitarum recentiorum iurisconsultorum ab Irnerio vsque ad Zasium libri....* He also produced an edition of the *Malleus maleficarum* and translated into German Jean Bodin's *De magorum daemonomania*.[31] Of Lutheran persuasion, he was extremely skilled at mediation in confessional matters, and interceded very successfully in disputes of that nature between the emperor and the Frankfurt city authorities. Fichard published his *Virorum qui superiori nostroque seculo eruditione et doctrina illustres atque memorabiles fuerunt Vitae iamprimum in hoc volumen collectae* in 1536 in Frankfurt, with Christian Egenolph. The collection shows us something of the way some authors continued in the antique mode of imitating Plutarch, remaining aware of the potential of biographies of famous men as intellectual history manuals regardless of confessional matters. The specific theme of interest to Fichard was the status of northern humanists as compared to their southern counterparts. The series of *Lives* Fichard published, none of which was actually written by him, was intended to explore in parallel the merits of Northern and Southern humanism. The slim volume contained eighteen *Lives* only, ten devoted to Italian men of letters and high clergy, six devoted to Germans, and two to Englishmen. The Italian *Lives* include Petrarch, Pius II, Joannes Campanus, Antonius Vrceus Codrus, Philippus Beroaldus, Giovanni Pico della Mirandola, Octavius Cleophilus Fanensis, Pomponius Laetus, Petrus

---

[31]   See R. von Stintzing, art. 'Fichard' in *Allgemeine Deutsche Biographie*, vol. 6 (Leipzig: Duncker & Humblot, 1961), pp. 757–9.

Philippus Corneus, and Cardinal Iacobus Papiensis.[32] The German *Lives*
comprise the biographical accounts of Conrad Celtis, Rudolf Agricola,
Wessel Gansfort, Petrus Mosellanus, Christophorus Longolius, and
Iohannes Oecolampadius.[33] Finally, the two English *Lives* turn out to be
nothing less than Erasmus' accounts of Colet and More.[34]

While Fichard does not adhere to Plutarch's strict parallelism, his preface
shows that he wishes to be seen as writing in the shadow of Plutarch and
ancient Greek and Roman biographies generally. Moreover, he considers
biography-writing to be part of history, sharing the latter's educational
aims. Echoing Cicero, he considers that the prime aim of all history is
to provide moral examples. But history takes two main forms, he notes.
One is the chronicling not of individuals' lives, but of the times in which
they lived. The other is more concise and more circumscribed, dealing
either with the causes, origins and outcome of one particular war, or with
a particular man's mind, morals, counsels, actions and end. He thinks
that those who practised the latter kind (*pars pro toto*) provided a greater
service as compared with the ones who practised the first sort of historical
writing.[35] The advantage of biography is first and foremost its brevity.
It is much easier to learn how to live morally if one has a short text at one's

---

[32]   See Johannes Fichard, *Virorum qui superiori nostroque seculo eruditione et doctrina
illustres atque memorabiles fuerunt Vitae iamprimum in hoc volumen collectae* (Frankfurt,
Christian Egenolph, 1536) [table of contents on verso of title-page], *Quorum vitae hoc libro
tractantur. Elenchus. Itali*

Fol. 1   Franciscus Petrarcha [per Hier. Squarzaficum Alexandrinum]
Fol. 10   Pius pontifex Max. [per Ioan. Antoni Cam episcopum Aretinum]
Fol. 27   Ioan. Ant. Campanus [per Michaelem Fernum Mediolanensem]
Fol. 55   Phil. Beroaldus [per Bartholomaeum Blandrinum]
Fol. 58   Ioannes Picus Mir. [per Ioannem Franciscum Picum]
Fol. 72   Octauius Celophilus Fanensis [per Fran. Polyardum]
Fol. 74   Pomponius Laetus [per Franciscum Maturantium Perusinum]
Fol. 76   Petrus Philippus Corneus [per Franciscum Maturantium Perusinum]
Fol. 80   Iacobus Papiensis Cardinalis [per Iacobum Volaterranum].
[33]   Ibid., *Germani*:

Fol. 81   Conradus Celtis Protucius [per sodalitatem literariam Romanam]
Fol. 83   Rodolphus Agricola [per G. Nouiomagum]
Fol. 87   Wesselius Gansfortius [ex primo libro illustr. Virorum inferioris
Germaniae G. Nouiomagi]
Fol. 88   Petrus Mosellanus [a Iustino Goblero]
Fol. 93   Christophorus Longolius [anon.]
Fol. 101   Ioannes Oecolampadius [per W. Capitonem].
[34]   Ibid., *Angli*:

Fol. 106   Ioannes Coletus [per Erasmum]
Fol. 112   Thomas Morus [per Erasmum].
[35]   Ibid., fol. a ijv.

disposal than if one has to work one's way through several volumes. This, in Fichard's view, is what impelled Plutarch, a man dedicated to the service of scholars, to publish *Lives* of illustrious men and to compare their vices and virtues, rather than commit to paper a general history drawn out over several periods and kingdoms.[36] Thus Fichard decided to follow in Plutarch's footsteps or, as he puts it:

> For this reason I too came to the conclusion recently that I would do something of great use, particularly to students, if following the example of this man [Plutarch] I published the *Lives* of those men who were famous for their learning in our own and in the previous century, in one volume so that others could read them and get to know them ....[37]

Fichard is fully aware that one important difference between him and Plutarch is his own lack of originality. Whereas Plutarch composed his *Parallel Lives*, Fichard simply collected *Lives* written by others, which he made into a small collection:

> For it seemed that it would procure great delight to readers if they could get to know about the most illustrious men's very diverse views, morals, conversations, friendships, virtues, vices, and so on, from one single work. What is more they would find it extremely profitable if they could view and study, as it were, in a common mirror, everything that pertained to the public and private life of these illustrious men ... For this reason I paid special attention to not relying on my own inventiveness when writing this book, but to collecting and summarising in one volume what had already been written by other people, who either had personal knowledge of these illustrious men or were their exact contemporaries or proved their trustworthiness as authors in other ways.[38]

In other words, Fichard thinks that a biographer, to be fully reliable, should either have known the subject personally or have been his contemporary. He does not detail the other proofs of reliability that a biographer should produce if his work is to be taken seriously. Thus despite his protestations to the contrary, Plutarch is not Fichard's exact model. The author of *Parallel Lives* did not know all his subjects personally, he did not collect biographical sketches written by others, and his interest in producing portraits of individuals complete with character defects was far removed from Fichard's concern with providing a collective mirror of morals. One thing Plutarch and our lawyer do have in common, however, is their concern with presenting a coherent group, be it military leaders or humanist scholars. Moreover, although Fichard does not say so in so many words, there is an attempt at parallelism in his presentation of a group of Italian humanists and Northern European humanist scholars. Both groups include theologians and clergy, as well as poets, rhetoricians and philosophers. At

---

[36]   Ibid., fol. a iijr.
[37]   Ibid., fol. a iiijr.
[38]   Ibid., fol. a iij r.–v.

the same time, the two groups possess their own distinctive characteristics. As far as the religious personalities are concerned, the Italian group includes a pope and a cardinal. The Northern group includes a reformer, a proto-reformer and a biblical humanist. The choice is not arbitrary. Pius II or Aeneas Silvius Piccolomini was as widely known for his literary talent and learning as for his anti-Conciliarist positions or his war against the Turks, and could be seen as a model of what a pope should be. Wessel Gansfort was famous for his rejection of scholasticism, while Colet's biblical humanism was very much to Fichard's taste. If we go no further than the religious personalities in Fichard's anthology, they are obviously meant to show the parallelism between North and South, but also the particularities of each part of the world and of each individual. Equally significantly, Fichard includes only moderate figures: Oecolampadius, but not Zwingli; Silvio Piccolomini, but not Savonarola; Colet, and not Wyclif. Of course, it could be argued that he included only those *Lives* he could find. However, the profile of the group is too coherent to be reduced to criteria of availability.

Fichard thus provided a model of how to choose the best representatives of humanism, including Christian humanism, from the North and from the South, so as to combine them in a collective portrait of best churchmen, theologians, poets, rhetoricians, philosophers, and so on. This model could not work for the *Lives* of first-order reformers whose very undertaking excluded collegiality of any kind. Although weak attempts at federating the reformers did exist from the 1560s, as is shown by the *Histoire d'excellens personnages*, these anthologies were less far ranging than Fichard's as they did not include biographies of religious adversaries, however pious. When Beza published his rather more federative *Icones* in 1580, he significantly included Savonarola, Wyclif and Erasmus, but not Pope Pius II or Colet. Fichard's anthology plainly augurs a different tradition, that of biographies of learned men, of which the culmination is represented by the Heidelberg lexicographer and literary historian Melchior Adam (1575–1622) and his *Vitae germanorum theologorum, Vitae theologorum exterorum principum, Vitae medicorum, Vitae iurisconultorum, Vitae politicorum*, and so on, all published within the first two decades of the seventeenth century.[39] Although, more confessionally biased than Fichard, Adam shared his forerunner's basically cultural, as opposed to religious, concerns. However, quite unlike Fichard, he wrote his biographical sketches himself and did not rely on existing models. Furthermore, living in the great era of biography which the seventeenth century had claims to being, his project extended

---

[39]   For a fuller account of Adam, see Robert Seidel, 'Melchior Adams Vitæ (1615–1620) und die Tradition frühneuzeitlicher Gelehrtenbiographik', in Gerhard von Kosselek (ed.), *Oberschlesische Dichter und Gelehrte vom Humanismus bis zum Barock* (Bielefeld: Aisthesis, 2000), pp. 179–204.

to several volumes and not to a slim pamphlet. Be that as it may, the sixteenth-century *Lives* of the reformers, which I shall be examining, had nothing to do with what I shall call in shorthand the Plutarch–Fichard–Adam school of *Life*-writing.

Life of Paul Fagius, or How to Fashion a Reformation Saint with Very Little Help from Antique and Medieval Models

None of the favourable sixteenth-century biographers mentioned so far raised any theoretical questions to do with the function of biography, religious biography, or indeed the problem of writing *Lives* of the reformers, as going against the Reformation ideal of not overvaluing individual humans at the expense of divine providence. We do, however, have indications that setting about writing a *Life* of a reformer could and did pose problems in some Protestant circles. One of the clearest contemporary statements of this is to be found in the anonymous life of the Strasbourg theologian and Hebraist Paul Fagius, who sought exile with Bucer in England after the 1548 *Interim*.[40] The volume containing the *Life* 'written in concise form (18 in-octavo folios) by a few ministers of the Strasbourg Church'[41] also includes several funeral orations on the death of Martin Bucer; the account of the exhumation of the bodies of Bucer and Fagius under Mary Tudor in 1556; a letter from Vermigli about the death of his first wife, Catharina; and the story (by James Calfhill) of her exhumation and reburial in Christ Church Cathedral. The volume was edited by Bucer's former secretary, Conrad Hubert (Hubertius), and published in 1562.

Unusually for the genre, the *Life* of Fagius is preceded by some theoretical remarks. Its authors specify that they have had to defend themselves against three accusations. Their detractors claim that, firstly, the writing of biographies is a perfectly useless occupation; secondly, it had in the past given rise to many superstitions (a veiled reference to *Lives* of the saints); and thirdly, there is no point in writing a biography of someone like Fagius, who has been dead since 1549, given that many more eminent and more eloquent theologians could have written one sooner and did not. The authors' justification in the face of the first two accusations is particularly

[40]   *Historia vera de vita, obitu, sepultura, accusatione haereseos, condemnatione, exhumatione, combustione honorificaque tandem restitutione beatorum atque doctissimorum theologorum D. Martini Buceri et Pauli Fagii quae intra annos XII in Angliae regno accidit. Item Historia Catharinae Vermiliae, D. Petri Martyris Vermilii castissimae atque piissimae coniugis, exhumatae eiusdemque ad honestam sepulturam restitutae*, ed. Conradus Hubertius (Argentinae apud Paulum Machaeropoeum, sumptibus Iohannis Oporini, 1562). Hereafter: Hubertius (ed.), *Historia vera*.

[41]   Hubertius (ed.), *Historia vera*, fol. a4r.–v.: *Catalogus eorum quae hoc libello continentur … Vita Pauli Fagii eruditione et linguarum cognitione clarissimi theologi breuiter conscripta per ministros aliquot ecclesiae Argentinensis.*

revealing of the tensions surrounding the genre. Making an oblique reference to pagan and Christian models, they claim that biographical writing has always been highly praised as there is nothing better than to commit to men's memory examples of the best virtues. According to them, pagan examples are generally considered to encourage the qualities of humanity, equity and justice. This means, they conclude, that no one will deny that Christian examples act as an even stronger encouragement to the true worship of God, piety and chastity.[42] They take the view that nothing that magnifies the glory of God can be bad. The prophet says 'the Lord is to be admired in his saints', but, they ask, how can God be admired in his saints (which they interpret to mean the faithful) if no memory of them is preserved? What is more, according to them, the examples of *Lives* of other faithful, more eminent and more devout, reveal something of the outer workings of divine grace and so compel the readers to turn to God in the anticipation of receiving the same grace. These reasons lead the authors to conclude that it was God himself who entrusted the writing of the *Lives* of the true faithful to His church to magnify His glory and to have perpetual witnesses to divine teaching. In the authors' view, the saints provide an example of virtues as if in a mirror.[43]

As for the accusation of the *Lives* of the saints (or the true faithful) being the cause of superstitions such as saint worship, they claim that truth cannot give rise to a lie and that piety cannot breed superstition. In their view, all superstitions can be traced back to two sources only: the devil, and natural, human perversity which is the fruit of the original sin. Thus if they follow God's counsel and truth, men cannot and will not leave any room for falsehood and superstition.[44]

---

[42]   Ibid., fols 97v.–98r.: 'Habet hoc genus scriptionis sem/98r./perque habuit cum summa vtilitate summam etiam coniunctam laudem. Quid enim vtilius et dignius esse potest quam Christianae religionis, pietatis, fidei caeterarumque pulcherrimarum virtutum exempla litteris hominumque memoriae mandare? Quod si gentilium exempla ad humanitatem, ad animi moderationem, ad aequitatem iustitiamque in omni vita colendam, non exiguum momentum omnium sententia conferre iudicantur, quis non maiora adiumenta ad verum Dei cultum, pietatem castitatemque Christianorum et eorum qui his praefuerunt, exempla allatura esse censebit?'

[43]   Ibid., fol. 99r.: 'Quamobrem sic statuimus hoc genus scriptionis ecclesiae diuinitus mandatum atque concessum esse, idque sapientissimo Dei consilio primum vt ex eo gloria gratiae suae elucescat; deinde vt perpetuos testes coelestis doctrinae haberemus; tum etiam vt exemplis gratiae suae in alios tam prompte tamque benigne effusae, ad eandem appetendam confirmemur. Postremo, vt omnium pulcherrimarum virtutum in sanctis exempla tanquam in speculo consideranda atque imitanda, nobis omnibus proponerentur.'

[44]   Ibid., fol. 99v.: 'Non igitur Deo aut veritati attribuendum est quod homines relicto Deo et veritate ad creaturarum venerationem cultumque et portentosa mendacia prolapsi sunt, sed Satanae et ipsorum hominum maliciae. Quis enim tam impius erit vt dicere audeat Deum sibi ipsi aut religioni suae contraria iussisse? Aut eorum memoriam sua authoritate consecrasse, per quos ipsius veneratio atque maiestas non cresceret sed imminueretur? Ex quo

In other words, the authors of the *Life* of Fagius have a vision of religious biography as a genre to be distinguished from both antique and humanist *Lives* and from the medieval *Lives* of the saints. While pious, religious biography differs from the pagan and humanist *Lives* only in so far as its object is to illustrate the glory of God, it is to be much more sharply distinguished from the traditional *Lives* of the Saints in that, unlike they, it rests on truth. The authors thus present Fagius as a saint cast in the literary mould of an antique hero. Their prime object is to offer an exemplary portrait. Now Fagius was no bishop, and could hardly have been claimed as the Christian equivalent of an emperor or a hero. He was no more than a reformed pastor, teacher and a Hebrew scholar, by no means the most eminent of his era. His life is thus to all intents and purposes concealed in a volume which is devoted for the large part to laudatory orations of Bucer, if one excepts the short biography of Vermigli's wife. Conrad Hubert, the editor and compiler of the volume, wants to commemorate Strasbourg-linked theologians and good Christians who emigrated to England after the *Interim*, and who thus incarnate resistance to idolatrous practices, all the more so as all three, Bucer, Fagius and Signora Vermigli, had their bodies dug up and burnt, the next best thing to a martyrdom. Because all three encountered adversity, idolatry and superstition in not just one country but two or more, they can serve as *exempla* for the faithful throughout Europe, while conserving their local appeal.

That said, the fact remains that Fagius was not a figure of prime importance, and the authors of his *Life* admit as much when they justify themselves against the reproach of producing an account of someone long dead whose *Life* had not been previously considered worth writing.[45] So Fagius was not a founding father of the Reformation, he was not an outstanding theologian or Hebraist; he did not occupy an important position in the hierarchy. He was neither Alexander nor Augustine, and

---

concludimus: si homines praeceptum Dei veritatemque sequentur, nullo modo superstitioni et vanitati locum esse relictum.'

[45]   Ibid., fols 99v.–100r.: 'Ad eos iam venimus qui forsitan consilium nostrum non improbabunt sed tamen tantam temporis moram reprehendent. Fatemur libenter haec citius a nobis eximiis illorum virtutibus praestanda fuisse. Sed cum et occupationibus et iniquitate temporum, adde etiam spe quadam nostra factum sit, non puto nos in eo iure accusari posse, praesertim cum de veritate nihil imminutum sit et quod morae intercessit, id diligentia et virtutum pulcherrimarum exemplis atque accessione facile compensari possit. Postremo iis etiam respondebimus qui huic oneri nos impares esse dicent et conatum hunc nostrum /100r./ aut in temeritatis aut arrogantiae crimen vocabunt. Quiduis potius patiemur, quam vt haec in nos conferantur, ab vtroque enim longissime semper abfuimus at adhuc abesse cupimus. Fatemur libenter nos ad illorum maximas virtutes parem orationem adferre non posse et alios esse quibus ea facultas a Deo tributa sit. Sed cum illi ad huiusmodi viros ornandos eloquentiam suam, quibus de causis nescimus, adhuc conferre noluerint, nos cum prae caeteris summis illis viris deuincti simus, gratitudinis potius quam eloquentiae rationem habendam esse iudicauimus.'

he was not a medieval saint whose life was likely to inspire its readers by
its spectacular miracles. In what way could he be presented as exemplary?
The *Life* starts off in the time-honoured Greco-Roman style presenting its
hero's lineage, and going on to his schooling, youth and studies. Unlike most
Greco-Roman *Lives*, however, it lays great stress on Fagius' commitment
to languages and especially Hebrew. More importantly, it emphasises
that he combined his Hebrew studies with a pastoral charge in Isny. His
Life contains a long and laudatory excursus on the Isny councillor Peter
Buffler, who so wanted to assist our hero in his endeavours that he actually
founded a printing press which he could use to print his works. As is only
fitting in one of such liberality, Buffler is shown as the perfect exemplum
of a Christian magistrate. Concerned to help the poor while furthering the
cause of the Reformation by encouraging learning and preaching of the
true Gospel, he was married to a wife who participated to the full in his
endeavours. It was due to his example that Strasbourg Council founded
the city's famous school.[46] Why devote this disproportionate amount of
space to Buffler? The general answer is that the authors want to make the
point that a pious Christian cannot flourish unless he has the support of
Christian magistrates. However, there is also another reason. As a result
of Buffler's dealings with Fagius over the printing press, the latter found
himself owing a thousand *écus* to Buffler, a sum which he could not pay
off. The Christian counsellor, however, was so impressed by his piety that
he let him off the debt.[47]

Despite his profligacy, Fagius is presented in the rest of the account as
first and foremost a devoted pastor. Although he wished more and more
to leave Isny, which he did not find suitable for his project of propagating
Hebrew studies, his love for his church and for his parishioners was such
that, after seeking Bucer's counsel, he resolved not to leave until he had

---

[46]   Ibid., fol. 103v.: 'Quamobrem Argentoratum vrbem florentissimam in qua literarum
et religionis studia prae caeteris tum vigebant, delegit. Iuuenes delectos ex singulis oppidis
ad quos beneficium suum pertinere volebat, Argentoratum mittit, qui liberalitate ipsius tam
diu aluntur, quoad cum vtilitate atque honore in patriam reuocantur. Quod vnius Bufleri
exemplum senatus amplissimus prudentissimusque Reipublicae Argentinensis mox secutus,
longe vtilissimum peulcherrimumque gymnasium maximis sumptibus aedificauit atque
collocupletauit, in quo cum omnium bonarum artium disciplinae, tum in primis diuinarum
literarum scientia traderetur.'

[47]   Ibid., fol. 104r.–v.: 'Ex qua re non modo quaestum nullum fecit sed ne ad summam
quidem expensorum vnquam peruenire potuit. Quae res et Fagium ab omni auaritia longe
alienissimum facile excusabit. Nam nisi tanta in Buflero liberalitas extitisset, frementibus
cognatis et haeredibus, omnibus suis fortunis, vna cum maximis suis laboribus fuisset
euersus. Buflerus igitur cum singularem Fagii industriam pietatemque perspectam haberet,
quam ei reliquam debebat summam aureorum plus mille totam condonauit, missoque
chirographo Argentoratum cauit ne ab haeredibus vllo modo /104v./ appellari posset. O virum
praestantissimum vna cum coniuge matrona pudicitia, pietate, elemosynarum omniumque
virtutum laude spectabili, memoria sempiterna dignissimum.'

found a suitable successor, who presented himself in the person of Johannes Marbach.[48] This did not happen until 1544. In 1541, when the region was being ravaged by the plague, he preached several sermons enjoining the wealthier citizens not to leave, as was their wont, but to stay and look after the poor and the sick. The section on Fagius' Strasbourg years is simply a catalogue of his writings. The authors stress, however, that his main object remained the spreading of God's word, so much so that he was judged a worthy successor to Wolfgang Capito after the latter's death. This remained his object after he left Strasbourg in 1548 to go to England with Bucer. He died in England of fever at the age of 45. He saw his illness as sent by God who thus made himself known to his children, and he never lost faith that God arranged things for the best. His death was peaceful and good.

In other words, Fagius was a reformed saint. He always put his parishioners and his church before his own ambitions. He devoted himself to learning in the cause of the Reformation, and not so as to further his own ambition. Although rather careless with money, he made up for it by his piety. He died in the faith of the Lord. All that is missing from this account are miracles, or indeed any hint that Fagius' experience of the divine marked him out from the run of men. The *Life* presents Fagius not so much as an *excellent personnage* as a *personnage très docte et très pieux*, undistinguished in many ways, and possessing character flaws such as any pastor could identify with.

Neither of the models we have just discussed could work for the *Lives* of sixteenth-century first-order reformers, which followed their own patterns and had their own purposes, depending on where they were written and by whom. As we shall see, despite the authors' protestations to the contrary, the early *Lives* of Luther, Calvin, Beza and the Swiss reformers were sui-generic and their purpose varied. They wavered between apologetics, hagiography, *exemplum* and the antique heroic model, with historical interest and method taking a varyingly strong hold. The favourable *Lives* spawned in their wake a wave of hostile biographies, a genre which was new (although not completely alien to classical models, especially Roman biography-writing in the context of the opposition to the first Principate), and not invariably ahistorical or mendacious by any means. These were directed particularly against Calvin and, to a lesser extent, Luther, while the very context of the Swiss reformers sheltered them from attacks of any consequence. The later sixteenth-century *Lives* of the reformers, regardless of whether they were friendly or hostile, helped create an image or images of the Reformation which survived into the twentieth century and beyond, although the original accounts remain for the most part forgotten and neglected.

---

[48]   Ibid., fol. 105r.

CHAPTER 1

Luther: Instrument of God or Satan's Brood. Main Developments in Luther Biography, 1546–81

Unlike the *Lives* of Calvin and Genevan reformers or the Zurich *Lives*, early attempts at writing a biography of the Wittenberg reformer, whether partisan or hostile, have been the object of a considerable amount of interest, especially among German church historians of the 1930s and 1940s. Among those, Herte's studies of Cochlaeus' *Commentaria* deserve a special mention.[1] To these we might add Volz's work on Mathesius.[2] Over the past decade, a resurgence of interest in the questions of reception and memory as an important factor of history writing in the Reformation has prompted further publications on Luther's *Lives*, some of which have yet to appear.[3] Of these more recently published works, Eike Wolgast's article on the early Lutheran biographies of Luther as attempts to establish the reformer's authority, Robert Kolb's study of Luther's image in the later phases of the Reformation, and Hans-Peter Hasse's article on Selnecker's *Life* of Luther deserve special mention, while bearing in mind that none of these deals with the Catholic side of Luther biography.[4] We should

---

[1]   Adolf Herte, *Das katholische Lutherbild im Bann der Lutherkommentare des Cochläus*, 3 vols (Münster/W: Aschendorff, 1943), vol. 1: *Von der Mitte des 16. bis zur Mitte des 18. Jhdts*, pp. 17–24. Herte offers an authoritative general discussion of the Catholic image of Luther, especially as conveyed in *Annals* and religious controversies of the period. He does not concern himself primarily with the biographical genre. See also Adolf Herte, *Die Lutherkommentare des Johannes Cochläus. Kritische Studie zur Geschichtsschreibung im Zeitalter des Glaubensspaltung* (*Reformationsgeschichtliche Studien und Texte*, vol. 33) (Münster/W: Aschendorff, 1935).

[2]   Hans Volz, *Die Lutherpredigten des Johannes Mathesius: Kritische Untersuchungen zur Geschichtsschreibung im Zeitalter der Reformation* (*Quellen und Forschungen zur Reformationsgschichte*, vol. 12) (New York: Johnson Reprint Corporation, 1971; reprint of Leipzig, 1930 edn). The work contains a detailed analysis of Mathesius' presentation of Luther, with a table of sources Mathesius used.

[3]   For example, Susan Boettscher's unpublished doctoral dissertation, University of Wisconsin (Madison). (Information communicated by the author.)

[4]   Eike Wolgast, 'Biographie als Autoritätsstiftung: Die ersten evangelischen Lutherbiographien', in Walter Berschin (ed.), *Biographie zwischen Renaissance und Barock* (Heidelberg: Mattes Verlag, 1993), pp. 41–72; Robert Kolb, 'Umgestaltung und theologische Bedeutung des Lutherbildes im späten 16. Jahrhundert', in Hans Christoph Rublack (ed.), *Die lutherische Konfessionalisierung in Deutschland. Wissenschaftliches Symposion des Vereins für Reformationsgeschichte 1988* (Gütersloh: Gütersloher Verlag, 1992), pp. 202–31;

also single out the first modern English translation with commentary of Melanchthon's *Life* of Luther and of Cochlaeus' *Commentaria* on the Wittenberg reformer.[5]

My aim in this chapter is not to repeat what Herte, Volz, Hasse and others have said, but to review the orientation and diffusion of the better-known biographies of Luther so as to offer a point of comparison for the orientation and diffusion of the Genevan and Zurich *Lives*. This is particularly important as Luther's *Lives*, partisan or hostile, stayed firmly within national boundaries although they did tend to cross those more easily, if they happened to be either written in Latin or translated into Latin from the vernacular. The upshot of this was that while the Catholic image of Luther was the direct outcome of Franco-German collaboration and became, so to speak, fixed on the European level fairly early on and for many years to come, his Protestant image tended to be diverse, regional and not fixed at all, ranging from that of a saint to the symbol of the *Augsburg Confession* and the unifying factor of post-Lutheran Lutheranism. It was also, as we shall see, close to the medieval ideal of sainthood. While it would have been inconceivable for Beza or Colladon to preach sermons or even to give lectures on the life of Calvin, this mode of recounting Luther's life and struggles was extremely common among the Wittenberg reformer's Protestant biographers. Another striking feature of Luther's *Lives* as written by his fellow Lutherans was their tendency not to view Luther as an individual, but as an instrument of God or embodiment of a set of doctrines incarnating the Reformation. Thus while there is no doubt that Wolgast is correct in seeing the early Lutheran biographies of Luther as attempts at establishing his authority, it is also important to stress that they all see this authority as first and foremost God-given.[6]

Melanchthon: Luther as an Instrument of God

Compared to the *Lives* of Zwingli or Oecolampadius, which we shall examine further on, Melanchthon's portrait of Luther was less well defined. The reason for this is that Melanchthon broke to some extent with the antique models and with the model of *Lives* of the saints by making his hero an integral part of history. Judging by the speech that Melanchthon

Hans-Peter Hasse, 'Die Lutherbiographie von Nikolaus Selnecker. Selneckers Berufung auf die Autorität Luthers im Normenstreit der Konfessionalisierung in Kursachsen', *Archiv für Reformationsgeschichte*, 86 (1995): 91–123, and literature cited in Kolb's and Hasse's articles.

5   *Two contemporary accounts of Martin Luther*, eds, trans. and ann. Elizabeth Vandiver, Ralph Keen and Thomas D. Frazel (Manchester and New York: Manchester University Press, 2002).

6   See Wolgast, 'Biographie als Autoritätsstiftung', pp. 70–71.

pronounced to his students on receiving news of Luther's death, the reformer was not seen by him as an ordinary man. Even allowing for the constraints of rhetoric, there is no question of describing Luther as a pious Christian, a hero or of having his death accompanied by miraculous portents, a concept which Melanchthon was otherwise not adverse to.[7] The speech is taken up mainly with a graphic description of Luther's last illness, 'an oppression of the humours in the stomach cavity', and his final prayer, in which he commends himself entirely to God. Melanchthon's concluding words make it clear that, in contrast with the perfectly human complaint which killed him, Luther was not of the mortal realm, for 'his doctrine of the remission of sins and faith in the Son of God was not the product of human intelligence but he was raised by God.'[8] With its very conscious effort to insert Luther not just into history but into sacred history or eschatology, Melanchthon's *Life* follows loosely the Suetonian format and is divided into the following commonplaces: Luther's lineage, birth, early years and schooling; his life as professor; his first attempts at reforming theology; his controversy with Tetzel; his relationship with Elector Frederick; the progress of Luther's Reformation; his dislike of change and innovation; his liking of moderation. There follows an excursus on the four main developments of the Christian doctrine after the time of the Apostles, and another one on the necessity of Luther's Reformation. Of the two final sections, one is on Luther's writings and the other is a *pia conclusio*.

In short, Melanchthon uses the format to present not so much a portrait of Luther – the character as such possesses fewer personal traits than Fagius, Zwingli, Oecolampadius, or for that matter Calvin – as to show him to have been an instrument of God. Why in that case is it necessary to do a Suetonian-type biography at all? Would it not have been enough to write up Luther's providential workings without going into his lineage, his studies, and so on? Apparently not. It is therefore legitimate to conclude that Melanchthon wanted to show his students and other readers not just Luther's instrumentality, but also something of his human characteristics; in other words, he wanted to demonstrate what sort of man God chose to restore the church. This imposed enormous constraints on any personal portrait, reducing it to the necessary minimum. Thus Melanchthon begins by regretting that Luther died before he could put into operation his plan of writing up his own *Life*. His biographer finds this regrettable not because of the providential aspect of Luther's life, but because (apart from refuting calumnies) 'a well-written account of his private life would have been useful,

---

[7]   On this, see for example Robin Barnes, *Prophecy and Gnosis: Apocalypticism in the Wake of the Lutheran Reformation* (Stanford, CA: Stanford University Press, 1988).

[8]   *Vitae quatuor Reformatorum*, ed. Neander: (*Vita Lutheri*), pp. 13–14: 'Neque enim humana sagacitate deprehensa est doctrina de remissione peccatorum et de fiducia Filii Dei sed a Deo excitatum vidimus fuisse.'

for it was full of examples which would have reaffirmed piety in good souls
and a catalogue of many events which would have kept his memory alive
for posterity.'[9] Melanchthon thus announces what his biography is not: a
biography in the sense of a chronological account of an individual's life. It is
an account of Luther as instrument of divine providence, which also praises
a selection of his extraordinary human qualities.

In other words, Luther, the exemplary human, is depicted by
Melanchthon as possessing only those features of character which are
of relevance to his divine mission. These happen to be his thirst for
learning, and more particularly humanist learning. Melanchthon stresses
his interest in rhetoric and the role of *bonae litterae* in his propaedeutic
studies. Although Luther was condemned to study the 'thorny dialectic of
the time' in Erfurt and although he found he had a gift for it, his mind,
according to Melanchthon, 'required much more and better.' Therefore, he
read authors such as Cicero, Virgil, Livy and others 'not as a child would,
just picking out words, but for instruction and as a mirror of human life'
seeking to apply their precepts. He thus became the object of admiration at
Erfurt.[10] This suggests that, in Melanchthon's view, the human God chose
to implement His design should be extremely intelligent and imbued with
classical learning and its moral values. The message here is the standard
Christian humanist message: only classical learning can lead to the right
understanding of the Bible, the implicit conclusion being that God could not
have chosen a scholastic as his instrument.[11] Indeed, Luther's biographer is
very keen to stress that his hero entered the Augustinian order not to profit
from scholastic learning and its methods, but for reasons of piety. This
meant that he could treat scholastic learning as a *parergon*, or incidental,
especially as he found it very easy. His principal concern was to 'read avidly

9   Ibid., p. 1: 'Spem nobis fecerat reuerendus vir Martinus Lutherus et curriculum se
vitae suae et certaminum occasiones narraturum esse quod fecisset, nisi ex hac mortali vita
ad aeternam Dei et ecclesiae coelestis consuetudinem euocatus esset. Vtilis autem esset et
priuatae ipsius vitae consideratio luculenter scripta, plena enim fuit exemplorum quae ad
confirmandam pietatem in bonis mentibus profutura essent et occasionum recitatio quae
posteritatem de multis rebus commonefacere posset.'

10   Ibid., p. 2: 'incidit Erphordiae in eius aetatis dialecticen satis spinosam, quam cum
sagacitate ingenii praeceptionum causas et fontes melius quam caeteri perspiceret cito arripuit.
Cumque mens auida doctrinae plura et meliora requireret, legit ipse pleraque veterum
Latinorum scriptorum monumenta, Ciceronis, Virgilii, Liuii et aliorum. Haec legebat non
vt pueri, verba tantum excerpentes sed vt humanae vitae doctrinam aut imagines. Quare et
consilia horum scriptorum et sententias propius aspiciebat et vt erat memoria fidelis et firma,
pleraque ei lecta et audita in conspectu et ob oculos erant. Sic igitur in iuuentute eminebat vt
toti academiae Lutheri ingenium admirationi esset.'

11   See also Irena Backus, 'Bullinger and Humanism', in E. Campi and P. Opitz (eds),
*Heinrich Bullinger. Life–Thought–Influence, Zurich, Aug. 25–29, 2004. International
Congress Heinrich Bullinger (1504–1575)*, 2 vols (Zurich: TVZ, 2007), vol. 2, pp. 637–59.
Although Bullinger too believed that only humanist learning paved the way to the Bible and
so to the truth, he never drew the providential conclusion that Melanchthon drew.

by himself the sources of celestial doctrine, in other words, the writings of the Prophets and the Apostles, so as to instruct his mind in God's will and to nourish fear and love by firm testimonies.'[12] Thus Luther the man possessed humanist learning and was pious. What other human qualities did God require of his instrument? Very few. Although Melanchthon never denies his subject's personal merits and virtues, that is not what is important. Indeed, having made clear to his readers that Luther followed the humanist course of studies, there was nothing much (in Melanchthon's view) about Luther the man that he, Melanchthon, needed to write about. As he puts it himself,

> And although the man's virtue as such is also worthy of praise for he used God's gifts with reverence, nonetheless it is necessary to give our thanks mainly to God because it was through Luther that He restored and restituted the light of the Gospel. And it is the memory of his doctrine which needs to be maintained and spread.[13]

He does, however, insist that Luther, far from wishing to trouble public order, firmly separated church and state, and that whatever he did pertained to the sacred realm only.

> The things that are of God he gave to God, he taught them correctly, he invoked the name of God when he should. He also had other virtues which are necessary in a man who is pleasing to God. As for political matters, he regularly avoided seditious counsel. I judge these virtues to be of such quality that other greater virtues cannot be sought in this life.[14]

In short, despite the Suetonian framework, and despite its periodic insistence on the protagonist's piety and his undoubted virtues, Luther's *Life* by Melanchthon turns out to be more of a handbook of the German Reformation than a *Life* of an individual. The real object of his work is not the man Luther, not even as an *exemplum*; it is Luther's place in God's plan. What then, according to Melanchthon, are the distinctive features of the movement that Luther implemented?

Firstly and most importantly, Melanchthon refuses to admit that his hero wanted to change anything. He therefore separates Luther's discovery

---

[12]   *Vitae quatuor Reformatorum*, ed. Neander: (*Vita Lutheri*), p. 5: 'haec studia tanquam parerga tractabat et facile arripiebat illas scholasticas methodos. Interea fontes doctrinae coelestis auide legebat ipse, scilicet scripta prophetica et apostolica vt mentem suam de Dei voluntate erudiret et firmis testimoniis aleret timorem et fidem.'

[13]   Ibid., p. 10: 'Et quanquam ipsius viri virtus etiam laude digna est, qui Dei donis reuerenter vsus est, tamen praecipue Deo gratias agi necesse est, quod per eum nobis restituit Euangelii lucem et ipsius doctrinae memoria retinenda et propaganda est.'

[14]   Ibid.: 'Ac talis quidem Lutherus ipse fuit: quae Dei sunt, Deo dedit, recte docuit, recte Deum inuocauit. Habuit et alias virtutes necessarias in homine, qui placet Deo. Deinde in politica consuetudine constantissime vitauit omnia seditiosa consilia. Has virtutes tanta esse iudico decora vt alia maiora in hac vita expeti non possint.'

of salvation by grace from his (later) quarrels with Rome. He insists that
Luther put forward his doctrine of salvation while he was firmly ensconced
in the Augustinian order and had no wish to invent anything new or to
foment quarrels. What he had to say is only what had been said before by
John the Baptist:

> Luther recalled men's minds to the Son of God and, just as John the Baptist
> pointed to the Lamb of God who took away our sins, so he showed that our
> sins are remitted gratuitously because of the Son of God and that this favour
> must be accepted by faith.[15]

This, according to Melanchthon, conferred him great authority so that
when he came to teach on penance, faith and remission of sins, those
who were more learned were thrilled by the sweetness of his teaching,
all the more so as Erasmus had already seen to it that the ground had
been prepared by giving new importance to the study of Greek and
Latin.[16] Melanchthon knew that, excepting the fact that Luther used
Erasmus' *New Testament* for his own German translation of the Bible,
nothing could be less certain than the reformer's direct indebtedness to
Erasmus. Furthermore, at the time when Melanchthon was writing, the
quarrel between Erasmus and Luther had become part of the theological
landscape. In his eschatological perspective, however, Erasmus and Luther
were indeed a part of the same renewal, the philology of one preparing
the ground for the theology of the other. At the same time, Melanchthon
admitted that it was Luther's, and not Erasmus', role in the history of
salvation which was of crucial import, and this is why he went to such
lengths to stress that Luther did not just put an end to a few abuses, but
he 'encompassed the whole of the doctrine necessary to the church, he
restituted purity of ritual and gave an example to the pious on how to
restore the church.'[17] Melanchthon's *Life* of Luther is part of his vision
of church history, which is determined solely by God and the devil whose
presence is subject to God's permission. If reformers such as Augustine or
Luther emerge at certain points (Luther being especially important as he
is the last reformer prior to the end of history), this is due solely to God's
providence. In that sense, all reformers are to be seen as no more than
divine instruments.[18] This view has important bearing on Melanchthon's

---

15   Ibid., p. 6: 'Reuocauit igitur Lutherus hominum mentes ad Filium Dei, et, vt Baptista
monstrauit agnum Dei qui tulit peccata nostra, ostendit gratis propter Filium Dei remitti
peccata et quidem oportet id beneficium fide accipi.'

16   Ibid., pp. 6–7.

17   Ibid., pp. 8–9: 'Quod ideo recito vt non solum considerant pii quos errores taxauerit,
quae idola sustulerit Lutherus, sed etiam sciant complexum eum esse vniuersam doctrinam
ecclesiae necessariam et puritatem in ritibus restituisse et piis exempla instaurandarum
ecclesiarum monstrasse.'

18   On this, see Backus, *Historical Method and Confessional Identity*, pp. 326–38.

concept of religious biography, as it causes him to break with the portrait method and to elaborate a distinct concept of a saint as one who is the instrument of God in his design to reform the church at certain periods in history. Although, as we have seen, Luther's biographer never denied that the purely human life of a providential reformer can have exemplary value, this in his view should be a suitable subject for an autobiography and not a biography. This explains why he devoted two whole sections of the *Life* to the 'four developments of Christian doctrine after the time of the Apostles' and to 'the necessity for Luther's reformation'.

The four developments are similar to those in the *Chronicon Carionis*, but the schema of Melanchthon's *Life* of Luther is simpler and leaves civil authorities out of the picture. He concentrates on Luther's importance within the history of the church, beginning with the apostolic era. After the purity of the apostolic era comes the *aetas origenica*, which represents a major perversion as 'in the minds of many it confused the Gospel with philosophy.' The same age, according to Melanchthon, 'abandoned all distinction between the Law and the Gospel, and untaught what the Apostles had taught.'[19] This gave rise to the Pelagian Age, the errors of which were then remedied by Augustine, whose era represents the second age in Melanchthon's chronology. Augustine was followed by some right-thinking men such as Prosper of Aquitaine and others right up until the time of Bernard of Clairvaux; they all represent the third age. Thereafter comes the *Gigantum aetas*, or the era of all the major errors, with the government of the church being taken over by lawyers, and with its introduction of Aristotle into the theology curriculum, all this being accompanied by the rise of the mendicant orders, and theology and piety coming to such a pass that the more pious scholastic theologians were longing for reforms.[20] Hence the necessity for Luther's Reformation, which has God as its sole author.

Although Melanchthon does not say so, he assumes six ages in all, of which Luther's is the fifth, the sixth being the final age. Melanchthon's biography found an echo outside of Germany, and was published in a French translation in Geneva in 1549 with a short poem in Luther's honour by Theodore Beza.[21] The translation itself is anonymous.

---

[19]   *Vitae quatuor Reformatorum*, ed. Neander: (*Vita Lutheri*), pp. 10–11: 'Origenica aetas, etsi aliqui fuerunt recte sentientes qualem fuisse Methodium arbitror, qui deliramenta Origenis improbauit, tamen in animis multitudinis inflexit euangelium ad philosophiam, hoc est, offudit hanc persuasionem, mediocrem rationis disciplinam mereri remissionem peccatorum et esse iustitiam de qua diceretur: "iustus ex fide sua viuet." Haec aetas paene totum amisit discrimen Legis et Euangelii et sermonem Apostolorum dedidicit.'

[20]   Ibid.

[21]   *Histoire de la vie et faitz de venerable homme M. Martin Luther, pur et entier Docteur de Theologie, fidèlement redigée par escrit par M. Philippe Melanchthon* (A Geneve, chez Iean Girard, 1549). The poem, signed by the initials 'D. D. B.' (Dieudonné de Bèze), is on

Johann Mathesius (1504–65): Preserving the memory of the 'Wundermann'

Johann Mathesius, sometimes mistakenly called 'Luther's first biographer',[22] was born in Rochlitz, north-west of Chemnitz. After studies at the University of Ingolstadt, he tutored children of noblemen in Munich for a brief period. He then went on to Wittenberg prior to moving to Jáchymov, Northern Bohemia, as school rector. He returned to Wittenberg in 1540 for further studies, and recorded some of Luther's *Tischreden*. In the same year he was granted his MA, and was ordained by Luther two years later. He then returned to Jáchymov as pastor and preacher, and protected the city from imperial officials during the Schmalkaldic War. He is known today chiefly for his sermons, many of which were printed in the sixteenth century, which provide a very interesting picture of the Lutheran Church during the period. His collection of seventeen sermons on Luther's life, preached between 1563 and 1565, is probably the best known of these.[23] First published in this form in 1566, the *Life* was basically pastoral in outlook as might be expected. Although not avoiding polemic at all costs,[24] Mathesius knew very well that he was preaching to the converted.[25] Given its homiletic form, which suggests on the face of it the medieval model of Sermons on the *Lives* of the saints, why did Volz credit Mathesius' work with being the first biography of Luther?

He gives a variety of reasons, not all of them equally convincing. He notes that when Mathesius published his *Historien*, two other *Lives* of Luther were already available. One of these was Melanchthon's *Life*, he says, and the other was Matthäus Ratzeberger's sketches on the history of Luther's time, a treatise situated halfway between biography and history which in fact did not appear until 1850. Volz does not consider either

---

the verso of the title page: '*Dizain*. Apres auoir longuement combattu, / et contre tous verité defendue, / De grands trauaux et vieillesse abbattu, / Luther le Grand à Dieu l'ame a rendue. / Quoy donc, sa force est elle ainsi perdue? / Non, car sa vie au vif icy descripte, / Dedans nos cueurs touts les iours resuscite, / Asseurant ceux qui de Foy ont vescu, / De veoir d'Enfer la puissance destruite, / Morte leur mort, et leur peché vaincu.' [After having struggled for a long time and defended the truth against everyone, the great Luther gave up his soul to God, beaten down by old age and sickness. Does this mean that all his impact is thus lost? No, his life, written down here, makes him come alive in our hearts every single day, assuring those who have lived in faith that they will see the defeat of the powers of hell, the demise of their death and the defeat of their sins.]

[22]   See, for example, Robert Rosin, art. 'Mathesius' in *Oxford Encyclopedia of the Reformation*, ed. Hans Hillerbrand, 6 vols (Oxford and New York: Oxford University Press, 1996), vol. 3, pp. 32–3.

[23]   See ibid., Bibliography, p. 33.

[24]   See Volz, *Mathesius*, p. 46.

[25]   I shall be referring here to the reprint of the 1566 edition: *Historien von dem Leben und den Schicksalen des grossen Reformators Doctor Martin Luther im Jahr 1565 in 17 Predigten beschrieben von Johann Mathesius, vormals Pfarrer zu Wittenberg* (Leipzig: bey Salomo Lincke, 1806). Hereafter: Mathesius, *Historien* (1566).

Melanchthon's or Ratzenberger's works as biographies. He founds his opinion of Melanchthon's work on nineteenth- and twentieth-century literature, which saw it mainly as a defence of Luther and of the evangelical cause against the attacks of the Romanists.[26] This is why he rejects its value as a biography, and not on the basis of Melanchthon's assertion that his biography of Luther does not contain sufficient personal elements to make it into an account of a life. Nor does he have anything to say to Melanchthon's open expression of regret that Luther died before writing his autobiography, which could have accommodated these personal elements. As regards Ratzeberger's long-unpublished account, Volz dismisses it as fragmentary and more akin to the genre of history than biography.[27] He also cites the *Sermons* of Cyriacus Spangenberg preached in Mansfeld at practically the same time that Mathesius preached his in Wittenberg. Volz reproaches Spangenberg with not keeping to the chronological order and with producing a work closer to *Sermons on Lives of the Saints* than anything else, on the model of Geiler of Kaisersberg, for example. It is indeed true that Spangenberg treats Luther under various headings or *loci communes* without taking much interest in his life. Among these *loci communes* we might mention Luther as Elijah, Luther as God's Angel, Luther as the true Evangelist and so on, which, as Kolb points out, go back to the early years of the Reformation, and which were only reinforced by the eschatological tones of Melanchthon's biography, much against the latter's will.[28] *Sermons* 14–21 treat Luther in an emblematic fashion.[29]

As against these and similar fragmentary and inaccurate portrayals of the reformer, Volz sets Mathesius' *Sermons*, which keep to the chronological order and which constitute the first ever (in Volz's view) account of the Wittenberg reformer based not just on personal acquaintance, but also on much documentary evidence. However, as we shall see below, it is the extremely hostile biography of Cochlaeus which rests on the most reliable documentary evidence as well as on the controversialist's personal knowledge of Luther. It also follows the chronology of the reformer's life rigorously year by year, and remains to this day an invaluable guide not only to the history of the Reformation, but, its inclusion of scurrilous myths apart, to the sequence and the nature of the reformer's *acta et gesta*.

---

[26]   See Volz, *Mathesius*, p. 36.

[27]   See ibid., pp. 36–7.

[28]   See Kolb, 'Umgestaltung', pp. 203–10, for Spangenberg's eschatological treatment of Luther. Kolb devotes only a few lines to Mathesius (p. 5) and thinks after Volz that 'Mathesius biography represented for the Lutherans the primary source for any new attempts at writing Luther's biography.' His remarks on Luther's portrayal by Selnecker, Dresser, and so on are valuable mainly for drawing our attention to Luther's portrayal in the context of controversies with the Crypto-Calvinists.

[29]   See Volz, *Mathesius*, p. 37.

Leaving aside the issue of friendly or hostile orientation and tone, and concentrating on the issue of method, what, if anything, makes Mathesius more of a biographer than Melanchthon and authors like Rabus, Spangenberg, for example, who saw above all the eschatological significance of the reformer and who preached sermons about him as if he were a saint? The quick answer is: attention to chronology, the presence of personal details and a fairly calm tone, but not very much else. Indeed, Mathesius' material was to be used and reused by Lutheran theologians in their defence of the Wittenberg reformer's doctrine of the Eucharist, in particular against Roman Catholic and Calvinist onslaughts in the latter half of the sixteenth and early seventeenth century.[30] Without being at all objective, Mathesius' *Historien* as such was as uncontroversial as it was possible for a Luther hagiography to be, which is very likely what contributed to its popularity as the *Urquelle* of later defences of Luther's authority.

So as to reach the widest possible public, Mathesius avoided any but the most general mention of theological issues while emphasising the pastoral angle. He also avoided any points that might be construed as contentious in such a way as to prove derogatory to Luther. Thus he mentions Erasmus' *Julius exclusus* as a precursor to Luther's reforms, but does not breathe a word about the 1525 quarrel between Erasmus and Luther.[31] In a similar vein, he does not give any details of the contents of Luther's theses of 1517.[32] His preface to the *Historien* in their published version is very revealing of his general stance and method, which has little in common with that of a biographer. Firstly, and most obviously, Mathesius' choice to commemorate Luther in sermon form and in the vernacular suggests that he was influenced by the same tradition of sermons on saints' lives as Spangenberg and, furthermore, that he was aware that this very form would, more than any other, make an impact not just on his parishioners, but on all his readers. In a vein very similar to that of Spangenberg, he makes it clear that Luther is no ordinary person and that he, Mathesius, having preached on the *Gospels*, *Samuel*, the *Psalms* and on *Paul's Epistles*, among other texts, has decided to preach on Luther[33] not because of any need to set down a correct sequence of events or to clear the reformer's *Life* from myths, but because Luther was, as he puts it, a miracle-man (*Wundermann*), a prophet of the German nation, sent by God in the last days, in other words the instrument of the Almighty (*Gottes Werkzeug*),[34] whose work has been largely forgotten especially by younger people, which has led to mingling his pure teaching with impurities. Not unlike Selnecker

---

[30]   Kolb, 'Umgestaltung', pp. 209–15.
[31]   Mathesius, *Historien* (1566), p. 19.
[32]   Ibid., pp. 28–32.
[33]   Ibid., p. [i].
[34]   Ibid.

after him, Mathesius aims to unite the conflicting Lutheran factions around the reformer. His work has a strong eschatological bent, and his conception of Luther as instrument of God is very similar to Melanchthon's, whose *Life* of Luther he obviously used as a source of inspiration.

He is fully cognisant, he explains (thus denying that he has any ambition to write an historical biography), that he has not kept to the narrative form that the appellation *Historien* implies. However, he conceives his task as preaching to the uneducated and to laymen in general. He has therefore handled his material so that his account could serve as consolation, instruction and admonition for all sorts of eventualities in the church and in the lives of the faithful, even if it meant oversimplifying. That same wish to reach as wide a public as possible has made him decide to publish the *Historien* in German, the same language they were preached in.[35] In a word, Mathesius sets out not to write a biography of Luther, but to commemorate the last prophet of the German nation and to set down his life as a spiritual and pastoral example to as wide a public as possible. His other reason for writing the *Historien* is that Mathesius feels that he owes a debt of gratitude to the Wittenberg Church and University, the two foundations that are due to Luther and of which he is a proud to be a member.[36] The preface ends with his declaration of loyalty to these two institutions on his own behalf and also on behalf of his children and parishioners.[37]

On his own admission, Mathesius' account of Luther's life is deliberately simplified and given an edificatory slant in an eschatological framework. In his conception of Luther as prophet and as God's instrument, our biographer, if he may be called that, does not distinguish himself sharply from Melanchthon or Spangenberg. Admittedly, he is more exhaustive on the details of the reformer's life than either of these, as well as being better documented. However, his aim is basically to edify, and not to chronicle. The terms *Gottes Werkzeug* and *Wundermann* constitute a *leitmotif* of the account. It is worth noting, however, that, despite the relative absence of references to contemporary controversies, Mathesius, like, after him, Selnecker in 1574/75, devotes particular care and attention to the chapter (Sermon 8) on the *Augsburg Confession*, detailing its theological content which he found obviously to be more important than that of the 95 theses which, as we have said, he passed over in silence. The account of the Augsburg Diet is thus one of the more historical parts of Mathesius' account. Naturally, writing in an edificatory mode, he makes no reference to the attacks of Surius, let alone Cochlaeus. However, his description of

---

[35] Ibid., p. [ii].
[36] Ibid., p. [iii].
[37] Ibid., p. [vii].

the emperor's arrival in Augsburg is obviously based on Cochlaeus,[38] while his summary of the articles of the *Confession* is equally obviously his own.[39] Mathesius' intention was obviously to commemorate the *Confession* as much as it was to commemorate the Prophet of the German Nation, God's instrument, Elijah, and so on – all names he currently uses as synonymous for Martin Luther in common with Spangenberg, Rabus and Selnecker.[40]

Mathesius' work is therefore very much in the mainstream of Luther hagiography of the late sixteenth century, with a chronological framework and a few personal details added. His perspective remains resolutely edificatory and consolatory. He is not unlike Melanchthon in his focus on the eschatological aspect of Luther's life and activity, and on his role as God's instrument. Like Spangenberg and Rabus, he sees the reformer as an incarnation of biblical figures and a latter-day prophet and apostle. Added to this is the fact that Mathesius communicated his account of Luther orally before writing it down, which was obviously the accepted way. Naturally, given the amount of fiction promulgated about the Wittenberg reformer in the form of idealised accounts, theatre plays, and so on, Mathesius' *Historien* is a model of sobriety.[41] However, this does not make him the first biographer of Luther, as Volz would have it. When it came to situating Luther in the context of his time, Cochlaeus' work, which I shall be examining further on, despite his obvious hostility to the person of the reformer, proved to be far more precise, as well as being more influential on the international scale and better documented, if not about Luther, then at least about the historical background to his life.

Nikolaus Selnecker. Biography of Luther as Statement of Faith

Nikolaus Selnecker, who was a friend of Mathesius, explicitly stated in the opening chapter of his Latin biography of Luther that he was not seeking to better either Mathesius' or Sleidan's work, but that he was simply concerned to restore the memory of Luther and the *Augsburg Confession* in the face of threatening oblivion.[42] Although a Crypto-Calvinist in the

---

[38]   Volz does not mention Cochlaeus in his table of Mathesius' sources for this chapter (cf. Volz, *Mathesius*, pp. 244–8). He only lists Luther's own writings, however.

[39]   Mathesius, *Historien* (1566), pp. 205–15.

[40]   See Kolb, 'Umgestaltung', pp. 206, 214–15.

[41]   See ibid., pp. 215–16, where Kolb notes that Luther's life by the seventeenth century was the object of religious plays which naturally mixed fact with fiction.

[42]   Nikolaus Selnecker, *Historica oratio vom Leben und Wandel des Ehrwirdigen Herrn und thewren Mannes Gottes D. Martini Lutheri. Auch von einhelliger und bestendiger Eintrechtigkeit Herrn Lutheri und Philippi* (Fürth/Bay.: Flacius-Verlag, 1992) (hereafter: Selnecker, *Historica oratio* (1576)), fol. A2v.: 'Quamuis enim alii in eodem argumento sudarint magna cum laude et extent inter caetera Sleidani de Luthero labor latinus ac D. Mathesii conciones de eodem grauissimae germanice habitae et scriptae, tamen cum viderem

early stages of his career, a member of Melanchthon's inner circle as a student in Wittenberg from 1549 to 1558 (the year when he became court preacher at Dresden), Nikolaus Selnecker was eventually drawn away from Philippist theology around 1570 and formed together with Martin Chemnitz and Jakob Andreae the nucleus of the team that worked in 1576–77 under the aegis of Elector Augustus of Saxony to compose the *Formula of Concord* and to win support for it.[43] The *Formula of Concord*, the first official document of Lutheran Unity, was founded on the *Augsburg Confession* which constituted its centrepiece. Selnecker was officially a Philippist during his years as court preacher in Dresden, albeit in some disagreement about doctrinal issues with his Crypto-Calvinist colleagues. Whether that was part of the reason for his dismissal from Dresden is uncertain.[44] After his departure from Dresden, he taught at the University of Jena between 1565 and 1568, and then at Leipzig (1568–86), where he was also superintendent and preacher at St Thomas's Church. Frequently sent on missions by Augustus of Saxony, he found himself involved alongside Chemnitz and Andreae in the reformation of Braunschweig–Wolfenbüttel (1570–74). It was on his return to Leipzig that he held the lecture on Luther's life which was to be published in Latin in 1575 under the title *Nicolai Selnecceri D. Historica narratio et oratio de D. D. Martino Luthero, postremae aetatis Elia et initiis, causis et progressu Confessionis Augustanae atque Lutheri ac Philippi homonoia sancat, Lipsiae publice habita et recitata, mensis novembris die XXII. ante enarrationem eiusdem Confessionis propter Historiam et alias utilitates studiosae Iuuentuti perquam necessaria. Anno salutis abundantis 1574.*[45] In 1576, at the very time that Selnecker was working on the *Formula of Concord*, the *Historica oratio* was translated into German by a student of his, Paul Heusler. Heusler published it in 1576 under the title *Historica oratio vom Leben und Wandel des Ehrwirdigen Herrn und thewren Mannes Gottes D. Martini Lutheri. Auch von einhelliger und bestendiger Eintrechtigkeit Herrn Lutheri und Philippi. Gehalten in der Universitet in Leipzig durch Nicolaum Selneccerum, der heiligen Schrifft Doctorn*

---

obliterari pleraque et iuuentuti erudiendae raro proponi ea quae Deus nostris temporibus potenter et successu mirabili et quidem nobis et ad nostrum vsum praestitit ...'. This passage is included in the 1576 German version of the work by Heusler (fols 1v.–2r.). Only the reference to Sleidan and Mathesius was suppressed by the translator so as not to complicate the task for the less learned readers of this version.

[43]   On Selnecker (1530–92), see Robert Kolb, art. 'Selnecker', in *Oxford Encyclopedia of the Reformation*, ed. Hillerbrand, vol. 4, p. 43, and literature cited ibid. For older but still valuable biographies, see Hasse, 'Die Lutherbiographie', p. 94, n. 8.

[44]   See Jobst Ebel, 'Die Herkunft des Konzeptes der Konkordienformel', *Zeitschrift für Kirchengeschichte*, 91 (1980): 237–82; Irene Dingel, *Concordia controuersa. Die öffentlichen Diskussionen um das lutherische Konkordienwerk am Ende des 16. Jhdts.* (Gütersloh: Gütersloher Verlagshaus, 1996), pp. 155–9, 245–8, 274–80.

[45]   (Lipsiae, apud haeredes Iacobi Berualdi, 1575.)

und Professorn etc. Aus dem Latein ins Deudsch gebracht und itziger Zeit nutzlich zu lesen, 1576.[46]

It is noteworthy that the German title omits all the details to do with the exact place and date of Selnecker's lecture. Further differences between the Latin and the German title and version suggest that the two versions were intended for two distinct circles of readers. As Hasse notes, Selnecker's Latin version contains a preface addressed by the author to Duke Christian I of Saxony (1560–91), who was 14 years old at the time.[47] In the preface, Selnecker urges the young duke not to forget Luther's Reformation and to do everything in his power to safeguard this great gift from God. He thinks that forgetting the essence of the Lutheran Reformation would lead to every possible evil such as arrogance, pride and rashness, culminating in the introduction of new (heterodox) teaching. The work, conceived in the midst of the Crypto-Calvinist crisis in Saxony,[48] was to undergo numerous reprints. The Latin version was revised in 1591. The German translation by Heusler dispensed with the foreword to Christian I, substituting for it the translator's foreword to Isaiah Heidenreich, preacher and superintendent of the Church in Breslau (Wrocław). While vehement in urging all true Christians to praise God and to thank Him for the Reformation, the translator's preface shows itself to be remarkably uninformative about the original. Heusler simply says,

> This *Oratio* was delivered here in Leipzig before studious youth by the honourable and very erudite Nikolaus Selnecker, my dear Latin teacher, highly regarded by the church, and, as I was asked to translate it into German for the high authorities,[49] I obeyed this wish. [... *und von mir, da es hoher Obrigkeit solte ins deudsch verfertiget werden, auff solch beger ins deudsch gebracht* ...] The reason for this was, that the work is about the wonderful works and blessings of God, of which He gave us ample proof through his faithful instrument Martin Luther of blessed and saintly memory, and through the *Augsburg Confession* which was promulgated despite all the difficulties. It also communicates many other excellent facts which are not generally known.[50]

---

[46]   Hasse, 'Die Lutherbiographie', pp. 101–3.

[47]   Ibid., pp. 102–4. Hasse reproduces ibid. (p. 103) Selnecker's autograph dedication to Christian I from the copy held by the Sächsische Landesbibliothek in Dresden.

[48]   On this, see especially H. J. R. Calinich, *Kampf und Untergang des Melanchthonismus in Kursachsen in den Jahren 1570 bis 1574 und die Schicksale seiner vornehmsten Häupter* (Leipzig: n.p., 1866); Ernst Koch, 'Der kursachsische Philippismus und seine Krise in den 1560er und 1570er Jahren', in Heinz Schilling (ed.), *Die reformierte Konfessionalisierung in Deutschland – Das Problem der 'zweiten Reformation'* (Gütersloh: Gütersloher Verlagshaus, 1986), pp. 60–77.

[49]   Very likely the Electress Anna of Saxony, who received the Latin copy intended for Christian together with a letter from Selnecker and who usually requested a German version of all writings sent to her. See Hasse, 'Die Lutherbiographie', p. 102, n. 37 and p. 105, n. 42.

[50]   I am referring here to the anastatic reprint of Selnecker's *Historica oratio* (1576), fols *iv.–*iir.

The omission of dates and of the reference to the *Augsburg Confession* in the title; the suppression of a collection of documents intended to illustrate the history of the *Confession*, which was appended to the original; the omission from the title of the description of Luther as 'latter-day Elijah', as well as the omission of Selnecker's preface to Christian I of Saxony; and finally the presence of Heusler's allusion to the author's wish to make the work available to civil powers, all suggest that the *Historica oratio* was to be marketed in German as a work of general import and no longer as an occasional piece intended for the quelling of Crypto-Calvinist feelings in electoral Saxony in 1574.[51] However, as against Hasse's contention that the *Oratio* in German became more of an edificatory *exemplum* and that it lost much of its profile as an apology of the *Augsburg Confession*, I should like to argue that the core of the treatise remained unaltered.[52] All that happened was that in its 'civil authorities' version, it was somewhat simplified and shortened, notably by the suppression of the appendices on the history of the *Confession*. As for the simplification of the title, the intention behind it was just that. It was much easier to sell the work to laypeople, however illustrious, as a *Life of Luther* than as a *Life of Luther* and a History of the *Augsburg Confession*, which gave it a technical slant.

Even so, Selnecker's work remained as much an apology for the *Augsburg Confession* as a *Life of Luther*, with the core of the work remaining the same. Thus in both versions, Selnecker argues in the opening lines that having finished the exposition of the early ecumenical Creeds – that is, the *Apostolic* and the *Nicene Creed* followed by the *Quicumque* –, he has now got to the point of starting his exposition of the *Augsburg Confession* 'called to it by the Son of God, the Lord Jesus Christ.' He thinks this absolutely fitting as the *Augsburg Confession*, according to him, 'serves us as a *Creed* at this time and contains the very essence of the word of salvation; that is, faith, holy doctrine and every single article invoked by the *militia Christi*.'[53] What is more, he says, he undertook to lecture on the text expressly with a view to 'informing our dear young people about the origins of the *Augsburg Confession* and its teaching, so called after the place where it was first set down and handed over, a place called Augsburg or Augusta, where the august princes our ancestors offered and presented it to the august Emperor Charles.'[54]

---

[51]   In Heusler's version, the *Historica oratio* was very often used as an introduction to Selnecker's edition of Luther's *Tischreden* (1577, 1580, 1581 etc.).

[52]   See Hasse, 'Die Lutherbiographie', pp. 105–6.

[53]   Selnecker, *Historica oratio* (1576), fol. 1r.–v. Selnecker lectured on all these *Creeds* in 1574. His lectures appeared in 1575 and were to be reprinted in 1577: *Symbolorum, Apostolici, Niceni et Athanasiani Exegesis fideliter repetens doctrinam perpetuam Ecclesiae Dei … scripta et edita Autore Nicolao Selneccero D. electorali professore in Academia Lipsica…* (Lipsiae, Joannes Rhamba, 1575).

[54]   Selnecker, *Historica oratio* (1576), fols 1v.–2r.

Similarly, both versions contain the polemical passages against the Carthusian Laurentius Surius (1523–1578) and his *Commentarius breuis rerum in orbe gestarum ab anno Salutis 1500 vsque ad annum 1566 ex optimis quibusque scriptoribus congestus*, which was printed in Cologne in 1566 prior to undergoing further expanded editions. Here, we should bear in mind that Surius set out to refute Sleidan's 'scientific' source-based historiography of the Reformation by portraying the movement as powered by demonic (in the sense of anti-Romanist) forces. Surius was first and foremost a compiler. His *Commentarius* was initially intended as a continuation of Nauclerus' *Universal History*, but finally appeared as a separate publication under Surius' own name. It relied mainly on hostile material such as Simon Fontaine, Kaspar von Gennep and, first and foremost, Johann Cochlaeus' *Commentaria Ioannis Cochlaei De Actis et Scriptis Martini Lutheri Saxoni*, published in 1549.[55] Because of its polemical anti-Sleidan orientation and fairly superficial use of sources, Surius' work encountered great success. Originally published in Latin, it was eventually expanded up to the year 1574 and translated into German and French. According to Herte, it underwent ten editions between 1566 and mid-seventeenth century.[56] Obviously, Selnecker saw its popularity as a major threat to the image of Luther and Lutheranism. Viewed in this light, it constituted as important an adversary as any Crypto-Calvinist movement. Selnecker lists it as such in the *Oratio* right from the outset:

> We must first of all recount the reason and the occasion for the *Augsburg Confession*, how it was written, handed over, accepted and confirmed, and we must tell it as it was, so that the chief leaders, electors, princes and parliaments are correctly and accurately informed, not just those who are well disposed to our Confession and who signed it, but also its detractors who are unable to lie in such a clear matter and who are a cause of shame to the righteous and the worthy among whose number Surius, the Carthusian monk and other birds of prey are not to be counted, as they oppose the truth ....[57]

Although apparently of a general nature, the allusion points clearly to Selnecker's preoccupations. Firstly, Surius is clearly named as an opponent of the *Augsburg Confession* and therefore implicitly as posing a major threat to Lutheran unity. Secondly, the passage makes clear that it is not just the Christian youth who is the prime recipient of the work, but all sovereigns and civil authorities, regardless of whether or not they subscribe to the *Confession*.

---

[55]   (Mainz, Franz Behem.) Cited hereafter as: Cochlaeus, *Commentaria* after the English translation in *Two contemporary accounts of Martin Luther*, eds, trans. and ann. Vandiver, Keen and Frazel. On Fontaine and Gennep, see Herte, *Das katholische Lutherbild*, vol. 1, pp. 9–17.

[56]   See ibid., vol. 1, pp. 17–21.

[57]   See Selnecker, *Historica oratio* (1576), fols 2v.–3r.

Other passages are even more explicit, as they attack a specific section of Surius' *Commentarius* and its portrayal of Luther. Selnecker says:

> Here we must not forget the shameful lies of the monk Surius, which would make the devil, who has been a liar from the beginning, ashamed of himself. He claims that one could have seen and recognised in Luther such things as made him suspect in the monastery of having concluded a pact with the devil, and in particular the fact that when one time during Mass, the Gospel passage about the driving out of the deaf and blind devil was being read out, he suddenly fell down on the ground screaming, 'it is not me, it is not me.' Such open lies ... do not even deserve an answer. But as Surius adds that Luther himself often testifies that he knows the devil and that he has eaten more than a grain of salt with him, we must insist that Luther is talking in the same spirit as all other Christian soldiers who strive daily against the devil's attacks, mockery and cheating ....[58]

The passage in Surius that Selnecker quotes was copied by the Carthusian word for word from the *Commentaria* of Cochlaeus.[59] It found its way into most hostile *Lives* of the reformer including that of Noel Taillepied, as we shall see later on. However, Selnecker obviously encountered it in Surius' *Commentarius* at some time when it was first published in 1566. As against this 'Cochlaean' image of Luther, Selnecker sets the image of the reformer as the providential saviour of the German nation who is symbolised by the *Augsburg Confession*. One of the more interesting features of the *Oratio* is the explicit link it makes between Martin Luther and his namesake St Martin of Tours, on whose feast day the reformer was born. There is no doubt that this reminder is not arbitrary, and that our biographer intended preachers to commemorate Luther by prayer and meditation on St Martin's Day. Selnecker makes a deliberate effort to show that the name 'Martin' was not given fortuitously, but that Luther's patron saint possessed all the virtues that the reformer was to equal and surpass. He therefore has recourse to material from *Lives of the Saints* to remind his readers that St Martin is said to have cut off with a sword a part of his own coat and to have given it to a beggar in Amiens who was suffering from hunger and exposure, neglected by all and sundry. The following night, St Martin apparently saw Christ, clad in the very garment that he had given to the beggar, in the process of telling the angels that it was Martin who had given it to him. Selnecker also evokes Martin's consecration as bishop 'or elder' of Tours, and his participation in the Council of Trier with Ambrose

---

[58]   See ibid., fol. 7r.–v. For the passage in Surius' *Commentarius* that Selnecker refers to, see for example its second edition: *Commentarius breuis rerum gestarum ab anno salutis 1500 vsque in annum 1567 ex optimis quibusque scriptoribus congestus et nunc recens multis locis non parum auctus et locupletatus per F. Laurentium Surium Carthusianum* (Cologne, Geruinus Calenius et haer. Joh. Quentel, 1567), p. 118. Cited hereafter as Surius, *Comm.* (1567).

[59]   See Cochlaeus, *Commentaria*, p.55.

and Jerome. He died peacefully, concludes Selnecker, in 412 AD, in the
reign of Arcadius and Honorius. His last words were, 'Lord, if I can carry
on serving your people, I shall not stint, but if you no longer want me to,
may thy will be done.'[60] The intention behind this excursus was obviously
to show Luther's illustrious spiritual ancestry, thus rejecting the slightest
insinuation of diabolical origins. Needless to say, Surius, who also knew
that Luther was named Martin after St Martin, did not comment on the
symbolic value of this.[61]

As well as the constant vein of polemic against Surius, another salient
feature of both the Latin and the vernacular *Oratio* is its insistence on
the basic agreement between Luther and Melanchthon, with Luther being
portrayed as clearly the more important of the two reformers, while
Melanchthon is portrayed not incorrectly as his most faithful disciple.
Selnecker makes no mention of any divisions in the Lutheran Church
after its founder's death: Luther emerges as the great unifying factor
whose teaching was (and is up to Selnecker's day) conveyed by all of his
colleagues and spiritual descendants, while the *Augsburg Confession* is
depicted as holding the whole church together after the fashion of the
early Christian *Creeds*. Referring to one of his own conversations with
Melanchthon on the subject of Luther, Selnecker reports the *praeceptor*'s
criticism of Karlstadt, who was reputed to have said that he (Karlstadt)
did not hanker after being greater than Luther or even after being seen as
greater than Luther. Melanchthon apparently retorted that Karlstadt was
being excessively arrogant and worldly, for Luther's greatness, honour and
merit were God-given; he did not raise himself above others, did not aspire
to it, and was an enemy of all personal ambition and arrogance.[62]

So, given that Selnecker shared this view of Luther, what was it that made
him important to our biographer? Predictably, it was the perfect accord
between the article on justification by faith in the *Augsburg Confession*
and the Wittenberg reformer's teaching. Given that Selnecker believed that
Luther's teaching was inspired directly by the Holy Spirit, it followed that
so was the article in the *Confession*. I have shown that, for Melanchthon,
Luther was the Reformation, the final eschatological renewal before the
end of history. For Selnecker, he was the agent or the instrument of the
Holy Spirit whose teaching found its institutional embodiment in the
Augsburg Confession, equal in importance to the early ecumenical Creeds
and having as much unifying power.[63] It would be wrong to claim that

60   Selnecker, *Historica oratio* (1576), fols 4v.–5r.
61   Surius, *Comm.* (1567), p. 117: 'Is natus est Islebii in celebri comitatu Mansfeldensi, anno
salutis 1483 pridie D. Martini cuius nomen accepit in baptismo.'
62   Selnecker, *Historica oratio* (1576), fol. 80v.
63   Ibid., fol. 83v.: '… das ist mein doctor Luthers eingebung vom Heiligen Geist und
warhafftiges und heiliges Evangelium etc.'

Selnecker's portrait of Luther did not have eschatological overtones, as might be expected of one whose commentary on Revelation situated the events described by the book in his own time and interpreted the male child in Rev. 12 as Luther.[64] However, the *Oratio* is by and large less overtly eschatological than the Revelation commentary, while stressing the parallel between Elijah and Elisha, and Luther and Melanchthon. Selnecker says,

> Master Philip, who followed Luther just as Elisha followed Elijah, when he got the letter announcing the great man's death during his lecture, said to his audience with much sobbing, lamenting and weeping: he is gone, he is gone. The great charioteer Luther has fallen with the chariot of Israel. May God have mercy on us.[65]

This – as it happens, true – account of Melanchthon's reaction was meant to show the reader that, contrary to Surius' claims, Melanchthon and Luther were at one. The former did not, as the Carthusian claimed, separate from Luther to found a new sect, nor was the *Augsburg Confession* to be taken as an unreliable and informal document, constantly revised only to be broken, a thin veil of unity over a multitude of sects, as Surius would have it.[66] Surius' *Commentarius* does indeed cite accounts by converts to Catholicism attesting that they never found the *Augsburg Confession* to provide a basis for concord and unity, be it in matters of doctrine or ceremonies, and that preachers who professed it disagreed among themselves.[67] He also insists throughout the work on the existence of divisions among the Lutherans, which constitute in his view a proof of the heretical nature of their teaching. The *Augsburg Confession*, he notes, has had to be altered several times so as to be adapted to the teachings of each new sect. Surius has a point when we consider the history of the document which was issued in various forms over the years.[68] It was partly to reply to these and similar criticisms that the *Formula of Concord* and, more particularly, the *Book of Concord* of 1580 restored the 1530 text of the *Confession* presented to the Augsburg Diet, efforts which issued in the famous *Invariata*.

This is the version that Selnecker defends in the final section of the *Oratio*, while passing the intervening versions over in silence. He stresses the public nature of the document, its approval by all the civil rulers and

---

[64] On this, see Irena Backus, *Reformation Readings of the Apocalypse: Geneva, Zurich and Wittenberg* (Oxford and New York: Oxford University Press, 2000), pp. 129–33.

[65] Selnecker, *Historica oratio* (1576), fol. 85v.

[66] Ibid., fols 86r.–87v.

[67] Surius, *Comm.* (1567), p. 936.

[68] See the critical edition by Heinrich Bornkamm in *Die Bekenntnisschriften der evangelisch-lutherischen Kirche herausgegeben im Gedenkjahr der Augsburgischen Konfession 1930*, ed. Deutscher evangelischer Kirchenausschuss, 10th edn (Göttingen: Vandenhoeck & Ruprecht, 1986).

the emperor. However, he still has to account for the eucharistic passages in the *Variata* of 1540 which made some concessions to the Philippists. Disclaiming any first-hand knowledge of this version, he stresses that he had been simply been told that these passages were introduced because there was some hope at the time of getting the 'Sakramentarier', or the Swiss churches, to sign the *Confession*, which is why the landgrave of Hesse asked Melanchthon to amend the text correspondingly. The changes, Selnecker notes, consisted only of leaving out a few words. Melanchthon, who introduced them, did it to obey the orders of the civil authorities, and it is the fault of neither the *praeceptor* nor other Lutheran theologians if their hopes of unity were dashed by the Sacramentarians.

By 1574, this was Selnecker's only possible line of argument, if he was to help put an end to Crypto-Calvinism in Saxony, as well as unite the warring Lutheran factions and provide a satisfactory reply to Surius' attacks. In general, the image of Luther as conveyed by Selnecker does not differ much from Melanchthon's image of the reformer. The main difference is its more specific, political, application. Whereas Melanchthon glorifies Luther as a prophet sent by God in the last days to restore the church, Selnecker, while not oblivious to this aspect, makes the Wittenberg reformer into a symbol of unity, and guarantor of the stability of the *Augsburg Confession* and of the Lutheran Church as an institution. It is in this context that he portrays Luther as Elijah, casting Melanchthon in the role of Elisha.

Hostile *Lives* of Luther: Cochlaeus and After

As I have already said, it was Cochlaeus' *Commentaria*, as filtered through Surius, that partly gave its shape to Selnecker's biography of Luther. As regards the highly influential *Commentaria*, I refer the reader to the recent English translation for a biographical account of Johannes Cochlaeus, one of the most famous pre-Tridentine Catholic controversialists.[69] The contents and sources of his account of Luther's Reformation were the object of a detailed analysis by Adolf Herte in 1935.[70] Herte notes quite rightly that the sheer number of document sources used explicitly or implicitly by Cochlaeus qualifies his *Commentaria* as a work of history. These sources cover a vast range of Luther's writings, as well as Cochlaeus' own correspondence with friends, papal briefs and bulls, pamphlets, disputation proceedings and oral accounts.[71] However, this does not make Cochlaeus into one of the first historical biographers in the modern sense of the term. His aim was not to write a *Life* of Luther, but to produce a

[69]   See Cochlaeus, *Commentaria*, pp. 40–52. Cf. ibid, pp. 357–67 for bibliography.
[70]   Herte, *Lutherkommentare*, cited above in footnote 1.
[71]   Ibid., pp. 1–225.

comprehensive albeit hostile guide to the Lutheran Reformation spanning the reformer's lifetime, so as to inform his readers about the nature of the enemy and his purpose. Needless to say, he wanted to stress the fact that Luther brought untold trouble and suffering to his fatherland. The work was written in Latin, which guaranteed it international and national recognition. It was also unusually detailed for a hostile biography as well as being very well researched, which did not stop the author from making use of a certain number of myths and rumours, which were to mark Luther's image for many years to come, not just in Germany but also in France and other countries.

In his account of Cochlaeus' working method, Herte notes that the work, while founded on an unprecedented wealth of contemporary documents and oral accounts, laid no claims to inserting Luther into universal history, let alone into eschatology. The account itself, according to Herte, follows no clear line of argument. However, despite being overcrowded with detail, all of it intended to improve the readers' knowledge of historical events such as the Augsburg Diet and the drawing-up of the *Augsburg Confession*, the *Commentaria* follow a clearer line of argument than Herte credits them with. What marks out the work is the dichotomy between the author's thorough description of historical events and his completely uncritical reliance on myths and rumours to do with the person of Luther. To stay with the example of the drawing-up of the *Augsburg Confession*, an exceptionally detailed part of the *Commentaria*, Cochlaeus draws on sources such as his own experience of the Diet; the proceedings of the Committee of seventeen and the Committee of fourteen, on both of which he sat in a last-minute attempt to find theological common ground;[72] Kaspar Sturm's account of the emperor's journey to Augsburg; and the official *Acts* regarding the *Confutatio* (of which he was one of the authors) published in 1530.[73] This means that to this day we can turn to the *Commentaria* for an accurate description of the emperor's arrival in Augsburg:

> However, the emperor's arrival was somewhat slower, due to the great honours and display of pomp with which he was most honourably received everywhere in the Venetian lands as he made his way through his ancestral Tyrolean territory. Here his brother King Ferdinand met him and entertained him with the greatest joy and splendour and his people of Swabia who had very famous silver mines gave him one silver coin that was equal in worth to 1700 gold coins and displayed very beautifully all the imperial family trees. And he travelled through the lands of the dukes of Bavaria, who together with King Ferdinand and Cardinal Campeggio, the legate of the apostolic see, retained him for four days in their very beautiful city which is called Munich ....[74]

---

[72]   Ibid., pp. 222–5.

[73]   See ibid., pp. 115–17.

[74]   See Cochlaeus, *Commentaria*, p. 247. Although the modern translators give a full bibliography of secondary literature, they unfortunately do not cite Cochlaeus' sources in

This is a perfectly factual account of the imperial itinerary, based mainly on Sturm's pamphlet (although Cochlaeus does not explicitly name it as one of his sources).[75] As against this and many other passages of undoubted factual value, we must, however, weigh up Cochlaeus' portrayal of Luther as a liar, Satan's associate, and a troublemaker doing everything in his power to perturb his country. One of the work's main objectives is to isolate Luther and brand him a heretic. Cochlaeus is less interested in Melanchthon and other members of the Lutheran faction. In other words, Cochlaeus' *Commentaria* are an interesting mixture of a chronicle (recounting year by year the events that took place in Luther's lifetime as accurately and in as much detail as possible) and a very successful attempt at creating a negative image of Luther, an image which was to be reproduced by most historians hostile to the reformer during the sixteenth century, and of which Surius was one of the most influential purveyors. Now, in order to create a successful negative image, Cochlaeus had recourse to a certain number of myths – some written, some oral – which were already in circulation about Luther and which, as we already saw, were to be reproduced by Surius (among others) prior to crossing the national frontiers.

It is of some significance, however, that Cochlaeus and his imitators were hesitant about resorting to some of the most sensational myths about Luther, in particular the myth of his diabolical origins, which deserves some attention here.[76] In 1533, a German priest called Petrus Silvius published a vernacular pamphlet against Luther under the misleadingly neutral-sounding title of *Zwey neugedruckte nützlichste buechlein, Aus welchen das erste handelt von der gmeynen Christlichen kirchen vnd mechtgiglich erklert.* The pamphlet was one of many published by Silvius, all of them, if Herte is to be believed, too boring to really influence the German public against the Reformation.[77] Silvius, initially a Dominican, left the order on grounds of ill health in 1514. In 1528, he was serving as chaplain to Georg of Saxony, and it was during that period that he took to writing against Luther. Weak and ineffectual though he may have been, nonetheless, Herte notwithstanding, Silvius made one major contribution to the Catholic Luther image: in nearly all his pamphlets, starting with *Zwey neugedruckte nützlichste buechlein*, he spread the story of Luther's association with the devil, asserting that Satan was Luther's real father. As sole source of this information, he quoted a 'truthful God-fearing

---

the footnotes, a task not as daunting as it might appear, given the preliminary work done by Herte.

[75] Kaspar Sturm, *Ain kurtze anzaygung und beschreybung Römischer Kaiserlicher Maiestät einreyten // Erstlich von Innspruck gen Schwatz, volgendt zu München, vñ zu letst gen Augspurg auf // den Rychstag, vnd was sich mittler // zeyt daselbst täglich verlauffen // und zugetragen hatt, //* Anno 1530.

[76] See Herte, *Lutherkommentare,* pp. 140–45.

[77] See ibid., pp. 141–2.

woman who knew of Luther's mother's secret games with the devil', the latter apparently having visited her on several occasions in the guise of a handsome young man during the carnival period of 1483.[78] Sylvius was obviously aware of the fanciful nature of this accusation, for he insisted that the 'God-fearing woman's' account was officially corroborated at the Leipzig Disputation. He asserts:

> This has not been invented by me; the woman had talked about it before, as I heard from others, and it was announced during the Leipzig Disputation, which is why I can keep to it with a clear conscience before God. And were I to be questioned by some official authority, I could easily say who the others were who first told me about it and who were there with me as the woman told her story and who heard it all from her own mouth. And were their conscience to be challenged, I am totally confident that they would say the same thing and retell it to others.[79]

Sylvius repeated more or less the same thing in two more pamphlets. Cochlaeus was familiar with the story and resorted to it in his personal polemic against Luther,[80] but not in his *Commentaria*, where he preferred to refer to Luther's own, famous joke about having eaten more than a grain of salt with the devil and to the fairly well-documented story of the reformer's fit during the Mass when a young Augustinian. It was this more sober account of Luther's demonic association that found its way into most hostile accounts of the reformer. Even before Surius' publication of his *Commentarius* in 1566, the French Catholic historian Simon Fontaine, who published his own anti-Sleidan *Histoire catholique de nostre temps* in 1558 made an extensive use of Cochlaeus' account.[81] Fontaine's *Histoire*, an account of the history of his era, was for the large part no more than a French paraphrase of Cochlaeus, albeit not without some qualifications, additions and, above all, suppressions. Thus, regarding the probability of Luther's satanic birth, Fontaine shows himself to be aware of Sylvius' account, but admits openly that he finds it suspect:

> His father was called Johannes Luder, a rather vulgar name in German parlance (which is why his son Martin took up the name of Luther instead of Luder),

---

[78]   Ibid., pp. 140–41. Herte does not note the importance or the influence of Sylvius' pamphlet on the image of Luther as the devil's spawn. Instead, he emphasises his lack of impact as controversialist.

[79]   Sylvius, *Zwey neugedruckte nützliche buechlein*, fol. iij r. Cited here after Herte, *Lutherkommentare*, pp. 141–2.

[80]   See ibid., p. 143. Herte does not point out that Cochlaeus' omission of the story from his *Commentaria* suggests that he has a good sense of how to use historical sources depending on the type of writing. What was permissible in a work of controversy could be viewed as suspect in a work of history.

[81]   Simon Fontaine, *Histoire catholique de nostre temps, touchant l'estat de la religion chrestienne contre l'histoire de Iean Sleydan composee par S. Fontaine, docteur en Theologie* (Anvers: Iean Steelsius, 1558). Hereafter: Fontaine (1558).

and his mother was called Margaret. I prefer to affirm this as the truth rather than dwell on the other view written down somewhere, according to which that the same Margaret conceived him thanks to the work of the devil who occasionally slept with her disguised as a young man before her marriage to Johannes Luder.[82]

However, he does not find at all suspect the section of Cochlaeus' *Commentaria* on Luther's association with the devil, and he translates it almost word for word:

> It is indeed true that during that time the brethren noticed something strange about him, which they had not noticed about anyone else, and this made them think that he suffered sometimes from fits of epilepsy or that he had some secret commerce with the devil. Among other things, one day when during the Mass they were reading the Gospel passage where it is written that our Lord chased out the devil, who was causing the possessed to be deaf and dumb, Luther fell down to the ground shouting: 'not I.' Independently of this, we know for certain that he said publicly in a sermon that he knew the devil well and that he and the devil had eaten together much more than one grain of salt ....[83]

Predictably, Fontaine shows himself to be less dependent on more factual parts of Cochlaeus' *Commentaria*, such as his account of the emperor's journey to Augsburg for the 1530 Diet. There is no reason at all to believe that he found these parts suspect, but it is highly probable that he thought them simply too concerned with Germany to interest his French readers. While abbreviating Cochlaeus, he inserts dates where the latter did not, again for the benefit of French readership. This is how he reformulates Cochlaeus' account of the delay in the emperor's arrival in Augsburg:

> The emperor could not be in Augsburg on 8 April, the day stipulated by the Diet, because he was delayed in Italy, in various Italian cities and in his territory of Tyrol, by the triumphant reception that each of these cities put on for him. But he finally arrived in Augsburg on 15 June, the day before the feast of Corpus Christi, accompanied by his brother Ferdinand, the king of Bohemia, and by Cardinal Campeggio, legate of the apostolic see.[84]

Fontaine got the dates from other passages in the *Commentaria* and he edited out altogether the story of the gift of the silver coin, which he judged

---

[82]   Ibid., fols 6v.–7r.

[83]   Ibid., fol. 7v. Cf. Cochlaeus, *Commentaria*, p. 55: 'However, he appeared to the brothers to have a certain amount of peculiarity, either from some secret commerce with a demon or (according to certain other indications) from the disease of epilepsy. They thought this especially because one day in the choir when during the Mass the passage from the Evangelist about the ejection of the deaf and mute demon was read, he suddenly fell down crying "it is not I, it is not I." And thus it is the opinion of many that he enjoyed some occult familiarity with the demon ... for he says in a certain sermon addressed to the people that he knows and is known very well to the devil, and that he has eaten more than one grain of salt with him ...'.

[84]   Ibid., fol. 158r.–v.

to be of little interest to his readers. His version of Cochlaeus, adapted to the use of the French-speaking public, was to prove highly influential.

Taillepied: The Background of the First Hostile *Life* of Luther in French

Luther's *Life* by Noel Taillepied first appeared in 1577, as one of four *Lives* in the *Histoire des Vies, meurs, actes, doctrine et mort de quatre principaux heretiques de nostre temps*. The volume contained *Lives* of Luther, Karlstadt and Vermigli by Taillepied, and the famous *Life* of Calvin by Bolsec (published with a separate title-page).[85] Born in 1540 at Pontoise, Taillepied studied at the Franciscan monastery there prior to becoming the in-house reader in theology. Around 1586, he left Pontoise to join the Franciscan monastery at Rouen. Seeking stricter discipline, he moved on in 1588 to the Capuchins in Angers, where he died during the following year. Author of several opuscules of religious controversy (including a reworking of Ludwig Lavater's treatise on ghosts[86] into a work which attacked non-belief in Purgatory, counteracting Lavater's defence of it) and some historical and philosophical works, Taillepied also published in 1587 *Les antiquités et singularités de la ville de Pontoise* and *Les antiquités et singularités de la ville de Rouen*, both characterised by theological preoccupations which take precedence over the chronicle proper.[87] Most revealing of his historical method and conception of biography, however, is without doubt his *Histoire de l'Etat et Republique des Druides...*, published in Paris by Jean Parant in 1585.[88]

Taillepied's preface to this work, addressed to Charles de Montmorency, *seigneur* of Dampville and Méru, and advisor to the king, stresses the importance of keeping written records. Taillepied has some unflattering comments to make about 'our [pre-Christian era] Gallic ancestors', who left no records for posterity. He contrasts this cavalier attitude with that of the Hebrews, who omitted no details, recording the *acta et gesta* of their synagogue, even noting down details as minute as the fact that the very

---

[85]   See also Chapter 4, pp. 154–5.

[86]   On this, see Irena Backus, 'Connaître le diable. Évolution du savoir relatif au diable d'Augustin à Martin del Rio', in Frédéric Gabriel and Pascale Hummel (eds), *La mesure du savoir* (Paris: Philologicum, 2007), pp. 33–54.

[87]   On Taillepied, see *Les antiquités et singularités de la ville de Pontoise. Réimpression de l'ouvrage de F. Noël Taillepied, lecteur en théologie des Cordeliers de cette ville. Edition revue et annotée sur les manuscrits des Archives de Pontoise et collationnée sur l'imprimé de 1587 par A. François.* Précédée d'une notice biographique et bibliographique sur l'auteur par Henri le Charpentier (Pontoise et Paris: H. Champion, 1876). Hereafter: Le Charpentier, *Taillepied*.

[88]   The full title (cf. ibid., pp. 17–22) is Noel Taillepied, *Histoire de l'Estat et Republique des Druides, Eubages, Sarronides, Bardes, Vacies, Anciens Français, gouuerneurs des païs de la Gaule depuis le deluge universel iusques à la venue de Iesus-Christ en ce monde* (Paris, Jean Parant, 1585). Hereafter: Taillepied, *Druides*.

aged Moses still had all his teeth when God recalled him to His bosom. Thus, continues Taillepied, the records set down by the Hebrews preserve models of virtue for us and steer us towards noble acts. As well as keeping a meticulous written record of their past, the Hebrew nation was also constantly reminded of it by their prophets, whom God sent expressly for the purpose.[89] The Hebrew nation was not the only one to honour and cherish its past. Among other ancient races, Taillepied evokes particularly the Trojans and the Romans. His remarks on the latter particularly are of interest, as what he praises the Romans for are not their historians such as Livy or Tacitus, but their custom of fabricating the images and statues of illustrious men:

> ... for they used to put up on portals which they called atria waxen reliefs of their ancestors so that children, on seeing their fathers, grandfathers, great grandfathers, uncles, great uncles dressed in all the honours which they had acquired and spilled blood for, might be incited and compelled to do likewise. And not content with that, [the Romans] used to put up at public expense, statues and trophies in gold and marble all over the city so that by seeing with their own eyes how richly their virtue was rewarded, those who examined these palpable portraits and representations could be moved to emulate them whose portraits, for example, they were.[90]

What is more, he continues, the Romans had public orators to praise publicly the deceased heroes and heroines from noble houses. They also constructed arches of triumph, pyramids, and other commemorative symbols. Finally, referring to Macrobius, he praises the Roman custom of children from good families wearing togas on the first day of the *Saturnalia* and on other solemn occasions. According to Taillepied, the Gaulois cut a sorry figure in comparison with the Romans, who devoted such care and attention to the commemoration of their own past. He notes ruefully that it was left up to foreigners such as Berosius or Julius Caesar to write early histories of the Gallic *acta et gesta*. The point he is making implicitly is that, although early *Chronicles* of the French and by French authors were by no means a rarity, these tended to date from the Christian era. A good example of this is the *Historia sancti Dionysii* by Hildouin, the first chronicle to identify Denis the bishop of Paris with Pseudo-Dionysius the Areopagite, which Taillepied knew, and which was one of the many works glorifying the French past to issue from the Abbaye de St Denis.[91] Surprisingly, Taillepied does not so much as allude to the fact that, at the

[89] See ibid., fols ā ijv.–ā iij r.: 'Pour ce mesme effet, Dieu autheur de noblesse, a enuoyé des prophetes pour esmouuoir le peuple à bien viure, luy proposant les actes heroiques de ses ancestres. "Prenez garde à Abraham vostre père (disoit le Prophete Esaie 51.) et à Sarra qui vous a enfanté."'
[90] Ibid., fol. ā iij v.
[91] On this, see Gabrielle Spiegel, *The Chronicle Tradition of Saint-Denis. A Survey* (Brookline, MA, and Leiden: Classical Folio Editions, 1978).

very time that he was writing, the Frankish myth was at its height and the writing of history showing the Celts and the Gaulois as the origin of all nations had never been practised so intensely.[92] Was Taillepied really unaware of this? The final part of his preface to Montmorency would suggest rather that the Frankish myth was of no interest to him, and that his real aim in writing the *Republique des Druides* was to create his own myth establishing a firm link between his patron and St Dionysius the Areopagite:

> From these [Berosius and Julius Caesar] and other authentic authors, I extracted and wrote down this minute fragment of history investigating the names, morals, laws and customs of the Druids and the ancient Gallic kings, which I make so bold as to present to your Highness, for I know from experience that you help and favour those who aspire and dedicate themselves to the right disciplines. You are moved to do so naturally and divinely by the supreme sweetness and humanity which has descended to you via your noble and chivalrous forefathers of the noble house and lineage of Montmorency. This line goes all the way back to the time when Christian faith implanted itself in France due to the help and assistance (better than that of any other patron) of one of your ancestors, St Lisbie, a French knight, issued from the dukes of Athens, who accompanied St Denis all the way to Paris and there married a most noble lady.[93]

In other words, given that his patron's line goes back to St Dionysius and Athens of the apostolic era, Taillepied finds it appropriate to acquaint him also with the history of the French pre-Christian period, which directly preceded the arrival of Montmorency's ancestor in France together with Dionysius. This betrays Taillepied's interest in establishing an historical tradition, regardless of whether it is document-based or fictitious. Moreover, his remarks about Roman concern with the commemoration of their ancestors show clearly his overriding interest in keeping records of noble deeds so as to edify future generations. He is no more concerned with truthfulness of records of noble deeds than he is with authenticity and reliability of historical tradition. However, at the same time he very carefully avoids giving the impression that his evidence is non-existent or unreliable. What one would expect therefore of Taillepied's historical works is a propensity to create myths while passing them off as historical truths and a wish to edify. How do these concerns manifest themselves in his *Histoire des actes, doctrine et mort de quatre Hérétiques de nostre temps*? For a start, he differs from Bolsec, who, as we shall see later on, was acutely aware of lack of precedents for the genre. Although Taillepied's *Histoire des vies* is, just like Bolsec's *Life of Calvin*, dedicated to Pierre

---

[92]   See Claude-Gilbert Dubois, *Celtes et Gaulois au XVIe siècle. Le développement littéraire d'un myth nationaliste. Avec l'édition critique d'un traité inédit de Guillaume Postel 'De ce qui est premier pour réformer le monde'* (Paris: Vrin, 1972).

[93]   Taillepied, *Druides*, fol. āvi r.– āvi v.

d'Espinac, archbishop of Lyon and primate of France, if the common title-page[94] is anything to go by, the Franciscan sees himself as very much part of an historiographical tradition of *Lives* of heretics, much of which is in fact constructed by himself.

In his preamble to the *Histoire des vies*, addressed to the reader, he explains the usefulness of hostile *Lives* of the reformers, which constitute, in his view, a perfect illustration of the evils wrought by the Reformation. He further claims that he is following the example of the church fathers, who made a point of writing down the lives of heretics as a warning. He does not go into any details, citing only Gregory the Great's maxim: *cuius vita despicitur, restat vt praedicatio contemnatur.*[95] In fact, there was no ancient genre of *Lives* of heretics, although patristic catalogues of heresies such as Epiphanius' *Panarion* contain some scattered biographical elements. Taillepied, in his efforts to establish an historiographical tradition, conflates *Lives* and notices on heresies as exemplified by the work of Epiphanius, and later by Bernard of Luxembourg, Wilhelm Lindanus, Gabriel Dupréau and others. Biographical information these notices contain is minimal. Authors such as Epiphanius and all those who came in his wake are above all concerned to identify heretical doctrines briefly and in simple terms. They naturally assumed that founders of heresies led wicked lives and died ignoble deaths, but rarely went into any detail, the best example here being Arius, known above all for his sordid (and historically unfounded) demise. In post-Tridentine Catholicism, such biographical information as there is in these collections of notices is overtly based on rumour and legend.

A good example of this is the Roman Catholic bishop of Roermond, Wilhelm Lindanus' *De fugiendis nostri saeculi idolis*, published in

---

[94]   *Histoire des actes, doctrine et mort de quatre Heretiques de nostre temps a savoir Martin Luther, André Carlostadt, Pierre Martyr et Iean Caluin iadis ministre à Genève. Recueillie par F. Noel Talepied C. [apucin] de Pontoise et M. Hierosme Hermes Bolsec docteur medecin a Lyon. Le tout faict pour aduertir et diuertir les Catholiques de ne se laisser abuser par leurs doctrines mortiferes. Dédié au M. Archeueque, conte de l'Eglise de Lyon et primat de France* (Paris, Iean Parant, [1577]). I shall be referring here either to this edition or to that of 1616, entitled *Histoire des vies, meurs, doctrine et mort des trois principaux heretiques de nostre tems à sçavoir Martin Luther, Jean Calvin et Théodore de Bèze jadis archiministre de Geneve. Recueillie par F. Noel Taillepied C. de Pontoise et Hierosme Bolsec...* (Douay, Iean Bogard, 1616). Hereafter: Taillepied, *Histoire* (1577), or Taillepied, *Histoire* (1616). In fact, the 1616 edition omitted the *Lives* of Karlstadt and Vermigli, long forgotten in France by then, but added Bolsec's *Life* of Theodore Beza. The title was altered accordingly. Taillepied's preface to the reader was reprinted from the 1577 edition with no changes. Bolsec's prefatory material was not included.

[95]   Taillepied, *Histoire* (1616), fol. 2v.: 'Car l'vn de raisons peremptoires par lesquelles on peut aysement confuter la doctrine de quelque heretique que ce soit, c'est de regarder si sa vie a esté bonne, sa perfection, quelle vacation il a tesnu, s'il s'est gouuerné honnestement ou non, selon Dieu et ses commandements, ainsi que testifie Sainct Gregoire pape en son homilie disant ainsi: *Cuius vita dispicitur restat vt et praedicatio contemnatur.*'

1580.[96] Lindanus considers the Reformation and its representatives as the equivalent of God's permission to the devil to act on earth. 'For, he says, there are many more signs given by God that Satan is speaking through Luther, Zwingli, Calvin, Campanus or the Anabaptists than were present in the time of the earliest founders of heresies such as Montanus, when they were spreading their demonic teaching throughout the world.'[97]

As regards Luther, Lindanus contents himself with repeating Cochlaeus and considers that it was common knowledge from 1518 onwards that he was possessed by the devil as witnessed by the edict issued by Charles V, as well as several testimonies from Luther's own mouth. He particularly singles out Luther's treatise on the private Mass, where the reformer describes the voice of his master, the devil, as so deep and terrible that, frequently, men who supped with him were found dead, having given up the ghost because they were so frightened. This, affirms Lindanus, is exactly what happened to Luther himself, who, according to Stanislaw Hosius (who also copied Cochlaeus), was found dead in bed after a bout of drunkenness.[98] The bishop of Roermond supplements Hosius' account with that of Claude de Saintes, according to which Luther after a drunken night was found dead in bed, his face black and his tongue hanging out.[99] He adds equally fictitious accounts of the deaths of Campanus and the Anabaptists and further specifies that Bucer died exactly the same death as Arius, when his bowels poured out of his 'incestuous belly' while he was in the lavatory.[100]

These notices have little to do with biography, either as we understand it or as Taillepied did. Their chief interest lies in their pedagogical function. There was little point writing books for laypeople on predestination or the doctrine of real presence. It was far more effective to put them off Protestant faith by showing, brutally and succinctly, that its leaders were instruments of the devil, degenerate as men and Christians, spearheading a degenerate movement.

Taillepied, for his part, wanted to do more than simply establish the equation between degenerate life and degenerate doctrine. He also wanted

---

[96]   De fugiendis nostri saeculi idolis nouisque ad vnum omnibus istorum euangelicorum dogmatibus nefariisque irreligiosorum quorundam moribus religiosa piaque ad omnes vbique Christianos piosque inprimis concionatores admonitio. Auctore Wilhelmo Damasi Lindano, ecclesiae Ruremundensis episcopo. Cui auctarii loco attexta est popularis Apologia qua ecclesia Christi Catholica defenditur... (Coloniae, apud Maternum Cholinum, 1580). Cited hereafter as Lindanus, De fugiendis. Armogathe, 'Les vies de Calvin', pp. 57–9, confuses the two literary genres in his bibliographical survey of sixteenth- and seventeenth-century Lives of Calvin.

[97]   Lindanus, De fugiendis, p. 78.

[98]   Cochlaeus, Commentaria, pp. 347–8.

[99]   Lindanus, De fugiendis, pp. 78–80.

[100]   Ibid., p. 91.

to justify his judgement by the appearance of historical research. This is what distinguishes his writings from Bolsec, who, as we shall see, had no qualms about openly having recourse to rumour and who wrote only two *Lives*, of Calvin and Beza, having personal scores to settle with both reformers. Taillepied knew neither Luther, nor Vermigli, nor Karlstadt, all of whose *Lives* he wrote. He wanted to give the appearance of offering historical proof that leaders of the movement that broke with the Roman Catholic Church had only one aim, which was to fulfil and live in accord with 'their carnal desires, giving themselves over to all sorts of lubricious and corrupt behaviour.'[101] He argues in the preface to the *Histoire* that reformers try to seduce the faithful just as the mermaids tried to seduce Ulysses and his companions, who reacted correctly by stopping their ears with wax.[102] His *Lives* of heretics are intended to edify, in the sense of showing the faithful what not to do rather than act as aversion therapy in the sense of provoking an instant adverse reaction, a job done much more effectively by short notices in catalogues of heresies.

Was Taillepied the French inventor of the genre that Bolsec took over and made his own, or were their enterprises conducted independently of one another? We shall be returning to this difficult question in Chapter 4 below.

Taillepied as French Remaker of the German Tradition

Taillepied's *Life* of Luther, albeit brief (14 fols in 8° in its first edition), is thus more than a quick paragraph on the reformer's sad end. Although he announces that his main sources for the *Life* of Luther were Simon Fontaine and Sleidan, it is obvious that he also had knowledge of Melanchthon's *Vita*, to which he obliquely refers. Moreover, several sections of his *Vie de Luther* are no more than a perversion of Melanchthon's judgement on the founder of the Reformation. His sources are naturally hostile accounts of Luther going back to Cochlaeus. As Herte pointed out,[103] Taillepied, despite stating that he relied on both Fontaine and Sleidan, resorts to the latter only very rarely and only to discredit him.[104] He relies mainly on Fontaine, while showing some awareness of Surius. His account of Luther's family, origins, place of birth, early education, and so on is copied almost word for word from Fontaine, and therefore indirectly from Cochlaeus, of

---

[101]   Taillepied, *Histoire* (1616), fols 2v.–3r.: 'Iay donc à bon droict esté induict (amy lecteur) d'escrire ces presentes vies des principaux heretiques de nostre temps, lesquels de no/3r./stre religion chrestienne et catholique se sont separez pour suiure et viure selon leurs libertés charnelles, s'adonnants à toutes lubricitez et autres meurs corrompus ...'.

[102]   Ibid., fol. 3r.

[103]   Herte, *Das katholische Lutherbild*, vol. 1, pp. 59–67, esp. p. 66.

[104]   The full title of the *Life* is *La vie de Martin Luther extraite des œuvres de M. Symon Fontaine et Sleidan*.

whose *Commentaria* Taillepied apparently had no first-hand knowledge. Similarly, Taillepied simply repeats what Cochlaeus, and Fontaine after him, had already said regarding Luther's entry into the Augustinian order:

> It is indeed true that at that moment the brothers became aware of something strange about him, which made them think that he suffered from epileptic fits or had some secret acquaintance with the devil. For example, when one day during the Mass, the passage from the Gospel was read out which tells how our Lord expelled the devil which made the possessed man deaf and dumb, Luther fell down shouting: 'not I.' Whatever one may think of this, we know for a certain that he said publicly in a sermon that he and the devil knew one another well and that they had eaten more than one bushel of salt together. And the book he wrote in his Saxon tongue on the private Mass is enough to convince us of this.[105]

He also repeats after Fontaine (who had got it from Cochlaeus' account) that Luther's marriage to Catharina von Bora was an immoral act and that she was a highly promiscuous woman. Furthermore, she had not escaped from the monastery in 1523 with ten other nuns, but was one of nine nuns kidnapped by Leonard Roppen with Luther's approval. Still according to Taillepied, Luther married her after she had been in Wittenberg for two years, an accurate piece of information transmitted from Cochlaeus via Fontaine, together with the fictitious comment that Catharina, instead of sagely serving the household of Lucas Cranach, had, prior to her marriage, been 'disporting herself among the students like a female donkey.'[106]

Along with sexual licence, another commonplace of heretical lifestyle was the intention of overthrowing the existing social order. Thus, Taillepied stresses: 'Luther made and implemented a new set of civil laws, seizing monastic property for himself and his own and incited the people to rise up against their natural lords and masters.'[107]

Far from having been raised by God as the second John the Baptist, as Melanchthon would have it, Luther, in Taillepied's view, is the cause or perdition and damnation of several hundreds of thousands of souls who fell into heresy because of him. He does not merit being written about

---

[105] Taillepied, *Histoire* (1616), fols 21r.–22v.

[106] Ibid., fol. 24r. 'Aduint en cest an et au temps de la saincte sepmaine qu'vn Leonard Roppen du bourg de Torgame, enleua neuf nonnains d'vn monastere, de nobles maisons et les emmena à Wittenberg, dequoy Luther le collauda grandement et pour monstrer que le faict luy plaisoit, deux ans passez, à scauoir quand Frederic fut mort, de la septiesme de ces nonnains Catherine de Bore, il en fit sa femme, apres qu'elle eust esté tout ce temps viuant à Wittenberg vagabonde parmy les escolliers comme vne Asnesse.' Cf. Cochlaeus, *Commentaria*, pp. 129–30.

[107] Taillepied, *Histoire* (1616), fol. 24v.: 'Luther d'autre part fit et ordonna lois ciuilles toutes nouuelles, saisissant les biens des monasteres pour luy et les siens, et incita le peuple de s'esleuer contre leurs Seigneurs naturels.'

except to show decent people how merciful God was towards them, not allowing them to fall into the trap of his teaching.[108]

According to Taillepied, Luther died as he lived: immorally and ignobly. Our biographer notes after Fontaine and Cochlaeus that 'on 17 February, he withdrew into the bedroom with his nun and never came out alive. Some say that he dropped down dead while going to answer a call of nature. One called Jonas, a Lutheran who having been called cook [Koch] called himself Just, wrote that he died of a sudden stomach ache.'[109] Whatever the immediate cause of his death, Luther, Taillepied implies, died after an illicit sexual act with a nun, and, what is more, he died alone without commending his soul to God. Our biographer, however, cannot dwell too much on the ignoble nature of Luther's death, for he is well aware that Luther was given a solemn and official burial in Wittenberg and that Melanchthon wrote a funeral oration for the occasion. Anticipating the Protestant argument that anyone who has been given the full burial honours cannot be considered to have died a bad death, Taillepied argues that this just shows the full madness of the reformers who gave the full burial honours to their leader, having always hitherto condemned what Taillepied calls 'Christian' (that is, Catholic) burial ceremonies. They of course will reply, he continues, that he was a holy man and that he deserved this honour. However, how could he be a saint seeing as he never managed to perform a single miracle although he tried?, counters Taillepied. In conclusion, he refers the reader to Laurentius Surius, who shows that Luther was nothing other than a seducer of innocents and that he should not be prayed for as he died obstinate in his disbelief.[110]

Whereas Melanchthon placed Luther in the scheme of salvation and identified the Reformation with him so closely that he left very little or no place for Luther the individual, Taillepied attacks the Reformation through the person of Luther. His biography is anything but original, being mainly an assemblage of rumours about the reformer's life, drawn mainly from Fontaine, who, as I said, had got all his information from Cochlaeus. What is remarkable about Taillepied's work is not its lack of originality, and not the fact that he apparently casually lifted whole paragraphs from Fontaine. Two features are striking. Firstly, Taillepied was the first to promulgate the Cochlean image of Luther in a biography and not in a work of history as Fontaine and Surius had done. By doing this, he guaranteed that the Cochlean image of Luther not only crossed national boundaries (Fontaine

---

[108] Ibid., fol. 26v.

[109] Ibid., fol. 27r.: '... le dix-septieme iour de feburier, ayant soupé se retira en sa chambre auec sa moniale de telle heure que iamais n'en sorit vif. Aucuns disent qu'en se leuant pour secourir nature, il tomba mort. Vn nommé Ionas, Lutherien, qui de cuisinier s'est surnommé le Iuste a escript que le mal d'estomach le print qu'il le fit mourir.' Cf. Cochlaeus, *Commentaria*, pp. 346–7; Fontaine (1558), fol. 241r.

[110] Taillepied, *Histoire* (1616), fol. 27r.–v.

had already made sure of that), but that it reached a wider public, thanks to its being presented in the form of a short pamphlet. The second striking feature of the work is the author's choice of passages to extract from Fontaine. Passing over in silence all the factual descriptions such as the emperor's arrival in Augsburg, and cutting out all the details of theological debates such as the religious colloquies or, for that matter, the proceedings of the Augsburg Diet – in short, cutting out all historical elements in the strict sense of the word –, Taillepied concentrated his portrayal of Luther on the less salubrious details of the reformer's personal life: his birth into a family who bore the coarse name of Luder ('poor sap'), his association with the devil when still an Augustinian, his marriage to a promiscuous nun whom he had kidnapped from a monastery with eight other nuns, and finally his ignoble death. Fontaine had already reduced the chronicle aspect of Cochlaeus' work down to a minimum. Taillepied cut it out altogether.

This made his work a highly sought-after commodity. It was soon to be translated or, to put it more accurately, paraphrased into Latin by the Scotsman James Laing, and published in Paris in the latter's collection of *Lives* of heretics, whence it found its way back to Germany via a vernacular edition of the very same collection. Before going on to discuss Laing's work in its context, a few words need to be said about the German translation of it, which shows how Cochlaeus' account in an abridged form, and with a few rumours added, returned to Germany in a popular version. The translator of Laing's *Lives*, Johann Engerd, professor at the University of Ingolstadt, who had recently converted to Catholicism, knew from reading Laing's preface that the original was in French, but did not know that Taillepied was the author.[111] The aim of Engerd's publication was very different from Laing's own intentions, which I shall be discussing below. Engerd found Laing's collection appropriate as a warning not just against the 'teachings of such doctors (as Luther, Calvin, Vermigli and Karlstadt)', but also against the *Formula of Concord* or 'the new Concordists', whose newly found agreement constituted a threat to the Catholic Church. Engerd was particularly interested in the *Life* of Luther, and less interested in the *Lives* of Calvin and the two reformers' 'helpers', as he calls them, which were a part of Laing's Latin version as they had been a part of the Taillepied/Bolsec *Histoire*. Engerd was also, needless to

---

[111]   See Herte, *Das katholische Lutherbild*, vol. 1, pp. 70–72. He entitled his translation: *Summarische Historia Vnd Warhafftig Geschicht Von dem Leben, Lehr, Bekantnuss vnd Ableyben Martin Luthers vnd Joann Caluini, auch etlich andrer jhrer Mitgehülffen vnd Diener dess Newoffenbarten Euangelii, Erstlich auss Frantzösischer Sprach durch Iacobum Laingaeum Scotum, der H. Schrifft Doctorem Sorbonicum zu Paris, ins Latein gebracht: An jetzo aber Zu guthertziger Warnung, vnd notwendiger Erinnerung, was von solchen Lehrern vnd anderen Newen Concordisten zu halten, auch wie sie aus Jhren Früchten zu erkennen seyn, trewlich verteuscht. Mit einer ernstlichen vnd sehr nützlichen Vorred obgemeltes Doctoris Laingaei* (Ingolstadt, 1582). For *Life* of Luther, see ibid, vol. 1, pp. 1–43.

say, familiar with Cochlaeus' *Commentaria*, and aware that it had recently been translated into German by 'the noble and very learned' Christoph Hueber, as he calls him.[112] However, he would have spotted that Laing's (that is, Taillepied's) *Life* of Luther presented the advantage of a convenient and entertaining digest of all the most insalubrious passages from Cochlaeus, for he justifies his undertaking on the grounds that the full version of Cochlaeus' *Commentaria*, despite its availability in German, is 'a thick volume and not everyone can afford it.'[113] He did use the original, but only in order to iron out some incongruities of spelling of German names; he did not incorporate any passages from the *Commentaria*, content with adding his own criticisms of Luther in the margin. He also stressed that he got support from highly respected, excellent theologians for his translation of Laing's 'wonderful little book', meant to act as a 'warning for the common man.'[114]

This recycling of material from Cochlaeus' *Commentaria* via France and Scotland shows the full importance of this work and of its adaptability to different cultures. Luther's negative image became fixed very early on among his opponents thanks to Cochlaeus and all those who copied or adapted him (Fontaine, Surius, Taillepied and Laing in particular).

Laing's *Lives* of Heretics and his Adaptation of Taillepied's *Life* of Luther

According to Thomas Dempster,[115] James Laing died in 1594 at the age of 93, which would mean that he was born around 1501. However, the authors of the new *Dictionary of National Biography* entry think 1530 a more likely date of birth. He studied initially at King's College, Aberdeen and then moved on to Paris, where he studied theology and took holy orders. In the University of Paris records, he is described as a Scot, of the diocese of St Andrews and of the German nation of which he was made *procurator* on several occasions (October 1556, August 1558, October 1560, February 1561, January 1571, and sometime in 1564 and 1590). This office entitled him to represent the German nation in the rector's court, the governing body of the university. He was also *quaestor* (bursar) of the German nation in October 1568. He became Bachelor of Theology in September 1571, and was Doctor by 1581. Bitterly hostile to the Reformation, especially in Scotland, he published in 1581 *De vita*

---

[112]   See ibid., vol. 1, p. 71.

[113]   Ibid., vol. 1, p. 71.

[114]   See ibid., vol. 1, p. 71, and references cited thereat.

[115]   Laing has not been the object of any detailed studies. Cf. *Oxford Dictionary of National Biography* online, s.v. Laing (http://www.oxforddnb.com/view/article/15887, accessed 7. May 2007). The most detailed account we have is that of Thomas Dempster in D. Irving (ed.), *Thomae Dempsteri Historia ecclesiastica gentis Scotorum, sive, De scriptoribus Scotis*, rev. edn, 2 vols (Edinburgh: Bannatyne Club, 1829), vol. 2, pp. 438–9.

et moribus atque rebus gestis haereticorum nostri temporis etc. Traductis ex sermone Gallico in Latinum quibus multa addita sunt quae in priori editione quorumdam negligentia omissa fuere. Authore Iacobo Laingaeo Scoto, doctore Sorbonico, Parisiis apud Michaelem de Roigny, via Iacobea sub signo 4 elementorum, 1581.[116] Although this was named as the second, improved edition of the work, the first edition does not seem to be extant. Be that as it may, Laing based his work on the *Histoire des actes, doctrine et mort de quatre Heretiques de nostre temps à scavoir Martin Luther, André Carlostadt, Pierre Martyr et Iean Calvin iadis ministre de Geneve*. Laing's translation was creative to say the least, and he added several supplements and *excursus* concerning the Scottish situation particularly.

The augmented *Life* of Calvin occupies pride of place and is followed by Taillepied's *Lives* of Luther, Karlstadt and Peter Martyr Vermigli in Latin.[117] The *Life* of John Knox is an original creation by Laing, who dedicated this 'rogues' gallery' to Mary Queen of Scots (who had abdicated in 1567) and to her son James VI.[118] The third edition came out in 1585, also in Paris from the presses of Michel Roigny. As well as all the *Lives* in the second edition, it contained an account of the martyrdom of Edmund Campion and the Latin version of Bolsec's *Life* of Beza.[119] Laing also added a new preface, addressed only to James VI although Mary was still alive. The comparison of the two prefaces (1581 and 1585) shows that Laing was not interested in either Luther or Calvin, or in any of the other heretics of his time except as a fateful warning to the Scottish sovereign of what would happen unless he returned to the Catholic faith.[120] We should bear in mind here that James VI's position in the early 1580s was ambiguous enough for him to be the object of solicitations from both sides. In 1580, Beza, acting on the advice of Peter Young, dedicated his *Icones* to the Scottish monarch, reminding him of the traditional links between Geneva and the Scottish Reformation.[121]

---

[116] I have used the copy held by the Bibliothèque de Sainte-Geneviève in Paris. Shelfmark: 8 Δ 65689 res.

[117] For Vermigli, see Chapter two, pp. 71–8.

[118] 'Illustrissimae serenissimaeque dominae suae Mariae Scotiae reginae et Iacobo Sexto eius filio omni virtutis genere abunde ornato, principibus potentissimis, fidei catholicae, apostolicae atque romanae propugnatoribus acerrimis et Albionis imperii haeredibus legitimis …'.

[119] *De vita et moribus Theodori Bezae, omnium haereticorum nostri temporis facile principis et aliorum haereticorum breuis recitatio. Cui adiectus est libellus de morte patris Edmundi Campionis et aliorum quorundam catholicorum qui in Anglia pro fide catholica interfecti fuerunt primo die Decembris. Anno domini. 1581. Authore Iacobo Laingaeo doctore Sorbonico* (Parisiis apud Michaelem de Roigny, 1585), cum priuilegio. Hereafter: Laing (1581).

[120] Cf. Chapter 4, pp. 167–9.

[121] *Correspondance de Théodore de Bèze*, eds Hippolyte Aubert, Alain Dufour, Henri Meylan *et al.*, 29 vols (Geneva: Droz, 1960–[continuing]), vol. 21 (1999), no. 1403, pp. 43–52.

What did James VI of Scotland and George Buchanan have to do with Taillepied?

The short answer to this question is: nothing. However, in order to understand the literary nuances and the timing of Laing's volume, and to appreciate the politics of his 'highjacking' of the Taillepied/Bolsec anthology, including Taillepied's *Life* of Luther, it is important to say something about the prefaces to the 1581 and 1585 editions, and especially about the nature of Laing's interest in certain key features and figures of the Scottish Reformation, James VI and George Buchanan in particular.

James, as is well known, was the offspring of the doomed match between Mary Queen of Scots and Lord Darnley, who was murdered early in 1567 before James was one year old. Mary was forced to abdicate in favour of her son when he was only 13 months old, and the infant king took up the Scottish throne. John Knox preached the sermon at James's coronation. James's childhood was turbulent, marred by a long and troubled minority which saw a succession of regents as well as civil war. He became the first Stuart king of England in 1603 under the terms of the Treaty of Berwick, which he had signed with Elizabeth I in 1586. The treaty pledged allegiance between the two countries and promised mutual help against invasion, thus protecting England from France. And so James acquiesced to his mother's execution and remained neutral when the Spanish Armada threatened English shores.

Although a firm Calvinist, partly due to having been taught by George Buchanan, James was vehemently opposed to the Presbyterian system of government, and his maxim 'no bishop, no king' went down in history. This led to his estrangement from his tutor in 1579, and also brought him into sharp conflict with Andrew Melville and other Scottish Presbyterians. In 1578, the strongly Presbyterian *Second Book of Discipline* appeared, which signalled the Scottish Church's rejection of the Concordat of Leith, the compromise solution devised in 1572 and condoned by Knox. In 1581, James sanctioned the publication of the *Second Confession of Faith* (which was approved by the Scottish Church, but was never submitted to Parliament), the object of which primarily was to flush out alleged Catholics in government at a time of heightened dread of the Catholic International. Crucially, it included a declaration of loyalty to the monarch. By 1592, the Presbyterian system of church government was approved by the Scottish Parliament, but not by the Crown. Both systems, however, continued to function for another 100 years.[122] One can thus appreciate Laing's attempts

---

[122]   See Gordon Donaldson, *The Scottish Reformation* (Cambridge: Cambridge University Press, 1960); idem, *All the Queen's Men. Power and Politics in Mary Stewart's Scotland* (New York: St Martin's Press, 1983); Alan R. MacDonald, *The Jacobean Kirk, 1567–1625: Sovereignty, Polity and Liturgy* (Aldershot: Ashgate, 1998).

to frighten the king into Catholicism, as well as Beza's attempts to placate him into maintaining the Presbyterian system.

As for George Buchanan (1506–82), to whom, as we are about to see, Laing devotes much of his preface, he was brought up by his widowed mother as one of five children. Eventually, his uncle sent him to study in Paris. On his return to Scotland, in 1523, he enrolled in the army until 1525, when he began to study again, this time in St Andrews under John Major, whom he accompanied to Paris in 1526. During his time in France, he came under the influence of the ideas of the Lutheran Reformation. In 1535, he returned to Scotland with his pupil, the Earl of Cassillis, and, during their period of residence in the country, he translated into Latin verse a pasquinade of Dunbar, *How Dumbar was desyrd to be ane freir*, which he retitled *Somnium*. It was Buchanan's first declaration of war against the Franciscans, the worst enemies, as he saw them, of reform in religion and learning. His engagement with Cassillis having expired, Buchanan was on the point of returning to France when an offer came to him from James V to become tutor to Lord James Stewart, one of James V's natural sons. As James's public policy showed, he was a Catholic, but happened to have a personal grudge against the Franciscans, and he charged Buchanan with writing against them. Although aware that he had already provoked the order, he wrote the piece entitled *Palinodia*, in which, by his own lights, he sought to express himself with such ambiguity as at once to satisfy the king and not to give further offence to the Franciscans. In point of fact, the satire turned out to be a more deadly attack than the *Somnium* on the vices and obscurantism of the order. But even this scathing satire did not satisfy James, and he demanded another. The result was *Franciscanus*, the longest and most elaborate of all of Buchanan's satires. The poem was not completed and published until 1560, the year that marked Buchanan's final return to Scotland. However, word of the poem's existence got out before its publication.

Supported by Cardinal Beaton, the Franciscans therefore accused Buchanan of heresy, and James V had no option but to put him in prison, from which, however, by James's own connivance, he escaped across the border, first to England, then to Bordeaux. He taught in Bordeaux until 1547, when he received an offer from the University of Coimbra. It was during his time there that he was condemned and imprisoned by the Inquisition. During his imprisonment, he produced his first translation of the Psalms into Latin, which was to win him lasting fame.[123] Freed in 1553,

---

[123]   On Buchanan, see especially Philip J. Ford, 'Georges Buchanan et ses paraphrases des Psaumes', in J. C. Margolin (ed.), *Acta Conventus neo-Latini Turonensis*, 2 vols (Paris: Vrin, 1980), vol. 2, pp. 947–57; idem, *George Buchanan*, *Prince of Poets* (with an *Edition* of the *Miscellanaeorum liber*, eds Ford and W. S. Watt) (Aberdeen: Aberdeen University Press, 1982); I. D. McFarlane, *Buchanan* (London: Duckworth, 1981).

he travelled in France and Italy until 1560. This coincided with his finally turning his back on Catholicism and becoming a member of the newly constituted Church of Scotland Assembly. Hitherto, despite his Erasmian anticlericalism, he had remained a member of the Church of Rome, but from 1560 his studies of the Bible convinced him that Calvinism was the true religion. This coincided with the adoption of the Reformation by Scotland, hence his return there after an exile of over twenty years. From his arrival until 1567, he remained in close connexion with the court, reading the classics with Mary in her leisure hours, composing a masque on the occasion of her marriage with Darnley, and celebrating the birth of her son, afterwards James VI, in a *Genethliacon*. In 1566, he became principal of St Leonard's College at the University of St Andrews. The murder of Darnley in 1569 turned him into a bitter enemy of Mary, as, like all Protestants, he believed that she was an accessory to the crime. Henceforth, therefore, he identified himself with the political and religious party which drove her from the throne, and it was in the interests of that party that his subsequent writings were mainly produced. Buchanan's greatest literary achievement of this period was his *Rerum Scoticarum Historia*, published in 1582.

In 1570, aged 64, he became tutor to the four-year-old James VI. Nine years later, in 1579, he was estranged from the then 13-year-old king, who had forbidden the sales of his book *De iure regni apud Scotos*, which pleaded for the right of subjects to reject an idolatrous and tyrannical ruler. He died in 1582, after having been considered in his lifetime as one of the most remarkable minds of the age.

By the time Laing came to publish his *Vitae haereticorum*, James was to all intents and purposes free from Buchanan's influence, and had recently forbidden his book as violating the principle of the divine right of kings which James held sacred. Laing saw a glimmer of hope for the conversion of James VI to Catholicism. His hopes, such as they were, were to prove misplaced. At the same time, Mary was imprisoned in England and there was still some hope of freeing her so that she could return to Scotland as the country's rightful ruler. The publication of *Vitae haereticorum* was thus a part of the very Catholic 'International' that prompted the appearance of the *Second Confession of Faith*, whose object it was to weed out Catholics in government. Indeed, Laing's 1581 preface, although addressed to Mary and to James (who was 15 at the time), does not see them as bearing the same hope. While retaining a highly respectful tone, the second part of the text, addressed to James, is an admonition bidding him to convert to his mother's religion. The section of the preface which addresses Mary, on the other hand, is more of a plea for her speedy liberation and return to Scotland as the last in the line of rightful defenders of its true, Catholic, faith.

Laing is not sparing of hyperbole as he apostrophises the Queen:

While I think on these things [hope of defeat of the heretics], we must beseech God and cause Him to bend with our prayers so that he frees you from your wicked enemies, so that, restored shortly by the grace of God and given back to your kingdom, you might restitute the Catholic faith which is, if not lost altogether, at least severely shaken and weakened. And that you thus make it come about that your very dear son, our prince, whom we all hold in very high esteem, might willingly begin professing and safeguarding the Catholic faith with all his heart, moved by the special love and respect for you, his mother, of whom he has no memory. And may he thus truly desire to adopt your faith, after having been deluded and deceived for so many years by wicked ministers and especially by the wretch Buchanan. And may you thus see to it that he James is instructed in the Catholic faith so that the Scottish Church, which for the past 400 years has adhered to no religion other than the Catholic, Apostolic and Roman, is restored to its former honour and ancient glory. If you do this, you will be honoured and praised as long as there are boars in the mountains, as long as fish like water and as long as heaven provides feeding ground for the stars that are attached to it.[124]

The tone of his address to James is very different. He thus explains his delay in writing:

Already several years ago, most excellent prince ... I found myself burning with great, nay hardly credible zeal ... which I do not judge as reprehensible in any way ... to counsel you about the honour due to God and about the salvation of the state, but as you were still too young to receive such admonitions and as those around you – some of whom were heretics, others ministers of the devil, others still, half-crazed with greed to despoil the church – had no regard for honesty, their salvation or honour of God, I deemed it wise to put off writing until now.[125]

In fact, James, in Laing's view, does no less than dishonour the memory of his ancestors, 'finding it more profitable to worry about his own glory than worry about his reputation in the eyes of those who came before him.'[126] After reminding him sharply about the glorious reign of his grandfather James V, under whom all heretics were consigned to the flames, a fate that Buchanan only managed to escape by seeking refuge abroad,[127] he appeals to the young king's family feelings, pointing out that the same heretics murdered his father Lord Darnley, who had been 'educated in the Catholic, Apostolic and Roman faith by his holy mother [Margaret Tudor].' He naturally says nothing about Darnley, a man who was anything but pious, conspiring with the Protestant lords in the murder of David Rizzio, Mary's private secretary. In short, the untold grief that the Protestants caused to his family should be enough to make James reflect about the pernicious nature of that religion, and convert to Catholicism. Laing wishes that James

---

124   Laing (1581), fol. ãvir.–v.
125   Ibid., fol. ãvi r.
126   Ibid.
127   Ibid., fol. ãvi v.

... might be able to spend a few months in France so as to be instructed in the Catholic faith and become acquainted with true worship of God, or in Spain, where there are hardly any ministers of the devil, so that [he] might witness the piety of its most holy king whose name shines in every corner of the world.[128]

It is difficult to say how much hope Laing really thought he had of converting James. However, his preface shows that he spared no efforts to persuade him. Obviously fearing that the cumulative picture of the Protestants' pernicious designs on the Scottish Crown and sovereignty would not prove sufficient, he had recourse to Buchanan as his 'secret weapon'. James had only recently cut himself off from his tutor because of their conflict over the divine right of kings, and Laing had every reason to think that a mention of Buchanan might turn James against the Protestant religion. Laing thus adds:

And besides your tutor George Buchanan, that most pernicious of heretics makes no secret of trying to persuade everyone that it is lawful for the people whenever it sees fit, to deprive you of your kingdom and to institute another in your place; in other words, to create a king. This is a wicked doctrine of the Mahomet, approved by John Wyclif in his article seven, and condemned by the Catholic, Apostolic and Roman Church at the general Council of Constance.[129]

Why did he decide on *Lives* of heretics as a genre that would be most effective in putting James off Protestantism? Laing explains his undertaking in the following terms:

So that, oh most illustrious prince, you might get a better grasp of the wiles, tricks, perfidies ... and seditions of these wicked ministers of Satan, I have laboured hard to render into Latin the lives of four of the most disgraceful heretics[130] and their ignominious, despicable and horrible deaths, and I dedicate all the labour to your dearest mother, our most excellent monarch, who, for the sake of Catholic, Apostolic and Roman faith, preferred to live out her days in perpetual darkness of the prison cell, which is to her eternal honour, than to be restituted among heretics, and also to you, oh illustrious prince ....[131]

He ends with a brief explanation of his choice of Latin as a civilised language: it is fit for princes together with Hebrew and Greek, by far to be preferred to *linguae barbaricae* suitable for heretics, and in this instance ranking above Scottish because it is accessible to a wider, international circle.

---

[128]   Ibid., fol. āvii r.

[129]   Ibid., fol. āvi v– āvii r.

[130]   The mention of *four* heretics points clearly to the existence of a first edition, seeing as the second, 1581 edition contains *five Lives*: Luther, Vermigli, Karlstadt, Calvin and Knox. This suggests that he used the same preface in the first two editions. Given that this preface alludes to the break-up of the association between Buchanan and the Scottish king (whom Laing addresses as prince, thus demonstrating his loyalty to Mary), we can assume that the first edition came out *c.* 1579–80. No copies appear to be extant.

[131]   Laing (1581), fol. āviii r.

Thus, it is not surprising to see that Laing does his best to apply Taillepied's *Life* of Luther to the Scottish and English circumstances, by adding to it incidents from these countries' Reformation history. As we shall see later on, he adopts the same strategy with Bolsec's *Life* of Calvin, to which he adds a virulent excursus on Buchanan, or with the *Life* of Vermigli, supplemented by an equally extraneous and virulent excursus on David Fergusson. His most substantial additions to Taillepied's *Life* of Luther, however, are concerned not with a particular Scottish or English 'devil's disciple', but with the English and Scottish Reformation's attitude to women, and especially their role in the church. It all began promisingly, according to Laing, with Henry VIII writing against Luther defending 'most clearly and truthfully' the doctrine of the seven sacraments and announcing himself as the 'Defender of the faith'. However, he notes, this auspicious beginning had a sad end as the king got older and his saintly and pious wife could no longer bear him the children he wanted. The king thus suddenly changed his mind and turned from a defender of the faith into its enemy. The sole reason for this sudden turn-around, according to Laing, was to do with carnal desire and the king's frustration after the pope had refused to grant him a marriage annulment, considering it a barbarous and impious act after twenty-four years of happy marriage. According to Laing, the queen (Catherine of Aragon) had borne Henry several children. Laing says nothing about the absence of a male heir, which was the real motive of Henry's first divorce.

Thus, under Laing's pen it was as a result of a carnal whim on the king's part that the 'schism which first arose in England was followed by the rise of the heresy which was the perdition of Scotland, the scourge of Ireland and which perturbed France, alienated Flanders from its sovereign, and, not to put too fine a point on it, infected the whole of Europe.'[132] Returning abruptly to Luther's reaction to Henry's pre-divorce *Defensio septem sacramentorum*, Laing dwells on the reformer's impudence. According to the Scotsman, Luther replied that God in His divine majesty was on his, Luther's, side, and therefore he did not care if a thousand Augustines, a thousand Cyprians and a thousand churches of Henry VIII rose up against him. What sort of a king was it anyway, who wanted to subject us to the supreme pontiff with his lies?[133] It was shortly afterwards that the unthinkable happened, notes Laing, and Luther's books fell into the hands of women who immediately began to discuss all sorts of difficult questions among themselves, so much so that one of them, Argula, even began to preach.[134] Laing is referring to Argula von Grumbach, who, while

---

[132]   Ibid., fol. 15v.

[133]   Ibid.

[134]   Ibid., fol. 16r. On Argula von Grumbach, see Peter Matheson, *Argula von Grumbach: A woman's voice in the Reformation* (Edinburgh: T & T Clark, 1995); Silke Halbach, *Argula*

never having ecclesiastical pretensions, actually did play an active part in Bavarian religious controversy and remained in correspondence with Luther until the end of her life. He notes that something similar happened in Scotland more recently. The Scottish woman who followed in Argula's footsteps invented the fifth Gospel, but was fortunately put to silence by other Edinburgh women who cited Paul's injunction against women preaching.[135] Laing's contention that the Scottish Reformation favoured women preachers seems particularly inappropriate when one considers John Knox's vehement stand against women's having any power in the church or state. Laing would not have been ignorant of this, and his accusation is obviously a jibe or an attempt at provocation which would have found fruitful ground among Scottish Presbyterians, who would have been outraged, as well as among Catholics, who would have found it an excellent reason not to adhere to Reformation doctrines.

As regards Laing's other additions to the Taillepied version, these are mainly to do with Luther's doctrines and come from unspecified sources. He thus notes that, so as to win more public acclaim, the reformer began to preach in a new way, trying to persuade everyone that the truth had been hidden from the time of the Apostles until his own era.[136] (Laing apparently does not realise that he is relaying Flacius' view of history rather than Luther's own.) He further notes that Luther's German version of the Bible was full of errors, and that various learned men including John Fisher and Johannes Cochlaeus wrote against his doctrines from early on. The main difference between Laing and Taillepied is that the former, in contrast with the Franciscan, finds it as important to attack Luther's work and impact as to denigrate the reformer's person. He wants to show that Luther's heresy led to all possible perversions and heresies, as much as he wants to demonstrate Luther's personal corruption. His Luther thus emerges as not just a degenerate and a sexual libertine, but also an author of unnatural and perverted doctrines and practices such as the intervention of women in church affairs. He is also the man responsible for the king of England's separation from the Roman Church for reasons of lust.

Taillepied's *Life* of Karlstadt

The reasons why Taillepied added a *Life* of Karlstadt to his anthology are obvious. The latter constituted a perfect example of the discordant nature of the movement, and could be read as a helpful appendix to the *Life* of Luther. It is much shorter than the *Life* of Luther, occupying

---

von Grumbach als Verfasserin reformatorischer Flugschriften (Frankfurt/M., Berlin: Peter Lang, 1992).
    [135]   Laing (1581), fol. 16r.–v.
    [136]   Ibid., fol. 16v.

barely two pages. Taillepied entitles it appropriately *Sommaire de la vie d'André Carlostad*, and although he does not name his sources, most, if not all, of the material is ultimately derived from Cochlaeus. He includes this biography of Karlstadt very deliberately in his anthology because it reveals the rivalry between Karlstadt and Luther. However, he confines himself to describing their struggle for power, and does not say anything about doctrinal differences. A disproportionately large section of the account is devoted to a condemnation of Karlstadt's marriage to Anna von Mochau, which took place on 24 January 1522 during Luther's 'exile' in the Wartburg. Taillepied describes it thus:

> He was Luther's friend and ally until the said Luther was banished to the city of Altstadt. During that time, going against the vow of chastity by which he was bound as a priest, he married and took a miss [demoiselle] for wife, to such joy and applause of the Lutherans that they composed a special sung Mass in his honour which was to be celebrated on his wedding day, and which begins: 'the Lord God said: it is not good for man to be alone, let us make a companion for him in his likeness.' And in prayer and during the collection, they referred to him as the blessed Andreas Karlstadt. And before his wedding, he asked one of the nobles to send him some venison, but the noble sent him a skinned ass cut up into pieces in a vessel, at the bottom of which lay the donkey's hooves and ears.[137]

The above passage reveals Taillepied's true reason for including a *Life* of Karlstadt as opposed to another 'heretic' who could have done the job equally well. Karlstadt is significant in his view not just because he fell out with Luther but because he was the first reformer to get married.

Taillepied's two pages devoted to the Franconian follow Cochlaeus' account almost word for word complete with Cochlaeus' slanting of facts and exaggerations. Typically for Cochlaeus, the chronology as regards the outbreak of iconoclasm, Luther's return and his opposition to it as well as the resulting breach between the two reformers, is correct. Like Cochlaeus, however, Taillepied exaggerates the violence of the quarrel claiming that Karlstadt was made to retreat to Orlamünde instead of requesting permission to do so.[138] He is quite correct, however, in saying, again after Cochlaeus, that the call to Karlstadt to teach in Wittenberg again came as part of an effort to stem his influence in Orlamünde, where he had gained a wide following.[139] His portrayal of Luther as instrumental in his former colleague's banishment is also derived from the *Commentaria*. Finally, both describe Karlstadt's period of asylum in Wittenberg as one of humiliation and total decline of influence. This is what Taillepied says:

> Having returned to Wittenberg, Karlstadt found himself despised so greatly by everyone and the object of their scorn and derision that he retired, taking his

---

[137] Taillepied, *Histoire* (1577), fol. 14v. Cf. Cochlaeus, *Commentaria*, pp. 153–5.

[138] Cf. Cochlaeus, *Commentaria*, p. 154.

[139] Ibid.

shame with him to a small village nearby where he lived for some time in poverty. Thus he who was an archdeacon and doctor of theology was a poor labourer until his death, constrained (something he had not learnt) to work every day behind the plough pulled by untamed horses so that he was the object of his neighbours' sneers and derision.[140]

Cochlaeus' account does not mention Karlstadt's flight from Wittenberg in 1529 (to avoid arrest), or the years he spent in Zurich and Basel until his death in 1541. Predictably, neither does Taillepied, whose *Life* of Karlstadt is meant to show that a heretic's life is not a merry one and that his death is bound to be miserable. Similarly, like his source, he never once adverts to the doctrinal aspect of Karlstadt's dispute with Luther, or indeed any aspect of his thought. The dispute as he depicts it is illustrative of quarrels and dissensions which necessarily arise among heretics.

Laing naturally included Taillepied's *Life* of Karlstadt in his translation of the Franciscan's anthology of heretical *Lives*. However, as Karlstadt was neither a founder of the Reformation nor a Calvinist, and as he had never had any particular connexions with either Scotland or England, Laing left it more or less intact, adding only the odd moralising sentence here and there, and sharpening up Taillepied's remarks on the German theologian's personal morality. Some of his additions suggest that he had done some research into sources. A few examples will suffice. Whereas Taillepied comments that Karlstadt violated the vow of celibacy by taking a 'miss' (demoiselle) for a wife,[141] according to Laing, the Franconian, after violating the vow of celibacy, took unto himself a 'whore, otherwise a distinguished woman of noble birth, under the pretext of matrimony, and he called her his wife, as heretics do.'[142] His identification of Anna von Mochau as a woman of noble birth implies access to another, unspecified, source. Where Taillepied relates the episode of the ass's carcass as damning enough in itself without any further comments, Laing adds some clarifications and his own reflexions:

> Karlstadt was the first among German priests to fornicate publicly with a prostitute under the pretext of matrimony, and so to open the way to wickedness and disgrace for all heretical clergy, German, French, English and Scottish, who had vowed to live chastely and purely, and for other monsters who now fornicate publicly with no shame.[143]

---

[140]   Taillepied, *Histoire* (1577), fol. 15r. Cf. Cochlaeus, *Commentaria*, p. 155.

[141]   Taillepied, *Histoire* (1577), fol. 14v.: 'Durant lequel temps contre l'obligation de continence, à laquelle il s'estoit soubmys recepuant l'ordre de prestrise, se maria et print une Damoiselle à femme ...'.

[142]   Laing (1581), fol. 22r: '... sed mox postea continentiae voto violato et meretricem, alioqui nobilem foeminam et claro sanguine natam, sub praetextu matrimonii, sibi adiunxit, quam vxorem, vt mos est haereticorum, vocauit ...'. In fact, Cochlaeus does mention that Karlstadt's wife was of noble birth. Cf. Cochlaeus, *Commentaria*, p. 155.

[143]   Laing (1581), fol. 22v.

Laing also elaborates on Taillepied's brief statement on the enmity between Luther and Karlstadt subsequent to the outbreak of iconoclasm. Whereas the Franciscan confined himself to saying,

> Luther, having come out of captivity, returned to Wittenberg, where he reprimanded Karlstadt severely in his sermons. The latter, angry at being made to look foolish in public, lashed out against Luther and preached violently against his opinions. The Wittenbergers found this insufferable, and Karlstadt was made to retire to Orlamünde …[144]

Laing elaborates as follows:

> Luther, having returned to Wittenberg from exile, preached against Karlstadt with great vehemence and humiliated and belittled him in public. He did this not because he, Luther, condemned or disapproved of changing the Mass or abolishing it – on the contrary, he greatly wished for any ill or scandal that could befall the Roman Catholic Church – but because it had been done by someone other than him, which made it wrong. For Luther was so greedy for popular approval and excess that it could be truly said of him, 'I cannot abide to have even Jupiter as rival.' Thus hostility increased between Karlstadt and Luther and became so deeply rooted that each became more than a heretic to the other, while each sought his own glory with total arrogance and Karlstadt saw that Luther, superior in intellect and teaching, was preferred to him.[145]

Laing's expansion of the original provides an excellent illustration of his method and goal. Rather than write a treatise against the marriage of the clergy, he prefers to show the true iniquity of clerical marriage by resorting to concrete, personal illustrations.

Conclusion

Lives of Luther in the second half of the sixteenth century fell sharply into two genres. The pro-Luther *Lives* were sometimes produced in Latin, at other times in German. Many took the form of sermons, following the model of late medieval *Lives* of the saints. Most had a distinctly national slant, Selnecker and Mathesius being the best examples here. Mathesius was distinctly pastoral, and had no ambition to go beyond German frontiers. Selnecker's work, although available in both German and Latin, treated of matters such as the issue of Crypto-Calvinism, which would not necessarily have aroused much enthusiasm outside Germany except among trained theologians, who were not his chosen public. Only Melanchthon, who cast Luther as the universal latter-day prophet and the emblem of the working-out of God's will before the Last Judgement, penetrated the international scene including the Genevan and French Calvinist circles of

---

[144] Taillepied, *Histoire* (1577), fols 14v.–15r.
[145] Laing (1581), fols 22v.–23r.

readers. Questions of influence apart, we have seen that the Lutheran Luther was generally presented as an emblematic intercessor, synonymous with the *Augsburg Confession*, which assumed the status of a universal *Creed*, especially in the eyes of those responsible for the *Formula of Concord*. The Catholic Luther, on the other hand, while also initially of German making, managed to attain to international status thanks largely to the authoritative nature of Cochlaeus' *Commentaria*, which were abridged, adapted and cited by a wide range of hostile biographers in Germany and France. Whatever they added or omitted, Cochlaeus remained their basic source. Neither the Lutheran nor the Catholic portrayal of Luther had much to do with biography as we know it today. Luther was a peg to hang the Reformation on; God's instrument; the last prophet, albeit one gifted with considerable (human) intellectual capacities; or, conversely, the devil's associate, responsible for all evils, including the Scottish Reformation. One feature shared by all his friendly biographers was the focus on Luther's doctrine as opposed to his person. In fact, in the eyes of men like Melanchthon, Mathesius or Selnecker, Luther was not a person at all, but an instrument of God, a miracle-man. Among hostile biographies, only Cochlaeus' *Commentaria*, which served as source to other anti-Luther *Lives* throughout Europe, includes historical information in the strict sense of the term, and even this work distinguishes sharply between recounting 'what happened when', with recourse to documentary evidence, and giving readers the most fanciful unsupported information about the reformer himself. Historians and biographers such as Fontaine, Surius, Taillepied or Laing, who all used Cochlaeus, extracted from his work particularly the rumours concerning Luther's sexual morality.

By the end of the sixteenth century, Lutheran portrayal of Luther was stuck in the strictly national framework, where it was situated somewhere between *Lives* of the saints and handbooks of theology, while the pan-European Catholic portrayal of him laboured between chronicle and libel designed to frighten and shock.

CHAPTER 2

Lives of Chief Swiss Reformers: Hagiographies, Historical Accounts and *Exempla*

Zwingli, a Christian hero complete with Miracles, and Oecolampadius, a Man too Saintly for Suicide

Oswald Myconius wrote Zwingli's *Life* shortly after Zwingli's death at Kappel in 1531.[1] The *Life* of Oecolampadius by Wolfgang Capito was first published as a preface to the Basel reformer's Commentary on Ezechiel, which appeared shortly after his death, also in 1531. The *Life* by Capito was prefaced by Simon Grynaeus, who gave a detailed account of Oecolampadius' death. The two *Lives*, Zwingli's and Oecolampadius', were then republished together in their collection of letters, *Epistolarum libri quatuor. Vtriusque vita et obitus*, in 1536.[2]

Myconius' *Life* of the Zurich reformer does not seem to have been primarily intended for public consumption, although it was to be eventually incorporated into the *Histoire d'excellens personnages* and into its English version, *A famous and godly history contayning the Lyves and Actes of three renowned reformers of the Christian churche, Martin Luther, John Oecolampadius and Huldericke Zwinglius*, which came out in London in 1561.[3] His *Life* of Zwingli was Oswald Myconius' sole venture into religious biography. Why did he write it?

Oswald Myconius (1488–1552) was first and foremost an educator. A native of Lucerne, he studied in Basel and spent many years in Zurich as schoolmaster at the Grossmünster before succeeding Oecolampadius in Basel. His friendship with Zwingli dated probably from *c.* 1516, or at any rate from his Basel period. Myconius had strong humanist inclinations, even though Erasmus referred to him disparagingly as *homo ineptus et quondam ludimagister frigidus*.[4] His *Life* of Zwingli, to whom he was genuinely devoted, takes the form of a letter addressed to a friend whose

---

[1] See Oswald Myconius, *Vom Leben und Sterben Huldrych Zwinglis. Das älteste Lebensbild Zwinglis*, ed. E. G. Rüsch (St. Gallen: Fehr'sche Buchhandlung, 1979). Hereafter: Myconius, *Vita Zwinglii* (ed. Rüsch).

[2] See Carbonnier-Burkard, 'Une *Histoire d'excellens personnages*', pp. 47–8.

[3] Translated nto English by Henry Bennet (London, John Awdley, 1561).

[4] 'A pompous individual, once a dull schoolmaster.' See Myconius, *Vita Zwinglii* (ed. Rüsch), p. 12, n. 15.

identity is concealed behind the appellation *Agathius Beronensis*. Melchior Kirchhofer, Myconius' nineteenth-century biographer, identified him as Gut, a canon of the chapter of Beromünster in Lucerne.[5] Walter Köhler, however, thought that it was more likely Ludwig Kiel (*Carinus*), also of Beromünster. Internal evidence seems to support this hypothesis. As Rüsch points out,[6] the questions the dedicatee addressed to Myconius suggest someone educated, of humanist tendencies and very favourable to the Reformation, who had heard of and read Zwingli, but who did not get to know him before his death. *Agathius*, so reports Myconius, considered Zwingli as almost divine, and was surprised at how often he was the object of vituperation and insult from his enemies. Having read the reformer's books, he wanted them to be as authoritative as possible, which is why he wanted an account of his morals and of his life from someone who had known him well.[7] He also wanted answers to specific questions. Were Zwingli's enemies right to reproach his taste for music as overly sensual? When did he begin his reforming activities? What was the nature of his relationships with Luther and the pope? Why did he not attend the Baden Disputation, given its importance? Why was he reproached with being 'bloodthirsty' (*sanguinarius*)? These concerns square with the person and the spiritual and intellectual itinerary of Kiel, who was a humanist canon of the Beromünster until his conversion to the Reformation in 1531. A friend of Erasmus, Glareanus and Amerbach, he knew Capito and Bucer but had never got to know Zwingli.

Thus it appears on the face of it that Zwingli's *Life* was an answer to a personal request, and that its author had no intention either of presenting Zwingli as a Reformation saint or using his *Life* to provide a distinguished ancestry to the new religious movement. Appearances, however, can be

---

    5   Melchior Kirchhofer, *Oswald Myconius. Antistes der Baslerischen Kirche* (Zurich: [n.p.], 1813), p. 89.

    6   Myconius, *Vita Zwinglii* (ed. Rüsch), pp. 14–16.

    7   *Vita Huldrici Zwingli ad Agathium Beronensem. Ab Oswaldo Myconio conscripta*, *Tiguri*, 1532, first published in 1536 in *Ioannis Oecolampadii et Huldrichi Zwinglii epistolarum libri IV ... Vtriusque vita et obitus, Simone Grynaeo, Wolfgango Capitone et Oswaldo Myconio autoribus* (Basel: Thomas Platter and Balthasar Lasius, 1536). It figured in all subsequent editions of the *Epistolae* (1548, 1592). See Myconius, *Vita Zwinglii* (ed. Rüsch), pp. 27–8. *Vitae quatuor Reformatorum*, ed. Neander: (*Vita Zwinglii*), p. 3: 'Petis Agathi mi carissime rem vt scitu dignam, ita longe supra vires ingenii mei. Nam magna vires magnas postulant. Equidem humi repere didici hactenus et est natura nescio quid humile vel a cunabulis in me. An vero non arduum vitam adumbrare Zwinglii? Non enim dico scribere, quemadmodum me tu petis, prudens certe, non nescius, a paruis quid exigendum. Requireret hoc non tam Plutarchum aliquem sed Ciceronem patronum. Adeo magnus est ille apud amicos et reuera tam paruus autem apud hostes, vt ipse tu scribis, Zwinglium saepe factum esse in auribus tuis Deum, contra non semel ita vituperatum vt mirareris quin terra deuoraret. Atque hanc causam esse dicis cur eum virum nosse vere cupias aliquo, cui vita et mores ipsius familiariter sint noti et hoc quidem propter libros quos reliquerit, tam solide conscriptos. Velles enim eosdem esse auctoritatis quam maximae.'

misleading. Firstly, the inclusion of the *Life* in the *Ioannis Oecolampadii et Huldrichi Zwingli Epistolae* and in other collections such as the *Histoire d'excellens personnages* would show that, regardless of Myconius' initial intentions, it assumed an emblematic value. Secondly, whether we consider Agathius Beronensis' questions about Zwingli as real or whether we take them to be a literary conceit, Myconius' reply shows that there was a need for an apology of Zwingli. We are thus confronted with a biographical preoccupation, which is specific to the Reformation and which will come to the fore much more clearly when we examine the *Lives* of Calvin and Beza. A biography, among its other functions, was seen as a good way of clearing a reformer's reputation. Myconius did this not by insisting on Zwingli's piety or his services to the church, but by portraying him as both *homo prudens* and a minister of Christ.

Familiar with antique models, Myconius starts off by saying that Zwingli's *Life* would require not so much the eloquence of Plutarch as that of Cicero. The short text itself is divided into eleven sections in chronological order. It is structured around Agathius' questions. After the introduction (addressed to Agathius), Myconius talks about Zwingli's lineage and early education, his early teaching career in Basel and his musical interests, and his studious time as priest in Glarus, an occupation which he pursued at Einsiedeln, prior to taking up his post as people's preacher in Zurich. One of the questions asked about Zwingli naturally concerned his early career in the Catholic Church. The obvious answer to any reproaches would be to insist on the reformer's conversion. However, under Myconius' pen, Zwingli never converts because he was never a papist:

> You must not think, Agathius: 'what, Zwingli preached the Gospel while a papist?!' Believe me; twenty-seven years earlier when he did not disapprove of Pico's resolutions, he had already had to endure an accusation of heresy from those who were stupid enough to make one. That is when hate, evil rumours, outcry arose and snares began to be set against him by the sons of the devil. These increased as his virtue increased.[8]

In the section on Zwingli's attitude to Luther's reformation, he makes a point of saying that Zwingli himself refrained from reading Luther's writings when they began to come out. He did, however, encourage others to read them so that people would recognise the similarity of doctrine and see that both were moved by the same spirit. Very obviously, one of Agathius' questions was to do with Zwingli's independence of Luther.

---

[8]   *Vitae quatuor Reformatorum*, Neander: (*Vita Zwinglii*), pp. 5–6: 'Non est Agathi vt apud te cogites: Zwinglius in papismo de euangelio? Crede mihi ante annos 27 propter hoc ipsum et quod resolutiones Io. Pici Mirandulae super eas quaestiones, quas Romae disputandas is olim frustra proposuerat, non improbaret, a pinguibus istis clam exprobratam audiuit haeresin. Hinc odium, hinc linguarum petu/p. 6/lantia, hinc clamores, hinc insidiae filiorum saeculi contra Zwinglium ceperunt initium et aucta sunt omnia, quoad virtutem auxit ipse.'

Myconius' reply suggests that he wanted to convey the image of Zwingli as the founder of the Reformation without making Luther into an impostor. Although his hero's pastoral preoccupations take back seat, he does insist that Zwingli preached against the rich, the mercenaries and those who oppressed the poor. In an excursus on Zwingli's reading, Myconius is concerned to stress not so much his love of sacred letters as his use of profane letters to provide a point of departure for the study of the Hebrew Scriptures. Thus in the midst of his duties as *Leutpriester*, he read Homer, Aristotle, Plato, Demosthenes, Thucydides, Lucian, Theocritus, Hesiod, Aristophanes and many more. This led him to learn Hebrew at the feet of Andreas Böschenstein and Jacob Ceporinus, with the help of his companions Leo Jud and Felix Manz, until he felt ready to comment on Jeremiah and Isaiah.[9]

Myconius says nothing about Zwingli's service as chaplain to the Swiss mercenary forces in papal service in 1513–15 any more than he mentions the condemnations of Anabaptists as anything other than a necessary measure in the face of this plague (*pestis*). His reforming activities after 1519 seem to centre on the dissolution of the monastic orders and on his campaign against military pensions. No mention is made of iconoclasm. He portrays Zwingli's non-appearance at the Baden Disputation as an act of civic obedience on his part, seeing as he was under council orders not to attend. After all, notes Myconius speciously, he was not afraid to attend the Disputation of Berne, no less risky than that of Baden, or to undertake the long trip to Marburg in 1529. As might be expected, a sizeable portion of the *Life* is devoted to clearing Zwingli of diverse calumnies and to citing cases of unwarranted verbal and physical attacks.

As for Zwingli's attitude to war, letters from him accusing the Five Catholic Cantons of offering war under the guise of peace suffice to show, according to Myconius, that he did not approve of war for its own sake. Thus far, besides his interest in the poor, there seems to be very little about Zwingli that is pastoral, if we go by Myconius' account. The biographer's main concerns focus on his subject's great learning, sacred and profane; on

---

[9]   Ibid., pp. 7–8: 'In tam anxiis laboribus Graecanicam lectionem haud vnquam omittebat vsque dum Homerum, Aristotelem, Platonem, Demosthenem, Thucydidem et facilioris notae Lucianum, Theocritum, Hesiodum, Aristophanem reliquosque perlustrasset. Et quia res postulabat et commodum, Andreas Boschenstein, Hebraicae linguae gnarus, Tigurum aduenerat ludum aperturus, discipulum agebat, valde strenuum. Arridebant statim hae litterae. Quamobrem posteaquam obtinuerat a senatu verorum studiorum et linguarum Latinae, Graecae et Hebraicae gymnasium, diligentius instabat vt Jacobus Ceporinus, iuuenis trilinguis, aduocaretur: sub hoc enim quod attinebat grammaticen perficiebat. Deinde LXX iugi collatione et translationis Hieronymi, sociis adhibitis Leone Juda, qui iam antea nonnihil in eas literas laboris et studii contulerat, et Felice Mancio, cui naeuum catabaptismus inussit postea non abstergendum, huc penetrauit vt Esaiam et /p. 8/ Hieremiam, prophetas excellentissimos, complanare sit ausus dexterrime.'

his preaching against wealth and mercenary service; on his elimination of his adversaries; and on his dissolution of monasteries. All in all, Myconius conveys a portrait of a political leader with religious convictions rather than that of a Christian pastor, let alone a saint. This impression is accentuated by the absence of a section on private morality, an omission no doubt due to the fact that Myconius did not need to clear his subject of the charge of sexual excess as neither Agathius nor anyone else raised any questions about it at the time. However, it would be a mistake to suppose that Myconius portrays his hero in lay terms. On the contrary, one of his aims is to demonstrate that Zwingli was in contact with divine forces just before and just after his death on the Kappel battlefield. He claims that Zwingli clearly foresaw his death, and actually 'whispered in a friend's ear' that the comet which was seen a few days before the Second Battle of Kappel would be fatal to him and to another unnamed person.[10] (Myconius understands the latter to have been Oecolampadius, who in fact died in the same year.) Even more significantly, as depicted by Myconius, Zwingli's death went one better than martyrdom, as it was accompanied by a miracle of the sort that is the staple of hagiographical legends:

> He [the messenger] said he [Zwingli] had been trampled by the pressing multitude three times, but had arisen every time. The fourth time his chin was transfixed by a spear and he fell to his knees crying: 'can this be misfortune? They can kill my body but they cannot kill my soul.' And so saying he slept in the Lord. After the battle when our soldiers had retreated, the enemy got the chance to look for Zwingli's body (but who told them so quickly that he had been there and that he died in battle?). They found it and after condemning it, they cut it into four, threw it in the fire and reduced it to ashes. Three days later, after the enemy had gone, Zwingli's friends came to see if they could find anything that remained of him and, miraculously, his heart emerged from the ashes, whole and unmarked. These good men were astonished, recognising the miracle but not understanding it. Attributing this event to God, they rejoiced greatly having been thus assured from above of the purity of the brave man's heart.[11]

---

[10]   Ibid., p. 13: 'Dixerat item intra dies quatuordecim ante profectionem bis, me audiente, pro suggestu dum feruerent omnia: "scio, scio, inquam, quid rei est. Es ist vmb mich zu tun. Vt ego tollar, fiunt omnia." Imo et cometen, quae visa est per aliquot septimanas, in aurem susurrat amico, fatalem esse et sibi et adhuc alteri cuipiam. Nos semper Oecolampadium intelleximus.'

[11]   Ibid., pp. 13–14: 'Prostratum aiebat prementium multitudine iam tertio sed in pedes semper restitisse. Quarto fixum cuspide sub mento et in genua prolapsum dixisse: "ecquid hoc infortunii? Age corpus quidem occidere possunt, animam non possunt." Atque his dictis mox obdormiuisse in Domino. Post cladem otium vbi datum hostibus (nam nostri retro in locum abierant securiorem) cadauer Zwinglii quaeritur (et quis indicarat tam cito vel adfuisse, vel occisum esse?), inuenitur, iudicio condemnatur, in quatuor partes secatur, in ignem coniicitur, in cinerem resoluitur.Hostibus digressis post diem tertium, accedunt amantes Zwinglii, si quid reliquiarum eius offenderent et ecce cor (mirabile dictu) /p. 14/ se offert e mediis cineribus integrum et illaesum. Stupebant boni viri, miraculum quidem agnoscentes, sed non intelligentes. Quare Deo tribuentes quicquid esset, nonnihil, tanquam certi magis de cordis viri sinceritate facti superne gaudebant.'

Myconius' *Life* thus presents Zwingli as the object of the very sort of miracle that the Reformation was supposed to combat. If that were not enough, the dead reformer was very quickly to become the object of relic worship, for, Myconius adds:

> Shortly afterwards, a man I knew very well and was on intimate terms with came to me asking whether I would like to see a piece of Zwingli's heart, which he carried about with him in a small casket.[12]

It was only awe, which, as he puts it, invaded his entire body, that stopped Myconius from agreeing to view the relic.[13] Apparently he saw nothing wrong or papist about conserving a portion of Zwingli's heart, and regrets that his reaction stopped him from being an eye-witness.

To sum up, Zwingli is not portrayed by Myconius as a person who is holy in terms of morals. There is little or no mention of self-abnegation, chastity, and care for his flock or, for that matter, preaching. Much more attention is devoted to the reformer's learning, and his attitude to civic and military issues of the time. His death is not depicted as martyrdom, but as an act of heroism. He is shown to be saintly only in so far as there is a miracle attached to his demise and in so far as no lesser part of his body than his heart is conserved as a relic. More importantly, the *Life* intends to put pay to rumours of crypto-papism, cruelty to the Anabaptists, cowardice and war-mongering, which arose in Zwingli's lifetime and were to influence the reformer's image until the present day, Myconius' efforts notwithstanding.

Oecolampadius

What of Johannes Oecolampadius? Although his *Life* was eventually published together with that of Zwingli, the two works could not be more different from one another. The *Life* of Oecolampadius is much more of a model life of a pious scholar of sacred Letters, as behoves a biographical notice included in a preface to a biblical commentary. The one feature it shares with Zwingli's *Life* is that it too is an apology, albeit an apology of a very different order. Capito wrote it at the express request of Simon Grynaeus, who was present at the reformer's death, which he described in a letter to Capito at the latter's request, asking the Strasbourg reformer for a *Life*. Grynaeus did not feel that he knew the deceased reformer well

---

[12]   Ibid., p. 14: 'Venit non multo postea vir mihi notissimus, sed et familiarissimus, rogans an portionem cordis cupiam videre Zwingliani, quod secum ferat in loculo.'

[13]   Ibid.: 'Quia propter sermonem hunc inopinatum horror quidam totum corpus peruaserat, negaram, alioquin et huius rei possem esse testis oculatus.'

enough to write one himself.[14] Moreover, it was Capito who had initially
asked Grynaeus for the account of Oecolampadius' death after hearing
'terrible' rumours of his suicide, or assisted suicide. Grynaeus felt that he
could quell any such suspicion in pious minds, having been present at the
Basel reformer's death and having closed his eyes himself.[15] The *Life* that
he requested from Capito was obviously intended to reinforce the image
of Oecolampadius as a man who would never commit the capital sin of
ending his own life.

Grynaeus insists throughout his account that he was present at the
reformer's death and that therefore his testimony is totally reliable.
He backs up his plea to Capito with apparently solid evidence of
Oecolampadius' persistent ill health; of the great weight of worries and
duties in the year he died, which caused an eruption of scabs all over his
body. He stresses that Oecolampadius, *egregius verusque Christi episcopus*
[outstanding and true minister of Christ] that he was, combined church
duties with preaching, while lecturing on the Old and New Testament in
the original languages, and editing, under much pressure, the works of
Theophylactus, Cyril and Chrysostom. On top of all this, he never ceased
writing and publishing biblical commentaries. We know that Grynaeus'
claims are vastly exaggerated, and that Oecolampadius, although he did
accomplish all these tasks, did not do them all in the year before his death.
Is Grynaeus trying to suggest that the deceased reformer was not in the
category of ordinary, overworked mortals? Is it for similar reasons that he
links chronologically the death of Zwingli at the Battle of Kappel with the
eruption of a sore on Oecolampadius' sacrum, 'the juncture of all the other

---

[14]   *Monumentum instaurati patrum memoria per Heluetiam regni Christi et renascentis
Euangelii, id est Epistolarum d. Iohannis Oecolampadii et Huldrichi Zwinglii aliorumque
eximiorum Iesu Christi seruorum libri IIII … Operi autem praefixa est apologia de istorum
twn hegoumenwn pia doctrina et historia de praeclarae illorum conuersationis praeclaro exitu*
(Basilaeae per Sebastianum Henricpetri, 1592) (hereafter: Capito/Grynaeus, *Oecolampadii
Vita*), fol. θ 4r.: *De d. Ioannis Oecolampadii obitu per Simonem Grynaeum Wolfgango
Fabritio Capitoni Simon Grynaeus salutem*: 'Peruelim autem vt tu Capito frater quo imprimis
autore, quicquid id est, ad te dedi, vitae ipsius summam perstringas. Nam te non fugit opinor
quantum in his momenti sit pietatis studiosos non tam in Domino mirifice oblectandi quam
etiam ad pie aemulandum potenter extimulandi. Abs te vero id non temere mihi videor
exigere. Alium enim qui istic maiori fide possit, arbitror esse neminem posteaquam inter vos
a multis annis tam arcta fuit consuetudo.'

[15]   Ibid., fol. η 4r.: 'De Oecolampadii nostri viri innocentissimi obitu horribilem apud
exteros famam vagari, quasi vel suisipsius vel suorum certe manibus clam peremptus sit
eamque scriptis quorundam aeditis confirmari et vulgo mortalibus qui longius hinc degunt
persuaderi, multorum iam saepe ad vos e Gallia partim, partim aliunde literis significatum
esse scribis, hortarisque vt qui rebus omnibus interfui ac diligentius etiam caeteris singula
notaui, quique extremum halitum illius legi atque oculos amici clausi, pro ea coniunctione
quae mihi cum eo semper fuit non superuacuum, sed necessarium iam propemodum officium
charissimi viri manibus exhibeam et suspicione graui piorum animos liberem, simul os
scelestum calumniatoribus istis fide digna narratione obturem …'.

limbs'? The sore spread, inflaming the whole body, he notes, until there was no doubt that the reformer was suffering from anthrax.[16] There follows a graphic and extremely detailed description of medical consultations, which proved to be of no avail. Grynaeus cites word for word Oecolampadius' last speech to those gathered around his bed. He makes a special point of saying that at the very moment that the reformer gave up the ghost, committing his soul to God, there were ten people praying around his bed and that, having been one of those witnesses, he thought it particularly important not to omit and not to disguise the truth because of the suicide rumours.[17]

The *Life* for which he asked Capito was to complete the rehabilitation of Oecolampadius, showing him to be the object of emulation to all pious Christians. Capito is thus asked implicitly to tread the delicate path between a medieval saint's life and the life of a human model of piety. Having known Oecolampadius personally and having had humanist training himself, what Capito comes up with is in fact a life of a pious Christian humanist, active in the affairs of the church. Without making any overt allusion to the rumours of suicide, Capito undertakes to obey Grynaeus' injunction to tell the truth without any rhetorical flourishes, 'lest the hidden faith of those who are about to convert turns to doubt.'[18] Naturally this tale of unadorned truth contains a fair amount of exaggeration, concerning not Oecolampadius' suicidal tendencies, but his scholastic training, his passage through the Bridgettine Order and his rather unfortunate intervention at the Disputation of Baden. In order to guarantee the truthfulness of his account, Capito very frequently uses the first person to show that he actually had a part in his hero's life.

[16]   Ibid., fol. θ 1v.: 'Iam infelici bello Heluetia efflagrabat, Zuinglius fortissimus restituendae apud suos innocentiae adsertor et sedulus euangelicae synceritatis vindex, ceciderat, conditiones pacis bonis vereque religiosis hominibus admodum graues coiuerant, aduersis rebus casu subito animi omnium fracti sternebantur, cum seu lue pestifera, quae per vrbem tum et in ipsius etiam domo grassabatur, seu repullulante et vim intus concipiente scabie, vlcus super os sacrum, qua compages membrorum omnium est, primum exeruit sese, mox auctis ignibus corpus totum mirabiliter inflammauit. Anthracem fuisse non est dubium.'

[17]   Ibid., fols θ 3v.–4r.: 'Decem fratres aderamus, in genua circum lectulum deuoluti, sublatis omnes in coelum manibus Dominum obtestantes. Iam prorsus illuxerat, iam sol horizonta nostrum plane contigerat, cum spiritum vir optimus redderet creatori Deo, tanta animi per omnia lenitate, tam certa in Christum dominum fi/θ 4r./ducia vt pii omnes ex obitu et illustri exemplo consolationem perceperint non minus quam e vita. Sic Oecolampadius vltimum vitae huius actum clausit, qui per omnem quam vixit aetatem se gessisset innocentissime. Me equidem quae autoptes vna cum fide dignissimis coram vidi, cum dissimulare, adeoque veritati denegare testimonium nefas duxi, ea potissimum vrgente causa, cuius initio commemini.'

[18]   Ibid., fol. θ 5r.: 'Rem enim ipsam et veritatem, non dictionis ornatum a me expectes illamque ipsam vt bonis omnibus in oculis est, ne fidem abditam conuertentis in dubium voces.'

After the usual preliminary remarks on Oecolampadius' birth and lineage, which is shown to be honest and illustrious, especially on the maternal side, Capito stresses particularly his thirst for truth, which was such that 'he did not even turn away from the hateful tedium of empty questions and sophisms, which prevented the more liberally disposed minds from so much as approaching the Holy Scripture.'[19] He thus studied Thomas, Richard of Middleton and, more particularly, Gerson, 'as he seemed to provide the most suitable food for piety.'[20] He neglected Duns Scotus. While stressing that it was Oecolampadius' thirst for truth that made him read even the hated scholastics, Capito wants to avoid making the reformer into a supporter of the scholastic method. He is therefore quick to point out that his hero steered away from the theatrical disputes which 'had been corrupting the minds of youth for several centuries', preferring instead to discuss his studies in a small group, in humanist style and caring more for *res literaria* than for winning a reputation for scholastic learning.[21] Thus, his biographer has conveyed the image of Oecolampadius as one who showed from very early on the makings of a reformer, ready to approach Scripture by methods other than those of the scholastics. However, as Capito is only too aware, things were not so simple: despite his liking for philology and his collaboration on Erasmus' New Testament, Oecolampadius was not quick to embrace Luther's ideas and went so far as to enter the Bridgettine Order so as to postpone his decision. Capito copes with this issue, insisting that the future reformer entered the monastery on special conditions. At the same time, he implicitly criticises this episode in his hero's life, pointing out that it was done against his (Capito's) advice.

According to him, Oecolampadius demanded on entering the monastery that he be granted freedom for his faith and studies and not be held by a vow. Neither the monks nor the bishop of Freising had any objections. The only person to protest was Capito himself, who, as he puts it, 'feared what in fact happened, that he would find neither the peace for his studies, nor the freedom to serve his neighbour and the church of Christ.'[22] This statement is not pure propaganda. We know that during his period in the monastery, Oecolampadius' religious position seemed to swing slowly but surely in favour of Luther. Although his attitude to pseudo-John of Damascus' *De his qui in fide dormierunt*, which he translated at the time, shows him to be fence-sitting with regard to prayer for the dead,

---

[19]   Ibid., fol. θ 6r.: 'Eo flagrabat cognoscendae veritatis desiderio vt quaestionum et sophismatum inanium odiosis taediis non auerteretur, quae fere ingenia liberaliter instituta a sacris literis vel obiter gustandis deterrent.'

[20]   Ibid., fol. θ 6v.: 'Post Thomam vero Richardum inter scholasticos praecipue amplexus est. Gersonem triuit non indiligenter quod is videretur ad alendam pietatem comparatior. Scoti acumen neglexit.'

[21]   Ibid.

[22]   Ibid., fol. θ 8r.

his *Iudicium de Martino Luthero* and *Paradoxon*, two treatises from the same period, show evidence of open support for the doctrine of salvation by faith.[23] Capito mentions neither of these works, but does refer to *De confessione*,[24] which was also written during Oecolampadius' monastic period, but was not published until 1525. He considers it was 'all the more pious for being unbearable to traffickers of ceremonies.'[25]

In Capito's view, all ambiguity ceased once Oecolampadius was out of the monastery and in Basel, where he preached on Isaiah by order of the council, 'despite criticisms from the sophists.'[26] The controversy, which was occasioned by his affirmation of the spiritual presence of Christ in the Eucharist, should not obscure the fact, according to Capito, that Oecolampadius never wanted either to hide the truth or to perturb the peace of the church.[27] Having shown his subject as a consistently brave man, Capito still has to cope with Oecolampadius' ineffectiveness. He thus transforms the Basel reformer's disastrous intervention at the Baden Disputation and his defeat at the hands of Eck into a heroic act. Oecolampadius, in his view, was the sole defender of truth present at the Disputation. To emphasise his heroism, Capito has to give a slightly pejorative account of Zwingli's role. Whereas Myconius had Zwingli doing his public duty by obeying the council's order not to attend the Disputation, Capito stresses that Zwingli actually did not want to go to Baden, as well as being asked not to go by the council. He adds that many reliable witnesses can still attest to Oecolampadius' skill and bravery against particularly numerous and pugnacious adversaries.[28]

In short, Oecolampadius' courage, his readiness to defend the truth, his dedication to the preaching of the Gospel, and his willingness to put his learning to use in the cause of the Reformation, show him to have been the sort of man who could not put an end to his own life. To remove any lingering doubts, Capito stresses:

---

[23]   See Irena Backus, 'What prayers for the dead in the Tridentine period? Pseudo-John of Damascus' *De his qui in fide dormierunt* and its "Protestant" translation by Johannes Oecolampadius', *Zwingliana*, 19/2 (1992): 13–24 (esp. pp. 13–14). See also Ernst Staehelin, *Oekolampad-Bibliographie* (Nieuwkoop: B. De Graaf, 1963 [repr. of 1917 edn]), nos. 28, 29, 31, 36, 38.

[24]   *Iacobi Latomi theologiae professoris de confessione secreta Ioannis Oecolampadii Elleboron, pro eodem Iacobo Latomo* (Basileae, per Andream Cratandrum, 1525). Cf. Staehelin, *Oekolampad-Bibliographie*, no. 112.

[25]   Capito/Grynaeus, *Oecolampadii Vita*, fol. θ 8r.: 'Iam in hoc instituto cum esset, praeter conciones certas quas edidit, scripsit etiam de confessione librum, quo magis pium, hoc magis ceremoniarum nundinatoribus ferendum.'

[26]   Ibid., fol. θ 8v.: 'Ibique senatu volente, vtcunque reclamarent Sophistae, publice Isaiam praelegere coepit.'

[27]   Ibid., fol. ι 1r.

[28]   Ibid.

This most saintly man kept to his life-course with constancy: his life was true, simple, sincere, well adjusted to piety, intent on furthering the kingdom of God and on combating the ploys of Satan. He maintained this attitude when he was dying: he stayed steady, unmoved and unaltered. Because he was founded on a firm rock, no tempests could even shake what he built, let alone damage it.[29]

The Strasbourg reformer achieves the goal he set himself. His readers would have come away from reading his account with a firm conviction that a man who was as brave, as pious and as constant as Oecolampadius could not and did not commit suicide. Coupled with Grynaeus' eye-witness account of the Basel reformer's last hours, the biography constituted a solid proof of all sorts of qualities that Oecolampadius himself never aspired to.

Life of Joachim Vadian by Johannes Kessler: Humanist Learning and Reformation Doctrine

Joachim Vadian (1484–1551)[30] was born, as Joachim von Watt, into a St Gallen family of wealthy and influential linen-merchants. After having gone to school in St Gallen, he moved to Vienna at the end of 1501, where he took up studies at the Faculty of Arts, under Conrad Celtis among other scholars. In Vienna, he changed his name to Joachimus Vadianus; like so many other humanists, he preferred a Latin name to express his admiration for the classic masters. He evaded the outbreak of the bubonic plague of 1506/1507 by moving to Villach, where he worked as a teacher and studied music. A study trip through northern Italy brought him to Trent, Venice and Padua, where he met the Irish scholar, Mauritius Hibernicus.

In 1509, Vadian completed his studies with the degree of Master of Arts and returned for a short while to St Gallen, where he studied the Scriptures in the library of the Abbey of St Gall. He then went back to Vienna, where he had some success as a writer. From 1512 on, he held the chair of poetry at the University of Vienna, having gained a reputation as an author of Latin poems. In 1513, he visited Buda, and the following year, he was named *poeta laureatus* by Emperor Maximilian I. In 1516, he was made rector of the University of Vienna.

---

[29]   Ibid., fol. ɩ 1v.: 'Hunc vitae cursum tenuit perpetuo vir sanctissimus: verum, simplicem, syncerum, aptum pietati, appositum iuuandis hominibus, promouendo regno Dei, impugnando Satanae molimina. Illa eadem ratio morienti per omnia constitit immota, certa, inuariabilis. Quia fundatus erat supra firmam petram, nullae tempestates quod inaedificauerat, non dico non euertere poterant, sed ne labefactare quidem.'

[30]   Cf. T. Pressel, *Joachim Vadian nach handschriftlichen und gleichzeitigen Quellen* (Elberfeld, [n.p.], 1861); Emil Arbenz, *Joachim Vadians Wirksamkeit von der Schlacht zu Kappel bis zu seinem Tode* (St Gallen: Zollikofer, 1910); Rudolf Gamper (ed.), *Vadian als Geschichtsschreiber* (St Gallen: Sabon-Verlag, 2006).

In the following years, Vadian studied medicine and natural philosophy, geography and history in particular, under Georg Tannstetter, also called Collimitius. In 1517, he graduated as a doctor of medicine, and subsequently moved back to his home town, St Gallen. On that voyage, he also visited many of his humanist acquaintances in Leipzig, Breslau and Cracow. In 1518, he was the first to climb Pilatus Mountain near Lucerne.

In St Gall, he was appointed city physician, and on 18 August 1519, he married Martha Grebel, the sister of Conrad Grebel, who would later become a leading figure of the Anabaptist movement. In 1521, he succeeded his father Leonard, who had died in December of 1520, as a member of the city council. The beginning of the Reformation in Switzerland (he was a friend of Zwingli) encouraged him to study the Scriptures and ecclesiastical texts for the first time. From 1522 on, he sided with the new Reformation exegesis and its methods, and henceforth was its most important proponent in St Gallen. When he was elected mayor of the city in 1526, he led the conversion of St Gallen to Protestantism, and managed to maintain that new state after the victory of the Catholic cantons in the Second War of Kappel. Vadian wrote several theological texts after 1522, helping to disseminate basically Zwinglian doctrines.

By the terms of his will, he donated his large private library to the city. His collection became the nucleus of the cantonal library of St Gallen, which is named 'Vadiana' to this day.[31]

Vadian's *Life* was written in Latin by his friend Johannes Kessler (1502–74), the chronicler of the St Gallen Reformation.[32] In the biographical account, he presents his friend's life and his considerable humanist learning as a necessary condition for the Reformation. This accent on Vadian's personal importance in the St Gallen events contrasts, as we shall see, with Kessler's portrayal of the same events in his chronicle. Moreover, he insists throughout the *Life* that only someone with as deep and broad a knowledge of the humanist culture as Vadian could have grasped instantly that the Scripture was the embodiment of Reformation doctrines and turned to the study of the Bible without any previous theological training. Kessler's agenda as regards his biographical endeavours is obviously not the same as his agenda as a chronicler. Even so, he never really departs from the chronicle genre, so that his *Vita Vadiani* pays greater (although not full) attention

---

[31]   Among his most important works are: *De re poetica et carminis ratione liber* (Viennae, 1518; modern edn, Munich: W. Fink, 1973); *Grosse Chronik der Äbte des Klosters St. Gallen* (St Gallen, 1529); *Epitome trium terrae partium, Asiae, Africae et Europae…* (Zurich, Froschouer, 1534); and *Aphorismorum de consideratione eucharistiae libri VI* (Zurich, Froschouer, 1535).

[32]   For Kessler's biography and a still authoritative study of the *Sabbata*, as he called his chronicle, see esp. Johannes Kessler, *Sabbata. St. Gallen Reformationschronik 1523–1539*, ed. Traugott Schiess, in *Schriften des Vereins für Reformationsgeschichte*, no. 103/104 (Leipzig: Rudolf Haupt, 1911), pp. 1–113. Hereafter: Kessler, *Sabbata* (ed. Schiess).

to chronology than other *Lives* of the period and adopts a fairly flat tone. Like his chronicle, entitled *Sabbata*, Kessler's *Life* of Vadian remained in manuscript form until the nineteenth century, when it was published by the St Gallen History Society in 1865.[33] However, as we are about to see, it was not a work intended for private use. The way it handles sources also suggests a chronicler at work. Although a friend of Vadian, Kessler never says so in so many words and does not invoke his own status as source, although he would have witnessed at least some of the events he describes. The *Life*'s most outstanding claim to veracity is its constant reference to Vadian's works in connexion with events that brought them about as well as references to other reformers, some of whom (for example, Bullinger) were still alive when he was writing. Kessler at no point apologises for or justifies his undertaking. He tries neither to still any doubts about Vadian's teaching nor to produce a work of apology for the reformer's personal life.

Given his predilection for chronology, he casts the *Life* in a fairly standard biographical mould of the time, starting with the subject's lineage, birth and upbringing, continuing through his life until his death, and including a physical description of him. He is more concerned with the detail of Vadian's studies than with their emblematic value, noting that Vadian initially attended the school in St Gallen, where his tutor was one Simon, a man of exceptional severity who inculcated the basics of literature and rhetoric into the boy.[34] The father (Leonard von Watt) was actively engaged in the son's education, and, noticing that he showed promise such that he could profit from a more advanced course of study than St Gallen could offer, he sent young Joachim to Vienna, which was famous at the time for its *studia humanitatis*. There, he benefited for a time from the teaching of several eminent men, but – and here Kessler distinguishes himself from other Reformation biographers by introducing a critical note – adolescence being a most dangerous age, Vadian did not escape its perils completely. Unlike the later Swiss reformers who, as we shall see, provide, under the pen of their biographers, a living example of how to study, young Vadian, according to Kessler, would have fallen by the academic wayside had it not been for the timely intervention of God and his parents:

---

[33]   *Joachimi Vadiani Vita per Joannem Kesslerum conscripta. E codice autographo Historicis Helueticis D. D. D. historicorum et amatorum historiae Sangallensium coetus nonis Septembribus anno 1865* (St Gallen: Zollikofer, 1865). Hereafter: Kessler, *Vita*. The *Sabbata* (lit. 'days of rest', so called because written in Kessler's spare time) were published for the first time in volumes 5–10 of the historical journal *St. Galler Mitteilungen* in 1866–68, but, unlike his *Life* of Vadian, they were to go through several subsequent editions. (See Kessler, *Sabbata* (ed. Schiess), p. 10.)

[34]   Kessler, *Vita*, p. 1*.

Vadian too had embarked on this path. His body was lively and exceedingly powerful and his heart aggressive; he never resisted provocation to a fight. Although he was endowed with exceptional intellectual gifts and possessed other qualities which are greatly commended in any man, opportunities for leading a more dissolute life began, which were of poor counsel in helping him to distinguish between the struggles he should embark upon and struggles he should leave well alone. And indeed he might well have continued giving into these, had the great God not preserved his head for dealing with greater things. At that time there was a man in Vienna on business from a certain Kobler, a St Gallen merchant. He was asked by Vadian's parents to give to the boy no more money than was sufficient for honest study and to watch out for his morals.[35]

Still according to Kessler, this man, on seeing the boy's rash, gladiatorial ventures and on apprehending him in his mischief, gave him a good talking to and bade him abandon his decadent ways and return to the course of study enjoined by his father, who had great hopes of him.[36] This admonition worked, and from then on Vadian began to work very hard.

As already noted, Kessler works very hard to make Vadian's career as a whole appear as an illustration of the very close link that exists between *litterae humaniores* and the Reformation. Unlike other Protestant writers of the sixteenth century (for example, Melanchthon), who tend to see *bonae litterae* as a propaedeutic stage to adopting the 'right' religion, Kessler is among those who see the two as inextricably joined together, so that *bonae litterae* lead to the Reformation, while the Reformation makes no sense without them. This conviction, we should add, was typical of the Swiss Reformation, and found its fullest expression in the writings of Heinrich Bullinger, who also thought that not just ancient languages but humanist education in general was what made us fully human and thus apt to receive God's word.[37] However, it is not so much the influence of Bullinger as the very nature of Vadian's literary endeavours that accounts for Kessler's emphasis of the inextricability of the profane and sacred realms.

Kessler describes carefully his subject's move to Villach in Karinthia, but does not say that it was motivated by a plague epidemic. He prefers

[35]   Ibid., pp. 3–4: 'Vadiano igitur in eo vitae tramite iam quoque versante, corpore vegito praeualidoque /4/ pectore animoso qui ad pugnam lacessitus nemini vnquam cesserit. Ingenii praeterea viribus praestantissimis aliisque dotibus quibus praeditus erat licet in homine praeclara magnaque commendatione visendae solutioris tamen vitae occasiones esse ceperunt et ad discrimina certaminum subeunda consultrices improbae. Et fortassis anuere perexisset ni Deus optimus maximus eximium hoc caput grauioribus gerendis rebus conseruasset incolume. Fuit autem eodem tempore Viennae vir quidam grauis et honestus a negotiationibus Kobleri ciuis Sangallensis mercatoris, cui a Vadiani parentibus iniunctum erat eam pecuniam ipsorum nomine numerare, qua honesta filii studia postulare necessario videbantur atque simul in illius mores animaduertere.'

[36]   Ibid., p. 4.

[37]   On this, see Backus, 'Bullinger and Humanism'.

to say that Vadian took on a schoolmaster's job so as not to be a financial burden to his parents.[38] He notes that by the time he returned to Vienna, his fame as orator had spread so that he succeeded the recently deceased Angelus Cossus of Bologne as professor of Greek and Latin. Kessler insists on and lists with great care the famous scholars that Vadian got to know while occupying this function. He also lists all the works by Vadian and makes much of his achievements as poet, which earned him the imperial title of *poeta laureatus*. Rather more unusually for the time, he also insists on the direct importance of geography to the Reformation and of his subject's contribution to it. He explains that Vadian first became interested in geography when he was rector of Vienna University, 'as he thought that it was a branch of Letters that was unclear and often badly presented.'[39] This conviction, Kessler continues, caused him to publish his *Epitome trium terrae partium* and his commentaries on Pomponius Mela. He was not afraid to travel to guarantee the reliability of his geographical works. At this point, Kessler gives details of Vadian's itinerary and stresses its dangers:

> For the sake of these investigations, he was not put off by the harshness and unpleasantness of a long journey. He saw both sides of Austria and the European part of Sarmatia. He went to Venice so as to see it for himself, he sailed round the bay of Triest, and he scaled the perilous mountain passes in the Swiss Alps, making very careful observations everywhere of phenomena, the knowledge of which had hitherto been based only on improbable hearsay and not on sound evidence. He was not at all discouraged by the rugged harshness or the steepness of valleys or the height of the mountains.[40]

Kessler plays around with the chronology of the journey, having it take place before Vadian's study of medicine for reasons which seem to do with the internal structure of his composition. Naturally, he also mentions Vadian's abortive legal studies as well as his medical studies which earned him the title of Doctor of Medicine by the time he was ready to go back to St Gallen in 1517. The moment he got there, Kessler notes, the council gave him a yearly stipend in return for working for them in any capacity he chose. The following year, he married the very chaste Martha Grebel. It was then, just as 'Letters began to flourish in Germany and as, by the grace of God, the study of theology took on a new life thanks to the efforts of learned men wishing to restore its conformity with Scripture',[41] that

[38] Kessler, *Vita*, p. 4.
[39] Ibid., pp. 4–5.
[40] Ibid., p. 5: 'Huius studii gratia non illi durum nec asperum fuit saepe longum iter facere. Vtranque vidit Pannoniam, Sarmatiam Europeam. Visendi causa Venetias perrexit, sinum nauigauit Tergestiuum, ardua per Heluetiam Alpium iuga conscendit vbique accurata obseruatione rerum quae incredibili rumore nec admodum firmis rationibus ferebantur, nihil fragosa asperitate nec praecipiti fossarum aut montium altitudine deterritus.'
[41] Ibid., p. 6.

Vadian decided to devote his literary gifts to the rebuilding of the Christian republic. Although some thought it not appropriate for a doctor to turn to religious matters, Vadian decided to follow the example of Luke and combine the two. His lack of theological training made it impossible for him to start his reforming activity by writing treatises on sacred subjects or biblical commentaries. His sole medium of expression was profane literature, and this is why, notes Kessler, Vadian expressed his early views on the restitution of pure religion not in a treatise of theology, but in the revised version of his commentaries on Pomponius Mela. These additions, he adds, were incorporated in sections on Ionia, Thracia, Macedonia, Spain, Ethiopia, and so on, all regions visited by Luke.

The modern reader cannot but be struck by the singularity of Vadian's approach. Theological works of the time, especially biblical commentaries, abounded in geographical descriptions of holy and less holy places. However, only Vadian expressly used a treatise of geography to express his early teaching of the Reformation. This gave the St Gallen Reformation its own intellectual and religious profile, as Kessler was quick to spot.

However, Kessler was also fully aware that Vadian's efforts did not stop at geography and that he did move on to theology proper, although never completely and never at the expense of *bonae litterae*. He therefore notes that, when the teaching of the St Gallen ministers became purer as a result of Vadian's conversion activities, he commented publicly on Acts and 'dictated at the same time the *Epitome trium terrae partium* [concentrating on localities mentioned in the Gospels and in the book of Acts], which was eventually published at the request of no lesser a man than Heinrich Bullinger.'[42]

Kessler describes with some care the Reformation events that Vadian directly influenced, dwelling on his subject's gentleness and his capacity to present both sides of any given question. Thus, he recounts, Vadian, faced with the anti-Reformation arguments of the Dominican preacher Wendelin Oswald, wrote at the request of the ministers a very learned work in German, which showed both sides of the issue.[43] Kessler further notes Vadian's readiness to combat the errors of the Anabaptists, and his role in the eucharistic controversy, as shown by the *Aphorismi* and the *Epistola*, written at Bullinger's request.[44] Finally, he insists on Vadian's intervention

---

[42]   Ibid., p. 7.

[43]   This remained unpublished.

[44]   *Orthodoxa et erudita D. I. V., viri clariss., epistola, qua hanc explicat quaestionem, An corpus Christi propter coniunctionem cum verbo inseparabilem, alienas a corpore conditiones sibi sumat, nostro saeculo perquam utilis et necessaria. Accesserunt huic D. Vigilii martyris et episcopi Tridentini libri V pii et elegantes, quos ille ante mille annos contra Eutychen et alios haereticos, parum pie de naturarum Christi proprietate et personae unitate sentientes, conscripsit* (Zürich, [Froschouer], 1539).

in the quarrel with Schwenckfeld following the request of Johann Zwick.[45]
A physical description of Vadian and an account of his death close this
remarkably factual account in which Vadian is presented first and foremost
as a man who influenced the course of the Swiss Reformation.

What does Kessler say about his hero in this unpublished biography
that he does not say in the *Sabbata*, and vice versa? A comparison of
the two works throws a useful light on his conception of biography. The
points the two works have in common and the differences between them
would suggest that Kessler saw Vadian's *Life* as neither a complement
nor an appendix to his *Sabbata*. First and foremost, the *Sabbata* is in the
vernacular, while the *Life* is in Latin. This would show that the former was
intended for the national and the latter for the international (and more
learned) readership. Moreover, unlike the *Sabbata*, which is organised in
the form of annals, the *Life* stays only fairly close to the actual chronology.
First and foremost, however, Vadian's role in the Reformation is barely
adverted to by the *Sabbata*, although the two works (the *Life* and the
chronicle) have in common their insistence on the connexion between
humanist learning and the introduction of the Reformation. Book Two of
the *Sabbata* is very largely devoted to Luther and 'other learned persons
whom God ordained foremost to reveal the truth in our time.'[46] Apart
from Luther, whom Kessler singles out as the most important ('rather like
the apostle Paul who, albeit not the first, surpassed all the Apostles who
preceded him'), all the other significant agents of God that he mentions
happen to have humanist background and to be skilled in classical languages
and learning. He singles out particularly Reuchlin, Erasmus ('to whom we
should be grateful despite the fact that he wrote against Luther in 1525'),[47]
but also Konrad Pellikan, Von Hutten, Oecolampadius, Melanchthon and
Bugenhagen (the only one whom Kessler knew personally). Although well
aware that the last three were, first and foremost, theologians, Kessler
praises them too not so much for the purity of their doctrine as for their
humanist learning. Interestingly enough, Kessler reveals in the second
book of the *Sabbata* that he aims to compile the *Lives* of these and other
learned men chosen by God to propagate his doctrine in his book *De viris
illustribus*.[48] As it happens, he never carried out his plan and the book

---

[45]   *Pro veritate carnis triumphantis Christi, quod ea ipsa, quia facta est et manet in
gloria, creatura, hoc est nostra caro, esse son desierit ... recapitulatio. Ad clarissimum virum
D. D. Ioannem Zviccium, urbis Constantiensis ecclesiasten* (Zürich, [Froschouer], 1541).

[46]   See Kessler, *Sabbata* (ed. Schiess), p. 28.

[47]   See ibid., pp. 28–9. Schiess notes that Kessler adds a rather touching description of
Erasmus at this point: 'he is still alive and living in Basel where I saw him myself: a dove-grey,
upright, man, aged and delicate looking, dressed in a long blue coat with a belt and wide
sleeves. Around his neck he has a velvet collar, which hangs down over the front of the coat,
both sides of equal length.'

[48]   See ibid., p. 29.

was never written. It does show, however, that Kessler regarded biography as integral to history writing while considering it a separate genre from chronicles and other accounts. His *Life* of Vadian was obviously the first in the series, and was intended to form one chapter of *De viris illustribus*.

How much, then, does he say about Vadian in the *Sabbata*? When all is said and done: little. He mentions Vadian's gentleness with regard to his adversaries, and his tendency to repay bad with good.[49] However, what he does not do is portray his role in the St Gallen Reformation as central or crucial. He is quite clear that in 1525 it was Zwingli, and not Vadian, who stopped most of the St Gallen population from turning Anabaptist and who brought about the conversion of many Anabaptists with his *Von der Wiedertaufe* and other writings.[50] As regards the abolition of the Mass in 1525, Kessler notes that by the time the preachers and the councillors, Joachim and Georg Vadian, were ready to issue an ordinance imposing the Zwinglian rite, the eucharistic quarrel between Zwinglians and Lutherans had penetrated as far as St Gallen. In the face of this, the councillors and ministers decided to play it safe and issued an ordinance on preaching only.[51] Were it included in the biography, this detail would detract from Vadian's image as a man thoroughly committed to the Reformation cause.

Nor is the humanist particularly singled out in the other sections. To take just one example, Kessler begins each book of the *Sabbata* by naming the mayor elected for that year. Although he goes beyond a routine mention of Vadian's first election in 1526, his account of it, which he accompanies by a prayer for divine blessing of the new mayor, can hardly be called detailed.[52] As 1526 happened to be also the year when the St Gallen citizens removed the remaining images and decorations from churches, Kessler goes into these events in considerable detail, but again does not depict Vadian's role as crucial in any way.[53] Detailing the events of 1532, when Vadian was again elected as mayor, Kessler considers his friend's renewed election as providential in the sense of wanted by God in view of new troubles on the horizon.[54] The troubles, once again described

---

[49]   See ibid., pp. 38–9.

[50]   Ibid., p. 50. Kessler does not exclude Vadian altogether, but mentions him only in a marginal capacity. Thus he describes him as volunteering to the council to write against the Anabaptists, which he did, showing that their preaching went against the teaching of the Apostles and was their own innovation. The Anabaptists produced a response, and when both the letters, theirs and Vadian's, were read before the council on 5 June of that year, the Anabaptists found that their reply was satisfactory and carried on with their teaching. (Ibid., p. 47.)

[51]   See ibid., p. 60.

[52]   Ibid., p. 61.

[53]   Ibid., pp. 62–5.

[54]   Ibid., p. 96.

by Kessler without adverting to Vadian's personal role, took the form of negotiations with the abbot, who not only returned to St Gallen that year, but also claimed restitution after the lost War of Kappel. His return meant the return of Roman Catholic worship. In order to stop any attempts at backsliding, the council issued an order that any citizen attending Mass would be summoned and fined.[55] The other troubles of 1532 took the shape of a disputation between the Anabaptist Johannes Marquart and St Gallen preachers, which ended with Marquart being expelled.[56] Again, just going by the *Sabbata*, Vadian does not seem to have participated actively.

The *Sabbata* ends in 1539. The year 1538 was the year that Vadian became mayor for the third time. Kessler notes that the year was marked, among other things, by the quarrel between St Gallen and Nürnberg concerning the taxing of Nürnberg linen-merchants coming to trade in St Gallen. Although Vadian and Ambrosius Schlumpf had already explained that the *Stockgeld* was not customs duty but was levied from both local and foreign merchants for the defrayal of costs incurred by trade, the Nürnbergers insisted until they were exempted from it.[57]

In Kessler's view, as conveyed in the *Sabbata*, Vadian was not central to the Reformation in St Gallen in the sense that theologians such as Zwingli or Bullinger were. Moreover, the *Sabbata* is very much a *Stadtchronik*, and as such aims to include all important events in any given year (including the appearance of comets, material difficulties affecting trade, for example[58]), and not just religious ones. It concentrates on events without much heed of individuals, the genre not lending itself to a biographical approach. Although some individuals, Vadian among them, are considered by Kessler as providential, this does not mean that all their actions are portrayed. Kessler's *Life* of Vadian throws a very different light on the St Gallen Reformation and its main protagonists. Although historically sound as far as chronology and the actual events in Vadian's life are concerned, it expressly exaggerates the role played in the Reformation by a man of Vadian's intellectual profile, incarnating the harmonious coexistence of profane and sacred learning.

Lives of Vermigli

Neither Bullinger nor any of the other second-generation Zurich pastors and Protestant intellectuals, with the notable exception of Vermigli, was ever the object of hostile biographies from their Catholic adversaries. While writers of catalogues of heretics, such as Lindanus, devoted brief notices

[55] Ibid., pp. 97–8.
[56] Ibid., p. 98.
[57] Ibid., p. 105.
[58] See, for example, ibid., pp. 102, 106–7.

to some of them (Bullinger in particular), showing them to be the spawn of the devil and/or sexual deviants, the writers of *Vitae* were silent. It was therefore not in self-defence that the Zurich Academy overtly adopted the policy of endowing each newly deceased professor with a *Life*. What was their purpose, and why was this 'cult of the individual' practised more intensely in Zurich than in Geneva? This question is of some importance, especially as some of the *Lives* I shall be considering seem to suggest that the practice was controversial and encountered opposition.

Simler's Life of Vermigli

Before turning to the *Lives* of Bullinger, I propose to examine Simler's *Life* of Vermigli, which was in fact a revised version of his funeral oration, hence the preservation of the word *Oratio* in the title. In form and content, however, it was more of a biography than a funeral oration, intended to throw light on two theological treatises by Vermigli published in the same volume.

Josiah Simler (1530–77), the son of Peter Simler, once prior of Kappel, was Bullinger's godson and was partly brought up by the reformer. He attended school in Kappel and Zurich, and then studied theology, Hebrew, Greek, natural philosophy and mathematics in Basel (1546) and in Strasbourg (1547/48), where he was taught by Vermigli. He married Bullinger's daughter, Elizabeth. In 1552, he started teaching the New Testament in Zurich, an office he combined with those of minister in Zollikon and, from 1557 onwards, deacon to Rudolf Gwalther in St Peter's. In 1560, he succeeded Bibliander as Professor of Old Testament, and so became Vermigli's colleague prior to succeeding him in 1563. Despite the difference in age, he was very close to Vermigli, although naturally not as close as he was to Bullinger.[59]

His *Oratio* on Vermigli's life and death contained two dedications, one to John Jewel, bishop of Salisbury, dated 1562, and one to John Parkhurst, bishop of Norwich, dated 1563. More importantly, the volume contained other writings of Vermigli too. Its full title was *Oratio de vita et obitu. Item scripta quaedam Petri Martyris Vermilii de eucharistia nunquam ante edita. His accesserunt carmina in eius obitum conscripta.*[60] It was the *Oratio* itself that was dedicated to Jewel, while Vermigli's hitherto unpublished eucharistic writings were addressed to Parkhurst. The choice of dedicatees

---

[59]   On Simler, apart from his *Vita* by Johann Wilhelm Stucki of 1577, which I shall discuss below, see also Hans Ulrich Bächtold (ed.), *Schola Tigurina und ihre Gelehrten um 1550* (Zürich & Freiburg/Br.: Pano, 1999), pp. 92–3 and bibliography.

[60]   I shall be referring to Edward Marten's translation, as published in *The Life, Early Letters and Eucharistic Writings of Peter Martyr*, eds J. C. Mclelland and G. Duffield (Sutton Courtenay: Sutton Courtenay Press, 1989). Hereafter: Simler, *Oratio* (ed. Mclelland).

was anything but arbitrary. Jewel had been a refugee in Strasbourg when Vermigli was there, and had personal links with him. Parkhurst, a close friend of Gwalther, was Jewel's former tutor and a religious refugee, like his former pupil. He had links of a more doctrinal and institutional nature to Vermigli, and would have been particularly interested to read his hitherto unpublished eucharistic writings, all to do with the theological debates that had taken place during the Italian reformer's stay in England. In short, the coupling of the *Oratio* with eucharistic writings in one and the same volume showed that Simler's interest was not purely that of a local biographer; he also wanted Vermigli remembered for his contribution to the English Reformation. In his dedication to Jewel, Simler is careful to outline his sources: not only did he know Vermigli personally, but he interrogated the reformer's former student and lifelong secretary, Giulio Terentiano.[61] Furthermore, having been entrusted by Vermigli's friends with the cataloguing of his correspondence, he drew much information from letters to and from him, as well as from his theological writings.[62] His aim was not to clear Vermigli's reputation, but, on the contrary, to make sure 'that eminent and eloquent men, favouring and loving Martyr (as I know many Italians, Englishmen and also Germans and Frenchmen to have done), could be stirred up by my example, to produce that which I for many causes could not do, namely, an excellent, eloquent and well-appointed oration to celebrate Martyr's praises.'[63] As a rhetorical flourish, Simler adds that Jewel would have been the perfect man for the task, were it not for his lack of time. He situates his own endeavour not in the tradition of pagan or saints' lives and not the early lives of bishops such as Possidius' *Vita Augustini*, but in the tradition of Christian funeral orations such as those of Gregory of Nazianzus commemorating Athanasius and Basil.[64] However, the analogy is more nominal than anything else. Although his real object is to give Vermigli posthumous publicity, he protests the contrary. His aim is not to make the reformer remembered as he will be anyway, but to guarantee that 'those who are mindful of his name may yet at the leastwise have this history, such as it is, of his life, wherein they may see both the beginnings and proceedings of his studies and from thence fetch examples of manifold and rare virtues.'[65]

---

[61]   On Giulio Terentiano of Piacenza (d. 1579), see Kurt Jakob Rüetschi, 'Gwalther, Wolf und Simler als Herausgeber von Vermigli-Werken', in Emidio Campi, Frank A. James III and Peter Opitz (eds), *Peter Martyr Vermigli. Humanism, Republicanism, Reformation* (Geneva: Droz, 2002), p. 258, n. 21, and also Paul Boesch, 'Julius Terentianus, Factotum des Petrus Martyr Vermilius und Korrektor der Offizin Froschauer', *Zwingliana*, 8/10 (1948): 587–601.

[62]   See Rüetschi, 'Gwalther, Wolf und Simler', pp. 251–74 (esp. p. 259).

[63]   Simler, *Oratio* (ed. Mclelland), p. 24.

[64]   Ibid.

[65]   Ibid., p. 25.

What Simler does not reveal at this stage is that, just as his *Life* of Bullinger was to be later, so the *Oratio* (at least, in its published version) is as much a treatise of reformed theology as a biographical account. It is also one of the rare partisan *Lives* to contain some slight criticisms of the subject's early convictions as well as an account of his conversion and a very detailed account not only of his two marriages, but also of his first wife. Although Simler takes into account every stage of Vermigli's career, it is no surprise that he devotes considerable attention to its early stages (as requiring the most explanation) and, because of the dedicatee, to the role Vermigli played in the theological and especially eucharistic disputes in Edwardian Reformation England. Simler devotes a separate section to his subject's writings and his last days. As regards its structure, although basically oriented towards England and the Italian's activity there, it also aims to highlight the impact he made in Zurich. That is why John Jewel, the dedicatee, is referred to in the third person in the section devoted to Vermigli's second stay in Zurich (1556–63), where the biographer stresses Vermigli's particular devotion to 'our commonwealth'.[66] The *Oratio* was thus intended for Zurich as much as it was for England. This of course did not stop it from being a very reliable piece chronologically.

I shall now examine in detail the most characteristic features of the *Oratio*, which are its description of Vermigli's conversion and its account of his two marriages. Vermigli was about forty-two years old when he fled Lucca, thus breaking openly with the Roman Catholic Church. This obviously required some explanation. Simler was not dealing with a case of a sudden conversion. He therefore had to describe his hero's intellectual and spiritual itinerary in such a way as to show that Vermigli was always a Protestant at heart, even in his time as abbot at Spoleto and prior at Lucca. However, Simler never uses the word 'Protestant' or 'reformed' in this context. He prefers to use the contrast between 'godly' and 'our men' on the one hand, and 'malicious' and those 'who wished to have the licentiousness of their lives restored to them' on the other. The latter two categories naturally represent the papal faction. This allows him to avoid entering into doctrinal differences between England and Zurich, and to associate 'godliness' not with any particular type of Protestantism, but with any or all anti-papal stances. He can thus portray the first forty-two years of his hero's life in as uncritical a way as possible, while glossing over any doctrinal differences between the Zurich Church and the Church of England.

---

[66]   Ibid., p. 73: 'when he was come to Zurich together with that excellent man John Jewel, an Englishman, now by the grace of God, bishop of Salisbury, he was very joyfully received both by the Senate of the College and by the ministers of the church and by all the godly.'

He describes Vermigli's conversion as being a gradual process entirely due to God. As he puts it, 'When I consider him, I cannot wonder enough at the proceeding and order whereby it seemed good unto the heavenly Father to bring him unto the knowledge of heavenly truth.'[67] In Simler's view, Vermigli was a sort of latter-day equivalent of St Paul, showing from a very early age the signs of what he would become after his conversion. (Simler makes no mention of Paul's persecution of Christians, or of the fact that he was converted as a result of a vision, neither of which applied to Vermigli.) This is how he describes the various stages of his hero's spiritual progress:

> For first he stirred up his will in the beginning of his age that he might endeavour with all his power to please and serve God, albeit He suffered him in the meantime to err in the manner of worshipping Him. Afterwards he so instructed his mind that he inclined the same to innocency of life and unto righteousness, whereby, although he could not deserve thanks of God, yet he showed himself unblameable before men. Lastly, He inflamed and kindled him with an incredible love of the Holy Scripture whereof, while he for a good space of time followed the letter, at length by the revelation of the Spirit of God he comfortably knew the hidden and spiritual mysteries. In this matter I might justly compare him to St Paul the teacher of the Gentiles, in whose life before his conversion there was an endeavour of worshipping God and of righteousness, which is according to the Law, wherein he was unblameable and moreover he used to read the Law as yet covered with a veil.[68]

Vermigli's intellectual evolution mirrors his spiritual itinerary. Initially versed in scholastic theology and in the writings of the Fathers, he gradually turned 'himself altogether to the fountains themselves'; that is, the Scriptures. As he read them, continues our biographer, his spirit became more and more enlightened so that he perceived more and more abuses in the church. This is when he began to read the writings of 'our men', especially Bucer's commentaries on the Gospels and Psalms, some works of Zwingli, and several of Erasmus' works.[69] Throughout, Simler emphasises his hero's exceptional moral integrity and lack of self-interest. Given Jewel's own integrity and rigorous handling of his diocese, it is difficult to say whether Simler presents Vermigli as a moral example or as a mirror image of his eminent dedicatee. Be that as it may, he does not in any way present him as a saint, or even as a special tool of God's providence (although naturally entirely determined by it). He is no more than a highly moral individual and excellent churchman likely to inspire others by his example.

Martyr's first marriage as such was of no particular interest to Simler. Nor was he at all interested in the person of Catherine Dompmartin. What

---

[67] Simler, *Oratio* (ed. Mclelland), p. 39.
[68] Ibid.
[69] Ibid., p. 41.

interested him was Catherine as a blueprint of a pious wife, and the fate
of her remains. His portrayal of her is correspondingly schematic. She was
'an honest and noble virgin, who, living at Metz and loving true religion,
was sent for to Strasbourg by godly men and afterwards was married to
Martyr.'[70] Vermigli's marriage was godly and chaste, like that of every
other reformer. It is possible that Simler had access to James Calfhill's
account of her exhumation and reburial of her remains, for, like Calfhill, he
stresses that she was a 'good and excellent matron', particularly generous
and kind in helping the poor.[71] More significantly, Simler is not afraid
of stressing that 'the common sort in Oxford' not only loved her, 'but
they also wondered at her as though she had been endowed with some
divine power, because, in sickness and especially in childbirth, their wives
by her counsel and help obtained for the most part undoubted safety.'[72]
Although he does not say that he himself thought her saintly, he does
attribute some saintly qualities to her while carefully avoiding any hint of
saintliness when talking about her husband. Her burial in Christ Church
Cathedral was thus fully appropriate, as was the subsequent restoration
of her bones under Elizabeth when they were mingled with the (supposed)
remains of St Frideswide, the patron saint of Oxford. Simler describes this
in some detail, concluding that it reflects 'a good and grateful mind of the
English men towards their master whose wife she had lately been.'[73] He
leaves open her saintly status, implying that the reformer's wife was in her
own way as saintly as St Frideswide and so fully deserving of being buried
in the same tomb.

By contrast, Vermigli's second marriage to Catherine Merenda is of
interest to Simler only because he needs to explain why his hero married
twice rather than remaining 'a chaste widower' after the model provided by
Bullinger or, for that matter, Calvin. Furthermore, the fact that the marriage
took place in Zurich added to its importance. In contrast with his portrayal
of Catherine Dompmartin, Simler does not assimilate Catherine Merenda
to a saint. She was simply a 'maid born at Brescia of an honest stock,
whose name was Catherine Merenda, which was come thither [Geneva]
for religion's sake.'[74] Further, according to Simler, Vermigli married her
on the basis of testimony of good men and of the whole church for the
sole purpose of begetting children, 'being persuaded by his friends since
he himself was very desirous of children, and that the more because he
alone was left of the family of Vermigli which once had flourished, he did

---

[70]   Ibid., p. 55.
[71]   Ibid.
[72]   Ibid., pp. 55–6.
[73]   Ibid., p. 56.
[74]   Ibid., p. 74.

determine to take another wife, six years after his first wife's death.'[75] The sole *raison d'être* of Catherine Merenda being to bear children, she does not get any further mention. In contrast with his description of Catherine Dompmartin, Simler does not try to make the reader believe that she did good works among the poor, let alone suggest that she was a saintly figure. He confines himself to mentioning the two children she bore, who died in infancy, and notes that she was 'great with' a third child when Vermigli died, 'whom I beseech the Lord may be delivered of a son, which living may represent his father in learning and godliness.'[76]

Simler is far more interested by the proviso in Vermigli's will that the child, when born, 'should not be brought up elsewhere than among us.'[77] This, according to the biographer, shows the full extent of Vermigli's predilection for Zurich, as does his refusal of calls to the ministry in Lucca and in Geneva.[78]

Undoubtedly, the most striking feature of Simler's biography is its dual orientation. The *Life* is intended for both the English and Zurich context. At the same time, he is rather more exhaustive than other biographers of the period and covers every stage of Vermigli's career, devoting particular attention to his conversion. Vermigli comes across as a model churchman, but no more than a model churchman. There is no hint of him as God's tool, endowed with some special eschatological mission, although Simler grants that divine providence is the sole determining factor of his calling. There are two main reasons for this relatively unheroic and unsaintly, albeit still extremely positive and pious, portrayal of Vermigli. First, he was not young when he converted; secondly, he was an Italian; and thirdly, he was never a leader of a reformed church.

The Hostile Life *of Vermigli by Noel Taillepied and James Laing*

As we have seen,[79] Laing did not publish an original *Life* of Vermigli, but paraphrased into Latin and considerably enlarged the *Life* by Noel Taillepied of Pontoise, which appeared in French in the collection *Histoire des actes, doctrine et mort de quatre Heretiques de notre temps*, published in 1577.[80] Vermigli, unlike Karlstadt, was of direct interest to Taillepied, mainly because of the Italian reformer's role at the Colloquy of Poissy and his disagreement with the Genevans on the question of real presence.[81]

---

[75]   Ibid.
[76]   Ibid.
[77]   Ibid.
[78]   Ibid., pp. 74–5.
[79]   See Chapter 1, p. 35.
[80]   On Taillepied, see Chapter 1, pp. 25–34.
[81]   On Vermigli's part in the Colloquy of Poissy, see Andreas Mühling, 'Vermigli, Bullinger und das Religionsgespräch von Poissy'. in Campi, James III and Opitz (eds), *Peter*

Taillepied explains that he drew most of his information about the Italian reformer from the latter's '*Dialogue on the two Natures of Christ* translated into French by one of his sect'.[82] He does not name any other sources, and the account he gives of Vermigli's life is anything but accurate. As we shall see from a more detailed comparison, Laing mistranslates, expands and adds to his original, of which he does not reveal the author.

Unlike Karlstadt or, for that matter, Luther, whose connexions with England and Scotland were less easy to establish, Vermigli had English connexions which were still remembered and which could be extended to Scotland, notably to show that all of Scotland's religious misfortunes (that is, the Reformation) were due to English influence. Within Laing's 1581 collection,[83] which it is important to remember was dedicated to James VI of Scotland and to his mother Mary, the biographical account of Vermigli (entitled *Vita et res gestae Petri Martyris Vermeliensis*) occupies twenty-six octavo-sized pages, which makes it considerably longer than Taillepied's original. However, of those twenty-six pages, fourteen are devoted to invective against David Fergusson (d. 1598), Scottish Presbyterian minister of Dunfermline (1563–72) and originally haberdasher by trade, who never so much as encountered Vermigli. The connexion between the two will become clearer after we have examined the salient parts of Laing's *Life* of the Italian reformer, and compared them with Taillepied's account.

As regards Vermigli's passage from Catholicism to Protestantism, neither Taillepied nor Laing could argue for a long and steady conversion culminating in the full 'seeing of the light'. Nor did they argue for the converse; that is, for the steady burgeoning of the seeds of heresy, present in their anti-hero from the beginning. Both writers argue for their subject's sudden contamination in Naples. Needless to say, Simler, who was very well informed about this period in his hero's life, considered it as the time 'when the grace of heavenly light began to shine more clearly unto him.'[84] For Taillepied and Laing, on the other hand, it is the time when out of nowhere Vermigli 'became infected by the heresy of a certain Spanish nobleman, Juan Valdes, who, because of his heretical views, had been forced to leave the court of Charles V after he had infected several Neapolitan citizens by his books in which he tried to make men into

---

Martyr Vermigli, pp. 241–9, and literature cited ibid.

[82]   Taillepied, *Histoire* (1577), fol. 15v.: '… selon que i'ay trouué en vn liure intitulé Dialogue des deux natures de Christ, translaté en françoys par vn de sa secte.' He is referring to the translation by Claude Kerquifinen (d. 1584?), French translator of several works of Juan Valdes. His version of the *Dialogus* is entitled *Dialogue des deux natures du Christ* (Lyon, à la Salemandre, 1565). The sole extant copy is available at the La Rochelle Public Library. (This translation is not mentioned by R. Kingdon and P. Donnelly in their *Bibliography of the Works of Peter Martyr Vermigli* [Kirksville, MO: The Sixteenth Century Journal Publishers, 1990]).

[83]   See Chapter 1, p. 35.

[84]   Simler, *Oratio* (ed. Mclelland), p. 41.

atheists, in other words, to convince them that God did not exist.' These books, according to Taillepied 'were founded upon [*sont fondez*] the errors of Anabaptists, Lutherans, Calvinists and others.'[85] For Laing, they 'drew their poison from the writings of Anabaptists, Lutherans, Calvinists and other monsters of that kind.'[86] In a word, according to Taillepied and Laing, Vermigli became infected not with a particular heresy, but with all heresies, including atheism.

As might be expected, given our biographers' perspective, from then on, things could only go from bad to worse. Unlike Simler, who was very careful to list all ports of call in the reformer's itinerary, Taillepied and Laing make no reference to his passage through Lucca, and have him come to Geneva from Rome together with Ochino.[87] As is his wont, Laing elaborates on the original, specifying that the two chose Geneva deliberately as being the 'refuge of all heretics'.[88] In fact, Martyr did refuse a call to the ministry in Geneva in 1543 when in Strasbourg, an event Simler does not mention and which Taillepied and Laing conflate with his escape from Italy in the company of Ochino in 1542. What really happened was that on that occasion, Ochino did come to Geneva, but Vermigli first went to Zurich and Basel before going on to Strasbourg. There is nothing surprising, however, about Laing's rhetorical device, which consists in 'sending' Vermigli and Ochino to Geneva, 'the vilest hiding place of all heretics'. Taillepied had already blown up the poor relations between Ochino and Calvin to make it seem that there was a general feeling of suspicion on the part of all Genevans towards the two Italians, which resulted in both of them leaving.[89] Both biographers (Laing more than Taillepied) thus exploit Vermigli's status as a religious exile to present him as an unwanted impostor, too suspect doctrinally to be accepted even in Geneva.

---

[85]   Taillepied, *Histoire* (1577), fol. 16r.

[86]   Laing (1581), fol. 25r.

[87]   Taillepied, *Histoire* (1577), fol. 7r.: '[Bernardin] soudainement se retira a Florence, ou Pierre Martyr le trouua. Ensemble delibererent laisser l'Italie et venir à Geneue, ou en peu de iours estans arrivez, on ne les voulut laisser seiourner en ladicte ville, craignant qu'ils ne fissent quelque trahison ...'. This chronological shortcut could of course be attributed to Kerquifinen, Taillepied's source. However, the value judgements are those of Taillepied and/ or Laing.

[88]   Laing (1581), fol. 26v.: '[Bernardinus] Florentiam venit vbi Petrum Martirem suum antiquum amicum reperit. In re tam dubia diuque soliciti ambo fuere quid consilii potissimum capiendum esset, tandem ... optimum rati sunt se conferre Geneuam omnium haereticorum miserrimam speluncam ac paucis post diebus ciues Geneuae ceperunt sibi cauere et non parum timere ne isti suae vrbis proditores forent ...'. Cf. Simler, *Oratio* (ed. Mclelland), p. 48: '... they both at length by common advice determined leaving Italy ... to go to Germany. And first Bernard departed from there, going first to Geneva and then to Augsburg in Rhetia. After two days Martyr followed him and first went to Bologna then to Ferrara and within a while to Verona ... At length he came over the Tyrol and the Swiss Alps into Switzerland.'

[89]   Laing (1581), fols 26v.–27r.

As might be expected, the Italian reformer's first marriage had nothing saintly about it in the eyes of his Catholic biographers. Taillepied, however, described it in fairly neutral terms, obviously keeping close to his source:

> As regards Peter Martyr, seeing as he did not have enough money to stay and wait for the final decision of the Genevan authorities, he went to Strasbourg, where after being received into the ministry, he married a young nun by the name of Catherine Dompmartin, who came from Metz.[90]

Under Laing's pen, the marriage never took place. Embroidering on Taillepied's account, he says:

> He went to Strasbourg, where, after a short time in the ministry, he fornicated publicly after the fashion of other depraved ministers with a beautiful young girl in orders, whom the impudent trickster called his wife, so that he could cover up his serious crime of breach of chastity.[91]

Neither mentions Catherine Dompmartin's good works or the exhumation and reburial of her remains. Vermigli's second marriage receives a similar treatment. Taillepied again describes it in fairly neutral terms:

> Shortly after [his arrival in Zurich in 1556] and six years after the death of his first wife, he got married for a second time to a nun from Bresse, called Catherine Meraude, who moved to Geneva to enjoy carnal liberties.[92]

According to Laing's account, six years after Catherine Dompmartin's death,

> [Vermigli] took a second prostitute unto himself, a nun called Catherine Merauda, who after leaving her monastery where she lived chastely and piously, fled to Geneva, the filthy hiding-place of all degenerates, where she could, after the manner of beasts, tender to the wanton desires of the flesh freely and without fear of reproach.[93]

Whereas Taillepied took some care to keep to the sequence of events in Vermigli's life, only slanting his source to show his readers what not to believe and how not to live, Laing was not at all interested in Vermigli's life as such. His sole aim was to show that Vermigli spread the Protestant contagion in England. Writing from Paris and seeing the Scottish Reformation very much as a Genevan product, he was more or less obliged to make the link between the Italian reformer and the city which he saw as the cesspool of all depravity. Zurich would not have fitted the bill nearly so well. Laing's Vermigli is thus formally similar to Bolsec's Calvin. Though not demonic, he is a sexual deviant, forced to exist on the margins of

90   Taillepied, *Histoire* (1577), fol. 17v.
91   Laing (1581), fol. 27r.–v.
92   Taillepied, *Histoire* (1577), fol. 18r.
93   Laing (1581), fol. 28v.

society. While both biographers dwell on the eucharistic disputes, Laing implies much more clearly than Taillepied that only someone as perverted as Vermigli could have come up with a Christology which was so inept that he fell ill and died of resentment when refuted by Brenz.[94] Taillepied comments:

> And on being asked [after the Colloquy of Poissy] by his fellow ministers to refute the writings of Johannes Brenz in which the latter asserts that Christ's body can be in several places at once,[95] Vermigli seized his pen and wrote a book entitled *The Dialogue of Two Natures of Christ*, a very pernicious work likely to do great damage to the soul. Brenz, after reading it, wrote a reply in which he taught Vermigli a lesson. Vermigli was getting ready to write a reply when on 5 November 1562, he fell ill partly through anger and frustration that no agreement between him and the ministers could be found ...[96].

Laing slants this account just enough to stress that of the two theologians, Brenz and Vermigli, it was the latter who was the real heretic:

> Therefore his comrades and fellow-ministers asked Vermigli to refute briefly Brenz's recent book, in which he asserted that Christ's body could be in several places at once, a doctrine which concurs with Catholic teaching. Peter Martyr began straightaway to compose the *Dialogue on the Two Natures of Christ*, a pernicious book to be condemned out of hand. Upon reading it, Brenz replied very aptly and with great subtlety, showing that Peter Martyr had no idea of ancient teaching of the fathers. On attempting to refute Brenz's response, Martyr fell ill on 5th November 1562, so that vanquished by sickness and stirred by anger that other ministers could not be brought around to his point of view, he died on twelfth [!] day of that month ....[97]

And here we come to the real object of Laing's *Life* of Vermigli, which, needless to say, has nothing to do with the Italian reformer. What Laing is trying to do, as I said, is to bring back Catholicism to Scotland via James VI. His attack on Vermigli's Christology provides Laing with a jumping-off point for attacking the Christology of David Fergusson (*c.* 1525–98), a glover by trade, first Presbyterian minister of Dunfermline, Latin scholar, chaplain to King James VI, and twice Moderator of the General Assembly of the Church of Scotland. This may seem a curious departure from the point for Laing, given that there was no record of Vermigli ever knowing Fergusson. What is more, as has been shown by Bruce Gordon, Vermigli's teaching was to exercise greater influence on the

---

[94]   Ibid., fol. 29r.–v.

[95]   He is referring to Vermigli's *Dialogus de vtraque in Christo natura* (Zurich, Chr. Froschouer, 1561), which is a reply to Johannes Brenz's *De vnione duarum naturarum in Christo* (1560).

[96]   See Taillepied, *Histoire* (1577), fol. 18v.

[97]   Laing (1581), fol. 29r.–v.

Scottish Episcopalian party than on the Presbyterians.[98] Now Fergusson was a hard-line Presbyterian and a major player in the Kirk's General Assembly for over thirty years, being identified with the Presbyterian party centred round Andrew Melville, and so a constant thorn in the side of the anti-Presbyterian Crown and the Episcopate. He had also agitated against Mary Stewart, and before that, Mary of Guise, the Regent.

More of a churchman than a theologian or writer, he did publish a number of small works. One of these was a plea for the idolatrous nature of the Mass (1563), written explicitly in response to one of Laing's colleagues at the Paris Theology Faculty, René Benoist. Benoist was in Scotland around 1561 as part of the Catholic entourage of Mary Stewart, and was one of her confessors along with Roche Mamerot and others. Fergusson's pamphlet against him was published in Edinburgh in 1563 under the title *An answer to one Epistle written by Renat Benedict, the French doctor, professor of Gods worde (as the translator of this Epistle calleth him) to John Knox and the rest of his brethren ministers of the word of God, made by David Fergussone minister of the same word at this present in Dunfermiling.*

The controversy, as we are about to see, explains why Laing selected Fergusson for his attack. However, it does not explain why he chose to attack him in the context of his *Life* of Vermigli. We can only note that it was apparently Laing's usual practice to attack figures of the Scottish Reformation via *Lives* of continental reformers who had never met the Scots in question. The best example here is Laing's swingeing attack on Buchanan in his annotated version of Bolsec's *Life* of Calvin.

Laing attributes Fergusson's heresy to his lack of education, and makes repeated insulting comments about his origins as a glover. Fergusson's sole reason for becoming a minister was greed, according to Laing. Apostrophising the Scotsman, he calls him an impertinent man completely ignorant of Latin, as all who have ever had any dealings with him know. The most eloquent witness of this, he explains, is the saintly doctor of theology from the Paris Faculty – an open allusion to René Benoist –, who wrote a letter to Knox in Latin to make him return to the bosom of the Catholic Church. Neither Knox nor Fergusson replied to Benoist when he was still in Scotland, notes Laing. Fergusson waited until Knox was dead and Benoist was back in France to write his response in his 'barbarous Scottish language', as Laing puts it, and to send it to Benoist. The latter, after asking Laing to translate it from English into Latin, was so stunned

---

[98]   See Bruce Gordon, 'Peter Martyr Vermigli in Scotland. A sixteenth century Reformer in a seventeenth century Quarrel', in Campi, James III and Opitz (eds), *Peter Martyr Vermigli*, pp. 275–94.

by its ineptitude, lies and insults against the pope, that he did not answer it.[99]

Not only does Fergusson not know Latin, insists Laing, but he does not know the biblical languages, despite the fact that he claims to admit no teaching that is not founded in the Scripture. As he does not know the languages of Scripture, argues Laing, the only source of scriptural knowledge open to Fergusson is the direct inspiration of God. If that is so, Fergusson is either a heretic (for heretics always claim to benefit from divine inspiration) or an apostle, prophet or a similar person sent directly by God. If he is sent directly by God, then, in Laing's view, he should be able to prove it by some miracle.

At this point in his invective, Laing produces a long list of anti-miracles produced by representatives of the reformed faith, starting with wars, and continuing through suicides of ministers and murder. He notes that such supernatural events as could be linked with the reformed constitute a proof of either divine punishment or the workings of the devil. These events include a certain heretic who cut off his hand with the very sword he used to smash images, and another, who, having built his house with materials of a dismantled sanctuary, found it exuding blood, and so on. The piece ends with Laing exhorting Fergusson to return to his glove-making.[100] As we have said, he establishes no link between Fergusson and Vermigli other than both sharing a false doctrine of the Eucharist.

That said, Laing's *Life* of Vermigli provides an interesting and rare example of a biography of a well-known 'heretic' (Vermigli) being used as a vehicle for invective against a less illustrious and lessser-known *minister cacodaemonis*. Presented in this way, the invective was guaranteed not to reach and anger merely James VI, to whom Laing dedicated his volume, but to get a much wider circulation than an isolated pamphlet against a fairly obscure Scottish minister. Laing, faithful to his models, Taillepied and Bolsec, saw no clear dividing line between the life of a reformer and its consequences in religious terms. His piece of invective against Fergusson shows this very well with every single biographical detail, none of which was in itself scandalous or linked to Vermigli, being used as proof of the former glover's heretical views.

Contrary to Laing's assertions, Fergusson wrote and published his *Answer* to Benoist in 1563, when Knox was still very much alive. He explains in his preface to the reader that he did not undertake to answer Benoist's *Epistle* 'as one more able to do so than the rest of my fellowes in office, but rather driuen thereunto by some zealous and godlie persons, who brought it to my hands for that purpose, after that it had been carried

---

[99]   See Laing (1581), fols 31v.–32r., esp. 31v.: '... tu tandem epistola barbara et scotica, mortuo iam sceleratissimo sycophanta Knox respondisti et huc Parisios illam misisti ...'.

[100]   For the invective, see ibid., fols 30v.–37v.

as a matter of great importance from one place to another and so at length (translated by a certaine freir out of latine into Inglish in favour of such persones as he thereby would gratifie) it was greatly boosted of: partlie therfor to satisfy the reasonable request of the aforesaid persons, and also to stop the mouth of the adversary from further bragging, but chiefly for the discharge of my conscience in the office whereunto God hath called me, I have occupied my pen in answering as after foloweth.'[101]

The conflict over the Mass between Mary Queen of Scots and Knox was naturally at its most acrimonious when she was in Scotland in 1561. It was obvious that Benoist's letter was one of many attempts on the queen's part to make Knox see reason. Contrary to what Laing leads the reader to believe, it was not a private document, but, as Fergusson puts it, 'was carried about from place to place as a matter of great importance.'[102] The English translation, which Fergusson mentions, was obviously intended to make it more widely available, although it was apparently never published. Knox could hardly reply to it himself, but either he or his entourage found it enough of a threat to charge Fergusson with a reply, which was no more personal than Benoist's *Epistle*. The ex-haberdasher explains that his treatise might be useful for those who are still in error. In other words, he sees it as an instrument of conversion. He also explains that he found Benoist's letter to be a piece of 'confused chaos'. He therefore divided it into four sections, to which he replied one by one with citations from Benoist's text. The four sections in Benoist's letter that Fergusson isolated concerned the usual issues. Benoist first addressed the matter of the dangers of the 'new religion', before going on to defend the Roman Catholic Mass, and warn Knox about the perils of becoming the instrument of Satan, especially active in these latter days. The final section recapitulated these three points. Fergusson's reply had nothing especially original about it, and was obviously intended to act as a spur to conversion. In a nutshell, he argued that there was no scriptural proof of the sacrifice of the Mass, and that neither Paul nor the early fathers ever referred to it.

Viewed in the context of his *Life* of Vermigli, Laing's outburst against Fergusson was something of a distraction, not to say a red herring. However, viewed against the Franco-Scottish religious context, it made perfect political sense. Firstly, it attempted to widen the breach between James and the Scottish Presbyterians. Secondly, it showed the latter to be a part of the great Genevan international conspiracy, of which Vermigli was, in Laing's view, one of the leaders.

---

[101]   David Fergusson, *An answer to one Epistle written by Renat Benedict, the French doctor, professor of Gods worde (as the translator of this Epistle calleth him) to John Knox and the rest of his brethren ministers of the word of God, made by David Fergussone minister of the same word at this present in Dunfermiling* (Edinburgh, [n.p.], 1563), fol. 2r.–v.

[102]   Ibid., fol. 2v.

The Lives *of Bullinger*[103]

Stucki's Encomium

Bullinger wrote a *Life* of Leo Jud, and would not have objected to having a biography devoted to himself.[104] As it turned out, he was the object of no fewer than three *Lives* in the year following his death. The first of these was a funeral *encomium* by Johann Wilhelm Stucki. Whereas Simler's *Oratio* on Vermigli was not a funeral oration at all by the time it was revised for publication, Stucki cast his piece in the classical *encomium* mode. How did he reconcile this basically profane genre with his religious convictions?

Indeed, his *Oratio* has very little, if anything, in common with the reformers' biographies we have examined so far. What is more noteworthy, it has hardly anything in common with Simler's account of the life of Vermigli other than the title. Stucki's piece is very much an oral exercice. It does not contain a single date and refers only to the barest outlines of the chronology of Bullinger's life, which is described in a totally schematic way. Stucki pays no attention to the reformer's personality, his psychological motivations or, for that matter, the specificity of his doctrine. The *Oratio* has its own particular dynamic. It begins with the evaluation of the role of religion for pagan thinkers such as Plato and others, and ends with a prayer for the Zurich Church and its ministers. Sandwiched between these two extremes, Bullinger is first introduced as incarnating all the civic virtues. As the account progresses, he shifts from being the most learned, the most cultivated and the most morally pure, to being the most pious and the kindest of Christians. In short, he is an *exemplum* not of a Christian hero, not of a pastor and not of a theologian, but of the perfect man acting in accordance with Christ's precepts. In other words, Stucki follows Bullinger's own humanist line. Indeed, as we noted above,[105] according to the reformer, profane learning and humanist learning in particular was what made us fully human and receptive to the study of sacred letters. Earlier, we noted the same strain coming to the fore in Kessler's *Life* of Vadian. However, Stucki's *Oratio* is a far more rhetorical piece than Kessler's account of the St Gallen reformer. It does not tell us anything about Bullinger's career, his marriage or his writings. Its object is to present the reformer as one who struck the perfect balance between the pagan and the Christian, thus constituting the model of the emblematic Christian. Stucki's *Oratio* is as far removed from the *Lives* of the saints' model as it is possible for an account of a religious leader to be. He argues:

---

[103] These *Lives* of Bullinger are in the process of being edited by Christian Moser of the Zurich Institut für schweizerische Reformationsgeschichte.

[104] This is currently being studied by Bruce Gordon, which is why I have not included it.

[105] See above p. 60.

> For the way of humanity and of divine wisdom has always been such that in order to teach men those things which pertain to the salvation of their bodies and souls, it uses not so much the works and help of angels as that of mortal men. It does this for various reasons, but chiefly so as to bind men together more tightly by the chain of love and solidarity.[106]

He stresses that God has used men to act as *exempla* to other men in all religions from the beginning of time. Indeed, according to Stucki, the best way to live this life and to prepare for the next is to lay a foundation of religion. Religion as revealed by human *exempla* is thus fundamental to all societies, not just the Christian society, although naturally Christian (Protestant) religion is the only true faith. Stucki further argues that the force of religion is such that even states which practised idolatrous cults produced men with the wisdom necessary to quell rebellions and instil basic civic values into the population. He gives a long list of examples, including Pompilius Numa, Lycurgus, Scipio Africanus and others. He thus establishes a direct continuity not between the good pagan and the good Christian religion, but between the pagan and the Christian state, the former being a forerunner of the latter. He further argues that, if what he calls 'idolatrous doctors of idolatrous nations', such as Gallic Druids, Indian Brahmins and Roman soothsayers, always enjoyed special honour, even greater honour should be given to the doctors of the only true religion, which is the Christian reformed faith. However, as Christians often do not honour their doctors as they should, God the ultimate avenger allows them to suffer under false doctors with the downfall of the state as the inevitable outcome.

After citing several biblical examples of this, Stucki turns his audience's attention to Zurich, a city particularly favoured by God since it restituted the true religion some fifty years previously. Now, Stucki obviously cannot argue that the Zurchers have been so ungrateful as to relapse into error, causing the downfall of their state. However, it is obvious that he feels that the death of Bullinger could leave an ideological gap, and that, with the *antistes* gone, political disorder could ensue. The prospect of the downfall of the state is thus intended as a warning. Even though this has not occurred, he contends that God has given other signs of his displeasure: it is because the citizens have been remiss with regard to the respect they accord their doctors, that God has taken unto Himself so many of the best of them in recent years. Among them, he mentions Pellikan, Bibliander, Peter Martyr Vermigli, Conrad Gesner and others. He particularly singles out Johannes

---

[106] Johann Wilhlem Stucki, *Oratio funebris in obitum d. Henrici Bullingeri*, in Josiah Simler and Stucki, *Narratio de ortu* (Zürich, Chr. Froschouer, 1575) (hereafter: Stucki, *Oratio*), fol. 2r.: 'Sic enim fert semperque tulit humanitatis ac sapientiae diuinae ratio vt ad homines ea quae ad illorum animi corporisque salutem pertinent docendum, non tam angelorum quam mortalium hominum opera ac ministerio vteretur, idque cum ob alias tum hanc potissimum ob causam quo illos hac ratione tanto firmiore inter se arctioreque charitatis societatis vinculo conglutinaret.'

Wolf (1521–71), preacher in Fraumünster and later professor of theology, mainly known as translator of Philo. His praise of Wolf, whose death preceded Bullinger's by some four years (and whose *Life* was written by Stucki in a hagiographical mode![107]), can thus constitute a prologue to Stucki's *encomium* of the *antistes*. He praises Wolf routinely for his profane and sacred learning; for his impeccable morals in public and private sphere; and for his sermons and lectures, German and Latin, which were invariably pious, learned and elegant. In a word, Wolf and the other departed doctors are to be mourned not because they were saintly, not because they were the instruments of God's providence and not for their outstanding services to the church; what gives them their unique value in Stucki's eyes is their sacred and profane learning which they put at the service of the state as well as the church.

The introduction of Wolf and the other deceased doctors of the Zurich Church changes the entire perspective of the *Oratio*: it becomes an *encomium* of a political and ecclesiastical system, and not just of Bullinger. As we shall see in the following chapters, this sort of *encomium* would not have been found acceptable in Geneva any more than a series of sermons on a reformer's life. The *encomium* particularly is the very genre that Beza wanted to avoid when he wrote his *Life* of Calvin, considering that the specificity of reformed biography was its capacity to show plainly and without personal glorification how God manifested Himself through a given individual. Moreover, the funeral *encomium* was to be specifically condemned by De la Faye in his biography of Beza in 1606.

To return to Stucki, having set the scene for his account of Bullinger, he points out that his recent death constitutes a very severe punishment of Zurchers for their impiety. This is the only indication in his opening paragraphs that he is dealing with a religious leader. Nothing in his plan suggests this:

> So as to avoid a disorderly account wandering here and there, I have decided to proceed as follows: I shall first of all describe as best I can all the illustrious qualities of his mind and soul, then his speeches, sermons and writings as well as his highly praiseworthy actions, then his physical attributes and finally his illness and glorious death.[108]

Plain language is not one of his concerns, any more than a guarantee of the truthfulness of his account. With his plan, he reminds his reader not to expect a chronological account of his hero's life. Beginning with Bullinger's mind and soul is not just a literary artifice, however. It enables Stucki to establish a very firm and clear distinction between the divine and human

---

[107] See my discussion of it, pp. 106–11 below.

[108] Stucki, *Oratio*, fol. 5r.–v.: 'Attamen ne sine omni ordine ... erret haec mea atque vagetur oratio, hac quidem via rationeque progredi certum est, vt primo de animi illius praeclaribus virtutibus, deinde orationibus actionibusque laudibilibus, tum de corporis externisque bonis egregiis, postremo de illius morbo atque morte gloriosa pro mea virili verba faciam.'

mind, and so avoid any risk of making Bullinger into a god. It also allows him to make the transition from spirit to the Holy Spirit, and to establish an almost perfect continuity between the pagan and the Christian, thus situating his narrative in the realm of humanist panegyric at the same time as having it point to superior, Christian truth. According to Stucki, ancient philosophers (Plato and the neo-Platonist tradition) wrongly thought that the human soul contained particles of divinity. Had they known Christ the supreme philosopher, they would have understood that it was his mind and his mind only that contained those particles of divinity that they attributed mistakenly to the human mind and soul. Bullinger's mind thus had nothing divine about it, although Stucki does consider it to have been inspired by the Holy Spirit. He thus implies that the deceased reformer owed his extraordinary intelligence, prodigious memory and other gifts to the action of the Spirit. This made his intellectual qualities divine (Stucki refers to his memory particularly as *plane diuina* at 6r.), although he did not share in any way in the essence of divinity.

Stucki then outlines the specificity of a mind which benefits from the action of the Holy Spirit. As might be expected, he argues that intelligence and good memory are not in themselves proof of it. They must be directed to specific ends, these being profane and sacred learning, and the ability to put the former at the service of the latter. He naturally considers Bullinger to have been quite outstanding in both areas:

> He was outstandingly well versed and accomplished in all the arts and liberal disciplines which serve theology, the queen and mistress of all learning, having studied them assiduously from a very early age but chiefly in Cologne.[109]

He goes on to praise not just Bullinger's knowledge of sacred writings, but the way he used the Scholastics particularly, whom he did not neglect altogether though referring to them only when their views concurred with the Scripture.[110] As behoves a Christian, this extraordinary intelligence and knowledge was coupled with a great purity of heart. It is only at this point, nearly halfway through the account, that Stucki's discourse acquires a distinctly Christian tinge. Without going into details of Bullinger's teaching, he describes at some length how the reformer taught all aspects of Christian faith, how he considered the Scripture as perfectly clear, disapproved of images, and was kind to the poor and the stricken. Interestingly, Stucki emphasises Bullinger's conciliatory attitude and his concern, on the model of early Christians, with helping everyone and not just those who shared his convictions. The most distinctive shift in orientation from an *encomium* to a Christian *encomium*

---

[109]   Ibid., fol. 6r.: 'Omnibus praeterea illis artibus et doctrinis liberalibus quae summae illi omnium reginae et dominae theologiae ancillantur, egregie instructus ac perpolitus fuit, in quibus ab ineunte aetate Coloniae praesertim multum operae studiique posuerat.'

[110]   Ibid., fol. 6v.

occurs in his description of Bullinger's last illness and death, which was nothing other than the 'beginning of eternal life'. Stucki comments at some length on the reformer's fortitude in the face of illness, concluding:

> ... he bore, conquered and overcame all these intolerable pains. Sometimes when they were so great that it seemed as if they could not get any worse, he nonetheless (oh heroic bravery!) prayed to God to make them increase and grow more intense for the sake of divine glory and for the salvation of his soul. We can thus easily see with what greatness of spirit he would have undergone and overcome in the name of Christ all those tortures, torments and sufferings whereby the tyrants of this world usually torture Christians and all those who practise true religion.[111]

Stucki obviously feels that some sort of explanation is necessary as to why the reformer did not suffer martyrdom, an apology that did not occur to any of the other biographers we have considered so far, all much closer to the Possidian model in their view of a 'good death' as a more appropriate end than martyrdom to a 'good life'.

The style and content of his *encomium* of Bullinger give us a good idea of Stucki's notion of the reformed exemplar. Unlike the Lutheran and Genevan biographers, he is not unduly concerned with doctrine and he does not insist on Bullinger as instrument of God, while considering him as inspired by the Holy Spirit. Five distinct features mark out the Zurich reformer as an example to all Christians. He instantiates together with other pious doctors the perfect civic order, as dictated by the classical *exempla*. Being a representative of the one true religion, he is also the chief doctor of theology embodying the true ecclesiastical order. Thirdly, he possesses great sacred and profane learning. Fourthly, he is kind to all afflicted, not just to those who share his convictions. Fifthly, he has an extraordinary capacity to suffer pain.

Josiah Simler's Vita Bullingeri: *Bullinger as Socrates and Anti-Pope*

Simler's work does not fall into the *encomium* genre. His object is not to present an idealised person or a saint. He has apparently no intention of defending remarkable individuals as instruments of God's providence. Nor does he set out to give a character sketch of his father-in-law, complete with psychological insights. Although it is the longest of the three contemporary *Lives* of Bullinger, the *Vita* does not contain a single intimate anecdote of the sort that Colladon included in his *Life* of Calvin. In fact, it tells us very little about Bullinger as a person, to the point of occasionally leaving him out of the picture altogether. Simler had a doctrinal rather than a biographical axe to grind, and he went about it in his own way. Written

---

[111] Ibid., fol. 18v.

in the form of *Annals*, the *Vita* concentrates first and foremost on a year-by-year account of Bullinger's writings, controversies he was involved in, and his relations with other reformers, both in Switzerland and elsewhere. Simler devotes a great deal of attention to the eucharistic disputes with the Lutherans, and even appends his own reply to Andreae's last pamphlet against Bullinger, which came out too late for the reformer to reply to himself. By contrast, he says relatively little about Bullinger's contribution to the Zurich institutions. The *Vita* was obviously intended for international as well as for national readership; its most personal section is the part dealing with the reformer's last illness and death. While God's providence is taken as given, it does not feature nearly as prominently as it does in Lutheran or Genevan biographies of their reformers.

However, Simler's preface to Johann Philipp, baron (*Freiherr*) of Upper Saxony, shows that, despite appearances, Simler is acutely aware of himself as biographer and of the nature of his endeavour, and he is very careful to place himself in the classical tradition as far away as possible from the *Lives* of the saints model. He says:

> It was an ancient custom, oh most generous master, to commit to the memory of posterity, through literary and historical works, not just the affairs of emperors and leaders, which they conducted bravely and gloriously, but also the deeds and opinions of those who were famous for their intelligence, their teaching and their wisdom. And Xenophon, who wrote both the account of Cyrus the Persian king and the commentary on the deeds and words of Socrates, the wisest of Greeks, is thought to have distinguished himself particularly in both types of writing. For although warlike virtues, which set off a lofty mind to its best advantage, have always been thought by society to be excellent and eminently worthy of commemorating, the studious pursuit of teaching and wisdom too has always enjoyed an excellent reputation. And it is no less glorious to teach religion and to serve as an example of virtue to others than to fight bravely and to wage war. For this reason, I do not think that anyone will hold it against me, if I commit to paper the deeds and words of men, illustrious for their doctrine, who lived in this century and whom I knew personally. Other similar writings of mine have been published before and more (if God will) remain to be published.[112]

---

[112]   Josiah Simler, *Narratio de ortu, vita et obitu reverendi viri d. Henrici Bullingeri, Tigurinae ecclesiae pastoris*, fol. 2r.: 'Vetus haec fuit consuetudo generose domine, ingenii et litterarum monumentis memoriae posteritatis consecrare non tantum imperatorum et principum virorum res fortiter et cum gloria gestas sed eorum quoque facta et consilia qui ingenii et doctrinae et sapientiae illustri fama celebres fuerunt. Ac Xenophon vtroque scirbendi genere praeclare de mortalium rebus meritus creditur qui et Cyri Persarum regis historiam et Socratis Graecorum sapientissimi dictorum factorumque commentarios conscripsit. Etsi enim bellica virtus in qua animi altitudo maxime elucet semper et excellens et memorabilis in societate humana extitit, suam tamen quoque laudem et famam doctrinae et sapientiae studia habuerunt. Nec minus gloriosum est alios de religione docere et virtutum illustri exemplo praelucere reliquis quam fortiter pugnare et belligerare. Quapropter neminem fore existimo qui mihi vitio vertat si doctrina excellentium virorum qui nostra aetate vixerunt et mihi noti fuerunt dicta et facta literis mandauero. Ac alia quidem huius generis ante a me publicata sunt et plura deinceps (si Deus volet) publicabuntur.'

Simler sees himself as a latter-day Xenophon, and Bullinger *qua* object of a biography as a latter-day Socrates, whose wisdom is to do with Christ rather than with the basic tenets of philosophy. Simler's endeavour is thus of a civic and humanist nature, and the issue of hagiography is not germane to it. Furthermore, as he makes clear, his *Vita* of Bullinger is only one of several *Lives* of heroes of the Reformation. Did Simler view his father-in-law as one in the line of heroes, or were there more particular reasons that led him to write about Bullinger? Indeed there were. On closer inspection, these turn out to have been not dissimilar from the reasons that spurred the production of all the other biographies, albeit with one important difference. Simler wanted not just to glorify Bullinger, but to make him better known among those who admired his works.[113] He also set out to defend the reputation of the Zurich Reformation by giving an account of the main events that took place in and around the Zurich Church during Bullinger's time at its head. He was very careful to point out, however, that he would only mention those events which were linked to Bullinger's life, leaving others to write down the full history of the Zurich Reformation.[114] The resulting work is as much a chronicle (albeit an incomplete one) as a biography, in contrast with Kessler's *Life* of Vadian, which, as we have seen, adopted two different methods in his *Sabbata* and in his *Life* of Vadian. Simler explains that his choice of method was dictated by his determination to scotch any rumours about Bullinger, similar to the ones of the *antistes'* death that were spread in 1565 when he fell ill with the plague:

> There are also those who approve of nothing except things which are their own and who try to obtain leadership of the church in our time. As they glory in besmirching the reputation of the dead, it seemed appropriate to forestall their calumnies by a true narrative containing not just the actions of Bullinger but also the main affairs of our churches ... I think you remember, generous master, although you were a mere boy at the time, when Bullinger was mortally ill some years ago and rumour of his death was spread abroad, how his adversaries danced for joy and how many lies they spread orally and in writing. As I do not doubt for one moment that the same people, who feed on lies like a chameleon on wind, will now spread similar lies, I thought it would be the right thing to do to write down a chronological account of Bullinger's life in a truthful and simple way ....[115]

---

[113]   Ibid.: '... quam vt in publicum emitterem, duae me praecipue causae impulere, primum quod scio quamplures esse per Germaniam et exteras quoque regiones qui Bullingerum propter scripta plurimum amarunt et historiam vitae eius scire desiderant ...'.

[114]   Ibid., fol. 2v.: 'Et quoniam ille praecipuus pastor nostrae ecclesiae multis annis fuit, intertextui mentionem praecipuarum rerum que toto hoc tempore in ecclesiis nostris vel gestae vel disceptatae sunt, quae poterant quidem et debebant copiosius exponi et pro dignitate sua elegantius explicari, quod forte alii facient, nos ea breuiter complecti voluimus et hactenus tantum quantum cum instituta historia vitae Bullingeri coniuncta fuerunt.'

[115]   Ibid.: 'Sunt deinde alii qui nihil nisi suum probant et nostra aetate imperium in ecclesia sibi vendicare conantur. His cum gaudeant mortuorum gloriam allatrare, visum est eorum calumniis vera narratione quae non modo Bullingeri facta, sed praecipuas res

The addition of the historical and theological background was, he explains, prompted by the fact that Bullinger was the chief pastor of the Zurich Church for several years. Simler shared one characteristic with Stucki and other members of the deceased reformer's inner circle: a worry about the future of the political and ecclesiastical commonweal with its leader dead. To reduce the risk, he chose, like Stucki, to express himself in the biographical mode, but a very different biographical mode from that adopted by Stucki. He opted for a chronological account of the life of a Christian Socrates, coupled with a chronicle of his time. The choice of Xenophon as role model was not just an aesthetic device. Simler might well have read the *Memorabilia* (which were available in print since 1521), and would have been struck by their simplicity as compared to the flowery language of funeral orations. There the resemblance ended, however. Unlike Xenophon, who transmits all sorts of anecdotes of uncertain historical value, Simler (who was much more intimate with Bullinger than his role model ever was with Socrates) gives a rigorous third-person account of his hero's religious and literary activity, which he sets against the background of the chronicle of his time. However, these differences are incidental. The point is that by mentioning Xenophon, Simler would have avoided any link with hagiography and would have also distanced himself from the funeral *encomium* approach.

The decision not to commemorate the dead *antistes* with an *encomium* was thus a deliberate one. As he says himself:

> I was linked to Bullinger by very close ties and I loved him like my own father when he was alive, and he in turn treated me like his own son. But this relationship, however close, should be taken as proof of accuracy of this account and not of its unreliability. For I had better first-hand knowledge than anyone outside his family, not just of what he did and said, but also of what he thought. Had I written an *encomium*, perhaps I would have deserved to be dismissed as a domestic flatterer, but what I wanted was to write down things as they were without any embellishment and to let the reader judge for himself.[116]

---

ecclesiarum nostrarum continet, occurrere. Etenim cum superioribus annis Bullingerus lethaliter decumberet et fama mortis eius a quibusdam diuulgata esset, meministi adhuc opinor generose domine, quamuis tum admodum adulescens esses, quae tripudia fuerint aduersariorum, quam multa vana literis quorundam et sermone sparsa fuerint. Quare cum mihi non dubium sit similia mendacia eosdem homines qui mendaciis vt chameleon vento aluntur, nunc quoque disseminaturos esse, existimaui me bonam operam nauaturum si seriem vitae Bullingeris vera et simplici narratione exponerem.'

[116]   Ibid., fol. 3v.: 'Fui equidem arctissima necessitudine Bullingero coniunctus eumque quoad vixit patris loco colui, ille me vicissim pro filio habuit, sed qualiscunque haec fuit coniunctio, ea non tam derogare quam confirmare fidem narrationis meae debet. Quod scilicet non tantum dicta et facta, verum etiam consilia ipsius mihi melius quam cuiquam alieno cognita et perspecta fuerunt. Quod si encomium scribere instituissem merito forte domesticus laudator reiici possem, nunc vero mihi propositum fuit simpliciter res ipsas narrare, iudicium lectori relinquere.'

As might be expected of a biography that lays as much stress on the history of the time as on its hero, its two principal interests tend to blend together. This is particularly obvious in the discussions of the eucharistic controversy, to which Simler devotes a disproportionate amount of space. However, the biographical part of Simler's account is still far more detailed than Stucki's. He is careful to give a full outline of Bullinger's education and a catalogue of his writings. He goes into the details of his marriage, giving the names of his children and their spouses. He is at great pains to outline his network of friends[117] and his relations with other reformers, including Calvin. He tackles his father-in-law's life year by year, which makes it very easy to fit in a chronicle of his hero's times. It is quite plain, however, that one of Simler's main aims is to stress that Bullinger played a central role in any given series of events, and that his main concern was to reconcile opposing parties, his attitude to the papacy constituting the sole exception.

Simler's description of the Wittenberg Concord of 1536, in which Bullinger played a minor role, constitutes a very good example of our chronicler–biographer's way of going about things. His account is based largely but not exclusively on Ludwig Lavater's *Historia de origine et progressu controuersiae sacramentariae de coena domini ab anno natiuitatis Christi 1523 vsque ad annum 1563 deducta*.[118] He augments Lavater's account with some reflexions of his own. Granting that Bucer was the chief mediator on the Eucharist between the Saxon and the Swiss churches, he insists that Bullinger 'was present at all these negotiations and took most of them upon himself', and that 'he worked particularly hard to establish firm agreement between Luther and the Swiss churches so much so that some accused him of plotting defection to Luther's side, an accusation of which he easily cleared himself in word and deed.'[119] What Bullinger would not and could not accept, however, affirms Simler, was the ambiguous phrase, 'the body of Christ is present with the bread and is thus exhibited physically, substantially, in an invisible, supernatural way' (*Christi corpus corporaliter et substantialiter et inuisibiliter atque*

---

[117] Ibid., fol. 9v.: 'Capellae ergo cum viueret Bullingerus, amicos habuit Vuolfgangum Ionerum, eius coenobii abbatem et Petrum Simlerum, cum quo et tum coniunctissime vixit et amicitiam ad obitum eius fideliter coluit, arctiore vinculo constrictam, filia sua elocata Iosiae Simlero Petri filio a quo haec descripta sunt. Iisdem annis cum doctissimis viris Heluetiae nostrae amicitiam contraxit et in eorum familiaritate peruenit cum Huldrico Zwinglio, Ioanne Oecolampadio, Ioachimo Vadiano, Leone Iuda, Bertholdo Hallero, Ambrosio Blarero et multis aliis viris doctis ...'.

[118] Published in Zurich in 1563, and translated into German by Johannes Stumpf.

[119] Simler, *Narratio*, fol. 16r.: 'Bullingerum non tantum his actionibus [Buceri] omnibus interfuisse et praecipuas partes sustinuisse sed in eo plurimum laborasse vt firma concordia inter Lutherum et nostras ecclesias constitueretur adeo vt quidam eum in suspicionem vocarint quasi ad Lutherum defectionem moliretur, verum ipse et verbis et facto suam innocentiam comprobauit.'

supernaturaliter cum pane praesens esse et exhiberi).[120] According to Simler, subsequent events were to prove him right. Once the wording was accepted, churches in the South of Germany agreed to adopt its correct (that is, pro-Zwinglian) interpretation provided that there were enough first-generation reformed ministers who understood the nuances. As soon as they were succeeded by younger men 'more militant than they and less well versed in religious controversies', there was a swing to the belief in what Simler calls 'gross, carnal presence', which resulted in an intense dislike of Zwinglians and, more to the point, the automatic association of the Wittenberg Concord position with Zwinglianism.[121]

It is true that Bucer's formula contributed to the aggravation of the eucharistic quarrel and the hardening of the Lutheran position. It is also true that, as Simler puts it, Bullinger and his church were 'alone in maintaining ancient simplicity' and not signing the concord.[122] However, there are several salient facts that Simler does not mention. He says nothing of the fact that Berne accepted the concord, but chose young Calvin to draft a *new* eucharistic confession in 1537, thus showing, without inclining to the Zwinglian position, that its acceptance of Bucer's formula was not wholehearted. Simler does not aim to be objective: he wants to show, without overtly criticising Bucer, that Bullinger's position would have proved to be far more conducive to the Zwinglian–Lutheran reconciliation. He thus has the dead *antistes* play a conditional key role in the history of the eucharistic quarrel.

His account of the *Consensus Tigurinus* of 1549 is far more conciliatory towards the other party to the agreement. He says:

> In the following year, the Genevans reached an agreement with the Zurchers about the Eucharist. Indeed, Calvin seemed to many to teach a different doctrine of the Eucharist than the ministers of the Zurich Church, and to be quite favourable to consubstantiation. Therefore, to free himself from this suspicion, he set out to Zurich in the company of Guillaume Farel, the pastor

---

[120]   Ibid.

[121]   Ibid., fol. 16r.–v.: 'Postquam enim huiusmodi phrases antea inusitatae a plerisque ecclesiis superioris Germaniae receptae sunt, paulatim commutatio doctrinae secuta est et primi quidem veteresque ecclesiarum ministri qui norant quo sensu haec recepta, ab ipsis et rursus quare a nobis repudiata essent, non adeo a nobis alieni fuerunt, sed amicitiam et fraternitatem nobiscum coluerunt. Postquam vero his alii minus exercitati in controuersiis ecclesiae sed magis feroculi successerunt, prorsus obtinuit crassa illa carnalis praesentia ac nunc non tantum explicatio illa Buceri sed ne ipsae quidem illae pacificatoriae propositiones amplius locum habent in illa ecclesia in qua olim Bucerus tanto studio summa cum laude docuit, sic vt Zuingliani sint, hoc est ipsorum iudicio omnium mortalium pessimi, qui docent et scribunt iuxta illarum propositionum sententiam.' See also Bruce Gordon, *The Swiss Reformation* (Manchester: Manchester University Press, 2002), pp. 146–90, 283–316.

[122]   Simler, *Narratio*, fol. 16v.: 'Bullingerus igitur ... solus cum suis veterem simplicitatem retinuit.'

from Neuchâtel, and discussed the question of the supper. And both parties easily reached agreement, as often happens between lovers of truth.[123]

Simler also notes quite rightly that the agreement led to sharpening of confessional divisions between the Swiss churches and the Lutherans, or, as he puts it: 'this consensus annoyed our adversaries even more, so that they insulted us even more in their writings.'[124] It is significant, however, that while granting that Calvin, Bullinger's opposite number, deserved the appellation of lover of truth, Simler does not so much as hint that that the Zurich *antistes* was anything but absolutely right and totally orthodox, as well as remaining endlessly ready to negotiate on what was no doubt the most divisive confessional issue for the Protestants of the second half of the sixteenth century.

As well as being the only man to have seen the truth about the Eucharist, Bullinger, as portrayed by Simler, was also the single most influential reformer, an image which has persisted among some contemporary historians.[125] The biographer is at pains to underline that his hero was consulted by everyone, and that he was implicated in all major religious and political events and negotiations on both national and international level. A few examples will suffice. He stresses that when Henry II of France wanted to renew the treaty between France and Switzerland, Bullinger and the Zurich Church were frequently consulted, not just by the royal emissaries, but by other Swiss cantons. The *antistes*, however, remained firmly opposed to the treaty, seeing it as a threat to Swiss independence.[126] His advice, Simler announces proudly, was followed, with no one raising any opposition. When the Bolsec affair erupted in Geneva, the other Swiss churches, especially the Zurich Church, were also consulted. According to Simler, Bullinger made use of this opportunity to show that his doctrine of predestination did not differ from Zwingli's, contrary to the malicious insinuations made by some.[127]

Simler refers to the 1560 debate between Flacius and Strigel as a synod, whereas it was more of a public disputation. He shows that Bullinger wanted the discussion to involve all Protestant parties, another sign of his pan-Protestant preoccupations that were always being thwarted by the extreme Lutherans – that is, the Gnesio-Lutherans.[128] A similar reproach of sectarianism is also made by Simler against the Council of Trent, but in much stronger terms. Here, he refers to Bullinger's unpublished work

---

[123] Ibid., fol. 24r.
[124] Ibid.
[125] See, for example, Fritz Büsser, *Heinrich Bullinger: Leben, Werk und Wirkung*, 2 vols (Zurich: Theologischer Verlag, 2003, 2005).
[126] Simler, *Narratio*, fol. 34r.
[127] Ibid., fols 26v.–27r.
[128] Ibid., fol. 34r.–v.

on the council, which was translated into Italian and published by Pier Paolo Vergerio.[129] In other words, one of the main objects of Simler's *Life* is to show that the *antistes* was both a witness to his time and one of its key actors, doctor of the Zurich Church and guarantor of political and ecclesiastical stability, not just of Zurich, but of the entire European Christendom, which was united under Bullinger's *aegis* for as long as he was alive, and which is threatened with decomposition after his death. The reformer under Simler's pen is not just a Christian Socrates; he is also Cyrus, combining the functions of a doctor of the church and local political leader with those of the Protestant equivalent of pope and emperor. Simler did not write an apology of Bullinger's teaching, character or personal life; neither did he present his father-in-law as an embodiment of a doctrinal statement, such as the First or the Second *Helvetic Confession*. His biography constitutes a political statement about the role of the Zurich Church on the Swiss and on the European scene.

Ludwig Lavater's Abridgement of Simler's Vita (1576)

Ludwig Lavater, Bullinger's other son-in-law,[130] produced an abridged version of Simler's biography in the vernacular.[131] His intention was to reach a more specific readership in Switzerland and Germany, and therefore to convey not so much an image of Bullinger as the head of international Protestantism as his importance for those two countries. Inevitably, this means that his work is considerably shorter than Simler's. He reproduces none of Simler's methodological reflexions, and does not put forward any of his own. Furthermore, he omits all references likely to puzzle the essentially German-speaking, general public, especially those to Bullinger's literary activity, as well as the list of his works. He also leaves out many details intended to show the extent of the *antistes'* influence. He makes only a minimal mention of Flacius, gives far less information about religious refugees in Zurich, lays far less stress on Bullinger's conciliatory efforts and on details of religious controversies in general, and, most importantly, gives the very minimum of historical background. In Lavater's *Vom leben und tod*, the chronicle of Bullinger's times, which characterises Simler's biography, all but disappears. Also absent from his account are any protestations of his love for the deceased reformer. These are replaced by one or two intimate anecdotes, which only a close friend or a relative could have known. On the other hand, Lavater brings out the main points

---

129   Ibid., fol. 26r.–v.
130   For further details of his life and writings, see pp. 111–16 below.
131   Ludwig Lavater, *Vom leben und tod dess Eerwirdigen unnd Hochgeleerten Herren Heinrychen Bullingers, dieners der Kyrchen ze Zürich* (Zürich, Froschouer, 1576). Hereafter: Lavater, *Vom leben.*

of Bullinger's doctrine in such a way as to explain, for example, the nature of the eucharistic controversy to readers who would have found the whole thing rather puzzling. In other words, he wants to render the reformer as agreeable as possible to his German readers, and perhaps even gain a few converts among Lutherans. In this respect, his work could be seen as a sort of counterpoint to the vehement attack by Simler on the Ubiquitarians.

Lavater announces his intentions in a very short preface, most of which is taken from Simler's account:

> It has seemed good and appropriate to me to write a short and simple account of the worthy Bullinger's life and death for two reasons. First, he was held in very high esteem, not just in Zurich and the Confederation, where he led the church for a long time with his pure and wholesome doctrine and his pious and blameless life, but also in many places in Germany, through his writings, of which he published many in Latin and in German, all for the edification of the faithful. For I have no doubt that many of those who read his writings will want to know something about the author, as is usual. Secondly, it is to be expected that there will be many rumours put about abroad concerning his death, as is the custom of those who hate true religion and who want to make its most outstanding servants hateful to people by telling all sorts of lies about them, so as to make their religion seem suspect. For when there was a plague epidemic in Zurich eleven years ago and Bullinger too fell sick with it, immediately outrageous rumours of his death spread around the country, which many people would have thought to be true, had God not made him better again so that he could show them in person where the truth lay. The same happened with Calvin and others ... This is why I will tell everything about Bullinger's illness and much else concerning him. Whoever wishes, will find all this described by Simler in Latin in far greater detail.[132]

Lavater thus does not deny his dependence on Simler. Indeed, to put out two biographies that were independent of one another might have rendered the authors liable to being accused of contradicting each other and spreading lies. This did not apply to Stucki's account, which did not claim to be the true account, but simply a funeral *encomium* with a minimum of biographical details. Lavater's reasons for writing, if we judge by the preface, seem to be very similar to Simler's. However, this is forgetting that his preface contains one omission and one addition, which puts his undertaking in a different category. Firstly, whereas Simler named as the most likely public for his *Life* people in Germany and other countries who admired Bullinger and wanted to know more about him, having read his writings (... *quam vt in publicum emitterem, duae me praecipue causae impulere, primum quod scio quamplures esse per Germaniam et exteras quoque regiones qui Bullingerum propter scripta plurimum amarunt et historiam vitae eius scire desiderant* ...), Lavater specifies that he has decided to publish his *Vom leben* on account of people in Zurich, in other parts of the Confederation,

---

[132] Ibid., fol. 2r.–v.

and in several regions of Germany, who were familiar with the reformer's work (*das nit nun zu Zürych ... und in der Eydgnosschafft, sonder ouch an vilen orten dess Tütschenlands ...*). He does not mention people in other countries. Secondly, unlike Simler, he explicitly mentions Calvin and other reformers as victims of scurrilous rumours surrounding their deaths.

With these two apparently innocent changes, Simler gives his work a very definite orientation: he identifies his readership as the middle-level literate and the young, and makes it clear to them that scurrilous rumours surrounding the death of any reformer are a common occurrence and are not to be taken seriously. Thus, he avoids the political message of a commonweal in danger, which, as we have seen, is present in Simler's and Stucki's accounts. Lavater aims to distract and instruct his readers, not to worry them.

His biography devotes proportionately more space to Bullinger's early years and education. Again, he does little more than abridge Simler, omitting notably any allusion to classical authors, which might have discouraged the non-classically educated. Instead, he adds a homely anecdote from Bullinger's Cologne days, especially for the intention of young boys (*umb junger knaben willen*), whom he includes among his potential readers. The story is about Bullinger as an adolescent in Cologne spending the money his parents gave him in the company of other youths in a grocer's shop, until finally the shopkeeper rebuked them for spending their parents' money in this light-hearted fashion and asked them not to come again. Still according to Lavater, Bullinger was later to praise the shopkeeper as an honest and pious man, for, Lavater concludes, 'there are many who take money from children without asking about the consequences this might have for the parents.'[133]

As might be expected, Lavater goes into some detail about the origins of the Zurich Reformation, Bullinger's progress to the office of *antistes*, and the beginnings of the eucharistic quarrel. However, he is not nearly as specific as Simler about the nature of, for example, Bullinger's objections to the Wittenberg Concord, confining himself to stating simply that Bullinger, while no less keen than Bucer to bring about unity, was opposed to ambiguous formulae. He does not say what the reformer found ambivalent about the phrasing of the concord. He does, however, repeat after Simler that the *antistes* was proved right by subsequent events.

He devotes the minimum of attention to the Council of Trent, but is much more interested than Simler in the details of the *Consensus Tigurinus*, which he describes in the simplest possible terms, stressing that it was necessary only because of rumours of disagreement between Bullinger and Calvin, not because there was ever any real quarrel between them.[134] In general, Lavater is much more insistent than his source about Calvin's and

---

[133]   Ibid., fols 5v–6r.
[134]   Ibid., fols 19r.–20v.

Bullinger's united stand in defence of a common cause. He emphasises this agreement especially in the paragraphs he devotes to Bolsec and Servetus, which he otherwise copies almost literally from Simler.[135]

Of the remaining issues that he addresses in his biography, we might single out the Worms Colloquy of 1557, the *Edict* outlawing Zwinglianism in Württemberg in 1558, the David Joris affair of 1559, the Polish Antitrinitarians, the controversy between Bullinger and Brenz in 1561, the plague epidemics of 1564 and 1565, the Second *Helvetic Confession*, and, of course, Bullinger's death. Needless to say, he abridges drastically Simler's very extensive account of French affairs, such as the St Bartholomew's Day massacre. Furthermore, apart from the odd anecdote of childhood extravagance, he includes fewer details on Bullinger as a person than his Latin source. Although he mentions some of his friends and associates, he does not say a word about his marriage, his children, his wife's and daughters' deaths, or his personal morals. Furthermore, he does not advert to his illness in anything but the most general terms, devoting much more space to Bullinger's parting letter to the Zurich Council, which he takes from Simler.

One feature of Simler's account that Lavater does not abridge are references to signs, portents and the miraculous, which were a part of the cultural landscape in German-speaking countries at the time. Both biographers mention the 'fiery sky' (northern lights[136]) towards the end of 1560 as a presage of the reconvening of the Council of Trent in 1562, albeit not quite in the same way. Simler limits its appearance to Switzerland,[137] whereas Lavater describes it in greater detail and extends its appearance to several countries.[138] Similarly, both mention a splendid new star which appeared in the constellation of Cassiopeia around the time of the St Bartholomew's Day massacre. Simler simply says that it gave rise to various interpretations by learned men, but that some thought it a sign that God wanted to strengthen His own in the face of persecution. Lavater is more explicit. He affirms that people explained its appearance as signifying that God, massacres or not, will allow His light to shine on

---

[135]   Ibid., fols 20v.–21r.

[136]   On this, see esp. Wiebke Schwarte, *Nordlichter. Ihre Darstellung in der Wickiana* (Münster: Waxmann, 1999).

[137]   Simler, *Narratio*, fol. 36v.: 'Sub finem huius anni pluribus locis per Helvetiam coelum arsit. Anno vero qui hunc sequutus est, concilium Tridentinum a Pio IIII. papa rursus est instauratum ac permultę ea de re consultationes ubique agitatae sunt. Per Germaniam principes et reliqui status protestantium id recusarunt.'

[138]   Lavater, *Vom leben*, fol. 24r.: 'Im ussgang diss jars ist der himmel fhürig erschinen, also dass man von einem flecken in den anderen gloffen unnd mengklich vermeint, es sye ein grosse brunst verhanden. Diss gesicht ist zu einer zyt in vilen landen gesehen worden. Darnach ist das Concilium zu Trient widerumb angangen. Die Tütschen Fürsten und die Stand des rychs, ob sy glych beschriben vom Bapst, habend uff dem Concilio nit wellen erschynen. '

His churches, and adds that some thought it was a portent of the Last
Judgement, when God would free His faithful from all persecution.[139] Still
à propos of the same year, both mention the incident of the fire of the tower
in the Grossmünster in almost identical terms.[140] However, it is Lavater's
turn to be more concise than his Latin source. Simler specifies that the
Grossmünster was where Bullinger preached, and that most people found
this a sad omen rather than a presage of their damnation, while Lavater
does not mention Bullinger and does not comment further, simply stating
that there was no damage.

Obviously, Lavater was writing for a public that was more sensitive to
signs and portents, which explains his wanting to announce them more
explicitly. It was far more effective to talk about the fiery sky in several
lands and to describe it as having the appearance of great heat than to
talk about a fiery sky in several parts of Switzerland. There was no point
referring his readers to 'judgements of learned men' on the significance
of the appearance of the new star, as they would only have found the
reference confusing. The impact was bound to be far greater if he simply
gave the two main interpretations. Similarly, it was important for his public
to know that the conflagration of the tower in the Grossmünster did not
mean that Protestantism was in danger.

Conclusion

Lives of some of the most prominent Swiss reformers show both the
importance and the evolution of the genre. From a hagiography of Zwingli
by Myconius to the historical accounts of Bullinger, we witness a constant

---

[139]   Simler, *Narratio*, fol. 46r.: 'Visa est etiam hoc tempore nova stella in ipso Cassiopeiae
sydere, tam splendida ab initio, ut caeteras omnes superare et cum Lucifero splendore
certare videretur. De ea diuisa fuerunt doctorum virorum iudicia, quorum multa publice
extant, plerique tamen existimabant Deum signum hoc dedisse ad confirmandos suorum
animos in tam atroci persecutione.' Lavater, *Vom leben*, 29r.: 'Umb dise zyt ist ein nüwer
sternen am himmel gestanden, welcher, wie es etlich ussgelegt, bedütet hat, on glychwol die
fürnemmen lüten erschlagen, werde doch Gott siner kyrchen nichts desterminder sin sternen
lassen glantzen. Andere sagend es sye ein verbott dess jungsten tags, an welchem gott sine
gläubigen uss aller verfolgung ussfahren werde.' It should be noted that according to modern
geophysical findings, 1571 and 1572 were both years noted for large numbers of remarkable
auroras. See M. Attolini, R. S. Cecchini, M. Galli and T. Nanni, 'Solar Activity Variations
in Historical Aurorae Records and Tree Radiocarbons', in W. Schroeder (ed.), *Advances in
Geosciences* (Bremen: Interdivisional Commission on History of the International Association
of Geomagnetism, 1990), pp. 28–35.

[140]   Simler, *Narratio*, fol. 46r.: 'apud nos hoc anno altera turris summi templi in quo
Bullingerus concionabatur de coelo tacta conflagrauit idque incendium non tam sui damno
quam tristi omine animos hominum terruit.' Lavater, *Vom leben*, fol. 29r.: 'In disem jar ist der
ein thurn am grossen Münster Zürych von der straal zu oberist angezündt und on wyteren
schaden abgebrunnen.'

attempt to record and to identify the nature and scope of the Swiss Reformation. In this context, Zurich particularly is presented as the blessed city. We are a long way away from the *Lives* of Luther, which emphasised the individuality of the Wittenberg reformer's relationship to the divinity, his unique place in the history of salvation, and his status as embodiment of key doctrinal statements of the Lutheran Church. Swiss reformers are not inserted by their biographers into the history of salvation, or, if they are, this is only implicit. On the other hand, their biographers consistently invoke classical models, without claiming to copy Xenophon, Plutarch or Cicero. Most of their accounts laid no particular claims to exhaustivity, while paying a varying amount of attention to the historical background depending on the intended readership. Their historical context is very different from that of the most important *Lives* of Luther. Establishing close links between the religious and the civic aspects of the Reformation, they reaffirm their religious, national, as well as city identity, and see the Reformation as a collective enterprise. Moreover, partly for this reason and partly because of a lack of authoritative adversaries on their doorstep, Swiss reformers were very rarely objects of hostile biographies, although they did receive their fair share of 'heretical' notices from Lindanus, Dupréau and others. Given the wealth of information all the biographers, especially Simler, provide, it is obvious that at the time they constituted a particular genre of religious propaganda, to be read by pastors but also by schoolboys and laypeople, according to the language they were written in and the amount and level of doctrinal information they provided. In its attention to this form of edification and commemoration, the Swiss and the Zurich Reformation in particular seems to constitute a unique case. As we shall see in the next chapter, religious biography in Zurich, although practised by only a few writers, was not confined to key doctrinal figures, and made up a very broad category of writings, ranging from school textbooks to reminders of certain key events such as the Battle of Kappel.

CHAPTER 3

Zurich *Lives* in the Latter Part of the Sixteenth Century

The Biography of Gesner by Simler[1]

Josiah Simler was, as we have seen, the author of the *Lives* of Vermigli and Bullinger. He also wrote the *Life* of the naturalist Conrad Gesner,[2] which he presents rather differently. It is neither a glorified portrait of a religious leader as the real head of Christendom, nor a portrait of a virtuous Italian reformer. Simler explains his motives for writing the *Life* in some detail. He considers it natural for us, when we see the intellectual legacy of certain outstanding men, to also want to see the men themselves and to find out what they were like. He notes that, in order to satisfy this desire, many have portraits painted, which convey a close likeness of those they admire. Simler, however, thinks pictorial representations frivolous as contributing solely to the 'vain albeit joyful pleasure of the eye', and finds that to commit to writing the lives, actions, words and main interests of the men is to perform a far greater service.[3] Thinking that many would wish to know more about the life of Gesner, whose name is great among the learned, Simler therefore decided to set down and publish those aspects of his life and achievements which he thought worthy of commemoration.[4]

---

[1] I am referring here to Josiah Simler, *Vita clarissimi philosophi et medici excellentissimi Conradi Gesneri Tigurini conscripta a Josia Simlero Tigurino. Item Epistola Gesneri de libris a se editis. Et carmina complura in obitum eius conscripta. His accessit Caspari Wolphii Tigurini medici et philosophi Hyposchesis, siue de Conr. Gesneri Stirpium historia ad Ioan. Cratonem S. Caes. Maiest. Medicum excellentis. pollicitatio* (Tiguri excudebat Froschouerus, 1566). (Hereafter: Simler, *Vita Gesneri.*) Cf. Manfred Vischer, *Bibliographie der Zürcher Druckschriften des 15. und 16. Jahrhunderts erarbeitet in der Zentralbibliothek Zürich* (Baden-Baden: V. Körner, 1991), no. C 774. See also ibid., no. C 775 for the second enlarged and improved edition, also published in 1566.

[2] On Gesner see, for example, Urs Leu, *Konrad Gesner als Theologe* (Berne: P. Lang, 1990).

[3] Simler, *Vita Gesneri*, fol. 2r.: ' Natura hoc nobis datum esse arbitror viri ornatissimi vt cum scripta et labores videmus quos memoria digni viri posteritati reliquerunt, eos ipsos coram videre et qui nam ac quales fuerint cognoscere cupiamus. Cui desiderio multi vt satisfaciant praestantium virorum icones depingi curant quae quam proxime vniuscuiuscunque vultum referant. Verum cum ingentium animorum virtutes intueri praestet quam vel optime ad viuum expressas effigies, inani quanquam iucunda oculis voluptate spectasse, rectius illi mihi facere videntur qui vitam eorum, dicta, facta studiaque praecipua literis commendant.'

[4] Ibid.: 'Itaque cum existimarem multos cupidos esse cognoscendi vitam Gesneri nostri cuius magnum est nomen inter omnes eruditos, volui literis mandare et in publicum edere

This introduction gives us a different insight into Simler's view of biography. He is no longer dealing with a religious leader, so the criteria he adopted for Vermigli's or Bullinger's *Life* no longer apply. There is no question of portraying Gesner as the exemplar for the Christian commonweal, and no need to show his specific contribution to the church or his divinely ordained mission. In short, the transcendent element is absent.

According to Simler, to qualify for a *Life* a layman has to be renowned for something, and only those aspects of his life which are intrinsically worthy of being set down for posterity should be recorded. The finished work can of course act as a way of paying his respects to a deceased friend. However, its prime function is that of a subject of study for schoolboys; in other words, a textbook providing a living, moral example. Simler cites Terence's *Adelphi* 3.3.61/74, who considers such *Lives* a 'mirror for youth.'[5] Simler explains:

> Philosophers have written excellently on all sorts of moral duties and theologians have been even more precise on the subject. But what their writings contain in the form of subtle and obscure disputations is illustrated by the lives and deeds of famous men. Therefore, given that the life of Gesner was full of piety, humanity and all sorts of moral values, I do not doubt that its account would be welcome to very many people.[6]

Given its aim, it is not surprising that a large portion of the *Life* is given over to discussing the best way of acquiring knowledge on the basis of the example provided by Gesner. An even larger part is devoted to a summary of his works, which shows that the text could be used by schoolboys as an introduction to Natural Science.

In respect of acquisition of knowledge, Simler, although he never departs from his laudatory tone, uses Gesner as an example of how not to go about it as well as a model of how to acquire it. His biographer portrays Gesner (as might be expected) as preternaturally gifted from a very early age. However, contrary to what might be expected, Simler does not draw a picture of a 'golden boy'. He explains that, after some years in Strasbourg studying Hebrew with Capito, Gesner went to study in Paris. It was not, however, time well spent. He was too young, and did not receive sufficient advice on which course of study to adopt. Because he enjoyed reading and was intellectually gifted, he tried to read too many authors on all sorts of

---

quae de illius vita memoratu digna cognoscere potui.'

    5   Ibid., fol. 2v.: 'Rectissime illi faciunt qui vitas praeclarorum virorum tanquam speculum iuuentuti proponunt, vnde praeclara exempla ad imitandum depromere possint, quando vbique occurrit de quo dicere possis: hoc facito, hoc laudi est.'

    6   Ibid.: 'Praeclare quidem de omni genere officiorum scripserunt philosophi et multo de eisdem exactius praecipiunt theologi sed ea quae illi verbis subtiliter disputant obscuriora plerunque sunt, vita autem et factis summorum virorum illustrantur. Quare cum Gesneri nostri vita, pietate, humanitate et omni virtutum officiorumque genere plena fuerit, non dubito hanc qualemcunque eius descriptionem multis gratam et vtilem fore.'

subjects, in both Greek and Latin – poets, orators, historians, physicians, philologists –, no doubt because he thought in his youthful daring that he could assimilate them all at once. As it was, he made his mind less incisive by this undisciplined reading, and would have been much better off had he read a few selected authors from beginning to end.[7] His poverty provided another obstacle and, in Simler's view, it was only due to his intelligence and good character that he managed to acquire as much learning as those for whom all things turn out well from a very early age.[8] These reservations on young Gesner's student years do not, however, make Simler's *Life* a critical investigation. He hastens to add that it is yet another proof of Gesner's outstanding intellectual qualities that he acknowledged openly the errors of his youth himself, and wanted them to serve as an example to young boys of how to go about studying.[9]

Simler devotes much of the rest of the *Life* to detailing Gesner's intellectual accomplishments and providing a summary of his works. He devotes the very minimum of space to Gesner's life and career, using the biographical genre to sketch out a programme of study for schoolboys. What should a Protestant intellectual know, and in what sequence is he to acquire his knowledge? Simler distinguishes between study of words (languages) and study of things (medicine). The first is indispensable, he thinks, because as man is the only rational animal capable of speech, the complete and supreme mastery of this skill in all its nuances is especially important for any scholar and philosopher. Granting that there are too many languages for any one single person to master, a serious student should concentrate his attention on those in which are written *res cognitu necessariae*, these being naturally Hebrew, Greek and Latin. What we have here is a humanist Protestant curriculum conducive to both intellectual and moral improvement of the student. What makes a scholar a Protestant scholar in Simler's view is knowledge not only of Latin, Greek and Hebrew, but also of vernacular languages, in which Gesner excelled. Simler reminds his readers that, as well as taking an interest in his native German and publishing a work on German proper names and their origins, Gesner knew French and Italian.

Given Simler's conception of two interlinked branches of education, one focusing on words and the other on things, it follows that to him first-rate knowledge of words entails first-rate knowledge of things. Here

---

[7]   Ibid., fols 4v.–5r.

[8]   Ibid., fol. 5r.: 'Fuit hoc praeter inopiam aliud impedimentum solidae eruditionis, incerta studiorum fluctuatio et scopi ignorantia in quo tamen ingenii simul vis quaedam diuina et naturae bonitas apparet, quod ex tot impedimentis eluctatus solidam et praeclaram eruditionem adeptus est, nihilominus quam illi quibus omnia a pueris ex voto obuenere.'

[9]   Ibid.: 'Est hoc ingenui animi praeclarum exemplum quod ipsum non puduit iuueniles errores cum apud amicos tum etiam in publicis scriptis agnoscere et fateri ac suo exemplo adolescentes monere quomodo rectius studia sua instituere debeant.'

again, Gesner proves to be the case in point. Simler stresses that, although he was a medical doctor by profession, he practised all philosophical disciplines, especially Aristotle's *Physics*, which is the closest to medicine, and *Ethics*. He taught both for over twenty-four years and, although his lectures on Aristotle were not nearly as illustrious as those of other teachers in other academies, he showed that a man of high intelligence, who has a mastery of Greek, is capable of making great progress in philosophy if he reads and teaches it on a daily basis.[10]

One of the *Life*'s most striking features is its appreciation of natural science. What Simler achieves via his account of Gesner is an apology for as well as a pocket guide to the study of natural phenomena, not something a reader of ancient, or for that matter modern, biographies would expect to find in a *Life*.

It goes without saying that Simler never uses the term 'natural science', a concept unknown in those days. He does not even talk about *philosophia naturalis*, but gets directly to the particulars. He explains that Gesner most enjoyed studying metals, plants and animals because one could gain more certain knowledge of them than of meteors and similar phenomena very far removed from the realm of the senses. Furthermore, he thought the study of metals, plants and animals was useful not just to medicine and other arts, but that it actually helped the student live his life properly and as it should be lived.[11] Simler insists:

> A great and enquiring mind follows up not just things that are probable or likely, but investigates by a proven method the hidden truth in particulars and publishes its findings given that the common good should be served as much as possible.[12]

Without once using the concept of 'natural science' Simler has defined it as the discipline uncovering the true nature of natural phenomena such as plants, metals or animals. Furthermore, he has integrated it into the pious Protestant curriculum as not only a respectable subject, but as a highly ethical branch of knowledge. As he is also meant to provide a concise guide to Gesner's writings, Simler also gives a summary of the naturalist's main treatises. He devotes particular attention to the *Historia animalium*, considering it his hero's most important work and one that was most often attacked. Simler defends it against the accusations of being merely a compilation; displaying poor ordering; having a barbarous style; and showing a 'lack of elegance' in its illustrations.[13]

---

[10]   Ibid., fol. 8v.

[11]   Ibid.: 'Et praeterea videbat vel mediocrem saltem istarum rerum contemplationem non solum ad medicinam et alias artes sed ad vitam commode degendam vtilem admodum esse et propemodum necessariam.'

[12]   Ibid.: 'Est autem hoc magni et ingenui animi in studiis non tantum probabilia et verisimilia sectari sed in singulis quatenus fieri potest et res ipsa patitur firmis rationibus latentem et abditam rei veritatem inuestigare et ea quae inueneris in publicum proferre, quando nobis commune commodum vel maxime spectandum est.'

[13]   Ibid., fols 12v.–14r.

The moral quality of a man's life being, in Simler's view, the perfect mirror of the quality of his work, he insists on his hero's orthodoxy and his piety fostered by a careful reading of the Bible and the church fathers, which enabled him to adopt the orthodox position in religious disputes. Furthermore, notes his biographer,

> Although he was a medic by profession, he thought rightly that the correct knowledge of religion was part of his duty, as it is of all those who want to preserve the appellation of Christians. He determined that the main fruit of his studies was that they could be of use to the church, which is why he devoted much effort in the *History of animals* to translating Hebrew names and translated correctly nearly all the Scriptural passages which mention animals so that his profession could also contribute something to the study of Scripture.[14]

Indeed, Simler notes, Gesner knew enough theology to condemn Antitrinitarianism. He was also tolerant in that he had friends whose religious convictions differed from his own, but never made him change or waver.[15] He also insists on Gesner's modesty and refusal of anything that might be thought remotely obscene, which is why he produced an expurgated edition of Martial. He was the perfect friend, perfect husband and, as might be expected, died a 'good death' in the arms of his wife after an illness.[16]

Simler portrays Gesner as the perfect Christian scholar and physician. He singles out his modesty, piety, gift for friendship and learning. He also establishes close links between his scientific pursuits and his interest in serving the church. He uses him as a blueprint for how to study, and provides readers with a concise guide to his works. More importantly, he has no problem with reconciling Christianity and the investigation of natural phenomena. Simler thus produces what we might call a pedagogical biography suitable for use as a school manual as well as an exemplary *Life*.

Stucki's *Life* of Simler

Simler's *Life* by Johann Wilhelm Stucki,[17] author of the *encomium* on Bullinger's death, does not subscribe to Simler's model of pedagogical

---

[14]   Ibid., fol. 16r.: 'Quamuis enim medicus esset professione, existimabat et recte, cognitionem verae religionis nihilominus ad se pertinere, et ad omnes qui modo omnibus commune nomen Christiani hominis tueri velint. Statuebat etiam hunc esse praecipuum fructum studiorum suorum qui ex illis ad vsum ecclesiae redundaret ideoque in animalium historia multum laboris impendit Hebraeis nominibus interpretandis et fere omnia illa loca scripturarum in quibus animalium mentio fit accurate interpretatus est vt ex sua professione aliquid studiosis sacrarum litterarum commodi afferret.'

[15]   Ibid.

[16]   Ibid., fols 16v.–17r.

[17]   *Vita clarissimi viri D. Iosiae Simleri Tigurini S. Theologiae in Schola Tigurina professoris fidelissimi a Ioanne Gulielmo Stuckio Tigurino descripta. Doctorum item virorum*

biography. However, Stucki is just as concerned as Simler to justify his undertaking. As we could gather from his *encomium* of Bullinger, Stucki sees all biography as a source of inspiration for its readers, and Christian biography as a particularly important source of inspiration to Christian readers. His justification of his undertaking gives very strong hints of the controversial nature of the biographical genre despite its popularity in Reformation Zurich. He is explicit that very many people mock and despise the biographies of men famous for their virtue and glory out of envy, malevolence and ignorance. In order to show that he is doing nothing new or heterodox, Stucki cites antique models, insisting that the custom of writing up sayings, deeds and views of those who brought great benefit to mankind through their teaching and virtue is very ancient.[18] To illustrate his point, he cites both pagan and Christian biographies, starting with Xenophon's *Life of Socrates* (Simler's model for his *Life* of Bullinger) and Plutarch's *Lives*. He also notes that, among Christians, Jerome and Epiphanius went to some lengths to write down the *Lives* of exceptional individuals.[19] Stucki is making an oblique reference here to a volume published by Cratander in 1529, which contained Epiphanius' *Lives and deaths of the prophets* and Jerome's *De viris illustribus*, with the Greek translation of Sophronius. The real object of the editor and translator Albanos Torinus (Thorer), a medical doctor, was to assemble all the biblical *Lives* and make them available in a bilingual edition not so much to act as *exempla*, but to encourage young people to learn Greek. Naturally, Stucki does not advert to this.

He places Zurich biographies in the same category as Xenophon's *Life of Socrates*, Plutarch's *Lives* or Jerome's *De viris illustribus* so as to avoid the slightest hint of hagiography. This genealogy is forced, and its object is not to establish a real tradition, but to give the Zurich endeavours at least some

---

quaedam in eiusdem obitum Carmina (Tiguri excudebat Frosch., Anno 1577). Hereafter: Stucki, *Vita Simleri*. Cf. Vischer, *Bibliographie*, no. C 925.

[18]   Stucki, *Vita Simleri*, fol. 2r.: 'Primo itaque omnium satis superque constat non nouam aliquam sed antiquissimam hanc esse consuetudinem, eorum dicta, facta, consilia, literarum monumentis consecrare qui doctrinae, sapientiae, caeterarumque virtutum fama clari et illustres extiterunt quique magna in genus humanum commoda atque beneficia contulerunt.'

[19]   Ibid.: 'Id testantur vt ex innumeris pauca tantum exempla commemorem cum Xenophontis de Socrate Graecorum sapientissimo, tum Plutarchi de multis Graecis atque Romanis illustribus viris, praestantissimi commentarii. Inter Christianos autem S. Hieronymus et Epiphanius duo clarissima ecclesiae lumina plurimum operae studiique in illustrium quarundam vtriusque sexus personarum vitis describendis posuerunt.' Stucki is referring to *Epiphanii episcopi Cypri De prophetarum vita & interitu commentarius graecus, una cum interpretatione e regione Latina, Albano Torino interprete. Sophronii graece & Hieronymi latine libellus de vita Evangelistarum, cum scholijs Eras. Rot. Parabolae & miracula, quae a singulis Evangelistis narrantur, graecis versibus a Gregorio Nazianzeno conscripta, addita interpretatione latina. D. Hieronymi Scriptorum ecclesiasticorum vitae, per Sophronium e Latina lingua in graecam translatae, & scholijs per Eras. Rot. illustratae. Gennadii illustrium virorum catalogus, ob historiae cognitionem lectu non indignus* (Basileae, Andreas Cratander, 1529).

respectability. In fact, none of the Zurich *Lives* bears any resemblance to Xenophon, Plutarch or, for that matter, Jerome. Although, as we have seen, Xenophon was cited as a role model by Simler himself in his biography of Bullinger, his anecdotal *Life* of Socrates was as far removed from the civic and religious Zurich model as were Plutarch's *Lives* with their psychological orientation. The same goes for Jerome's *De viris illustribus*, the aim of which was to provide a repertory of Christian authors and their writings. Stucki exaggerates slightly when he says that in his time it is the custom of every academy 'of good moral standing' to publish laudatory *Lives* of those who were its ornament in their lifetime. He considers this custom very praiseworthy, as there is no denying that it is just and good to publish the biographies of those who devoted all their lives to the glory of God and salvation of men. Since this honour is granted to those who did not have true religion and who therefore had only the shadow of virtues, it is all the more apt to reward thus those who were really virtuous and who performed great deeds for the whole of humankind and particularly for the Christian republic.[20] Thus far, Stucki echoes, sentiment for sentiment, Simler's own preamble to his *Life* of Bullinger.

Where he goes further than Simler is the extent to which he identifies civic virtues and Protestantism. A good state to him is a Protestant state with its own illustrious individuals who give it an identity, rather like Plutarch's heroes or Suetonius' Caesars who conferred an identity on the Roman Empire. He notes that:

> The more a city or a district abounds in pious and learned men, the more deserving it is of high praise. Not buildings or fortifications resplendent with gold, silver and marble, but men remarkable for their piety and religious opinion should be thought to be the real ornaments and props of all republics and kingdoms.[21]

This is a far cry from the self-abnegating, miracle-performing saint or the suffering martyr. It is an equally far cry from Luther the eschatological

---

[20] Stucki, *Vita Simleri*, fol. 2r.–v.: 'Quae sane consuetudo vt olim, ita hodie quoque valde, vti dictum est, trita et vsitata, multis sane nominibus siue honestatis siue vtilitatis ratio ducatur, videtur esse laudanda. Nam primo omnium cuinam quaeso non aequum iustumque esse videatur, illorum orationibus scriptisque publicis honorificam mentionem fieri qui ad Dei gloriam hominumque /2v./ salutem, ad quam nati, seu potius a Deo ipso nobis donati fuerunt, omnia sua studia atque consilia contulerunt ? Etsi hic olim honos iis tributus est, qui verae religionis expertes, non tam veris virtutibus quam virtutum imaginibus quibusdam siue vmbris praediti fuerunt, quanto iustius idem honos iis impertiri debet qui vera religione veris solidisque virtutibus ornati, cum vniuersum genus humanum, tum vero atque in primis Christianorum rempublicam plurimis commodis ornamentisque cumularunt?'

[21] Ibid., fol. 2v.: 'Nam quo vrbs regioue aliqua piis doctisque viris est abundantior, tanto maior et illustrior illius laus merito censeri debet. Non enim aedificia vel munita, vel auro, argento, marmore refulgentia sed viri pietate doctrinaque praestantes vera rerumpublicarum atque regnorum ornamenta simul atque firmamenta existimari debent.'

divine instrument or the edifying model, as set up by Calvin's biographers. Stucki applies the pagan model to Christian biography much more blatantly than Simler ever did. He considers Simler and similar illustrious departed to be the heroes of the fatherland and objects of veneration similar to, but infinitely better than, images. He encourages the cult of the individual, but his individuals blend with the community and take their life from it while defining it in their turn. This is what Stucki says:

> Therefore by praising them, we also praise their fatherland which nurtured them, just as by praising children, we praise their parents and others who brought them up. Need I also add that these accounts of their lives reflect the glory of God to which all our merits are ultimately due. For all men, but especially those endowed with special gifts and virtues by the Holy Spirit, are clear and bright images of God, and we should study and contemplate them with great diligence.[22]

At times, he seems to forget that he is writing a Christian biography, as when he affirms:

> The *Lives* of famous men should be studied with great care if only because they are so effective in encouraging young people to be virtuous and in discouraging them from vice. For as Sallust attests, once upon a time people attributed great power to statues and bodily images because they encouraged virtue. Therefore we must believe that verbal effigies of souls and virtues, which are much more accurate and more reliable, have an even greater power to do so.[23]

While removing any suspicion of image-worship, he does place Zurich Protestant heroes on the same level as either pagan gods or saints. Indeed, he more than suggests that human beings can be given special honour. In a word, in Stucki's view, biographies of eminent Zurich Protestants contain all the characteristics of antique *Lives*. The only difference is that, being Christian, they are better and contain more moral truth than the efforts of Xenophon or Suetonius. As we have said already, one startling characteristic of his approach and of the Zurich School generally, when compared with the *Lives* of Luther or with the Genevan *Lives* of Calvin and Beza, is the absence of emphasis on the role of providence. Simler,

---

[22]   Ibid.: 'Laudari itaque illi non possunt quin patria simul illorum parens atque nutrix laudetur, sicuti laudes liberorum plaerunque in illorum parentes et alumnos videmus redundare. Quid dicam quod ad ipsius quoque Dei Optimi Maximi gloriam, quo nostra omnia merito sunt referenda, illae ipsae descriptiones pertinent? Nam cum omnes quidem homines tum vero atque in primis illi qui eximiis sancti Spiritus muneribus et virtutibus sunt ornati clarae quaedam et illustres ipsius Dei sunt imagines ac proinde diligenter nobis cognoscendae ac contemplandae.'

[23]   Ibid., fols 2v.–3r.: 'Praeterea vel hoc quoque nomine clarorum virorum descriptiones minime sunt negligendae quod ad posteritatem partim ad virtutes incitandum, partim a vitiis deterrendum, maximam vim obtinent. Nam vt Salustius testatur, corporum imaginibus atque simulachris magna olim tributa est vis, homines ad virtutem inflammandi, multo certe magis atque ve /3r./ rius huiusmodi ipsorum animorum atque virtutum effigies literis expressas, eam vim vel maximam habere credendum est.'

Stucki and Lavater prefer to stress that their subjects, because of their contribution to the commonweal, are special members of a special group deserving of special honour.

Stucki's *Life* of Simler is less of a manual than Simler's *Life* of Gesner. Nonetheless, it is still highly didactic. He states openly that one of his aims is to encourage people to read Simler's works,[24] and divides his literary production into three categories: theological, mathematical and historical. Simler, according to him, excelled in all three fields. In theology, he singles out his defence of orthodox teaching on the Trinity and Christology, and especially his treatise on the Holy Spirit against the Antirinitarians, 'which greatly pleased Theodore Beza, that very learned and intelligent theologian of our time, and also many other learned men.'[25] Simler's mathematical works provide his biographer with an opportunity to discourse on the usefulness of mathematics to the theologian. His excursus throws an interesting light on the status of mathematics in Christian learning and education in sixteenth-century Zurich. Replying to those who think that mathematics is 'quite foreign to theology',[26] Stucki appeals to Augustine to show its relevance for biblical exegesis, and to Plato and Aristotle to prove its importance for theology generally:

> For first of all many obscure passages of the Holy Scripture cannot be understood correctly without the art of numbering and measuring correctly. As Augustine says in *De doctrina christiana* 2, Chapters 16 and 38: 'ignorance of numbers means you cannot understand many passages in the Scripture which are figurative or mystical.' This also holds good for geometry, without which we cannot understand scriptural passages to do with architecture. And besides, who can doubt that a theologian needs to know something about physics, ethics, economics and politics ... And as Pythagoras, Plato ..., Aristotle and experience itself attest, the principles of mathematics are necessary if we are to understand all of these disciplines ... And finally, mathematics is vital for understanding all arts, for lifting up man's mind from things perceived by the senses to seeing the truth, to understanding more easily the number, the measure and the weight of not only human but also divine works whereby the omnipotent architect of heaven and earth created all things out of nothing and governs them to this day with great constancy. And who dare doubt that this is of relevance to theologians?[27]

---

[24]   Ibid., fol. 3v.: 'Adde quod cum illius scripta forsan nec omnia, nec ab omnibus adhuc sint lecta, hac ratione plures forsan ad illa legendum incitabuntur, qui ea ante vel ignorarunt vel non tanti quanti par erat fecerunt.'
[25]   Ibid., fol. 7v.: 'Hi libri mirifice Theodoro Bezae doctissimo acutissimoque nostri saeculi theologo aliisque compluribus doctis viris placuerunt et quidem merito ...'.
[26]   Ibid., fol. 9r.: 'Sunt enim nonnulli qui illa a theologo alienissima esse iudicant cum potius magna illorum cum theologia sit affinitas atque cognatio neque parua theologo ad munus suum melius obeundum adiumenta afferant.'
[27]   Ibid., fol. 9r.–v.

Simler's *Life* thus provides his biographer with an opportunity to issue a programmatic statement on the importance of mathematics in theology, which was obviously challenged at the time. Similarly, we have seen that Simler's own *Life* of Gesner enabled him to defend the natural sciences, albeit somewhat less insistently. Among contemporary authorities in favour of mathematics, Stucki mentions Philip Melanchthon, Simon Grynaeus and Peter Ramus. Stucki's and Simler's view of mathematics and natural sciences is directly opposed to the view of another theologian of the same period, Lambert Daneau, who refused to link the science of numbers with the knowledge of things divine considering that our knowledge of Christ via the Scriptures provided us with all the Christian mathematics we required.[28] As mathematics involved astrological predictions, the debate that Stucki merely alludes to suggests a basic difference of opinion on the usefulness of numbers to theology between Zurich and Geneva.

Stucki also singles out Simler's knowledge of history. The issue of usefulness of history to theologians was not controversial at the time, and required no lengthy justification. He therefore rests content with listing Simler's historical works (making sure to include his *Lives* of Gesner, Vermigli and Bullinger) and pointing out that, to a theologian, nothing is as useful as history for refuting errors.[29] The rest of Stucki's biography of Simler follows the standard pattern: private life, appearance, morals and character, and finally death.

While its strictly biographical part contains nothing of startling originality, Stucki's *Life* of Simler provides the theoretical backing for interlinking civic and religious virtues in a biography, and illustrates the pertinence of this type of biography to education, especially scientific education. At the same time, as we have seen, it creates a vast ambiguity. Just from reading Stucki's preface, it is difficult to see where profane biography ends and Protestant biography begins.

Stucki's *Life* of Johann Wolf (c. 1521–71)

Stucki included Wolf in his *encomium* on Bullinger, as we have noted, but he also devoted a separate *Life* to him.[30] Johann Wolf was first of all chaplain

28   See Irena Backus, 'Le Tertullien de Lambert Daneau dans le contexte religieux du 16ᵉ siècle', in Maria Rosa Cortesi (ed.), *Atti del convegno 'I Padri sotto il torchio', le edizioni dell'antichità cristiana nei secoli 15–16* (Florence: SISMEL, 2002), pp. 33–52.

29   Stucki, *Vita Simleri*, fols 9v.–10r.: 'Theologus certe vt hoc breue dicam, sine historiarum cognitione, minus commode munus suum tueri potest. Nulla enim /10r./ ratione facilius atque commodius quosuis errores atque superstitiones quam hac ipsa (vt eam Cicero scite admodum appellat) teste temporum, luce veritatis, vita memoriae, magistra vitae, nuncia vetustatis refelli ac refutari posse satis superque constat.'

30   See pp. 80–81 above.

to the Zurich Hospital. In 1551, he became preacher in the Fraumünster, and from 1565 onwards professor of theology at the Zurich Academy. He had the reputation of someone well-versed in several disciplines, and was the author of Old Testament commentaries on I Ezra and also on Deuteronomy, as well as other theological treatises. Most of his works were published posthumously. Despite his relatively short life and fairly modest literary production, like most other Zurich intellectuals of the latter half of the sixteenth century, he was found worthy of a biography. Stucki appended his *De vita et obitu [Johannis Wolfii] narratio* to the second edition of the latter's commentary on Ezra in the form of a preface.[31]

This determines his reading public, which would have comprised for the most part preachers, teachers and some students of theology. Now Wolf himself had a short and relatively unspectacular life. However, putting his *Life* in the form of a preface to one of his biblical commentaries provides Stucki with an ideal opportunity to produce an emblematic and highly moralistic biography which required no methodological justification; a very different undertaking from Stucki's *encomium* on Bullinger or his educational biography of Simler. He depicts not just Wolf, but his entire family as the absolute model of godly individuals; in other words, as saints. What distinguishes them from Roman Catholic saints? Naturally, they are not an object of prayer and are quite incapable of performing miracles, while being heavily dependent on divine providence. More importantly, however, it is the inclusion of the entire family as well as the depiction of Wolf's career against the background of certain key events of the Reformation that gives Stucki's *Life* of Wolf its distinctly Protestant slant.

He places under the *aegis* of divine providence Wolf's birth in 1521, which also happened to be the year of the holding of the Diet of Worms. In fact, referring obliquely to the Book of Revelation, he notes that 'some men of great intelligence and judgement ... saw that very year as putting an end to the period of 1260 years ... prophesied by the Apocalypse of John 11 ... of the church being tormented by cruel nations and by the Antichrist ...'.[32] Stucki certainly does not see Wolf as living in the time of the final

---

[31]   Johannes Wolf, *In Esdrae librum primum de reditu populi Iudaei e captiuitate Babylonica in patriam et templi ... Item de vita et obitu eius narratio scripta a clarissimo viro D. Io. Gulielmio Stuckio sacrae theologiae professore* (Tiguri, Frosch., 1584), fols aa4v.–bb4r. Cf. Vischer, *Bibliographie*, no. C 1038. The first edition of the commentary was published in 1570, when Wolf was still alive.

[32]   Wolf, *In Esdram*, fol. b2r.: 'Fuit annus hic insignis celeberrimis illis comitiis Imperii Vormatiae a Carolo V. imperatore habitus in quibus Lutherus piae memoriae coram imperii Romani proceribus frementibus ac dira quaeuis illi minitantibus suis hostibus, doctrinae suae rationem magno excelsoque animo non sine magno certe vitae periculo reddidit. Vnde viri quidam magni ingenii atque iudicii hoc ipso anno menses illos 42, hoc est annos 1260 quibus secundum illud antiquum Ioannis vaticinium quod extat 11. Cap. Apocalypsi sancta Dei ciuitas, hoc est Ecclesia, immanissimarum gentium et Antichristi tyrannide sit diuexanda, finitos fuisse volunt ...'. Stucki's interpretation of history is also that of the *Centuries of*

unleashing of Satan. That he lived when he did is due solely to God's providential counsel, which wanted Wolf to be born 'when languages, liberal arts, true faith and true religion were beginning to re-emerge from the darkness in which they had long been buried.'[33]

In his biographer's view, however, it was not just the year of Wolf's birth that was providential. His entire family was marked out by God. Accordingly, Stucki devotes almost as much space to his parents as he does to his hero. He dwells particularly on the details of Wolf's father Heinrich, learned in Hebrew, Greek and Latin – a rarity in those barbaric (pre-Reformation) times –, who was taken prisoner at the Battle of Marignano during a journey to Rome. Because he was an expert lute- and lyre-player (both of which were very effective in softening aggression), he won his captors' sympathy and was soon released. Three years after his release in 1519, he went on a pilgrimage to Santiago de Compostella in the company of Jakob Aescher, Ulrich Sturm and Diethelm Reyst (who was later to become the president of Zurich Council). They established very close links during the pilgrimage, and vowed to be godparents to one another's children when married. Stucki also puts down to divine providence the fact that Diethelm Reyst's daughter married Johann Wolf's brother, Caspar, and that Johann himself officiated at the marriage.[34] Heinrich returned home from the pilgrimage in the providential year of 1519, when Charles V became emperor and when Zwingli began to preach the Reformation in Zurich. He married and embarked on a public career, but fell at the Battle of Kappel.[35] Heinrich Wolf's life and career is above all marked out in Stucki's view by his exceptional learning and culture, and by his presence at all the crucial events of Swiss history: the Battle of Marignano, the beginning of Zwingli's Reformation and the Battle of Kappel. Although he was never an active proponent of the Reformation, Wolf's father instantiates the Zurich burgher who does the right thing. We might go so far as to say that he represents the humanist-educated, patriotic middle classes who laid the foundations for Zwingli's movement.

Unlike most sixteenth-century biographers, Stucki devotes a considerable amount of space to Wolf's mother. However, she is no more than a symbol

---

Magdeburg, the authors of which saw Luther's Reformation as a return to the apostolic era after thirteen centuries of heresy. As regards the specific issue of John's prophecies referring to Luther and his Reformation, see Backus, *Reformation Readings of the Apocalypse*, pp. 129–33.

[33]   Wolf, *In Esdram*, fol. b2r.–b2v.: 'Quicquid sit, hoc ipso certe foelici et aureo saeculo Deus Ioan. Wolphium pro singula sua prouidentia nasci et in hanc lucem aedi voluit, quo et linguae artesque liberales et vera fides atque religio e tenebris quibus diu sepulta iacuerat, rursus ex /b2v./ citata in lucem emergere coepit, ad quod ipsum tam salutare et admirabile suum opus, illius quoque optima fidelissimaque opera vti voluit.'

[34]   Ibid., fols b2v.–b3r.

[35]   Ibid., fol. b3r.–v.

under his pen, providing him with an occasion to moralise on the duties of a mother if left a widow with young children to bring up. We have seen that sixteenth-century men earned more praise from their biographers if they did not remarry after their wives' death. Simler went to some lengths to justify Vermigli's remarriage by the need for children in the commonweal. Remaining a widow was even more important for women, if Stucki's account of the elder Mrs Wolf is anything to go by. He stresses that after losing her husband in service to the fatherland, she remained a widow for thirty-seven years despite the solicitations of various suitors. She devoted all her energies to the practice of piety, to managing and augmenting the modest inheritance left by her husband, and particularly to bringing up her children. Still, according to Stucki, God rewarded her for her labours: all the daughters made good marriages; Johann the eldest son became a faithful servant of the church and the academy; Heinrich his junior by six years followed in his father's footsteps; while the youngest son Caspar became a Greek scholar and a physician responsible among other things for the publication of Conrad Gesner's works. Mrs Wolf under Stucki's pen is even more of any empty symbol than her husband. She has no life other than her exemplary function of a widow with children. Stucki confirms his lack of interest in the person when he affirms that all her efforts were all the more admirable in that day and age when maternal indulgence weakens the children's moral fibre. He harks back nostalgically to the models of Roman matronhood, such as Cornelia, mother of the Gracchi, or Aurelia, the mother of Julius Caesar.[36] Two features of his account of Mrs Wolf are worth singling out. Firstly, she has no individual existence. Secondly, as a symbol, she is based not on any Christian figures, but on paradigmatic Roman matrons.

Symbolic too is the main protagonist, Johann Wolf, whose way of going about his education Stucki takes as the prime example of 'how it should be done'. After basic schooling in Zurich and at Kappel, Wolf travelled to other places of learning: Tübingen, Marburg and Leipzig. There, Stucki emphasises, he listened very carefully to all his teachers, and took extensive notes which he subsequently kept in his library so that they formed a part of his literary heritage. Stucki seizes this opportunity to advise young men travelling abroad for their education to take down in writing anything they learn which is of interest. This will enable them to go over their notes with profit and enjoyment when they get older. Only too many, he laments, neglect to do this either because of idleness or placing excessive trust in their memory.[37] Other features of Wolf's study period abroad are found to be equally exemplary. Stucki stresses that despite his fairly short absence – barely two years –, he encompassed all the liberal arts, and many other

---

[36] Ibid., fol. b4r.–v.
[37] Ibid., fols b4v.–bb1r.

useful subjects which others do not master during a much longer stay. He insists that this was due only partly to the workings of divine providence: first and foremost, Wolf had his own intelligence and capacity for hard work to thank.

What emerges very clearly thus far is that the Wolf family provides an example to all the middle-class Protestants in Zurich, not just because God has decreed that this should be so, but also because of their intrinsic qualities. However, the biographer does not really concern himself with any member of the family as an individual. Their virtues are depicted as paradigmatic, fulfilling a purely didactic role. They show their readers how to behave correctly in a civic manner: how to love the fatherland, how to bring up children, and how to get maximum profit from a period of study abroad.

In contrast with his mother and father, Wolf does actually receive an account of the main events of his life, albeit in a very schematic way. Stucki describes his marriage to Regula Hegner (worthy daughter of a worthy father, exemplary housekeeper, and bearer and upbringer of beautiful children, as well as a lifelong companion) and his sons' careers as equally worthy of imitation.[38]

The same goes for the way Wolf fulfilled his public functions, particularly that of tutor to young men, many of whom were of noble descent. According to Stucki, he treated them as if they were his own sons. In addition to having them repeat what they learnt in class, he taught them the *Progymnasmata* of Aphthonius and other precepts of rhetoric and dialectic. Aware that theory is worthless without practice, he had them apply the precepts to specific exercises. He also had them do physical training to keep their bodies and their minds healthy – all this, according to Stucki, in contrast with most tutors, who hardly devote any care to their charges.[39]

Stucki's *Life* of Wolf provides a new insight into uses of religious biography in Zurich in the latter half of the sixteenth century. As well as serving as funeral *encomia*, heroic accounts of founders of the Reformation in their context, and educational textbooks defending the study of science and mathematics or manuals for tutors, biographies could be made to act as a vehicle for transmitting middle-class family values. Using his account of Wolf to do just that, it is not surprising that Stucki leaves until the very end a brief description of Wolf's appearance, health, last illness and death.

He places the paragraph on Wolf's death in a providential framework: just as his death was a sign of God's anger, so his birth had been a sign of the Almighty's clemency and favour. Correspondingly, just as the year of his birth was the best of years because of the Diet of Worms, so the year 1572 was the year in which several catastrophes presaging the end

---

[38]   Ibid., fols bb1v.–bb2r.
[39]   Ibid., fol. bb2v.

of history occurred. It was also the year, Stucki notes, in which a new star appeared, sent by God to announce the imminent coming of Christ and to console His faithful:

> The whole year 1572, in which God sorely tried our fatherland by the death of such a great man, was also sadly marked by other terrifying signs of God's anger and fury, which preceded Wolf's demise. Among these was the death of the Queen of Navarre, who had always shown herself to be a steadfast protector of the true church and true religion. There was also the assassination of Admiral Coligny and very many others in France, the most gruesome event in living memory. And there was the terrible fire of the Grossmünster struck by lightning, an account of which Wolf sent to his son Heinrich in Leipzig. And finally there was the new bright star which God, despite everything, seems to have lit up to announce the imminent coming of Christ our Saviour, and thus to console His church which was so sorely afflicted at the time.[40]

Similarly, Stucki notes that many dire events occurred subsequently to Wolf's death: the Siege of La Rochelle, the burning-down of the *curia rhetorum* and the death of Heinrich Bullinger, to mention just a few.[41] What is significant here is that Stucki evidently feels that a morally emblematic life such as Wolf's has to be situated in a prophetic context if it is to assume its full religious significance and its full Protestant identity. Wolf is neither a martyr nor a saint, nor a cipher. He belongs to the category of remarkable individuals issued from model, middle-class families, whom God raises at a particular time in history to help 'fight the good fight'.

Stucki's *Life* of Ludwig Lavater

Ludwig Lavater (1527–86), biographer and son-in-law of Bullinger, and author of a very popular treatise on the supernatural,[42] was the son of Hans

---

[40]   Ibid., fol. bb4r.: 'Fuit, vt hoc quoque postremo loco addam, totus hic annus 72 quo Deus patriam nostram tanti viri morte grauissime afflixit, multis etiam aliis horrendis irae atque furoris diuini signis valde funestus, quae eius mortem praecesserunt. Huiusmodi fuit luctuosus et inopinatus ille reginae Nauarrenae quae fidissima verae ecclesiae religionisque semper patrona extiterat, interitus; illa post hominum memoriam funestissima Amiralli et innumerabilium aliorum per totam Galliam trucidatio; terribilis apud nos turris summi templi de coelo facta conflagratio, cuius historiam diligenter conscriptam Io. Vuolphius ad Henrichum filium suum Lipsiam miserat; noua denique splendidaque illa stella quam tamen Deus ad Christi Seruatoris nostri vicinum aduentum significandum ac proinde ecclesiam suam tum temporis valde afflictam consolandum videtur accendisse.'

[41]   Ibid.: 'Vt autem mortem eius praecesserunt, ita eandem consecuta sunt plurima et publica et priuata mala, cuiusmodi fuit obsidio Rupellanae grauissima totius ecclesiae Gallicae afflictio, curiae rhetorum funesta conflagratio, Henrichi Bullingeri patris nostrae patriae fidelissimi obitus et alia quae enumerare omnia nimis longum foret.'

[42]   *Von Gespänsten / unghüren / fälen / u. anderen wunderbaren dingen / so merteils wenn die menschen sterben söllend /oder wenn sunst gross sachen unnd enderungen vorhanden sind / beschähend / kuirtzer und einfaltiger bericht* (Zürich, Froschouer, 1569).

Rudolf Lavater, the *landvogt* of Kyburg. After studies in Kappel, Zurich, Strasbourg, Paris and Lausanne, he travelled in Italy. He became ordained in 1549, and was made the first archdeacon of the Grossmünster. In 1585, he became the head pastor of the Zurich Church. His sole venture into biblical exegesis was his commentary on Nehemiah, which Stucki decided to publish posthumously, just as he did with Wolf's commentary on Ezra. Here too, he appended the author's life instead of a preface,[43] but did not make quite the same points. He did not want to use Lavater to provide an exemplum of how to study, how to bring up a family and how to teach young boys. What he insisted on instead were his communication skills as a preacher. The other distinguishing feature of his account is his insistence on showing that the entire Lavater family was exceptional, a feature which also characterised his account of Wolf. Ludwig Lavater, however, unlike Wolf, was in a slightly uncomfortable position as object of a biography, having a father more famous than himself. Stucki got over this by stating bluntly that the more praiseworthy the father, the greater the glory that devolved to the son. However, his real reason for devoting literary effort to the two Lavaters, father and son, was personal. Stucki admits openly that Ludwig surrounded him (Stucki) with a more than paternal love right from his (Stucki's) boyhood until the day of his own death. Moreover, he frequently counselled Stucki, and entrusted him with his commentary on Nehemiah, his last work.[44] Hans Rudolf, as it turns out, also had close personal links with our biographer and his family:

> But why, asks Stucki, talk so much about the father? If we consider his virtues, not enough has been said. Moreover, he was the biological father of our Ludwig and the spiritual father of our entire fatherland, and we should add a father in holy baptism for the sake of which he took on my father and then me in 1542 and became the father in Christ of my father and myself; these are all reasons why I think I should always nourish and sing his praises. And finally the more praiseworthy the father, the greater the praise and the glory that is due to the son, who sedulously imitated his father's virtue.[45]

---

[43]   Ludwig Lavater, *Nehemias. Liber Nehemiae qui et secundus Ezrae dicitur* (Zürich, Froschouer, 1586). Cf. Vischer, *Bibliographie*, no. C 1089.

[44]   Lavater, *In Nehemiam*, fol. α2v.: 'Ac quoniam ille vt nostis omnes, me a pueritia mea ad vitae vsque suae finem singulari ac plus quam paterno amore est complexus, multis magnisque beneficiis ornauit, studiorumque atque commodorum meorum omnium non modo fautor sed etiam adiutor fidelis exstitit, consilia familiarissime plurima et arcana sua mihi communicauit, denique extremum hunc ingenii sui foetum praelo tam commissum ante suum obitum fidei meae commendauit, me quoque prae aliis omnibus virtutum eius atque laudum, etsi nequaquam illis parem at gratum, tamen ac memorem praeconem esse debere confiteor.'

[45]   Ibid., fols α4v.–β1r.: 'Sed, cur, inquies, haec de patre tam multa? Imo si virtutes illius spectes, nimis pauca; deinde cum ille natura quidem nostri Ludouici, amore vero atque beneficiis totius nostrae patriae, denique baptismi sacrosancti nomine, ex quo et ille me anno 42 et patrem quoque /β1r./ meum suscepit et meus et patris mei in Christo pater extiterit, me quoque virtutes illius et laudes merito grata mente atque voce recolere semper atque

Just as his *Life* of Wolf and just as Simler's and Lavater's *Lives* of Bullinger, so Stucki's *Life* of Lavater and his father is full of prophetic events, starting with the date of Ludwig's birth, 1 March 1527, the year of the sack of Rome and the year preceding that of the Berne Disputation, 'which put an end to idolatry and superstition in the entire region of Berne.'[46] Stucki finds equally significant Ludwig's birthplace, the fortress of Kyburg, a symbol of Helvetic glory which was restored by Ludwig's father, who was its governor for eleven years.[47] He also comments at length on Lavater Senior's legation to Rome in 1524 to retrieve the Swiss mercenaries' wages from Pope Clement VII. Stucki commends Hans Rudolf's refusal to kneel in front of the pope and kiss his hand, and disregards the total failure of the embassy.[48] Above all, however, Stucki seeks to exculpate Lavater for the defeat at Kappel. True, he admits that Hans Rudolf became the object of calumnies after the defeat, but this is the fate of all good military commanders. He adds that Lavater's name was cleared subsequently.[49] Stucki's account of Lavater Senior does not stop there. It also includes an anecdote about the commander saving the life of a common soldier at Marignano, only to have his own life saved by the same soldier eight years after, and goes through all of his public functions stressing that, although ignorant of Letters himself, he took particular pleasure in the discourse of learned men, as witnessed by his friendship with Vadian.[50]

Stucki has naturally less to say about Ludwig's mother, Anna Reuchlin, stressing that she came from an illustrious family and was chaste. He adds that her father was a supporter of the Reformation 'avant la lettre'.[51] Whereas, as we have seen, it was all to Mrs Wolf's credit that she did not remarry after her husband's death, it is all to Lavater Senior's credit that he *did* remarry after Anna's demise, just as it is to the younger Lavater's credit that he honoured and respected his father's second wife, Vasula Stapfer, 'not as one would a stepmother, but as a mother.'[52]

There is very little substantial difference thus far between Wolf and Lavater. Stucki inserts both in the wider context of the Zurich Reformation, and gives them and their families emblematic value: they provide two models of good Protestant households. The two distinctive features that mark out his *Life* of Lavater from his *Life* of Wolf are on the one hand the

---

praedicare debere existimo. Adde quod quo laudatior fuit pater, tanto maior quoque filii, qui paternam virtutem sedulo imitatus est, laus atque gloria censeri debet.'

[46]   Ibid., fol. α3r.
[47]   Ibid.
[48]   Ibid., fols α3v.–α4r.
[49]   Ibid., fol. α4r.
[50]   Ibid., fol. α4v. On Lavater's role at the Battle of Kappel, see Olivier Bangerter, *La pensée militaire de Zwingli* (Berne: Peter Lang, 2003).
[51]   Lavater, *In Nehemiam*, fol. β1r.
[52]   Ibid.

personal element (Stucki knew the Lavaters better than the Wolfs), and on the other the Lavaters' more prominent social position.

When it comes to the main protagonist, Ludwig, he was rather better known than Wolf outside the city limits of Zurich, not least because of his marriage to Bullinger's daughter. Because of this and the close links between them, Stucki presents his *Life* rather more like a personal homage, and less a prefabricated exemplum. Accordingly, he gives a fairly detailed portrayal of Lavater. He dwells particularly on his tireless desire to serve the church the moment he returned from his travels abroad. He started preaching when very young, and became preacher at Grossmünster, where he was to remain for thirty-six years. He was a constant source of solace and support, not just to his wife, but also to his father-in-law in the latter's declining years.[53] However, it is not so much his personal qualities as his sermons that are presented as exemplary. In other words, Stucki's biography acts as a preaching manual:

> His sermons were prepared without adornment or colouring, not for show but for edification, for the use of the flock. They were adapted for both the learned and the simple ears, and full of doctrine and consolation. He stuck remarkably well to the maxim, 'whatever you teach, be concise', and eagerly respected both brevity and clarity (which is a great art indeed), for he would say that especially in the winter cold any speech or sermon by any man, however eloquent, was more of a burden than of use to the public. I should add that his ordering of material and method was so excellent that any man who was not altogether slow or stupid could encompass and retain his entire sermon in his mind and memory.[54]

For this reason, Stucki adds, he won the admiration of no lesser an Old Testament scholar than Konrad Pellikan, who attended his sermons frequently and even asked Lavater to make him copies; this accounts for the large number of Lavater's sermons available in manuscript. In all, whereas the Wolfs provided first and foremost an example of middle-class Protestant morals and education of children, the Lavater family provides first and foremost an example of middle-class Protestant piety and communication.

---

53   Ibid., fols β4v.–γ1r.

54   Ibid., fol. γ1v.: 'Fuerunt autem conciones illius sine fuco et pigmentis non ad ostentationem sed ad aedificationem, hoc est vtilitatem auditorum comparatae, cum doctorum, tum idiotarum sensui et intelligentiae accommodatae, denique doctrinae consolationisque plenissimae. Praeceptum illud: 'quicquid praecipis, esto breuis', egregie obseruauit ac breuitati simul et perspicuitati (quod magnae artis est) studuit, hyemali praesertim tempore atque frigore, cuiusuis vel facundissimi hominis orationem si horae spacium excessisset, maior iam auditoribus taedio quam vsui esse. Ordinem atque methodum (vt hoc quoque addam) tam egregiam adhibebat vt vel integra eius concio a quouis non hebetis omnino et obtusi ingenii homine facile mente memoriaque comprehendi ac retineri potuerit.'

Stucki was able to use Lavater as an example of a Christian communicator all the more easily as he was well known outside of Zurich and had received a number of accolades from Genevan and foreign theologians. Some of his treatises, notes Stucki, won the approval of Theodore Beza, 'the greatest of all theologians', who thought that his commentaries had the defining characteristic of what constitutes a good commentary: total absence of digressions and ambiguities.[55] Moreover, Stucki adds, he always acknowledged any help he received, unlike other commentators who copy their colleagues shamelessly. Stucki also cites Lawrence Humfrey's view of Lavater in his *Life* of John Jewel:[56] it shows, as Stucki puts it, how much the eminent and pious bishop of Salisbury respected Lavater's work. The latter apparently sent Jewel two works of his for an opinion: his Commentary on the Proverbs of Solomon, and his treatise against the Lutherans, entitled *De controuersia sacramentaria*. Jewel is reported by Humfrey (as reported by Stucki) to have said that it was only on reading Lavater's commentary that he understood some of Solomon's Proverbs for the first time. He also reports Jewel's rather more nuanced response to *De re sacramentaria*: Jewel apparently declined to express an opinion, claiming lack of first-hand knowledge of the events referred to. However, he thought that the book's candour and modesty would contribute to calming the malice of Brenz and other adversaries.[57]

The last part of Stucki's account concentrates on Lavater's pastoral activities, which it depicts as just as model in their own way as his capacity to communicate. He describes Lavater as morally perfect in every way,

---

[55]   Ibid., fol. γ3v.: 'Vt autem conciones uiua voce prolatae, ita hae quoque illius scriptiones breues, perspicuae, piae et eruditae doctissimis quibusque viris maxime probantur inter quos Theodorus Beza theologus ille … talem quodam in loco de iis sententiam tulit: "id, inquit, adhibuit in scribendo iudicium vt neque sit alienum consectatus neque lectorem incertum et suspensum reddat quas duas vel principes boni interpretis virtutes arbitror." Haec ille.'

[56]   *Ioannis Iuelli Angli episcopi Sarisburensis vita et mors, eiusque verae doctrinae defensio cum refutatione quorundam obiectorum, Thomae Hardingi, Nicolae Sanderi, Alani Copi, Hieronymi Osorii Lusitani, Pintaei Burdegalensis, Laurentio Humfredo, S. theologiae apud Oxonienses professore Regio* (Londini apud Johannem Dayum, 1573).

[57]   Lavater, *In Nehemiam*, fols γ3v.–γ4r.: 'Iuelli quoque Angli episcopi Sarisburensis viri eloquentia, doctrina ac pietate florentissimi quodnam fuit de eiusdem lucubrationibus iudicium Laurentii Hunfredi theologi Oxoniensis verba in Iuelli vita clarissime testantur. "Transmisit, inquit, in Angliam ad Iuellum, Ludouicus Lavaterus doctus et diligens Tigurinae ecclesiae ecclesiastes, librum suum in Solo-/γ4r./monis Prouerbia et alium De controuersia sacramentaria." In altero Iuellus (quoniam eius iudicium requirebatur) multiplicem et variam lectionem et doctrinam reconditam agnouit, ita vt nihil in eo genere putarit extare cum eo conferendum, ingenue confessus est se multa illius sapientissimi regis prouerbia tum demum intellexisse quae antea ignorabat. In altero autem libello, ait se, quod ad rem ipsam et ad historiae veritatem attinet non habere multum quod dicat: difficile esse iudicium ferre de illis rebus quibus cum gererentur non interfuerit, de fide autem scriptoris nihil se dubitare orationisque perspicuitatem, candorem, modestiam D. Brentio atque adeo liuori ipsi omnibusque aduersariis non posse non placere.'

most kind and welcoming to religious refugees from France, Italy and other countries. He also visited the sick and the dying without being called, and offered consolation to criminals when they were led to their place of 'just punishment'; that is, the scaffold.[58]

We can see that Stucki gave each of his subjects a different type of biography designed for a particular purpose, emphasising a particular set of strong points to be contemplated and imitated. Simler was singled out for his integration of mathematics into theology; Wolf for his educational capacities; Lavater for his embodying all the virtues of a good pastor. We have seen also that Stucki's accounts of Wolf and Lavater particularly enabled him to stress the importance of the family, and the transmission of certain religious and ethical values via the family. His biographies, like all the second-generation Zurich biographies of second-order figures, were not chronicles or theological treatises; nor did they seek to sanctify their heroes in any way other than by ascribing to them all the virtues and none of the vices of good Christian citizens. For this reason, they provide a unique insight into the city's Protestant culture in the second half of the sixteenth century, and the way this culture integrated historical events such as the beginnings of the Reformation or the First War of Kappel.

The Autobiography and Biography of Konrad Pellikan

Autobiography as opposed to biography in the German-speaking areas in the early modern period has been the object of fairly intensive research in recent years in the context of study of the so-called 'first person literature', or *Selbstzeugnisliteratur*.[59] I do not propose to duplicate those studies, but simply to point up the difference between an autobiographical and a biographical account in the second-generation Reformation Zurich. For this reason, I shall concentrate on the autobiography of the Hebrew scholar Konrad Pellikan (1478–1556), near-contemporary of Zwingli and Bullinger, which functioned as a biography in sixteenth-century Zurich after having been edited by Ludwig Lavater. Pellikan was above all a philologist, and was never actively involved in confessional polemics.[60] Born in Rufach in Upper Alsace, he was brought up in Heidelberg by his uncle, who was a member of the humanist circle of Bishop Johann von Dalberg. In 1493, he

[58] Ibid., fol. δ1r.

[59] See particularly in the series *Selbstzeugnisse der Neuzeit*: K. von Greyerz, H. Medick and P. Veit (eds), *Von der dargestelleten Person zum erinnerten Ich. Europäische Zelbstzeugnisse als historische Quelle (1500–1800)* (Cologne: Böhlau, 2001); G. Jahnke, *Autobiographie als soziale Praxis. Beziehungskonzepte in Selbstzeugnissen des 15. und 16. Jhdt in deutschsprachigem Raum* (Cologne: Böhlau, 2002).

[60] On Pellikan, see Christoph Zürcher, *Konrad Pellikans Wirken in Zürich, 1526–1556* (Zürich: P. Laing, 1975).

was placed as a novice in the Franciscan monastery in Rufach. Two years later, he moved to the monastery in Tübingen, where he studied Greek, Latin and theology. After studying Hebrew with Johannes Reuchlin, he became the first Christian to publish a Hebrew Grammar, in 1501. As lector at the Franciscan monastery in Basel, he was part of the circle of Bishop Christoph von Utenheim. From 1516, he was closely associated with Erasmus. He contributed to the propagation of Luther's ideas in Basel by publishing his works. In 1523, he was appointed Professor of Theology at Basel, at the same time as Johannes Oecolampadius. In 1526, Zwingli called him to the Old Testament Chair in Zurich, where he was to remain for the rest of his life. He was the only Reformation author to write a Latin commentary on the complete Bible. His autobiography[61] is similar in tone to Kessler's biography of Vadian. It is as much an account of a life as a chronicle of the times, albeit of a far more intimate and objective nature than Kessler's piece. Zürcher, Pellikan's modern biograper, finds it especially interesting for its descriptions of the Franciscan Order in the Upper Rhine torn between scholasticism and humanism on the eve of the Reformation, and for its account of education in Zurich in Zwingli's time.[62] In fact, it would be more accurate to say with regard to his descriptions of the Franciscan Order that he reconstructs with great precision the ambivalent intellectual and religious climate of the times, something that a sixteenth-century biography was not supposed to do. Whatever the approach it adopted, it had to draw clear confessional and moral lines, or share the fate of many autobiographies and remain confined to obscurity

Pellikan himself called his autobiography a *Chronicon*, not a *Vita*, but this title did not resurface until the appearance in 1877 of Riggenbach's edition of the full text. In 1582, however, Ludwig Lavater published edited extracts from it under the title *Narratio de ortu, vita et obitu eiusdem [Pellikani] iam primum in lucem edita*, and appended this as a preface to the first volume of his 1582 edition of Pellikan's Latin Bible Commentary.[63]

Lavater's choice of title *Narratio de ortu, vita*, and so on is perfectly predictable given the Zurich biographical taste of that period. Lavater also added the end (in the third person), describing Pellikan's death. This flowery ending in the third person contrasts sharply with the autobiography proper,

---

[61]   Available in a nineteenth-century edition by Bernhard Riggenbach, *Das Chronicon des Konrad Pellikan* (Basel: Banheimer, 1877). Hereafter: Pellikan, *Chronicon* (ed. Riggenbach).

[62]   See Christoph Zürcher, art., 'Pellikan', in Hillerbrand (ed.), *The Oxford Encyclopedia of the Reformation*, vol. 3, p. 241.

[63]   *In Pentateuchum siue quinque libros Mosis, nempe Genesim, Exodum, Leuiticum, Numeros, Deuteronomium, Conradi Pellikani sacrarum literarum in schola Tigurina Professoris commentarii. His accessit narratio de ortu, vita et obitu eiusdem, opera Ludouici Lavateri Tigurini, iam primum in lucem edita...* (Tiguri excudebat Christophorus Froschouerus, Anno 1582). Hereafter: Pellikan, *In Pent.* (ed. Lavater).

which is written in fairly austere style in the first person. The question
we should ask ourselves at this stage is, what did Lavater include and
what did he omit from Pellikan's *Chronicon* so as to make it fit the style
and dimensions of a prefatory *Narratio*? Did he effect any confessional
changes in Pellikan's original account? All these questions can be answered
if we replace Lavater's extracts, which amount to sixteen folio pages in the
context of the complete *Chronicon* numbering 183 closely printed quartos
in Riggenbach's edition. Given the disparity between the two works, I shall
point only to the most significant omissions. Pellikan's intention in 1544[64]
was not to write in praise of himself, or to make himself into an emblem or
a hero. Lavater naturally omits the introduction to the *Chronicon*, in which
Pellikan explains that his purpose was of anything but public nature. The
manuscript bears the title *chronicon C. P. ad filium et nepotes* ('the chronicle
of Conrad Pellikan to his son and to his nephews'), showing that its author
intended it for members of his family only. In the opening words, Pellikan
addresses his son Samuel and his nephews, explaining that he intends the
work not to 'boast about the fathers, but to instruct the sons.'[65] He refers to
the *Chronicon* as 'my private Chronicle' (*Chronica priuata mea*).[66]

However, he does not see his literary undertaking as an expression of
individualism: he situates himself in a long tradition of fathers writing down
their lives to preserve family memory and to edify their sons. He hopes
that his son will perpetuate this tradition. He notes that he is following
the literary example of his uncle Jodocus Gallus, rector of Heidelberg
University, and subsequently preacher at Speyer Cathedral. Gallus made
brief notes of his genealogy and life on the inside covers of his books, and
particularly, his copy of Terence. Pellikan greatly regrets that the latter
was not transmitted to his sister's children with the rest of the inheritance,
but was taken by Gallus' friends, who found it of value for the general
information it contained about the times.[67]

In Pellikan's view, what is intended as family history should remain
in the family. It is neither to be perused by friends, nor published. In a
word, had he lived until 1582, he would not have been pleased to learn

---

[64]   On the manuscript of the *Chronicon* and its date, see Pellikan, *Chronicon* (ed.
Riggenbach), pp. 1–3. In fact, Pellikan's account ends in 1555. However, the last pages for
years 1545–55 are written in the form of notes covering a year at a time, whereas the rest
takes the form of a continuous narrative.

[65]   Ibid., p. 1: '... vt tu quoque aeuo tuo victurus similiter attendere, annotare et ad
successorum sancta exempla conscribere consequenter studeas et adhorteris, ad memoriam
sanctam et vtilem, non ad iactationem patrum sed ad institutionem filiorum ...'.

[66]   Ibid., p. 2.

[67]   Ibid.: '... studuit annotare diligenter sed breuius cognationis suae genealogias et sua
quoque fata passim adscripta coopertoriis librorum, maxime cuidam libro Terentiano, quem
ex omnibus suis libris post mortem eius testamento legatis filiis sororis meae vnicum indolui
cum aliis non inuentum, sed a familiaribus suis amicis subtractum ob multa huiusmodi
annotata temporaria gesta ...'.

of Lavater's publication, which is no doubt partly why the latter omitted the original introduction from his *Narratio*, and chose to begin with details of Pellikan's birth.[68] Lavater also omits another essential part of the *Chronicon* which traces the origin of the family name and its genealogy. Having thus suppressed all information about the original scope and purpose of the *Chronicon*, he can edit the rest to suit the public requirements of the biographical genre. He keeps the details of Pellikan's education, but omits all his social and cultural comments such as his remarks on the appearance of embroidered and chequered clothes, as well as new type of shoes which he calls 'slippers' or *pantofflen*, all fashions brought back by soldiers returning from abroad in the late 1480s, which proliferated during Pellikan's childhood.[69] Also absent is the very detailed account of Pellikan's journey to Rome at the request of his provincial. The object of the journey was to attend the general chapter of the Franciscans of both observances which Leo X convened for 1528; Pellikan was selected to represent his province together with the ex-provincial Johannes Machysen. Lavater does not pass over the Roman episode altogether; thus he shortens considerably, but does not leave out, Pellikan's description of the city's churches.[70]

What he does omit altogether are the details of the life of his hero's uncle Jodocus Gallus (d. 1517), where Pellikan speaks quite openly about his uncle's illegitimate daughter (begotten when he was still young), whom Gallus had brought up well and honestly although he never acknowledged as his.[71] He also speaks quite openly about the same Franciscan uncle's dislike of the celibacy vow and the stratagem he used to cope with the strains of it, which, if publicly known, would have discredited Pellikan's image forever in Zurich of the late sixteenth century, which was keen to propagate solid family values. Gallus, like many clerics, had a mistress whom he kept away from home so that he could contain himself better and fall less often than if he had her living close at hand. Apart from the fact that he violated the rule of celibacy, Gallus, in his nephew's view, was a most pious man and would have shared the reformers' views on celibacy.[72]

These details provide valuable, first-hand information to the modern reader about sixteenth-century attitudes to sexuality in religious orders and in general. However, they would have been inappropriate in a biography for public use which acted as a preface to biblical commentaries. Even more surprisingly, Lavater omits all the details of Pellikan's work on Luther editions, which led to or was concomitant upon his conversion.

---

[68]   Pellikan, *In Pent.* (ed. Lavater), fol. B1r. Cf. Pellikan, *Chronicon* (ed. Riggenbach), pp. 3–4.
[69]   See ibid., pp. 8–9.
[70]   See ibid., pp. 59–67. Cf. Pellikan, *In Pent.* (ed. Lavater), fol. B6r.
[71]   See Pellikan, *Chronicon* (ed. Riggenbach), pp. 69–70.
[72]   See ibid., pp. 70–71.

Whereas the *Chronicon* explains in some detail the nature of the Hebraist's involvement with the Luther editions published by Adam Petri in 1520, Lavater introduces the confessional issue between the Franciscan provincial Caspar Schatzgeyer and Pellikan rather abruptly,[73] making it seem as if Schatzgeyer has no apparent reason for calling Pellikan 'a promoter of Luther's works'. This could simply be due to pressure of space and a wish on Lavater's part not to devote too much attention to Luther. Unlike Pellikan, he does not conceive his role to be that of an accurate chronicler of the Reformation. His publication of Pellikan's biblical works is a celebration of the 'Zurich School' of biblical studies.

For the same reason, Lavater also leaves out all the details to do with the Hebraist's transfer from Basel to Zurich, which was anything but straightforward. Pellikan makes it clear that it took two letters from Zwingli to make him leave Basel. He admits freely that he replied to the first letter without much enthusiasm, giving two reasons for his hesitation. Firstly, he was not sure that the Basel authorities would grant him release from his duties. Secondly, he was not clear about what Zwingli wanted him to do in Zurich.[74] However, seeing that the progress of the Basel Reformation was slow and that he was no longer safe in his order, he gave in to Zwingli's requests, partly aided by the counsel of friends, especially Jacob Meyer. As well as giving numerous other details of this episode in his life, Pellikan explains exactly under what conditions he was to move to and work in Zurich. The situation turns out to have been infinitely more complex than Lavater's three-line account allows us to understand.[75] Pellikan reproduces the text of Zwingli's letter specifying his working conditions and salary. Zwingli promised him a canonry with a salary of 60 or 70 florins per year (a salary equal to Zwingli's own), an elegant and conveniently situated house, and some holidays 'to make the work bearable' [*ut labor sit tolerabilis*]. In return for this, he was to read daily and comment on 'a certain quantity of text in Hebrew'. Zwingli's remarks in the letter about Pellikan's use of the Franciscan habit are particularly telling, and show that although it was not encouraged, it was not condemned outright. Zwingli's exact words were:

> Monk's hoods are an object of derision here, and even if you always wear one, there is no point in bringing it just to put it away. However, you must absolutely wear it for the journey because of the impending civil war and the wickedness of tyrants raging not here in Zurich, but in other cantons.[76]

---

[73] See bid., pp. 74–6, 80. Cf. Pellikan, *In Pent.* (ed. Lavater), fol. B6v.

[74] See Pellikan, *Chronicon* (ed. Riggenbach), p. 106.

[75] Pellikan, *In Pent.* (ed. Lavater), fol. B6v.

[76] Pellikan, *Chronicon* (ed. Riggenbach), p. 108: 'Cucullae ridentur apud nos sed si perpetuo vtaris, prorsus autem nihil si adferas vt ponas, cucullato autem tibi veniendum est ad nos propter instantem tumultum tyrannorumque improbitatem non apud nos sed apud alios saeuientem.'

Even the slightest hint of confessional ambivalence had no place in Lavater's account. By the 1580s, the religious parties were polarised to the extent that a bare mention of Pellikan's custom of wearing a Franciscan habit and Zwingli's view that it was advisable to conserve it in some circumstances was likely to discredit both men with Lavater's readers, and throw doubt on the orthodoxy of the very commentaries he was promulgating.

The rest of Lavater's biography concentrates on Pellikan's activities as Hebraist and Bible commentator, with only the minimum of space devoted to his marriage and other aspects of his life. Furthermore, Lavater consistently omits any mention of events that might throw a negative light on Zwingli's Reformation. This is why he does not repeat the *Chronicon*'s account of the Baden Disputation, and especially the discussion of Zwingli's absence and reasons for it. Admittedly, as Riggenbach points out, Pellikan's knowledge of the Baden Disputation and its chronology in relation to the Berne Dispute was anything but accurate.[77] However, Lavater would not have been embarrassed by that, but by his hero's mention of Thomas Murner's *Acts* as being the official record and also by his insistence on the precarious state of the Reformation at the time of the Disputation.[78] Among other significant details omitted by Lavater, we might single out Pellikan's words addressed to his son Samuel, the chief dedicatee of the *Chronicon*, towards the end of the text. This omission is due more to lack of space than to embarrassment. Pellikan's exact words are very revealing of Zurich's view of itself, and throw an important light on the reasons for the popularity of biography in the city:

> To replace Zwingli, from 1532 onwards [the Lord] raised up for His church many excellent and most learned men, of whom it has been said ... that you will not find easily in Germany another city so productive of good authors and writings. This has been plain for anyone to see in Zurich up until now and will hopefully continue thus. And it is a pleasure to give their names here for the perpetual honour of our church so that you and your descendants know which and what sort of men reformed the Zurich Church, in the hope of preserving it by the grace of God, temptations notwithstanding. The commander and leader of them all, strong in word and deed, unparalleled in diligence and constancy, is Ulrich Zwingli. He is joined by Leo Jud and others [here follows a list of some twenty names of doctors who followed in Zwingli's footsteps, including Bibliander and Bullinger] who are all famous through their publications of useful and pious writings. All of these have come from the presses of Christoph Froschouer, most faithful man and highly industrious and skilled printer,

---

[77] Ibid., p. 115, ns. 2–4; p. 116, n. 1.

[78] Ibid., pp. 115–16: 'Eodem mense [=February 1527!] disputatio peracta est Badenae vbi Oecolampadius contra Eckium et Fabrum aliosque multo favore Heluetiorum adiutos coactus est disputare, modo quo descripta est disputatio et impressa ab Heluetiis Lucernae ... Timor et opinio vehemens erat quod si Zwinglius interfuisset disputationi, ipse et propter eum alii quoque Basilienses docti excidium non euasissent, verum absentia eius seruasse creditur reliquos doctos et bonos viros ...'.

thanks to his efforts and opportunities he has provided. Praises in his honour bear witness to his labours and merit ....[79]

Pellikan expresses the same profound conviction that all Zurich *Lives* of the period illustrate: Zurich's theologians and Protestant scholars generally made it into a golden city. All those who were part of the *aeropagus* deserved to be commemorated. In setting down his *Chronicon*, Pellikan never envisaged for one moment becoming of those who gave the city its distinctive profile. Still less did he imagine that Lavater would extract sections from his 'private Chronicle' so as to put together an official *Life*. One thing remains certain: in setting down his account of his life and times for the use of his children, Pellikan was writing what the modern reader would recognise as an historical account of the Reformation with all its doctrinal and political ambiguities and uncertainties. By the time Lavater had abridged the *Chronicon* into *Narratio de ortu, vita*, and so on, much of the information was lost, and it was no longer a piece of historical writing in the sense that we would understand today. At the same time, Lavater rendered a service to historians of historiography. By extracting certain points from the *Chronicon* at the expense of others, he pointed up the difference between biography and chronicle or history in sixteenth-century Zurich. He made it clear that a biography, as understood then, should treat of the subject's intellectual and moral qualities and make a number of didactic points intended to edify the readers so that they follow the biographee's example. For this reason, he ignored all the information on contemporary attitudes to dress, sexuality, difficulties encountered by the Reformation, ambiguities attendant upon its beginnings. However, while presenting Pellikan out of his historical context, he did answer quite clearly certain cultural and theological questions that were drowned in the mass of other information in the *Chronicon*. One such question was to do with the status of the vernacular. Lavater's account pinpoints it very clearly by reproducing Pellikan's remarks on this word for word. Obviously he considered the Hebraist an authority on this matter, supplementing, if need be, the authority of Bullinger himself:

> I also wrote in German a commentary on the Pentateuch, Joshua, Judges, Ruth, Samuel, Malachi, Jeremiah and Isaiah so as to refute the Jews. For the same reason I also translated into German Ludovicus Vives' very elegant disputation with the Jews. I translated many books of Aristotle and Cicero into the vernacular so that their philosophy could shortly be learned by clever men in the language of the people as was the custom in Greece. The Romans too when they became aware of works written in Greek that could be useful to them, had them translated into Latin. Why should our language suit the communication and learning of philosophy less than the others? It would be very helpful to have the new philosophical concepts and methods in a German

---

[79]   Ibid., pp. 141–3.

version. Furthermore, it would be highly profitable to learn Turkish ... so that
we could finally soften them up and civilise them by our teaching. In German
churches, true religion has been preached in German these many years by pious
and learned preachers. Moses who now speaks very intelligibly to our people
is better understood by ordinary people nowadays than formerly by Parisian
doctors and monks, even though they were Thomists or Scotists. The Prophets,
Christ, the Evangelists and the Apostles speak to our people in German and
there is nothing so abstruse in the biblical canon that our Bullinger cannot
explain with total clarity and profit so that the people understand it. Even
though he himself understands all the sacred languages, he only ever uses
the common language of the people in church assemblies. He is clearer, more
perspicacious and more eloquent than anyone else when it comes to explaining
individual details.[80]

The passage raises the point of extending the use of the vernacular to liberal
arts. It also explains the importance of the vernacular in the church, and
finally it pays a tribute to the *antistes*. Appearances to the contrary, there
is no contradiction with the language of the *In Pentateuchum* itself, which
is Latin. Pellikan carefully limits the use of the vernacular: it is a language
of conversion, a language which facilitates the learning of liberal arts and
makes the Bible readily available to the common people. Moreover, citing
the example of Bullinger, he makes it clear that any minister must also
master the sacred languages so that he can explain theology and Scripture
in the vernacular clearly and correctly.

What was a minor digression in the *Chronicon* has thus become, in
Lavater's *Narratio*, an important programmatic statement on the respective
merits of Latin and the vernacular languages in the religious instruction
of the laity.

Conclusion

As noted in our conclusion to the previous chapter, *Lives* played a unique
role in Reformation Zurich. Whereas the first-order reformers were seen as
pillars of the religious movement, with Zwingli being raised to the status
of a saint and Bullinger to that of the Protestant head of Christendom, the
biographies of their followers and disciples served as religious, cultural
and historical propaganda destined for all classes and age groups. In the
latter years of the sixteenth century particularly, the biographical genre
was a crucial factor in the cohesion and continuity of the Reformation, its
education system, its spiritual and ethical values, and its culture. As well
as providing examples, *Lives* of men such as Gesner, Simler, Wolf, Lavater,
Stucki and Pellikan served as a justification for the teaching of natural
history or mathematics, and inculcated the correct pedagogical methods,

---

[80] Pellikan, *In Pent.* (ed. Lavater), fol. B8r. Cf. Pellikan, *Chronicon* (ed. Riggenbach),
pp. 135–7.

the right family and patriotic values, the correct way to preach, and the right use of vernacular in religious instruction. They also served as a reminder of the beginnings of the Zurich Reformation if, as in the case of Lavater, they happened to have famous ancestors who had witnessed key events such as the Battle of Kappel. Whatever the level and type of readership intended, their orientation was primarily national, although all the biographers were fully aware of their European, particularly German, context. There was an implicit understanding, partly based on the classical tradition of *Life*-writing, as to what a biography could and could not say, as we have seen from the comparison of Pellikan's autobiographical, private *Chronicon* with Lavater's edition of it. The object of biographies was not to go into the historical background of the biographee, or to describe customs or events which were likely to throw even a hint of unfavourable light on the Reformation or, for that matter, on the biographee. Similarly, they did not go into any detail regarding the biographee's character or motivation. An individual's Roman Catholic past was referred to routinely, if at all. It was often reduced to a veritable minimum, as with the fathers of Wolf and Lavater, who were depicted as Protestant *avant la lettre*. By the same token, a biography was not supposed to invent or add legendary material, or invoke models other than classical.

At the same time, anthologies of *Lives* of reformers and teachers found no place in Reformation Zurich. No Plutarch or Suetonius came along to compare and contrast. One senses from their determined reliance on classical models and from their repeated justifications of the practice of *Life*-writing in the face of arguments against it that there was quite a lot of opposition to the genre on the grounds that it would resuscitate the *Lives* of the saints with the attendant cult. While obviously seen as a powerful pedagogical tool, *Lives* of distinguished figures of the Swiss Reformation enjoyed something of an apocryphal status. Often hidden in the form of prefaces to other works, they never became a part of official, religious literature and were never given the prominence of the much shorter and less substantial funeral orations and poems, which is probably why they have received so little attention from modern historians.

CHAPTER 4

Early *Lives* of Calvin and Beza by Friends and Foes

Compared to Lutheran Germany and Switzerland (Zurich in particular), Geneva was anything but a centre of Reformation *Life*-writing. Nobody preached sermons on the lives of Calvin or Beza or any of their colleagues; no one used either reformer as a symbol of Protestant unity or social cohesion. No one in the sixteenth century thought that the Geneva Reformation should be commemorated via the *Lives* of its pastors, theologians or scholars, or that their *Lives* could or should be used as models of family values, patriotism or pastoral skills. In all, Calvin was the object of three partisan *Lives*, two of them by Beza and one by Beza and Colladon. Beza for his part only interested one contemporary biographer, Antoine de la Faye. This discretion stands in sharp contrast with the amount of attention both the reformers, Calvin especially, received from hostile Roman Catholic biographers, starting with Bolsec, continuing through Jean Papire Masson, and ending with Richelieu. In fact, as we shall see, the most important methodological developments in Calvin *Life*-writing were the work of sixteenth- and early-seventeenth-century Roman Catholic biographers and annalists. It was they who shifted the focus of his biography from the realm of the *exemplum* to the realm of history. At the same time, it was they too who managed to generate a very powerful, negative image of the reformer, which proved far more influential and lasting than the Beza/Colladon attempts to make Calvin's life into an *exemplum*. Independently of full-length *Lives* of Calvin and Beza, it is noteworthy that the only work about figures of the Reformation to come out of Geneva in the sixteenth century was the volume of Beza's *Icones*.[1] These, however, cannot qualify as *Lives*, being composed of engravings with at most a paragraph of text identifying each figure. This situates them in the Varronian portrait genre that Simler in his *Life* of Gesner considered as inferior to and less instructive than written accounts of *Lives* of illustrious men.[2]

---

[1]   On the *Icones*, see Chazalon, 'Les *Icones* de Théodore de Bèze (1580)', pp. 359–76, and literature cited ibid. See also C. Chazalon, 'Théodore de Bèze et les ateliers de Laon', in Irena Backus *et al.* (eds), *Théodore de Bèze (1519–1605). Actes du colloque de Genève (septembre 2005)* (Geneva: Droz, 2007), pp. 69–87.

[2]   See Chapter 3 *ad* note 3 above. In fact, the portrait genre was by no means widespread in Geneva, Beza's *Icones* being its sole representative. Simler was no doubt referring to Renaissance collections of portraits of famous men. For these, see Chazalon, 'Les *Icones*'.

Protestant *Lives* of Calvin and Beza. Attempts to Find a Distinctive
Calvinist Style

As is well known, Beza wrote the first version of his *Life* of Calvin in French
as a preface to Calvin's Commentary on Joshua, which the reformer left
unpublished on his death in 1564, and which his successor had published
by Perrin in Geneva in the same year.[3] Also in 1564, Beza published
the *Life* separately under the title *Discours de M. Théodore de Besze,
contenant en bref l'histoire de la vie et mort de Maistre Iean Caluin avec le
Testament et derniere volonté dudict Calvin. Et le catalogue des liures par
luy composez.*[4] Gardy lists four separate imprints of the leaflet all dating
from 1564. All of these were printed without the printer's name. However,
Gardy identifies one as emanating from the presses of Thomas Bouchard
in Saint-Lô,[5] and another as being the work of Eloi Gibier of Orléans.[6] Of
the remaining two, one bears the place of printing as 'Orléans'; the other
neither the printer's name nor his address. All four imprints contain the
printer's preface to the reader, but only the Saint Lô imprint also includes
the preface by Antoine de la Faye.[7] The imprint cited below[8] is a plaquette
of 63 pages with the preface by the printer (who could be Eloi Gibier),
which points to a fundamental difficulty surrounding the publication.
The printer emphasises that Beza's *Life* is too short, having been intended
only as a preface, and the reader must not think that the remembrance of
someone as important as the Genevan reformer can be encompassed in
such a short work.[9] However, this does not make it worthless. What, then,

---

[3]   See Frédéric Gardy, *Bibliographie des œuvres de Théodore de Bèze* (Geneva: Droz,
1960), no. 173, p. 105. Hereafter: Gardy.

[4]   I shall be referring to the 1564 printing without the printer's address. Hereafter:
Beza, *Discours*. See Gardy, no. 175, p. 105.

[5]   See ibid., no. 176, p. 106 (contains preface by Antoine de la Faye as well as the
printer's address to the reader). Cf. Geneva: Musée historique de la Réformation copy
(shelfmark: B 24, 1 (64) b). De la Faye's preface figures on fol. A ij r.–Aij v.: *inc.* 'Quand Dieu
nous propose quelques excellens personnages …' *des.* '… qui est la parole de Dieu.' De la Faye
distinguishes the *Life* of Calvin from the Catholic hagiographical genre, and stresses that *Lives* of
saintly individuals are intended by God not to obscure His glory but to highlight it. By imitating
the example of Calvin and other saintly men, we are able to obey God's commandments.

[6]   See Gardy, no. 174, p. 105.

[7]   See ibid., no. 175, p. 105; no. 177, p. 107

[8]   See ibid., no. 175, p. 105.

[9]   Beza, *Discours*, p. 2: *Imprimeur au lecteur*: 'Cependant ne trouue estrange si ce
discours ne commence par la forme accoustumee aux Hystoriographes, car l'intention de
l'autheur qui est M. Theodore de Besze, semblablement bon seruiteur de Dieu, et compagnon
de M. Iean Caluin en l'oeuure du Seigneur, n'a esté de le publier comme une histoire, ains
seulement pour vne preface aux commentaires dudict Caluin sur le liure de Josue, mis en
lumiere depuis son trespas. Ie t'ay bien voulu aduertir de ce, affin que tu ne pensasses que la
memore d'un si grand personnage se peut contenter d'vn si petit discours (combien qu'il soit
diligemment et veritablement fait) …'.

is the specificity of Beza's biography? According to the printer, its object is above all to edify the reader. Calvin's life is his doctrine, and his doctrine is both the way he lived and what he taught in his struggles to establish orthodoxy. As Gibier puts it:

> Dear reader, I am offering to you this summary account containing the life and death of the faithful servant of God, John Calvin, in whom you will see marvellous examples of assaults which he bore to defend the doctrine of the Son of God and also the help God gives to His own when his honour and glory are at stake.[10]

The *Life* also has an introductory function in the printer's view, 'as it will surely give you hope of expecting a fine and complete account of everything he did, which will profit greatly the progress of God's Church.'[11] As neither Gibier nor Beza view Calvin as an instrument of God's providence in the sense that Luther's biographers did, Gibier's complaint or *caveat* concerning the brevity of the text is particularly striking. In fact, it helps us to identify the intended audience of the *Discours* as not being an audience of the converted, or one that was overly familiar with Calvin, contrary to the Lutheran and Swiss biographers, who were writing for their own faithful. The *Discours* is obviously intended for France as much as (or more than) Geneva, and is meant to serve as a brief and simple introduction not so much to Calvin's life as to his piety and doctrine. It presents the reformer as an edifying example of someone who bore countless assaults in his struggle to establish the true doctrine of God. Knowing about Calvin the man and what he had to endure is not matter for an autobiography, contrary to what Melanchthon thought about Luther, but for an official biography which will profit the church. This may seem surprising when we bear in mind Calvin's own discretion about himself and his open aversion to becoming an *exemplum* or any sort of cult figure after his death, and a fear of this happening despite his wishes.[12] The tone set by the preface to Beza's *Discours* suggests that his disciples feared on the contrary that Calvin's discretion, if extended to biography-writing, would hamper the evangelisation of France and the conversion of new faithful.

The *Discours* proved something of a bestseller. Between 1564 and early 1565, it underwent eight further French imprints including the *Histoire d'excellens*

---

[10]   Ibid.: *Imprimeur au lecteur*: 'Amy Lecteur, ie t'offre ce present sommaire contenant la vie et mort du fidele seruiteur de Dieu M. Iean Caluin par lequel tu verras de merueilleux examples des assaux qu'il a soustenus pour deffendre la doctrine du Fils de Dieu, et aussi quelle assistence Dieu fait aux siens quand il est question de son honneur et gloire.'

[11]   Ibid.: *Imprimeur au lecteur*: '... lequel te servira seulement de te donner esperance d'attendre vne belle et ample histoire de ses faits et gestes, qui profitera grandement à l'aduancement de l'Eglise de Dieu ...'.

[12]   He forbade any identifying mark on his grave, and its exact location in Geneva's Plainpalais cemetery remains unknown to this day.

personnages and a reprint of Calvin's Commentary on Joshua.[13] It was also translated into Latin, English and German.[14] However, it created as many problems as it solved. In fact, unlike all the other *Lives* we have examined so far, Calvin's *Life* was to undergo extensive revisions and transformations, in a way which suggests not so much a concern with reaching different audiences as a methodological problem. Thus the French version of the *Discours* was first of all augmented and reorganised by Beza and Nicolas Colladon, and published as a preface to Calvin's *Commentaires svr le liure de Iosué* in 1565.[15] This version was then reprinted five times between 1565 and 1663, both separately and in preface form. Finally, in 1575, Beza completely rewrote this second *Life* of Calvin, appending the new version to his edition of *Ioannis Caluini Epistolae et responsa*, which was subsequently re-edited in 1576 and 1657.[16] This third *Life* of Calvin was also inserted into the 1617 edition of Calvin's *Opera theologica* and the 1654 Leiden edition of the *Institutes*.[17]

Why was it necessary to redo Calvin's *Life* twice when the *Lives* of the other Reformers never underwent more than one version by any one author? Given that none of the *Lives* produced was as extensive as the printer of the 1564 version of the *Discours* would have liked, the wish for comprehensiveness cannot have been the sole motive. Before examining the three versions, it is important to say something about the role played by Nicolas Colladon. His name never appears in the work, and we know him to have been the co-author of the second *Life* only because Beza reveals as much in his *Apologia altera ad F. Claudium de Xaintes*, which figures in the second volume of the *Tractatus theologici*. In fact, Beza asserts that Colladon was the sole author of the second *Life*:

> You say that it was I who called Elisha's words 'my father, my father' after Calvin as he was leaving this life. But, as everyone here knows, it was not I who wrote or published this *Life*, but my erstwhile colleague, Nicolas Colladon,

---

[13]   See Gardy, nos. 175–182, pp. 105–9.

[14]   See ibid., nos. 184–187, pp. 109–12.

[15]   *Commentaires de M. Iean Calvin svr le liure de Iosué. Auec une Preface de Theodore de Besze, contenant en brief l'histoire de la vie et mort d'iceluy: augmentee depuis la premiere edition deduite selon l'ordre du temps, quasi d'an en an...* (A Geneve, De l'imprimerie de François Perrin. 1565). Cf. Gardy, no. 189, p. 112. References here to the text in *Ioannis Caluini opera quae supersunt omnia*, eds G. Baum, E. Cunitz and E. Reuss, 59 vols (Braunschweig: Schwetschke etc., 1863–1900), vol. 21 (1879), cols. 50–115. Hereafter: *Calv. Opp.*, vol. 21.

[16]   *Ioannis Caluini Epistolae et responsa. Eiusdem I. Caluini Vita a Theodoro Beza Geneuensis ecclesiae ministro accurate descripta ... Omnia nunc primum in lucem edita* (Geneva, Pierre Saint-André, 1575). Cf. Gardy, no. 200, p. 119. For later editions, see ibid., nos. 201–203, 206, pp. 119–21, 122.

[17]   See ibid., nos. 204–205, pp. 121.

although admittedly he did include in it the preface which I wrote to the French version of Joshua and which treats of Calvin's life and death.[18]

In 1983, Daniel Ménager,[19] following Herminjard, argued that it was far more likely that Beza himself was the author, as the references in the first person could only apply to him and not to Colladon. Why, then, the subterfuge on Beza's part? According to Ménager, it was due to the reference to 2 Kings 2, 13, which acts as an epigraph: 'my father, my father, the chariots and the horsemen of Israel' – Elisha's cry at seeing Elijah translated into heaven. The phrase in itself was innocent enough as it stood, and need not have been taken as an eschatological statement. Johann Haller used it in a letter to Beza without any eschatological overtones, meaning simply that a figure of reference had gone.[20] However, Calvin's Catholic opponents, especially Claude de Saintes in 1567, were quick to see it as a sign of Protestant idolatry. This was coupled with the fact that some Protestants such as Simonius expressed the view (also in 1567) that biographies of Calvin were likely to render the Protestants, particularly the Genevan Protestants, vulnerable to the accusation of being worshippers of Calvin rather than Christ.[21] According to Ménager, these factors sufficed to make Beza deny the authorship of the second *Life*. However, this does not explain why he then wrote another *Life* in 1575. There are further difficulties. Admittedly, Beza could have been resorting to a white lie in his *Reply* to De Saintes, but why then attribute the 1565 *Life* to Colladon, who was very much alive at the time and who could have denied his authorship? As it was, he neither declared himself openly to be the author, nor denied Beza's allegation. Furthermore, it is a well-known fact that Colladon, as his Commentary on the Apocalypse shows, was far more explicit than Beza (or, for that matter, Calvin)[22] about the eschatological significance of the Reformation, and far more given to revealing hidden

---

[18]   See *Calv. Opp.*, vol. 21, col. 10: 'Ego historiam illam quod omnes hic norunt neque scripsi neque edidi sed qui tum erat mihi collega Nicolaus Colladonius, quamuis in eam sit translatum quod de Caluini vita et obitu quadam in Iosuam praefatione Gallica fueram praefatus.'

[19]   See Ménager, 'Théodore de Bèze, biographe de Calvin', pp. 244–7.

[20]   See *Correspondance de Théodore de Bèze*, eds Aubert, Dufour, Meylan *et al.* (hereafter: *Correspondance de Bèze*), vol. 5 (1964), p. 85: Haller to Beza, 23 June 1564: 'Quamuis non possim non plurimum dolere propter obitum clarissimi et maximi viri D. Caluini et cum Elizaeo clamare: "currus et auriga Israelis", tamen illi gratulor quod Dominus ipsum ex miseriis huius mundi et praesenti saeculo malo liberauit et ad regnum suum coeleste transtulit.' Ménager, who cites the passage (pp. 245–6), sees it as indicative of the fact that his friends and disciples identified Calvin with Elijah. However, the contrast of tone between the apocalyptic reference and the rest of the sentence (thanks to God for having freed Calvin from his mortal coils) suggests that Haller is using the reference topically.

[21]   Ménager, p. 246.

[22]   See Irena Backus, 'The Beast. Interpretations of Daniel 7.2–9 and Apocalypse 13.1–4, 11–12 in Lutheran, Zwinglian and Calvinist Circles in the Late Sixteenth Century',

details of Calvin's life which he prided himself on knowing. Thus any biblical reference with eschatological overtones and any intimate details such as we find in the 1565 *Life* would be more likely to be his work. Moreover, the radical difference of tone between this *Life* and the other two speaks for a different authorship, at least in part.

The Pattern of Revision in the Three Lives of Calvin

I shall examine the three *Lives* in chronological order, in an effort to trace the pattern of change. Basically, the issue that Beza faced was that of establishing intellectual and literary criteria for the biography of a major reformer. The three *Lives* represent a process of searching for these criteria.

As regards the *Discours*, did Beza draw any inspiration from Possidius' *Life* of Augustine? As we have seen, Possidius first of all gave a chronological account of Augustine's life, followed by a section on his hero's morals and a section on his last days and death. Throughout his account, he emphasised the role of grace, Augustine's services to the North African Church, and his struggle against heretics. He gave a detailed account of both his public and private morals, and stressed that he died a good Christian death. Beza wrote his biography of Calvin in rather different circumstances. He did not have anything like the *Confessions* to draw on, and he wanted to underplay the personal element, without removing it altogether, given his dual aim of promulgating the man and his teaching, the two being in his view inseparable. This is also why the *Discours* starts not with a chronology of the reformer, but with an account of Calvin's doctrine and his struggles against the heresies of his time:

> Indeed, as for his doctrine, which I shall address first, it is so far from the truth that the very number of its opponents renders it suspect to all people of sound judgement that, on the contrary, it can serve as a good argument of its solidity. This is especially true as no one who ever opposed it was aware that they were criticising not just a man, but one who was a true servant of God.[23]

There follows a chronological catalogue of all the heresies combated by Calvin. Beza divides it into two parts: main heresies and second-order heresies. Among Calvin's main opponents, Beza lists the Anabaptists, Caroli, Servetus, Bolsec, and the Antitrinitarians. Second-order heretics include Pighius, Sadolet, Joachim Westphal and Tillemann Hesshusen. All

---

Reformation and Renaissance Review, 3 (2000): 59–77; Backus, *Reformation Readings of the Apocalypse*, pp. 66–74.

[23]   Beza, *Discours*, p. 4: 'Or, quant à sa doctrine, de laquelle je veux parler en premier lieu, tant s'en faut que la multitude de ceux qui luy ont contredit la doivent rendre suspecte envers toutes gens de bon jugement qu'au contraire cela seul pourroit servir de certain argument pour l'approuver, d'autant que nul ne s'y est jamais opposé qui n'ait expérimenté qu'il s'adressoit non point contre un homme, mais contre un vray serviteur de Dieu.'

these, unlike the first category, issue from established churches. Castellio and Bauduin get a section to themselves. One of the distinctly 'un-Possidian' features of Beza's biography is a long excursus on his own disagreements with Castellio, which ended on the latter's death in 1562. Even though he feels qualms about including it, he does nothing to remove it and justifies this by appealing to the edifying value of such warnings:

> I know that this long discourse will displease some as if I were speaking as a man of immoderate passions who could not even let the dead rest in their tombs, but I can protest before God that I never hated him when he was alive and that I never had any personal dealings with him, good or bad. So, far be it for me to hate and persecute the dead who are given over to the judgement of God. But I wanted to voice this so that everyone keeps away from his books and from disciples that he left behind.[24]

The excursus is not arbitrary. It shows that the *Discours* was intended first and foremost for a French audience, one which might have been familiar with Castellio's name, reputation and at least some of his works. In the midst of the Wars of Religion, Castellio's *Conseil à la France désolée* and his warnings about Calvin's intolerance would have found followers. If Beza was to make Calvin attractive to the French public, he had no option but to show the Basel professor in the worst possible light while making it clear that Calvin (rather like Possidius' Augustine) was the model churchman who spent most of his time combating heresies. Beza concludes that his account of Calvin's teaching and doctrinal struggles exhausts the major part of Calvin's life, which was in his view 'one perpetual doctrine, in what he said, what he wrote and in his morals and way of life.'[25] However, Beza does not stop his biography there. After the idealised account of Calvin's origins and education, and an idealised account of his expulsion from and return to Geneva, he interweaves Calvin's private and public morality. In this, he again shows himself to be quite unlike Possidius, who separated the factual account of Augustine's life from a description of his public and private morals. According to Beza, Calvin had more integrity and worked harder than any man in the service of the church. He had extremely fragile health, but, despite this, supported the heavy charge that

---

²⁴   Ibid., p. 15: 'Je sçay bien que ce long discours sera trouvé mauvais par aucuns, comme si j'en parlois en homme passionné et ne pouvois même souffrir les morts se reposer en leur sépulchre, mais je puis protester devant Dieu que jamais je n'ay hay le personnage vivant, avec lequel aussi je n'eus jamais affaire particulier en bien ni en mal; tant s'en faut que maintenant je voulusse hayr et pourchasser les morts qui sont remis au jugement du Seigneur. Mais il a falu que cecy fust entendu afin que chascun se garde de ses livres et disciples qu'il a laissez après luy.'

²⁵   Ibid., p. 17: 'Voilà les principaux combats que ce bon personnage a soustenus heureusement pour la vérité du Seigneur. Au reste par ce discours je pense avoir traité la pluspart de sa vie, car qu'a-ce esté autre chose de sa vie qu'une perpetuelle doctrine, tant par paroles que par escrits, et par toutes ses mœurs et façons de vivre?'

God placed upon his shoulders. He was of exceptional temperance, and most of the time content with one meal taken every twenty-four hours. Contrary to the accusations of some, he was not in the least vainglorious or ambitious, never abused his position, and never made any important decisions without consulting his colleagues. His attire and the furnishings of his home were of the utmost modesty. He never dedicated his works to important patrons.

Although, in contrast with Augustine, Calvin was married, Beza stresses that his marriage was of the most chaste, despite the accusations of adultery levelled not so much at him as at those close to him (in fact, his sister-in-law). But according to Beza, similar things happened in the house of Jacob and David.

> But he has yet to be born, the man who could so much as suspect him of whom we speak ... He lived for about nine years in the state of chaste matrimony. After his wife's death he remained a widower for sixteen years until his death ... Who could be a stauncher enemy of any adultery? It is true that the Lord tested him on this through persons who were close to him. Far worse things happened in the house of Jacob and David.[26]

Does Beza mean that during his nine years of marriage Calvin abstained altogether from sexual intercourse with his wife, or is he saying that during that time their conjugal act was limited to a minimum necessary for procreation? Calvin and Idelette did in fact have one son, who died a few days after his birth in July 1542, as attested very briefly by Calvin's correspondence with Pierre Viret and Jean Sturm.[27] Apart from his chastity, Calvin was characterised, according to Beza, by his clemency towards heretics and his vehemence, which no one could confuse with a choleric temperament. It goes without saying that he had a good death.[28]

This summary suffices to show that Beza's first *Life* of Calvin follows a similar pattern to Possidius' *Life* of Augustine although Beza never mentions Possidius. Allowing for difference of context, period and public, Beza, like Augustine's biographer, insists on his subject's struggle against

---

[26]   Ibid., pp. 33–4: 'Mais il est a naistre qui jamais en ait mesmes soupconné celuy dont nous parlons en lieu où il ait conversé. Il a vescu enuiron neuf ans en mariage en toute chasteté; sa femme estant décédée, il a demeuré en viduité l'espace d'environ 16 ans et jusques à la mort ... Qui a esté le plus rigoureux ennemi de toute paillardise? Il est vray que le Seigneur l'a exercé sur ce fait en des personnes qui le touchoyent de près. Il est arrivé pis encore en la maison de Jacob et de David.'

[27]   See *Correspondance des réformateurs dans les pays de langue française*, ed. A. L. Herminjard, 9 vols (Geneva: H. Georg, and Paris: G. Fischbacher, 1866–97), vol. 8, no. 1149 (letter from Calvin to Viret, 19 August [1542]), p. 103, and no. 1173 (letter from Jean Sturm to Calvin, 29 October [1542]), p. 170.

[28]   Wilhelm Lindanus in his *Historia tragica* of 1564 (French version: *Discours en forme de dialogue ou histoire tragique* [Paris, G. Chaudière, 1566]) mentions that most of the reformers encountered bad and ignoble ends (cf. ibid., fol. 147r.).

heretics, his services to the church, the interference of divine grace in his activities, his high level of public and private morality, and more especially his chastity. He presents Calvin as inseparable from his teaching in such a way that the man is the doctrine and the doctrine the man. Beza's concern to make Calvin as acceptable as possible to the French public accounts for the long excursus on Castellio, and for Beza's constant emphasis on the presence of Satan, who tempted the reformer at every juncture. A man as besieged as Calvin by demonic forces would have appeared more sympathetic than a man with acknowledged character defects.

Irrespective of that, Beza's identification of the man with his teaching and the highly idealised, not to say hagiographical, portrait of the reformer would have rendered the Genevans vulnerable to the accusations of trying to start a Calvin cult. Admittedly, Claude de Sainctes raised explicit objections not to the first, but to the 1565 *Life*. However, the printer's cautious preface and the subsequent attempts at a new biography by Colladon and Beza suggest that Calvin *Life*-writing had difficulties in establishing itself.

As stated, we know Colladon to have been the author or, more accurately, the co-author of the 1565 *Life* only because Beza reveals as much in his *Apologia altera ad F. Claudium de Xaintes*. There is no doubt that Ménager[29] is correct when he identifies the first-person references as applying to Beza only,[30] but there is equally no doubt that all the intimate anecdotes and eschatological references could only be the work of Colladon. This suggests that Beza and Colladon collaborated. The *Life* keeps intact most of the contents of the *Discours*, but reorders them in a strictly chronological framework, adding material such as additional facts, dates and detailed information on Calvin's works, without removing the catalogue, which had figured in Beza's *Discours*. The Possidian model was abandoned, and with it the identification of Calvin the man with his doctrine. Calvin's *Life* in its second version focuses much more on events, and this means that the reformer is shown not so much as a static model as someone interacting with the environment. This should make the *Life* much closer to the modern conception of historical biography. However, this is not the case for a variety of reasons. Firstly, the biographers' objective is not to situate Calvin in the history of the period, but to prove that his life shows him to be called by God and armed by Him 'with holy perseverance until the day of his death to edify his own orally and in writing.'[31] Thus, given that the text stresses that anything that happens,

---

[29]   Ménager, pp. 244–7.

[30]   For example, *Calv. Opp.*, vol. 21, col. 51: '... c'estoit Melchior Volmar duquel ie me souvien d'autant plus volontiers que c'est celuy mesme qui a été mon fidele precepteur et gouuerneur de toute ma ieunesse, don't ie louerai Dieu toute ma vie.'

[31]   Ibid., vol. 21, cols 52–3.

happens only because of God's will, Calvin's life only makes sense because it is ruled by providence. We might at this stage make the comparison with Melanchthon's *Life* of Luther, or, for that matter, with Beza's *Discours*, and leave it at that. However, what is interesting about the 1565 account of Calvin is that, despite being couched in this providential framework, it contains several perfectly human anecdotes about the reformer and devotes a great deal more attention to the exact chronology of Calvin's works. As Ménager[32] pointed out, Colladon introduces anecdotes such as the theft of Calvin's horse on his way to Basel in 1536,[33] his risking his life to quell a rebellion of the Council of 200 on 16 December 1547,[34] or joking with his friends that he did not produce a second edition of the *Traité des reliques* (1546) because they failed to provide him with further examples of fake relics.[35] He also shows privileged knowledge of Calvin's intellectual gifts, his memory in particular, concerning which he cites several examples of its prodigious capacity.[36] These anecdotes are not arbitrary, and neither are they intended just to liven up the account, as Ménager claims, but to identify Colladon as co-author and, even more importantly, to render Calvin more human.

Another feature of this *Life* of Calvin is its construction on a yearly basis according to the chronicle model, a device which further humanises Calvin by portraying his life as a series of struggles fought by a man. This emphasises the break with Beza's first portrayal of the reformer as identical with his teaching. We might further note that the frequency with which the *Life* cites dates[37] enables it to show that God intervened directly in the history of Geneva during Calvin's time, beginning with his return in 1541:

> Thus he was re-established in Geneva on the thirteenth of September 1541 with Master Viret as his colleague. And thus God showed His wonderful mercy towards the people of Geneva. For given that when the ancient nation rejected Moses, God delayed their deliverance by forty years, did not the people of Geneva who had rejected Calvin and his companions, all good and faithuful servants of Christ, deserve to be enslaved forever to the tyranny of the devil and the Roman Antichrist? And yet, God allowed them to reconstruct their Church after only three years.[38]

---

32   Ménager, p. 243.

33   *Calv. Opp.*, vol. 21, col. 53.

34   Ibid., vol. 21, col. 69.

35   Ibid., vol.21, col. 68.

36   Ibid., vol. 21, cols 108–9.

37   See, for example, ibid., vol. 21, cols 62–3: 'Davantage il commença à escrire sur sainct Paul, dediant son commentaire de l'Epistre aux Romains à M. Simon Grynée, le plus docte des allemans et son grand ami. La date dudit Commentaire est de l'an 1539, le 18 octobre. Aussi il escrivit en François un petit Traité et bien familier, de la Cene du Seigneur pour l'usage de ceux de la langue Françoyse …'.

38   Ibid., vol. 21, col. 64: 'Par ainsi il fut restabli derechef à Genève, l'an 1541, le 13 de septembre trouuant là pour son compagnon M. Viret. En cest endroit se monstra merveilleuse

Calvin's *certamen* comes to an end with his death, described by Colladon at great length as the paradigm of a death of a true servant of God exercising a public function. This is followed by the expanded section of the *Discours* on Calvin's lack of ambition, morals and so on, which takes on a more expressly apologetic colouring than in the 1564 version. What Beza and particularly Colladon have done is write a much more personalised account of Calvin's life and work. These elements alter completely the *Discours*, which has been reordered to fit into this framework. While no biography in the modern sense of the term, the *Life* now conveys more of the specificity of Calvin than Beza's first account. Removing Beza's identification of the man with the doctrine and referring the reader to Calvin's works for the latter, the Beza/Colladon effort substitutes for it a portrait of someone more human but nonetheless sent by God at a particular time. That model too proved unsatisfactory if we go by the reactions of De Sainctes and Simonius, and only served to reinforce the impression that Geneva was promoting a Calvin cult instead of Christianity.

Beza waited ten years before trying his hand at a new biography of Calvin, aiming this time at a more restricted readership of theologians. This 1575 *Life* was written in Latin, and was not to be translated into French until 1681. Beza appended it to his edition of Calvin's letters, thus linking implicitly the biography with the letter as its documentary source. Nowhere does Beza suggest that he based his work on the letters, which we know to have been very carefully selected for public use.[39] Their function is to confirm a certain public image of the reformer as founder and leader of the church, and not bring the reader closer to the man or to reveal hitherto unknown facts about him. Gone are all the anecdotes of 1565 judged unsuitable for a biography of a churchman and a public figure. Gone too is the long apologetic passage judged likely to expose the Genevan Church to accusations of instituting a Calvin cult.

Beza in 1575 was facing a similar problem to that confronted by the biographers of Fagius in 1562. It was obviously under the weight of similar criticisms that he decided to publish yet another version of the *Life*. Like his English near-contemporaries, he had to strike a delicate balance between pagan *Lives* and hagiography, if he was going to determine and defend the role of religious biography in the context of Calvinism. Beza thus did not even attempt to revive the *Discours* model, refining the content

---

la misericorde de Dieu envers le peuple de Genève. Car si le peuple ancien reiettant Moyse, la deliurance fut retardee quarante ans, le peuple de Geneve n'estoit-il pas bien digne d'estre à iamais asserui sous la tyrannie du diable et de l'Antechrist romain, quand il auoit reietté Calvin et ses compagnons, fideles et excellens seruiteurs du Seigneur? Et toutesfois Dieu n'a permis que pour cela ait esté différé l'edifice de ceste Eglise que trois ans seulement.'

[39]   See Ménager, pp. 249–51, esp. p. 250: 'La Correspondance, déjà soigneusement triée pour n'offenser ni la mémoire de Calvin, ni la susceptibilité des destinataires, ne passe pas finalement dans la biographie.'

of the 1565 *Life* instead, especially by adding factual details of Calvin's (but not his own) disputes with the Antitrinitarians and with Castellio. More importantly, however, he added a methodological and ideological justification for Calvinist *Life*-writing in the face of doubts and criticisms:

> Let them clamour, those who got hold of the idea through ignorance and those who are wicked, that we worship Luther, Zwingli and Calvin as if they were gods while very frequently decrying as idolaters those who worship saints. Let them shout, I say, as loudly and as long as they want. We have an answer ready. It is one thing to commemorate the labours, the words and the actions that holy men performed or uttered in the cause of religion – for good men become better through knowing these things while the wicked are condemned, that being our sole purpose in this sort of writing. It is, however, quite another thing to do as they do, which is either to deface the lives of truly holy men with tales which are as impious as they are inept (this is what Abdias, whoever he was, did with the Lives of the Apostles), or to fabricate tales from the most disgusting lies (generally called golden legends in barbarian vocabulary, but I call them stinking legends suitable for removal) and finally to bring back into use the images of pagan gods, with only the names changed.[40]

Despite its more militant tone, Beza's answer to criticisms is basically no different to that given by the biographers of Fagius. The function of the reformers' *Lives* is moral and edifying. They bear no relation to the *Lives* of the saints, as they do not mingle fact and fiction. They do not attribute supernatural powers to their subjects, nor are they meant to encourage people to worship them. This is how Beza defines the genre:

> There is no one in my view [he says] who does not admit that amidst all God's works men are to be recognised and honoured above all, and among these mortals, especially those who have distinguished themselves by their teaching and saintliness. It is not for nothing that Daniel [12, 3] compares saintly men to stars whose splendour points the road to blessedness to others. Those who allow their light to be completely extinguished at their death deserve being invaded by darkness much thicker than before.[41]

By acknowledging this, Beza ratifies the tradition of *Life*-writing while giving it a distinctly Calvinist stamp. This means that he distinguishes his endeavours from the hagiographical tradition more sharply than the Lutherans did. At the same time, in contrast with the Zurich biographers, he separates himself from the antique *Life*-writing tradition by declaring that he is following a biblical precept and nothing else. This enables him to claim with a clear conscience that select individuals are crucial for the fulfilling of God's design, and that their *Lives* have a definite purpose in the spiritual, moral, social and doctrinal itinerary of the faithful. However, he has still to define the correct style for this biblically founded biographical venture:

---

[40]   *Calv. Opp.*, vol. 21, cols 119–20.
[41]   Ibid., vol. 21, col. 120.

I did not want to imitate those who do not so much point up the truth as render it suspect to some by adopting a panegyric or epideictic style. Therefore I have striven to write not as ornately but as truthfully as possible and have preferred to use a simple narrative style.[42]

This apparently routine sentence reveals an increase in methodological awareness since the appearance of the *Discours* and the 1565 *Life*, all the more striking as it is not shared by any of the Protestant biographers we have so far examined. Beza in 1575 consciously departs both from the antique model of biography as a variant of a funeral panegyric and from the model of saints' *Lives*. The *Life* of a reformer, especially one as important as Calvin, should obey its own laws. The 1565 *Life* had set the tone, by stating that it set out Calvin's *Life* in chronological order for the sake of simplicity, but it is Beza who defines the genre in 1575. A Protestant biography is supposed to be truthful in the sense of not containing any admixture of the miraculous or legendary. It is also supposed to be plain, so as to distinguish it from the *Lives* of heroes of pagan antiquity. However, Beza would have been fully aware that he could not escape antique and hagiographical tradition altogether. As the aim of Calvinist biography is to edify, it conserves important elements of Roman imperial biographies by providing a role model or a source of inspiration with which the faithful can identify. It is not for nothing that this third biography of Calvin is also the first Protestant biography to publish a physical description of its subject *à la* Suetonius and in the spirit of Varro's *Imagines*, albeit in a summary form and only after the account of his death. Beza describes him as of medium height, of very pale and dull complexion, with eyes which remained bright until he died, a sign of penetrating intelligence.[43] Beza was obviously in the process of developing a conception of Protestant biography which would crystallise five years later in the *Icones*. In keeping with this conception, he situated his subject in a biographical tradition going back to the Roman Empire, while retaining a distinctive Christian colouring. This entailed a certain standardisation or emblematisation, which is another reason why Beza reduces Colladon's detailed defence of Calvin's character and morals as well as cutting all intimate anecdotes. Although fully aware that Calvin is still being accused of all sorts of excesses including false miracles,[44] Beza feels that no detailed apology is called for. Furthermore, he dismisses the accusations of ambition, cruelty, greed, and so on, as routine. All great men of pagan Antiquity were accused of these and similar crimes, he

---

[42]   Ibid.

[43]   Ibid., vol. 21, col. 170: 'Statura fuit mediocri, colore subpallido et nigricante, oculis ad mortem vsque limpidis.'

[44]   This accusation was first made by W. Lindanus in 1564. In the French version of the work, *Discours en forme de dialogue ou histoire tragique*, it figures on folio 128r. It was taken up by several Catholic writers.

contends. As for true servants of God, they have always been the object of opprobrium. In this third version of his biography, Calvin is raised to the status of a *Hercules christianus*,[45] or a remarkable individual who gave his life over to the service of the church.

Beza's *Life* of Calvin in its final version thus marks the beginning not only of a new style of religious biography, but also of a new perception of the role of individuals in implementing God's plan. Calvin is neither a saint nor an antique hero, but, contrary to what might be expected, given the Protestant concept of predestination, he cannot be reduced to the role of divine instrument either. With his second *Life* of Calvin, Beza put forward the more specific notion of the emblematic Christian hero, which was to propagate itself until well into the twentieth century and which finds its full expression in the Geneva Reformation Monument.

Antoine de la Faye's Life of Beza

Antoine de la Faye's *Life* of Beza provides a perfect illustration of the problems and the tensions attendant upon the Genevan production of *Lives* of reformers. De la Faye (1540–1615), a French religious refugee, obtained the Genevan *bourgeoisie* in 1568. In 1575, he became principal of the *Collège*, and a year later he began to lecture in philosophy at the Academy of Geneva. From 1578 until 1580, he held the chair of philosophy at the academy (which he obtained thanks to Beza's backing) while in charge of two parishes. He became professor of theology in 1581, and was to hold the chair until 1610. He was also rector of the academy from 1580 until 1584. In 1586, he accompanied Beza to the Colloquy of Montbéliard. Apart from a few biblical commentaries, the bulk of his theological production is contained in several volumes of disputation theses. He was also responsible for French translations of Livy and Flavius Josephus.

De la Faye saw himself as Beza's natural successor at the very time when the council was intent on making the Company of Pastors into an instrument of the civil authorities. They did not want to extend to Beza's successors any of the privileges they had accorded to him and to Calvin before him, so that De la Faye's claims encountered scant enthusiasm. He undertook to write Beza's *Life* in January 1606, while occupying the house that had previously been occupied by Calvin and later by Beza. He had not sought the council's permission for writing up his mentor's life, and did not even submit the matter to the Company of Pastors. The council got wind of this (probably via De la Faye's adversary, Jacques Lect),[46] and ordered all copies of the book to be seized, having heard

---

45   *Calv. Opp.*, vol. 21, col. 170.

46   On the attempts of the council to censor Beza's Biography, see Ingeborg Jostock, *La censure négociée: le contrôle du livre à Genève, 1560–1620* (Geneva: Droz, 2007), pp.

that it contained 'des poincts deshonorables et au defunct et à l'Estat', and, what is more, was written in a 'stile bien plat.'[47] Several councillors then read the manuscipt and confirmed that De la Faye 'touche plusieurs poincts qui sont contre l'heureuse memoire du defunct.' More concretely, the council objected to the publication of extracts from Beza's Will, finding two of these unacceptable. The first adverted to the difficulties Beza had encountered in Lausanne because of the *Poemata*. The second concerned the Company of Pastors' absolute authority in all matters to do with the continuity of Calvin's doctrine. On 24 February 1606, the council ordered that the work be suppressed. However, the Company of Pastors objected and found that it would be enough to amend the offending passages, which Jacques Lect then struck out. De la Faye was not to be deterred, and the work was printed by his brother-in-law, Jacques Chouet.[48] On 22 March, the council ordered the imprint to be brought to the Town Hall so that all the copies could be destroyed. At that point, De la Faye offered to have printed at his own expense a sheet correcting the two offending clauses.[49] The council agreed to this provided that all the copies were amended. Naturally, some uncorrected copies survive,[50] which enable us to make comparisons. These turn out to be highly revealing not of hidden aspects of Beza's personality, but of the political climate in Geneva in 1606 and the status of biographies of religious leaders as perceived by the civil authorities. Herewith a synopsis of the uncorrected and corrected passages in clauses 2 and 7 of Beza's Will:

> Uncorrected copy: p. 73, clause 2: 'Quod Lausannae peste correptus grauissimisque appetitus calumniis, ab vtraque lue, per Dei misericordiam liberatus sit'. Cf. Beza's Will: in *Registres de la Compagnie des Pasteurs*, vol. 9, p. 133: 'Durant lequel temps il m'a préservé en la maladie de peste et en plusieurs épreuves de calomnies et querelles.' (Cf. ibid. for another copy of the Will, which reads erroneously: 'Et esquelles' instead of 'querelles'.) Corrected copy: p. 73, clause 2: 'Quod Lausannae peste corruptus, per Dei misericordiam liberatus sit.'[51]

262–7, and literature cited ibid. Jostock attributes the entire censorship scandal to the enmity between Lect and De la Faye, which is probably an oversimplification.

[47]   Cf. ibid., p. 263.

[48]   Cf. ibid., p. 264.

[49]   Cf. ibid., pp. 263–7.

[50]   *De vita et obitu clariss. viri, D. Theodori Bezae Vezelii, Ecclesiastae et Sacrarum literarum Professoris, Genevae, 'hypomnêmation'* / *autore Antonio Fayo* (Geneuae: apud Jacobum Chouet, 1606). Hereafter: De la Faye. Geneva's Bibliothèque publique et universitaire holds one of these under the shelfmark MD 707 (2). Another copy is held by the Geneva Musée historique de la Réformation (MHR Ba 2a).

[51]   De la Faye, uncorrected copy (Geneva: MHR: Ba 2a), p. 73: 'Sick of the plague when in Lausanne and attacked by most serious calumnies, he was liberated from both these scourges by God's mercy.' French version in *Registres de la Compagnie des Pasteurs de Genève* (hereafter: *RCP*), ed. R. Kingdon, J. F. Bergier *et al.* (Geneva: Droz, 1962– [continuing]), vol. 9, ed. M. Campagnolo, M. Louis-Courvoisier and G. Cahier (Geneva: Droz, 1989), p. 133: 'During which time He saved me from the plague and from undergoing several trials on

Uncorrected copy: p. 73, clause 7: 'Hortatur ad mutuam concordiam <u>monetque</u>
<u>vt neque in</u> doctrina <u>neque in disciplina quicquam mutari aut nouari sinant</u>, sed
constanter retineant ea quae sancto et sano iudicio a nunquam satis laudato D.
Caluino, ex S. Dei Verbo deprompta sunt instituta.' Cf. Beza's Will in *RCP*,
vol.9, p. 134: 'Dieu leur veuille accroistre ses grandes graces de plus en plus
pour estre bien unys, tant en la doctrine receuë en ceste Eglize, qu'en la discipline
d'icelle, se souvenants non seulement ce que eux et moy ont receu, mais de ces
grands personnages desquels nous l'avons receu, et singulierement de ce grand
serviteur de Dieu, feu Monsieur Jean Calvin, de la sagesse, pieté, erudition
et prudence duquel ce sera bien assez s'ilz peuvent estre bons imitateurs ...'.
Corrected copy: p. 73, clause 7: 'Hortatur ad mutuam concordiam monetque
vt doctrinam ac disciplinam aliaque quae sancto et sano iudicio et nunquam
satis laudato D. Caluino, ex S. Dei Verbo deprompta, sunt instituta, sancte
tueantur ac retineant.'[52]

In fact, the changes are minimal.[53] In clause 2, we can see that De la Faye
was made to falsify Beza's own words. In clause 7, however, it is plain
that he was compelled to remove the phrase he had put in himself: '[Beza]
urges them to agree among themselves and *advises them to disallow any
changes or innovations in teaching and in church discipline.*' Beza's Will
read: '[Beza urges them] to remain united in the doctrine they received
from this Church and in ecclesiastical discipline, remembering not only
what they received but also and especially the great servant of God, John
Calvin, from whom they received it.' De la Faye's use of Beza's Will was
at once too candid (he referred to a shameful incident in Beza's past which
the council judged unfit for public reading) and too slanted (it was plain to
the council that our biographer was attempting to use Beza's purportedly
last words to secure his own elevation to the role of *antistes* of the Genevan
Church). Just as the council was in the process of gaining more power over
the church, there was no question of the syndics allowing an interpolation

---

account of calumnies and accusations.' De la Faye, of *De vita et obitu* corrected copy (MHR
Ba 2), p. 173: 'Sick of the plague he was liberated by God's mercy.'

[52]   De la Faye, uncorrected copy (MHR: Ba 2a), p. 73: 'He exhorts them to agree among
themselves and advises them not to allow any changes or innovations in doctrine or discipline
but to keep instead to what was instituted by (the highly venerable) Calvin's holy and sound
judgement on the basis of God's Word.' French version in *RCP*, vol. 9, p. 134: 'may God grant
them his grace more and more generously if they remain united in the doctrine they received
in this church and in its discipline, remembering not only what they and I have received but
also of the great men from whom we received it, and especially remembering the late Master
John Calvin; whose wisdom, piety, learning and prudence they will do well to imitate exactly
if they can.' De la Faye, of *De vita et obitu* corrected copy (MHR Ba 2), p. 173: 'He exhorts
them to agree among themselves and advises them to keep to the doctrine and discipline that
was instituted by (the highly venerable) Calvin's holy and sound judgement on the basis of
God's Word.'

[53]   I have compared the uncorrected copy held by Geneva's Musée historique de la
Réformation (MHR Ba 2a) with a corrected copy (shelfmark: MHR Ba 2). See notes 51 and
52 above.

in Beza's Will suggesting that the model which gave more autonomy to the church was to remain in place.

The incident shows that in early seventeenth-century Geneva, a biography of a reformer such as Beza was a public, political document, and its contents were not subject to the criteria of historical accuracy. Furthermore, it shows the importance of the reformer's Will as a document declaring not so much personal intentions as dictating the public and ecclesiastical order to be kept after his death. Thirdly, it shows that a reformer such as Calvin or Beza was not just a pious individual to be remembered as an example, but a public symbol and a guarantee of continuity within the church and state. The Geneva Council's accusations of inaccuracy or forgery are interesting because they show that the magistrates and the biographer had exactly the same conception of what a biography of Beza should be. Where the two differed was the nature of the political and church order that Beza's biography should commemorate, as well as the status of the reformer's Will with its mention of his 'profane' past. Be that as it may, the council prevailed. Significantly, the French version by Pierre Solomeau of De la Faye's *Life* of Beza, published in 1610,[54] omitted the extracts from the Will.

As regards the literary criteria of what a reformer's biography should be, those which Beza himself set in his final *Life* of Calvin had become the accepted method by the time Antoine de la Faye came to write his *Life* in 1606. However, precisely in Beza's case, the *Hercules christianus* model posed problems, as De la Faye was well aware. Given the opprobrium attached to Beza's early epigrams, pagan references of any sort had to be kept to a minimum. In his preamble to the Latin *Vita*, De la Faye sets out his method very clearly. Although very familiar with the Catholic attacks on Beza's personal morality, he does not see his venture primarily as an attempt to clear Beza's reputation. More importantly, he is intent to stress that he does not aim to write a funeral panegyric after the manner of antique writers, who listened to what others were saying about the deceased and set down rumours or suppositions as if they were the truth. Such fables were in his view far too easily believed, and this did untold harm to the accuracy of our knowledge of both public and private affairs.[55] De la Faye knows that Beza despised this sort of airy nonsense when alive, so it is neither necessary nor fitting to honour his memory in this way. He thus

---

[54]   *Brief Discours de la vie et mort de M. Theodore de Beze de Vezelay, personnage très renommé. Pasteur et professeur des sainctes lettres à Geneve. Avec le catalogue des livres qu'il a composez* (Genève, Jean Cartel, 1610).

[55]   De la Faye, p. 6: 'Nec vero nobis propositum est hoc loco panegyricum sermonem stylo ad id elaborato componere vt Bezae encomia in aperto ponamus, quae nunquam in obscuro fuere. Mos erat ille veterum quorundam, magna ex parte alienis auribus seruientium et incerta pro certis plerumque affirmantium, quae quidem ab ipsis prodita et ab aliis credita, dici non potest quantum vulnus historiae, siue priuatae siue publicae, iam olim intulerint et etiamnum hodie inferant.'

deliberately distances himself from the Greek way of writing biographies even more explicitly than Beza had in 1575. According to De la Faye, Hebrews, Persians, Chaldeans and Egyptians entrusted all significant writing to the most serious and learned men, who would scrupulously respect the truth. As for the Greeks, those writing more for pleasure than in the name of truth have been rightly exposed as unreliable.[56]

As well as distancing himself from the Greek panegyric style of writing biography, De la Faye thus established new criteria for a biography of a model Protestant individual:

> It is of great importance for the common good of the human society to accord pride of place in the public theatre of memory and in the sanctuary of reputation to those who put above all else their love of God, the church and the commonweal, and who for their zeal deserve the best from all good men. For it is thus that they survive in living memory and receive and gather on earth a testimony of their piety and a small reward for their virtue (not that they ever sought it), a sort of harvest from the seed of their labours. And all the while they are enjoying the eternal and blessed harvest in the heavens with God. Not forgetting that they thus offer a gracious challenge to those who remain, spurring them on to imitate them. They also help blunt the evil words and the sharp stings of slanderers. For it is possible to learn piety from the dead when the servants of God who have led a praiseworthy life and whose morals are saintly, converse with their posterity, and – all malice (which tends to flourish among the living) gone – their virtue, perceived by all from high up, beckons to us and incites us to tread the same path as they so that we may get to where they got to.
>
> For the true and not the passing glory is that which leads from God as centre and is reflected back to God, its centre, and rests in Him ....[57]

De la Faye takes Beza's theory of Protestant biography a step further, and defines a Protestant saint as one who is a public figure, not an individual (famous or obscure) recognised after his death via his miracles and elevated to the status of sainthood by a papal decree or canonisation. He also insists, as Beza had in 1575, that one of the characteristic features of the genre I shall call 'lives of exceptional Calvinist individuals' is its strict respect of truth. What are his criteria for truth? As he defines them, a true biographical narrative is one that allows us to admire the gifts of God in a given individual without any human admixture. It is this that particularly distinguishes Christian Calvinist biographies from pagan ones. A Christian

---

[56]   Ibid., pp. 6–7: 'Atque in huiusmodi rebus laudabilis et imitanda inprimis videtur Hebraeorum sapientia, qui rerum insignium describendarum prouinciam demandabant lectissimis grauissimisque viris quos veri obseruantissimos esse sibi persuadebant. Idem fuit institutum Persarum, Chaldaeorum et Aegyptiorum. Graecorum autem nonnullorum ad voluptatem potius quam ad veritatem scribentium iampridem traducta est nimis lubrica fides.'
[57]   Ibid., p. 7.

biography merits the appellation if, and only if, it sets out to show God's workings through a person and aims to instruct rather than please. Phrased like this, De la Faye's theory implicitly admits that the biographer can criticise or at least take into account his hero's failings, as these by definition cannot be of divine origin. The same theory automatically excludes all anecdotes such as the ones that Colladon introduced into the 1565 *Life* of Calvin. It differs from the Lutheran concept of religious biography by placing emphasis on God's workings as opposed to the instrumentality of the human individual. It also differs from the Zurich *Lives* of the period by paying rather less detailed attention to the value of religious biography as a civic or an educational model.

De la Faye continues:

> Let us therefore talk about Theodore Beza in such a way that we can admire and worship the gifts that God made manifest through him ... A discourse which is commendable is that which, content with a bare and simple account of facts, sets out to be useful rather than agreeable. In accord with its purpose, it does not understate or exaggerate or make things seem worse than they are. With this foundation laid, the *Life* of that excellent man Theodore Beza shall be fittingly superposed on it. And it is the Almighty God, worshipped by Beza with mouth and pen in his lifetime, who, with Beza dead, shall be the subject of this account rather than Beza himself.[58]

He thus legitimises and confirms Beza's own theory regarding the commemoration of remarkable pious individuals, who held public office, in the form of *Lives*. They do not intercede with God for those who are left behind. They are not to be prayed to, and they never performed any miracles or had any posthumous miracles associated with them. However, their activity for God, the church and the republic, coupled with their saintly morals, reveals what God expects from mankind. They deserve glory because of this. Theocentric though this conception of Calvinist biography is, it does not mark, any more than Beza's *Life* of Calvin, a complete break with antique biography or hagiography. Although De la Faye is by no means averse to using documents such as letters, prefaces, Wills, and so on, he does not submit them to a critical assessment, as what matters is not the individual but his place in God's purpose.

Large portions of the chronological year-by-year *Life* deal with Beza's services to the church. De la Faye devotes a lot of attention to the Colloquy of Poissy, to Beza's struggles and writings against heretics, his relationship

---

[58]   Ibid., p. 8: '... De Theodoro Beza ita loquamur vt Dei in ipso dona potissimum demiremur et osculemur ... Illa ratio et oratio commendabilis videtur et est, quae nuda et simplici rerum expositione contenta, prodesse magis quam placere quaerat, quaeque rebus ipsis non impar, eas dicendo neque auget, neque minuit, neque deterit. Hoc fundamento posito, non absone superstruetur ornatissimi viri domini Theodori Bezae vita, Deusque optimus maximus (quem vita, ore et calamo dum potuit Beza laudauit) in Beza mortuo potius quam Beza ipse nobis depraedicabitur.'

with key church and political figures abroad, and others. He also uses the pretext of a biography to give a very careful and detailed exposition of Beza's doctrine of key theological issues such as the Eucharist. An account of the reformer's writings is interwoven with the narrative; there is no separate catalogue. More tellingly, perhaps, there is no section devoted to exaggerated praise of Beza's private morality. In fact, personal or anecdotal interjections are few and far between. Beza blends with the religious events of his time. In contrast with Melanchthon's *Life* of Luther, De la Faye does not give his role eschatological overtones or consider it prophetic. Beza has not been raised by God to reply to abuses that have been undermining the church since the time of the Apostles. He has, however, been elected to manage some of the Almighty's causes at a particular moment in history.

With that proviso in mind, it is obvious that Beza's early epigrams, which earned him the reputation of a sexual deviant or a licentious man of the world among his Catholic adversaries, are something of an embarrassment to De la Faye. In keeping with his minimalist view of human powers, he does not pretend, however, that Beza never wrote them, but insists that the memory of this human error of youth is artificially kept alive by Beza's adversaries:

> Imitating not so much the morality as the style of Catullus and Ovid, he published some epigrams which he later found too licentious. And he himself was the first to condemn them shortly afterwards and to conceive a great dislike of them. And despite this they live on due to a contrary tendency which functions with regard to them quite unlike with regard to his other works. For whereas religious adversaries usually declare war on their adversaries' works and go to great lengths to suppress them, a pertinacious and inextinguishable flame of hatred for their author prolongs the life of these epigrams. The poems that Beza himself wanted buried and extinct, they still raise from the dust. Again and again in their wickedness they make them publicly available by republishing them as often as they can. And what do they achieve by this *kakoetheia*? Nothing other than to show that they deserve the wrath of God, while demonstrating that Beza was the most worthy of their goodwill, love and tolerance. For he made the heavenly angels happy after transforming for the better the Muse of his youth and earnestly turning her to the worship of God.[59]

He expressly avoids giving any details of the controversy surrounding the *Juuenilia*, which, as we shall see, were exaggerated and embroidered upon, notably by Bolsec, to provide the staple of Catholic accusations.

Be that as it may, the very existence of the epigrams makes it impossible for De la Faye to portray Calvin's successor as a model of chastity. Nor does he wish to do so. In contrast with Beza, who was keen not to say anything about Calvin that might be construed as damaging, our biographer has no hesitations about going into detail with regard to Beza's worldly lifestyle prior to his conversion, which made even the future reformer himself feel

59   Ibid., pp. 9–10.

that he was falling into the snares of Satan.[60] While stressing that his hero always hated vice, De la Faye freely admits that he did spend a part of his youth in pursuit of pleasure, ambition, and so on.[61] He does nothing to conceal Beza's secret marriage, concluded partly 'so that he would not be vanquished by his youthful desires and partly to avoid being deprived of ecclesiastical benefices.' He adds that the marriage (to Claudine Denosse), if made public, would have meant abandoning all the ecclesiastical benefices, which Beza had received from his uncle Nicholas, the prior of Saint-Éloi-lès-Longjumeau.[62] Most of his account is copied word for word from Beza's Latin preface (addressed to Melchior Volmar) to his *Confession of faith* of 1560,[63] the one major difference being that De la Faye sees the converted Beza as a saint in the sense of someone exempt from any criticisms or reservations. Thus, from 1548 onwards, Beza begins a new career as a man who points to God's workings on this earth. De la Faye hastens to assure his readers that the seeds were there already prior to the final conversion. His secret union with Claudine Denosse was accompanied by a solemn promise of public confirmation and a vow to renounce his status of cleric.[64] And, he announces proudly, Beza did punctiliously keep both solemn promises,[65] although not until after his conversion at the moment of grave illness. Moreover, the conversion was in no way due to Beza, at least according to our biographer. It was the Lord in person who called Beza back to the straight and narrow by sending the illness which caused him to beg forgiveness and to devote himself to God's service with all his being. Still, according to De la Faye, it was the same illness that brought

---

[60]   Ibid., p. 10: 'Iuuentute autem florens, otio, pecunia rebusque aliis omnibus potius quam bono consilio abundans, sensit a Satana sibi circumiici infinitas tendiculas.'

[61]   Ibid., pp. 10–11: 'Quanquam enim vitia odisset et natura abhorreret ab eorum consortio, in quibus vel improbitatis, vel pestiferas labes vel minimum agnoscebat, bonas tamen horas in rebus ludicris collocabat. Nam et voluptatum illecebris et ambitiosula gloriae dulcedine quam ex Epigrammatum suorum editione erat adeptus … honorumque amplissimorum spe irretitus, aliquandiu detinebatur.'

[62]   Ibid., p. 10: '… quos tamen omnes alter patruus (nam prior ille mortuus erat) abbas Frigidimontanus studio et amore in illum propenso facile superabat. Hic enim illum in abbatia illa cuius reditus annuus ad coronatos quinquies mille aestimabatur, successorem designabat, praeter duo beneficia quibus Beza, licet talium rerum inscitus et ignarus, oneratus fuerat.' Ibid, p. 11: 'Id ita faciebat partim ne caeteros offenderet, partim quod a scelerata illa pecunia, quam ex sacerdotiis illis percipiebat non satis posset adhuc absterreri.'

[63]   *Correspondance de Bèze*, vol. 3, pp. 46–7. See also Alain Dufour, 'Théodore de Bèze', in Académie des inscriptions et Belles-Lettres (ed.), *Histoire littéraire de la France, vol. 42* (Paris: De Boccard, 2002), pp. 315–470, esp. pp. 322–3.

[64]   De la Faye, p. 11: 'Sponsalibus tamen addita est expressa promissio fore vt illam primo quoque tempore, perruptis impedimentis omnibus in ecclesiam Dei abduceret et palam cum ea matrimonium confirmaret, itemque vt interea temporis nullo ex sacris illis papisticis ordinibus initiaretur.'

[65]   Ibid.: 'Vtrumque autem postea sancte praestitit.'

about true health.[66] In keeping with the biblical model, once recovered, Beza left his homeland, his parents and his friends (but not his wife, whom he married openly in Geneva in 1548) in order to follow Christ.[67]

De la Faye's reliance on autobiography as source for biography and his emphasis on Beza's services to the church call to mind Possidius' *Life* of Augustine. Although De la Faye's work cannot be said to be a carbon copy of it, he is the only one of the biographers we are considering here who openly mentions Possidius in his very detailed account of Beza's death. The way he mentions Possidius' account suggests that it was recited as a deathbed consolation to the reformer, who was apparently seen as a latter-day Augustine. What is more, it shows that De la Faye knew not only Possidius' *Life* of Augustine, but also Paulinus' *Life* of Ambrose. This is what he says:

> On that day, when I Antoine de la Faye went to visit him together with the very honourable doctor Perrot (it was Saturday, 12th October), he mentioned the immensity of God's mercy imparted through Jesus Christ. Whereupon I recited this verse from Psalm 130[3]: 'if thou, Lord, should keep account of sins, who, oh Lord, could hold up his head?' He could not hear what I said and asked me to repeat it. I then expounded these words at greater length more loudly and added this saying of Ambrose as cited by Possidius in his *Life* of Augustine: 'there is no reason to be ashamed for the way we have lived for our Lord is good.' And Dr Perrot drawing attention to men's unpraiseworthy desire for staying alive cited the following words from Possidius: 'you are afraid to suffer; you do not want to die. What is to be done with you?'[68]

The two quotations from Possidius[69] and the allusion to Ambrose suggest regular use among Genevan ministers of the time not only of the penitential Psalms, but also of exemplars from the past as a source of consolation and edification. While *Lives* of the saints were severely condemned, *Lives* of bishops of the Early Church were obviously accepted and used.

---

[66]   Ibid., p. 12: '... nondum tamen poterat ex tam perplexis ambagibus et oppositis obstaculis sese extricare. Ecce vero dum ita anxius animi in dubio versatur, illum a deuio itinere in rectum reuocat Dominus. Morbum enim grauissimum, velut sui iudicii nuntium et apparitorem mittit adeo vt pene de vita desperaret ... cum lachrymis veniam petit votumque illud de vero Dei cultu palam amplectendo renouat totum denique se illi consecrat. Sicque factum est vt morbus ille verae sanitatis illi principium attulerit. '

[67]   Ibid., p. 12: 'Simul atque igitur lectum relinquere licuit, abruptis omnibus vinculis, sarcinulis compositis, patriam, parentes, amicos semel deserit vt Christum sequeretur seque in voluntarium exilium cum sua coniuge recipit Geneuam, anno 1548, nono Kal.Nou. Ibi primum palam in ecclesia solenni inter Christianos ritu matrimonium celebrauit et sedem fixit.'

[68]   Ibid. pp. 65–6.

[69]   See *Vite dei Santi*, ed. Mohrmann, vol. 3: *Vita Augustini* 27, 7, p. 200: 'non sic vixi vt me pudeat inter vos viuere, sed nec mori timeo quia bonum Dominum habemus.' The same saying is put into the mouth of Ambrose by his biographer, Paulinus of Milan. See *Vite dei Santi*, ed. Mohrmann, vol. 3: *Vita Ambrosii* 45, 2, p. 112. The second quotation is to be found in *Vita Augustini* 27, 11, p. 202, where it is cited by Possidius as a phrase from Cyprian (= *De mortalitate*, 19).

Naturally, in contrast with Possidius, De la Faye does not credit Beza with any miraculous actions. However, he does rather undo the sobriety of his account by evoking the eclipse of the sun, which accompanied Beza's last hours.[70] Its biblical connotations would have been plain for all to see!

Like Beza in the 1575 version of his *Life* of Calvin, De la Faye gives a physical description of his subject which he appends to the account of his death. The reason for including the description is theological and has nothing to do with the wish to liven up the account or the desire for exhaustivity. This is how he describes Beza:

> Beza was of sturdy build, of striking good looks and of such sound health that he often said he did not know what a headache was. He had great intelligence, accurate judgement and a particularly retentive memory. He was extremely eloquent and second to none when it came to affability and liking for his fellow men, so much so that, because of these gifts, to which was added longevity (although they were all inferior to his excellent doctrine and piety), some called him a phoenix of his age.[71]

This shows the adversaries of the Reformation that good health and physique do not tell us anything about a given individual's relationship to God and to divine providence. De la Faye points out not unjustly that they used Calvin's frail health and daily physical pain as proof of God's hostility to him. Now what will they say about Calvin's successor and implementer of his doctrines, who never had a day's illness in his life?[72] A brief vindication of Beza and the paraphrase of portions of his Will, 'a mirror of his life', close the biography. Apart from the subversive elements we have already discussed, the Will evokes Beza's wish to be buried in the public cemetery which, De la Faye notes, was disobeyed by the civil authorities *propter grauissimas rationes politicas*.[73]

De la Faye has thus erected a reformed exemplar. Once again in contrast with Luther, Beza is not assigned a place in the eschatological order. Nor is he a Christian Hercules, in contrast to Beza's Calvin. De la Faye's *Life* is a devotional guidebook. It also makes the point already made more timidly by Beza's and Colladon's *Lives* of Calvin: God can and does use remarkable individuals to fulfil His purpose. Most importantly, however,

---

[70]   De la Faye, p. 65: 'illo die eclipsis erat solis eiusque valetudo aliquantum immutari in deterius deprehensa est adeo vt de eo actum domestici putarent. Adfuere praesto omnes et piis colloquutionibus per horas aliquot habitis precibusque ardentissime a Iohanne Pinaldo conceptis gratiae Dei commendatus est.'

[71]   Ibid., p. 67: 'Fuit Beza statura corporis quadrata, forma conspicuus, valetudine firma adeo vt quid esset capite dolere se nescire saepe diceret; ingenio summo, iudicio accurato, memoria tenacissima, facundia singulari, affabilitate et comitate nulli secundus, adeo vt propter commemoratas dotes, adiuncta illis vitae longaeuitate (quae tamen omnia erant inferiora summa doctrina et pietate) quidam vocarent Bezam aetatis suae phoenicem.'

[72]   Ibid.

[73]   Ibid., pp. 72–4.

De la Faye lays down the criteria for Protestant sainthood as applicable to individuals holding a public function in the church, chosen by God at a particular time to fulfil a particular part of the divine purpose. De la Faye was in fundamental agreement with the council about the importance of publishing *Lives* of men of God. Where differences arose was in their respective conceptions of what God's plan was.

Teissier's Edition of Lives *of Calvin and Beza in 1681*

Antoine Teissier's French translation[74] of Beza's second (1575) *Life* of Calvin and his adaptation of De la Faye's *Life* of Beza is an important historical document attesting a reuse of these *Lives* in a context very different to the one for which they were initially intended. Teissier's choice of translating Beza's 1575 *Life* of Calvin in preference to reprinting the 1564 *Discours* and the changes he makes to De la Faye have nothing accidental about them, and tell us much about the reception of sixteenth-century biographies by an author who had claims to being an official historian of French Protestantism, whose literary production dealt to a large extent with biographical writings and whose concordism was at the antipodes of Calvin's and Beza's theological stance.[75]

Who was Antoine Teissier? Born in 1632 in Montpellier, in a family which originally came from Nîmes, he studied classics at Lunel and Orange. Wanting to become a minister, he went on to Nîmes and then to the Academies of Montauban and Saumur. However, he never finished his training, apparently on grounds of ill health, and decided to become a lawyer. He obtained his doctorate from Bourges, but quickly abandoned his legal career in favour of literary endeavours. In 1682, he co-founded the Nîmes Academy of Belles-Lettres. On the revocation of the Edict of Nantes, he took refuge abroad, stopping off in Geneva for a few days prior to settling in Zurich, where he remained (barring the years 1689 and 1690, when he was in Berne as editor of a French newsletter) until 1692 living off his writing as best he could with the support of the city council. In 1692, he arrived in Brandenburg, with a letter of recommendation from the Zurich Council, where he obtained the post of the official historian and later tutor to the electors of Prussia. He died in Berlin in 1715. His literary production consists of translations from Greek and Latin, many

---

[74]   The work appeared without the translator's name: *Les Vies de Jean Calvin et de Théodore de Bèze mises en françois* (Geneve, Jean Herman Widerhold, 1681) (Hereafter: Teissier). Eugène and Emile Haag attribute it to Teissier quite unequivocally on the basis of external evidence. See *La France protestante*, eds Eugène and Émile Haag, 10 vols (Paris: Joël Cherbuliez, 1846–59), vol. 9 (hereafter: Haag, vol. 9), col. 349.

[75]   In 1687, he published the *Traité de la concorde ecclésiastique des Protestants dans lequel on fait voir que la différence des sentimens qu'il peut y avoir entre eux ne doit point empêcher leur réunion* (Amsterdam [Geneva], 1687).

of biographies.[76] Apart from the *Lives* of Calvin and Beza by Beza and De la Faye, he translated, among other works, the *Epistle of Clement to the Corinthians*,[77] the *Life* of Galeas Caraccioli and the *Account of the death of Francesco Spiera*,[78] selected letters of Calvin,[79] and the *Lives* of the electors of Brandenburg (from the Latin of Cernitius).[80] Among his other contributions to the biographical genre, it is worth singling out the *Abrégé de la vie de divers princes illustres avec des refléxions historiques sur leurs actions*.[81] The work consists of short accounts of lives of princes of Antiquity such as Scipio, Tamburlane and others, some real and some fictitious, intended to serve as an example to the elector and his male offspring. Another work revealing of Teissier's interests is his *Catalogus auctorum qui librorum catalogos, indices, bibliothecas, virorum litteratorum elogia, vitas aut orationes funebres scriptis consignarunt*, which appeared in Geneva in 1686. Based on Labbe's *Bibliotheca bibliothecarum*, it adds 1700 entries to Labbe's 800.

In a word, Teissier was a Protestant man of Letters who had done some theology. Already before migrating to Prussia he had come under the influence of Samuel Pufendorf's theory that a civil government in any given country can authorise the coexistence of two religions so that the adherents of each can coexist peacefully in a civil society. He translated several of Pufendorf's treatises into French before settling in Brandenburg.[82] His convictions influenced his presentation and adaptation of the *Lives* of Calvin and Beza, as we are about to see.

His literary production falls into two main categories: biography and translation from Greek and Latin into French of historical and legal treatises, ancient and contemporary. After the revocation of the Edict of Nantes, his readership was composed of (fairly) cultivated French religious refugees, who wanted to keep intact the memory of the Reformation, but also German princes whom he taught in the latter part of his life. His translation/adaptation of the *Lives* of Calvin and Beza dates from the period just preceding the Revocation, when Louis XIV was taking an increasing number of measures against French Protestants.[83] The *Lives*

---

[76]   See Haag, vol. 9, cols 348–50.

[77]   *Epître de S. Clément aux Corinthiens* (Avignon, 1685).

[78]   *Vie de Galéas Caracciol, mise en françois et Hist. de la mort horrible de François Spierre* (Lyon, 1681). Published under the pen-name of Sieur de Lestan.

[79]   *Lettres choisies de Calvin* (Berlin, 1702).

[80]   *Les Vies des électeurs de Brandenbourg* (Berlin, 1707).

[81]   Published in Amsterdam, 1710.

[82]   For a not very accurate list of Pufendorf's works translated by Teissier, see Haag, vol. 9, col. 350. For Pufendorf's religious thought, see Detlef Döring, *Pufendorf-Studien: Beiträge zur Biographie Samuel von Pufendorfs und seine Entwicklung als Historiker und theologischer Schriftsteller* (Berlin: Duncker & Humblot, 1992).

[83]   On this, see for example Olivier Fatio and Louise Martin, 'L'Église de Genève et la Révocation de l'Édit de Nantes', in Société d'Histoire et d'Archéologie de Genève (ed.),

were thus intended to edify, console and incite to steadfastness in the face of persecution, and to prevent an increasing number of conversions to Catholicism. (Teisssier himself, it must be remembered, refused a lucrative position in France in 1690, preferring to remain a poor Protestant exile in Zurich.[84]) What, in those circumstances, were Teissier's aesthetic and doctrinal criteria for what a reformer's biography should be?

His preface is quite unequivocal. He thinks that Calvin and Beza were the greatest luminaries of the Reformed Church, whom God used to promulgate His plan to spread the light of the Gospel in France. He therefore finds it surprising that the two reformers' *Lives* have not been translated into French. As there is no doubt that their virtue and their knowledge were quite out of the ordinary, the memory of everything they did could not but profit every pious soul.[85] In the Plutarchan tradition, Teissier sees biography as a *peinture*;[86] in this instance, pictures or portraits to be exhibited especially in France, valuable both as historical documents and as models of piety.[87] Teissier finds two characteristics common to the two reformers that perfectly answer his purpose: firstly, their self-denying stand for truth, and secondly their status of religious refugees. And he concludes: 'Just as in their lifetime they were miraculously successful in their efforts to rebuild the walls of the heavenly Jerusalem, perhaps, after their death, the memory of their strength and virtue will be able to stop the city from falling into total ruin.'[88] This, he says, is the aim of his literary endeavour.[89] As the original *Lives* are extant in Latin only, he wants to make them available to a wider public. However, he is quite explicit that not any *Life* will do. Although aware that Beza's 1564 *Discours* on Calvin is available in French, he explicitly voices a preference for the *Vita* of 1575.

Genève au temps de la Révocation de l'Édit de Nantes 1680–1705 (Mémoires et documents publiés par la Société d'Histoire et d'Archéologie de Genève) (Geneva: Droz; and Paris: Champion, 1985), vol. 50, pp. 164–91.

[84]   Haag, vol. 9, col. 349.

[85]   Teissier, fol. *2r.–v.

[86]   Ibid., fol. *3r.

[87]   Ibid., fols *3v.–*4r.

[88]   Ibid., fols * 4v.–*5v.: 'Veuille ce Dieu miséricordieux qui est adoré parmi nous avec tant de pureté, faire cesser entierement ces désertions scan/*5r./daleuses qui causent une si vive douleur à son Eglise et inspirer à tous les membres qui la composent une constance si invincible, qu'ils ayent la force de resister à tous les efforts, que le monde pourra faire pour les attirer à soy. On a crû que rien n'estoit plus propre à leur faire concevoir ce généreux dessein que de leur représenter la vertu héroïque de Calvin et de Bèze, qui tous deux renoncerent avec plaisir à /*5v./ toutes les douceurs de leur patrie et à tous les avantages qu'elle leur offroit, pour suiure Jésus-Christ qui les appelloit aux souffrances et aux tribulations. Et comme pendant leur vie ils travaillèrent avec un miraculeux succès, à rebâtir les murailles de la céleste Jérusalem, peut-être qu'après leur mort la mémoire de leur vertu sera capable d'empécher qu'elles ne tombent en une entière ruine.'

[89]   Ibid., fols *5v.–*6r.: 'Voilà le principal but /*6r./ que l'on s'est proposé, en mettant au jour les vies de ces grands hommes.'

As regards De la Faye's *Life* of Beza, Teissier feels that it can be made available to the general public only after some changes, suppressions and additions. What is more, he considers the polemical style of both the *Lives* as out of keeping with the spirit of his time. He explains:

> We took the liberty of toning down certain expressions which Beza and De la Faye used because we noticed that they did not conform to the taste of our age and that they could shock persons of contrary belief, for whom we have great esteem and respect out of duty and inclination.[90]

Times had changed since 1606! While it was obviously still acceptable for a Protestant writer to present Calvin and Beza as the greatest luminaries of the Protestant Church, it would not do to present them as the scourge of all those who happened to disagree with their doctrine.

This is also why Teissier would not reproduce Beza's 1564 *Life* of Calvin. Although it was widely known in its French version, it was out of keeping with the spirit of the times and so likely to do more harm than good. Teissier naturally does not say so in so many words. He asserts instead that the *Discours* of 1564 is somewhat careless, unworthy of the subject-matter, and that it is therefore legitimate to claim that there is no *Life* of Calvin in French. Beza was aware of it himself, he adds, which is why he wrote another *Life* in 1575, which, unlike the *Discours*, was accurate or *accurate conscripta*.[91] Teissier does not mention the 1565 *Life*. This could be because he has no knowledge of it, or because he finds its eschatological overtones and anecdotal style even less in keeping with the spirit of his age (or, rather, with his own convictions) than the *Discours*. Be that as it may, at no point does he suggest that Beza was the author of any *Life* of Calvin other than the *Discours* and the 1575 *Life*, which in Teissier's view required only minor changes to make it publishable. De la Faye's *Life* of Beza required rather more editing. Noting that De la Faye's style was verbose and that he devoted far too much space to relating various insignificant (*peu considérables*) events in Beza's life, Teissier explains that he cut out all the speeches (*discours*) that he found to be unnecessary and all the details that he found unworthy (*indignes*) of figuring in the reformer's biography. For these he substituted summaries of Beza's first speech at the Colloquy of Poissy and of the compliment he paid to King Henry IV on the promulgation of the Edict of Nantes.[92]

---

[90]   Ibid., fol. *7r.: 'L'on a encore pris la liberté d'adoucir certains termes dont Bèze et de la Faye se sont servis, parce qu'on s'est persuadé qu'ils ne seroient pas au goût de nôtre siècle et qu'ils pourroient choquer les personnes d'une contraire créance, pour qui nôtre devoir et nôtre inclination nous obligent d'avoir beaucoup d'égard et de respet.'

[91]   Ibid., fols *7v.–*8v.

[92]   For the best modern succinct account of both Beza's speech and of his reconciliation with Henry IV, see Dufour, 'Théodore de Bèze', pp. 362–6 and 461–2.

It is difficult to say whether Teissier had any knowledge of the controversy over De la Faye's *Life* of Beza, which preceded its appearance in 1606. He does not include the problematic extracts from Beza's Will, but this could simply be due to the fact that he had no knowledge of the uncensored version of the work. Be that as it may, Teissier sets out to purify Beza's *Life* of all polemical elements, and to make him into a symbol of religious unity. His interpolation of the summary of the reformer's first speech at the Colloquy of Poissy and of his reaction to the promulgation of the Edict of Nantes was not due to an arbitrary whim on Teissier's part. At the time when he was writing, French Protestantism was threatened by the ecclesiastical policy of Louis XIV, to which both the incidents constituted a perfect counterpoint, while retaining the conciliatory 'Pufendorfian' perspective. Thus Beza's first speech at the Colloquy of Poissy was intended to show that the points of discord between Catholics and Protestants were surmountable, and that Protestants were faithful and obedient subjects of the Crown. Teissier insists on these points, knowing that they would meet the approval of the French Catholic sovereign:

> Then, having shown the points of agreement and discord between us and the Roman Catholics, he explained and proved the chief articles of our faith in a manner suited to the place and the occasion. And above all, he was intent on showing that our religion teaches us the respect and obedience which is due to kings and sovereigns in general and that those who rebel against their prince have no enemies more ferocious than we.[93]

By contrast, Teissier leaves out entirely De la Faye's discussion of the publication of *De officio pii viri* and its possible attribution to François Bauduin. He also cuts his account of the controversy between Bauduin and the Genevan ministers.[94] Still in the same spirit, he leaves out De la Faye's account of the rumour 'put about in 1597 by Jesuits who know no shame' that Beza was dead after having reconverted to Catholicism.[95]

As for Beza's reconciliation with Henry IV, this is how Teissier, following Jacob Spon's *Histoire de Genève*,[96] describes the meeting between the two men at L'Eluiset:

> Indeed, King Henry IV having pitched camp before the Fort of St Catherine ... Beza went to see him despite the exceptionally cold weather ... and complimented him in those terms: 'Sire ... I shall leave it to the angels to proclaim the praise which is due to thee for having poured his most precious blessings upon thy person in such a way as to make your Majesty appear as

---

[93]   See Teissier, p. 225.
[94]   See De la Faye, p. 33.
[95]   See ibid., p. 59.
[96]   Teissier, pp. 283–4, includes the account with marginal annotation: '*Hist. de Genève* par Iac. Spon, Tom 2, livre 3, pag. 135.' He is referring to the first edition printed in Lyon by Thomas Amaulry in 1680.

one made in Heaven for the happiness of France. I therefore pray God that He bestows all that is best upon your Majesty and makes thy people live in profound and eternal peace.[97]

In other words, Teissier's adaptation of De la Faye's *Life* of Beza is not so much a detailed portrait of a Christian leader, who imposed an ecclesiastical order to be followed under all circumstances (which was De la Faye's intention), as an account of the Golden Past of French Protestantism, which ushered in the Edict of Nantes. Teissier contrasts this implicitly with the grim present and Louis XIV, a sovereign to all intents and purposes as Catholic as the late Henry IV, who appears to be undoing all prospects of confessional coexistence.

Hostile *Lives* of Calvin and Beza

Although many reformers were the object of biographical opprobrium in some form or other, Calvin, more than anyone else, became the object of biographical controversy, which extended up until the latter half of the seventeenth century. Indeed, we might argue that traces of it persist to this day, and that the image of the reformer as either a sexual maniac or a ruthless inhuman dictator, or both, goes back to the French Catholic reception of him in the sixteenth century. His successor, Theodore Beza, excited far less interest from biographers, regardless of whether they were friendly or hostile.

Jerome Bolsec

Jerome Bolsec, who needs the minimum of introduction, wrote his *Life* of Calvin in 1577 as a response to Beza's first *Life* of the reformer. Originally a Carmelite friar in Paris, he converted to the Reformation *c.* 1545 and settled first on the estates of the duchess of Ferrara and subsequently in the Chablais, which was then (1547) under Bernese jurisdiction. He worked as a physician, but frequented theological gatherings in Geneva, which is where he came into conflict with Calvin. Bolsec argued that predestination to salvation or reprobation amounted to no more than man's own faith or lack of faith in God. Arrested in October 1551, he was put on trial and banished from Genevan territory. This relatively light sentence was due to Bernese intervention. Bolsec then travelled in France and Switzerland, continuing his attacks on Calvin. His doctrines were condemned by the Protestant Synod of Lyon in 1563. In his last years, he returned to the

---

[97]   Ibid., pp. 283–4.

Catholic Church, settled in France, and published his *Lives* of Calvin (1577) and Beza (1582).[98]

Although he spent much of his life in conflict with Calvin, the two *Lives* he published were intended to strike at Beza rather than at the author of the *Institutes*, who had been dead since 1564. More particularly, Bolsec intended his *Life* of Calvin as a response to Beza's *Discours*.[99] What is significant about both the *Lives* is not that they were hostile, but that they were published as *Lives* as opposed to the biographical notices on Calvin by Dupréau, Lindanus, Florimond de Raemond or Laurentius Surius, which were concealed within larger works of history of heresy. This would suggest that Bolsec saw the threat of reformers, Calvin in particular, attaining to the status of saints thanks to their biographies by Beza and others, and that he wanted to strangle the idea at birth with his own *Lives*. In this, he was to be successful: his image of Calvin, Beza and the Genevan Reformation was to prove as pervasive in the centuries to come as the image of the Christian hero or Protestant saint promulgated by Beza and De la Faye respectively. Bolsec wanted to destroy the image of Geneva as quickly and effectively as possible, which is no doubt why he published a biography of Beza while the latter was still alive.

Whether Bolsec's works were factually true or false is not something that need concern us here. To say that they arose in a polemical context is to say very little. It is far more important to note that any hint of the existence of Protestant saints posed a threat to some Catholic circles; otherwise, Bolsec's works would not have encountered their enduring success.

Although always treated in isolation, Bolsec's *Life* of Calvin should be viewed in the context in which it appeared. Initially a monograph published simultaneously in Paris by Mallot and in Lyon by Jean Patrasson,[100] it was

---

[98]   On Bolsec, see Philip Holtrop, *The Bolsec Controversy on Predestination from 1551 until 1555* (Lewiston, ID, and Lampeter, UK: Edwin Mellen Press, 1993), and literature cited ibid. There is no authoritative historical study of Bolsec and the circles he moved in after his departure from Geneva. As for Frank Pfeilschifter's study of Bolsec's image of Calvin and its reception in French Catholicism, *Das Calvinbild bei Bolsec und sein Fortwirken im französischen Katholizismus* (Augsburg: FDL, 1983), it deals only with generalities and does not measure the full impact of Bolsec. It also lacks precision when it comes to detail.

[99]   See Bolsec's quatrain on the verso of the title page of the 1577 Patrasson edition: 'Iamdudum latui et silui satis: exeo tandem // Et loquor intrepidus Bezae commenta revincens // Falsa quibus sanctum Christi deturabt ovile: // Nitere doctrina patrum optime lector. // Pelle nouos impostores qui toxica melle // Fucato obducunt. Cur vincit opinio verum? [I have been hiding and keeping silent for long enough, at last I am coming forth without fear in order to speak and to lay low Beza's figments. Excellent reader, you must have trust in the doctrine of your fathers. Drive away the new impostors who spread poison which they disguise as honey. Why is truth being vanquished by opinion?]

[100]   *Histoire de la vie, mœurs, actes, doctrine, constance et mort de Jean Calvin...*, *Recueilly par M. Hierosme Hermes Bolsec* (Paris, G. Mallot, 1577). [Another imprint: Lyon, Jean Patrasson, 1577.]

incorporated in the same year into the *Histoire des actes, doctrine et mort de quatre Heretiques de nostre temps à savoir Martin Luther, André Carlostadt, Pierre Martyr et Iean Caluin iadis ministre de Geneve. Recueillie par F. Noel Talepied, C. de Pontoise et H. Hierosme Bolsec...*, first published in 1577 in Paris by Jean Parant. Despite the title page, we are dealing with two separate publications which would have been sold together. The one with the main title page does not contain Calvin's *Life* by Bolsec, but only the *Lives* of Luther, Carlstadt and Vermigli by Noel Taillepied (Talepied).[101] Bolsec's work is appended to it in the 1577 Lyon imprint by Jean Patrasson: *Histoire de la vie, mœurs, actes, constance et mort de Iean Calvin, iadis ministre de Geneue, recueilly par M. Hierosme Hermes Bolsec* [...]. The Taillepied collection and Bolsec's work have each their own separate preface addressed to Pierre d'Espinac (1540–99), archbishop and count of Lyon, primate of France and leading counsellor of the House of Lorraine active in the League.[102] In his preface, Bolsec shows full awareness of ancient biographical genre and his own distortion of it. He knows that hostile *Life*-writing was not practised in Antiquity. Ancient lawyers preferred to exercise their rhetorical skills in their clients' defence rather than as prosecuting attorneys. Of Cicero's extant prosecuting speeches, he singles out those against Verres, governor of Sicily notorious for his avarice and lasciviousness.[103]

As well as deviating from the antique biographical style, Bolsec knows that he is flouting the basic rhetorical rule of not speaking ill of the dead.[104] However, he considers that one way of avoiding that accusation is to reinterpret the proverb 'praise only is to be bestowed after death' so as to mean:

---

[101]   See Le Charpentier, *Taillepied*. For Taillepied and his *Life* of Luther, see Chapter 1. For Taillepied's *Life* of Vermigli, see Chapter 2, pp. 71–8.

[102]   He was Henry III's ambassador in England for a time, but the latter had him imprisoned in 1588 after the assassinations of the duke of Guise and the cardinal of Lorraine. See H. Brown and H. di Lorena, 'The Assassination of the Guises as described by the Venetian Ambassador', *The English Historical Review*, 10 (1895): 304–32.

[103]   The preface is included in the 1580 Latin translation of the *Life*, *De Ioannis Caluini magni quondam Geneuensium ministri vita, moribus, rebus gestis ac denique morte. Historia ad reuerendissimum archiepiscopum et comitem Lugdunensem per Hieronymum Bolsecum medicum Lugdunensem conscripta et nunc ex gallico eius Parisiis impresso exemplari Latine reddita* (Coloniae, apud Ludouicum Alectorium et haeredes Iacobi Soteris, anno 1580) (hereafter: Bolsec, *Calvin* (1580)), pp. 3–7, but disappears from subsequent editions and translations, including those by James Laing. I have consulted the 1580 Latin version after ascertaining that it is a faithful rendering of the French original of 1577 (cf. pagination in parentheses).

[104]   Ibid., p. 3: 'Et surdo maledicendum etiam non esse vulgo iactatum prouerbium est, quod de absente vel de vita functo potest intelligi. Atque huc etiam pertinet quod non minus vulgo dicitur, nimirum vt post funera atque mortem laudes.' (Cf. 1577, p. 3: 'C'est aussi un proverbe commun en la bouche de plusieurs qu'il ne faut medire d'vn sourd, par lequel mot se peut entendre l'absent et le passé de ce siècle.')

... not that we should praise all men once they are dead, but that men who did
do great and illustrious deeds in their lifetime should not be given excessive
praise while still alive in order not to encourage adulation and more importantly
because it is only at the end of their lives that we can say what they did that was
good and what that was bad.[105]

Bolsec thus justifies himself in the eyes of many people who he knows will
hold it against him that he 'wanted to bring out into the open the many
vicious deeds of John Calvin after his death', in contrast with Beza and his
laudatory *Discours*.[106] In his defence, he cites Plato, according to whom,
'he who is immersed in sordid deeds and who nonetheless passes for a good
man and is elevated to the highest public position, wreaks more damage
upon the common weal than all those citizens generally acknowledged as
bad of whom nothing is expected.'[107]

He insists on the reformer's calamitous influence on France and on his
role in the wanton destruction of his native country 'and the neighbouring
lands'. According to Bolsec, Calvin was directly responsible for turning
countless simple souls away from the Roman Catholic Church. However,
Bolsec's real adversary is not so much Calvin himself as Beza, whose main
crime, in Bolsec's view, is daring to contend that his mentor was more
important and led a purer life than all the Apostles, doctors and their
successors put together.[108] With its hagiographical overtones, the *Discours*
could have influenced some Catholic faithful to defect to the Protestant
camp, hence Bolsec's determination to 'counter Beza's lies.'[109]

He takes God as witness that he is not motivated by any personal dislike
of either of the two reformers, but solely by zeal to let the truth come
to the fore and by sympathy for all those simple souls whose ruin and
perdition the Genevan reformers brought about.[110] One obvious question
arises at this point: why did Bolsec wait so long before publishing his *Life*
of Calvin? He justifies the delay by claiming that he had planned to do this
for some years, but that all sorts of hindrances and impediments had been
put in his way by God's ancient enemy so that the first opportune moment
did not come until thirteen years after Calvin's death.[111] The moment was

---

[105]   Ibid., pp. 3–4. (Cf. 1577, p. 4.)
[106]   Ibid., p. 4. (Cf. 1577, p. 4.)
[107]   Ibid. (Cf. 1577, p. 4).
[108]   Ibid., pp. 4–5. (Cf. 1577, pp. 4–5.)
[109]   Ibid., p. 5: 'silentium abrumpere coactus sum vt eodem zelo atque spiritu qui me
anno 1552 incitabat vt praesens praesenti in eo quo ipsi Geneuae coegerant coetu atque
concilio palam resisterem etiam nunc permotus et instigatus manum calamo admouerem et
Bezae me obuium obiicerem eiusque mendacia confutarem quibus in magnum diuinae gloriae
praeiudicium et ad ecclesiae domus Dei euidentem, qui malitiosissimus Sathanae minister
fuit, eum syncerum ac praecellentem Dei seruum fuisse asserere ac praedicare est ausus.'
(Cf. 1577, p. 5.)
[110]   Ibid. (Cf. 1577, p. 5.)
[111]   Ibid., pp. 5–6. (Cf. 1577, pp. 6–7.)

well chosen indeed, as it coincided with the time when France was at its weakest after the seventh War of Religion, which ended with the Treaty of Bergérac in June 1577. It was also the time of hardening positions. D'Espinac, who had links to the League and who introduced Tridentine reforms in his diocese as well as having undoubted political influence (he was Henry III's ambassador to England), was the perfect dedicatee, and very likely played a concrete part in the project. Bolsec was the obvious choice as author, as he had known Calvin and was seeking revenge not so much on Calvin himself, but on Beza and Calvin's other disciples who conspired to blacken his name, or, as he put it:

> The followers and servants of the Calvinist sect have not only set all sorts of deadly traps against my person but have also waged and do to this day wage a war against me aiming to make me the object of general hate. Not only do they write vicious invectives against me and spread all sorts of rumours about me through a variety of fabrications ... but they also secretly send clandestine letters against me to their comrades, as has frequently come to my knowledge.[112]

What better way to counter his enemies and clear himself than to blacken the reputation of the leader of the Calvinist Reformation, against whom he had stood over twenty years previously?

On what sources is Bolsec's account based? Although he swears to their soundness, if we examine his statement, we see that he all but openly admits to relying on fabrication, rumour and hearsay. This is how he describes them:

> And I call the same God to witness that I am not aware of having written anything that goes against my knowledge of the facts and my conscience, but that what I write is based on truth. I have taken it either from the official documents and accounts in Calvin's own hand or got knowledge of it from the oral accounts of men of highest authority or saw it with my own eyes and touched it with my own hands.[113]

There were no official accounts, let alone ones written by Calvin himself, which attested to the reformer's iniquity. The phrase simply conveys an illusion of an objective use of written sources. As for oral accounts of men of highest authority, sixteenth-century readers would have expected some mention of names, but here again, none was forthcoming. That left the

---

[112] Ibid., p. 6. (Cf. 1577, p. 6.)

[113] Ibid., p. 5: 'Iam hoc quoque eundum testor Deum nihil me hoc tractatu complexum quod contra meam conscientiam scriptum esse mihi conscius sim, sed quae scribo omnia veritate niti et vel ex tabula ac testimoniis ea me manu ipsius Caluini conscriptis desumpsisse vel referentibus maximae auctoritatis viris cognouisse vel meis oculis conspexisse manuque palpasse.' (Cf. 1577, pp. 5–6: 'Semblablement que je n'escry chose aucune en ce traicté qui soit contre ma conscience, mais selon verité approuvée par tesmoignages d'escrits de la main mesme d'iceluy Caluin: par relation de personnages dignes de foy et selon que j'ay veu de mes yeux et touché de ma main.')

reader with Bolsec's own guarantee of his privileged status of eye-witness, which could not be verified thirteen years after Calvin's death.

Bolsec's *Life* of Calvin falls into twenty-six chapters, and it is difficult to situate it in any genre given that his intention is to write a purportedly historical account which flouts the convention of 'not speaking ill of the dead' for which no literary models were established. Bolsec obviously had no knowledge of Cochlaeus' *Life* of Luther, and if he did, he was not influenced by it. Bolsec's work, as noted above, was contemporary with Taillepied's anthology: both were sold together from 1577, as well as being dedicated to one and the same patron. However, Bolsec's *Life* of Calvin adopts a different approach, as we shall see, and while there is no doubt that both are powered by similar motives and by the same political forces, there is no concrete indication of collaboration between the former Carmelite and the Capuchin. Bolsec's work has two important characteristics: firstly he evokes as his model antique *Life*-writing and not notices on heretics; secondly, while Taillepied had no personal knowledge of Luther, Vermigli or Karlstadt, Bolsec not only knew Calvin personally, but also suffered under his regime.

He anticipates the accusation of 'speaking ill of the dead' by situating Calvin in the long line of heresies going back to the Sadducees and the Pharisees and continuing in an unbroken line to Calvin's Geneva. By definition, within the Christian tradition, a heretic, let alone a heresiarch, dead or alive, could not be portrayed in a favourable light. He had to be persuasive, hypocritical and acting for his own glory, while leading numerous souls to perdition, an ignoble life which ended fittingly with an ignoble death.

Bolsec therefore opens his work with a short general account of ancient heresies, Jewish and Christian, without worrying too much about the chronological order. Among the Christian heresies he has Carpocrates (a second-century Gnostic) follow Arius. Carpocrates, with his licentious ethic, is followed by Ebion, and his introduction of Mosaic ceremonies into the teaching of the Gospel. He then groups together Basilides, Marcion and Manes, who postulated dualism and determinism. They in turn are followed by Pelagius, with his denial of original sin. This, Bolsec specifies, is only the start of *aliorum phanaticorum caterua* [the crowd of other heretics] who came in their wake. He is no more concerned with giving a history of heresy than with the personalities of different heretics. His succinct account is simply intended to show that Satan used Calvin as a tool to bring back all these heresies previously condemned and to reassemble them in Geneva. Taillepied, as we have seen, showed that Luther was in personal league with the devil, relying on the tradition going back to Silvius and Cochlaeus. Bolsec prefers to portray Calvin as the reincarnation of all heresies, an impersonal tool of the devil rather than a consenting accomplice. In symmetry with Beza's *Discours*, he concentrates on the reformer's morals, actions and death on the one hand, and his doctrine on the other, in an attempt to counter Beza point by point. Although, as we shall see, those were to be refuted soon enough by the Protestant and the Catholic camp, they nonetheless played an important part in generating a certain image of Calvin and Geneva, which proved extremely tenacious.

Indeed, Bolsec's *Life* encountered considerable success if we go by simply the number of editions and translations it received at the time. The French version was published simultaneously in Lyon and Paris in 1577, and reprinted in Paris in 1582. It was translated word for word into Latin by an anonymous translator in 1580 and 1582, and published in Cologne. James Laing, Scottish doctor of the Paris Faculty of Theology, incorporated it in Latin, with some additions and marginalia, into his *Vitae haereticorum*, published in Paris in 1581 and 1585.[114] Its existence in Latin from 1580 onwards also meant that it could be and was translated into other vernacular languages. The German translation appeared in 1580, and was reprinted in 1581 and 1631; a Dutch translation was published in 1581; and a Polish version came out in 1583. Although it was rapidly discredited, it continued to be printed in Catholic circles until 1875, and was to exercise a lasting negative influence on the image of Calvin and Geneva.[115]

As has been shown by other sixteenth- and particularly seventeenth-century Catholic biographers of the reformer, Bolsec's account of Calvin's youth conflates at least two people from Noyon called Jean Cauvin.[116] To this conflation, he adds a certain amount of rumour and fiction, intending to give his reader a full portrait of Calvin's iniquitous youth, the hallmark of any heretic. He begins by claiming that already the reformer's father Gérard Cauvin was a blasphemer.[117] We know in fact, thanks to Canon Jacques Le Vasseur, the chronicler of Noyon Cathedral, that although Gérard Cauvin

---

[114]   See Chapter 1, pp. 34–45.

[115]   Doumergue was still defending Calvin against Bolsec's calumnies in 1912. See E. Doumergue, *Calomnies antiprotestantes*, vol. 1: *Calvin* (Paris: Foi et Vie, 1912), pp. 10–27. Cf. also, for example, the popular historical biography by the Catholic authors Jean Moura and Paul Louvet, *Calvin* (Paris: Bernard Grasset, 1931), which is almost entirely founded on Bolsec's account.

[116]   Cf. also Théophile Dufour, 'Calviniana', in [no editor], *Mélanges offerts à M. Émile Picot, membre de l'Institut, par ses amis et élèves* (Paris: Librairie Damascène Morgand, 1913), pp. 1–16, esp. pp. 13–16.

[117]   *Histoire de la vie, mœurs, actes, doctrines, constance et mort de Jean Calvin, jadis ministre de Genève. Recueilly par M. Hierosme Bolsec, docteur médecin à Lyon*. Cited after Taillepied, *Histoire des trois principaux hérétiques* (1616), fols 39v.–124v. (Hereafter: Bolsec, *Calvin* in: Taillepied, *Histoire* (1616).)

speculated with his clients' money[118] and died excommunicated, there is no record of him ever having been convicted of blasphemy. Bolsec further claims that Calvin himself was convicted of sodomy as a young cleric in Noyon, a crime for which he would have been burned at the stake had the sentence not been commuted at the last moment to branding with a *fleur-de-lys* on the shoulder. Under the weight of this opprobrium, Calvin, according to our biographer, sold his benefices and left for Germany and Ferrara. In fact, as is well documented by the same Le Vasseur, a certain Jean Cauvin, Roman Catholic vicar of Noyon, was deprived of his livings for refusing to abandon his dissolute lifestyle. The description might have well suited young Calvin were it not for the date, January 1553; Calvin had been well and truly settled in Geneva since 1541.[119] Furthermore, still according to Le Vasseur, no records of branding exist in connexion with any of the Noyon clergy of the 1530s. As we shall see, this piece of information had already been discredited as a myth in 1583 by Jean-Papire Masson. Bolsec stresses that before leaving Noyon, Calvin changed his name from Cauvin to Calvin, 'either through ignorance or in full knowledge of the fact that it went well with his morals, very similar to those of that vindictive and wicked Calvinus to whom Juvenal attributes the words "vengeance is the sweetest good".'[120] It is in fact very doubtful that Calvin, given his classical background, would have taken the name of the greedy, vindictive anti-hero of Juvenal's 13th Satire. He was much more likely inspired either by the Roman advocate mentioned by Cicero or by the proconsul of that name. As we shall see, Jean-Papire Masson affirms in 1583 that it was the proconsul who provided the inspiration.

It follows, at least in Bolsec's view, that given his general depravity, Calvin's initial attempts to reform Geneva were nothing other than incitement to revolt against the civil authorities.[121] As regards his morals, they never improved. Not content with the charge of sodomy, considered a heresy in itself, Bolsec accuses the reformer of having sexual intercourse with most of the city's married women under the cover of pastoral guidance. Although admitting that he has no proof of the reformer's promiscuity,

[118] See Jacques Le Vasseur, *Annales de l'Eglise de Noyon jadis dite de Vermand, ou le troisiesme liure des Antiquitez, Chroniques ou plustost Histoire de la Cathedrale de Noyon. Par M. Iacques le Vasseur, docteur en theologie de la Faculté de Paris, doyen et chanoine deladite Eglise*, 2 vols (Paris: Sara, 1633), vol. 2, ch. 90, p. 1151. Hereafter: Le Vasseur, *Annales*, vol. 2. Cf. also Chapter 5.

[119] See ibid., vol. 2, pp. 1170–71. Le Vasseur points out the confusion. For other examples of confusion of Calvin with his different namesakes, not exploited by Bolsec, see Dufour, 'Calviniana', pp. 11–16.

[120] Bolsec, *Calvin* in: Taillepied, *Histoire* (1616), fol. 40v. (1577: p. 26.)

[121] Ibid., fol. 49r. (1577: p. 38): 'Et d'auentage, ils dirent mille opprobres et vilenies contre les sindiques et seigneurs du Conseil, tachans à esmouoir sedition et d'inflammer le peuple contre les gouerneurs et magistrats, entreprise vrayment diabolique ...'.

Bolsec weaves together rumours put about by 'several people of sound judgement' and calculated to make Calvin appear as the local lecher and his home as a seat of depravity. Interestingly enough, he makes no mention of the reformer's marriage. This is how he describes the reformer's dealings with the opposite sex:

> I know that ... there was talk of many married and unmarried women who regularly went to see him at his home unaccompanied, except for a small child carrying a Bible under his arm. If they met a relative or a friend along the way who asked where they were going, they would say demurely that they were going to visit that holy man to get a resolution to a doubt. And they stayed for a long time. There was particular talk and rumours concerning the wife of a foreign nobleman who took refuge here for religious reasons and whose name I shall not reveal out of respect. I will say though that he lived near Geneva, just next to Saconay in the territory of Gex. The lady in question was young, beautiful and vivacious. She often went to dine with Calvin and stayed overnight when her husband was out of the country ....[122]

Appearances to the contrary, the phrase 'rumours concerning the wife of a foreign nobleman' does not refer to Calvin's fairly close relations with Jacques de Falais (d. 1556) and his wife Yolande de Brederode, both of whom he converted to the Reformation. Yolande was initially more responsive than her husband, and the reformer no doubt made use of her to influence her consort.[123] However, things did not turn out as Calvin would have wished: De Falais did indeed convert and settle in 1548 for a short time in Veigy, in the proximity of Geneva, but the couple's friendship with Calvin did not survive De Falais' sympathies for Joris and Castellio. De Falais' support of Bolsec sealed the breach between him and the reformer. Bolsec mentions Yolande and her husband separately and by name in his *Life* of Calvin, but does not imply adultery on Yolande's part, showing her rather as a victim of Calvin's machinations.

Predictably, Bolsec has Calvin die of phthiriasis (infection due to crab lice) after a miserable life, his diverse maladies proving in Bolsec's eyes his ungodliness. 'For [he says] apart from the many illnesses mentioned by Beza, Calvin was also tormented by an ill with which, or so we read, God in his justice vexes those enemies, who wanted to usurp His glory and honour, that is, their whole bodies itch being eaten by lice and other vermin, and they develop a particularly stinking and virulent ulcer at the base of their private parts where they are wretchedly chewed by crab-lice.'[124] Furthermore, still according to Bolsec, Calvin died cursing all his writings and desperately rewriting for the last time his *Institutes*, the

---

[122]   Ibid., fol. 70r.–v. (1577: pp. 69–70.)

[123]   The best recent treatment of the De Falais episode is by Mirjam van Veen, '*In excelso honoris gradu*. Johannes Calvin und Jacques de Falais', *Zwingliana*, 32 (2005): 5–22. See also sources and literature cited ibid.

[124]   Bolsec, *Calvin* in: Taillepied, *Histoire* (1616), fol. 101v. (1577: pp. 112–13.)

ultimate proof of inconstancy. Indeed, he concludes, if the first *Institutes* were as perfect as Beza claims they were, why did Calvin rewrite the work so many times?[125]

What may seem surprising is not so much the fact that Bolsec accuses Calvin of sexual depravity, but that his image of the reformer encountered enduring success despite him openly admitting to its being founded on rumours. However, we must not forget that Bolsec's aim was to contradict Beza's *Discours*. As such, his *Life* of Calvin turns out to be the perfect and extremely convincing obverse of Beza's 1564 composition. Whereas Beza praises Calvin's chastity and austerity, Bolsec credits him with total licentiousness. To Beza's praises of the reformer's zeal and capacity for hard work, Bolsec opposes an obsessive interest with the rewriting of one work, in itself a proof of inconstancy. Where Calvin's successor expounds on Calvin's marriage as a model of what a pious marriage should be, the ex-Carmelite does not even advert to it in his treatment of Calvin as the local seducer of married women. Whereas Beza praises Calvin's good death, Bolsec has him die a miserable death in solitude, as behoves a heresiarch, who embodies all ancient heresies. While Beza exalts Calvin's kindness to heretics, Bolsec has him bear the entire responsibility for the death of Servetus, a myth which turned out to have an astonishingly long life, despite many attempts to disprove it.

When he reacted against Beza's *Discours* with his *Life* of Calvin, Bolsec did not know Beza's 1575 *Life*, in which Calvin's successor explicitly lays down criteria for truthfulness as one of the hallmarks of Protestant biography. Had Beza established these criteria in 1564, Bolsec's job would have been much more difficult. As it was, however, Beza's first *Discours* seemed to augur the birth of Calvinist hagiography, an impression Beza and Colladon strove to wipe out with their subsequent attempts at the Genevan reformer's biography. Bolsec's *Life* of Calvin is the only hostile biography of a reformer that can be considered as a sort of upside-down saint's life. Bolsec, however, as we have seen, did not take medieval hagiography as his model. His *Life* of Calvin therefore assumes the form it does only because it responds to a text which would have been seen very much as a life of a saint, minus only the miracles. Although no external evidence for this is available, it seems highly probable that Bolsec's effort, viewed in conjunction with Taillepied's *Lives* of Luther, Vermigli and Karlstadt, represents a new type of anti-Reformation propaganda, launched by D'Espinac and other members of the League at a time when reconversion of at least a portion of the French Protestant population seemed a real and realistic prospect. As we shall see, other hostile biographies of Calvin, notably that of Jean-Papire Masson, were to be oriented by very different concerns.

---

[125]   Ibid., fol. 103r.–v. (1577: p. 115.)

Bolsec's Life *of Beza*

Bolsec's *Life* of Beza[126] has the interesting particularity of having appeared not after the protagonist's death, like most biographies, but during his lifetime.[127] Beza never replied to it. Bolsec knew far less about Beza than he did about Calvin. He left Geneva before Beza's arrival and, more to the point, did not have a biography to work from. He was thus unable to do with his *Life* of Beza what he did with his *Life* of Calvin; that is, to overturn the existing biographical models so as to make his protagonist look like the antithesis of both civic virtue and saintly abstinence. All he could do was put together the little that he did know about the reformer from the writings of Catelan, Florimond de Raemond and other hostile sources, and add it to a completely negative account of the Genevan Reformation. Thus, under Bolsec's pen, Beza became a symptom of the general depravity of Calvin's religious movement.

The biography for the most part is not a biography in any strict sense of the word, but a long indictment interspersed with a catalogue of incidents and value judgements, most of which are only loosely connected with Beza, if at all, such as the long excursus on Bolsec's dispute with Calvin on predestination. Again unlike most biographies, which are not expressly addressed to a particular recipient, Bolsec addresses his *Life* of Beza 'to their venerable and much honoured lordships the syndics and to the members of the Great and Small Council.' Was Bolsec under orders from the French Church to produce a defamatory work on Beza, his *Life* of Calvin proving itself to be successful? No evidence for this exists. Be that as it may, Bolsec perhaps took advantage of what was an exceptionally difficult period for Geneva's economy to try to convince the authorities of the iniquity of the Reformation, seeing as the influx of religious refugees made considerable inroads into the public finances. However, he makes no reference to this in his preface, where he sets out to convince the council that Beza and the Reformation recapitulate all the most abominable ancient heresies and should therefore be done away with. In contrast with his *Life* of Calvin, he makes no mention of his sources and does not punctuate his account with

---

[126]   *Histoire de la vie, mœurs, actes, doctrines et deportements de Theodore de Beze, iadis archiministre de Geneue. Aux magnifiques et honorez seigneurs sindicques et assistans du petit et grand conseil de la ville de Geneue, desire, salut, sapience et assistance du S. Esprit, Hierosme Hermes Bolsec, theologien et medecin, leur bon et sincere amy.* First published in Paris in 1582. (Cf. following note.) Cited here after Taillepied, *Histoire* (1616), fols 127r.–192r. (Hereafter: Bolsec, *Beza* in Taillepied, *Histoire* (1616).)

[127]   Bolsec was aware of this and invited Beza mockingly to 'add the rest if he so wished' in the title of the first edition: *Histoire de la vie, moeurs, doctrine et déportements de Théodore de Bèze dit le Spectable, grand ministre de Genève selon que l'on a peu voir et cognoistre jusqu'à maintenant, en attendant que lui mesme, si bon luy semble adiouste le reste, par Hierosme Bolsec* (Paris, chez Guillaume Chaudière, 1582).

'they say that ...' or 'rumour has it that...'. All these features put together
are more evocative of a prosecuting counsel's address than a biography.
After a summary account of all the heresies encapsulated in the movement,
he begins not with details of Beza's lineage and birth, but with an anecdote
of Calvin's failed attempt to perform an exorcism, which he had omitted
from his *Life* of Calvin, probably because he did not know of it in 1577.[128]
There follow several pages of reflexions on the general iniquity of Calvin
and his associates (more or less copied from his own *Life* of Calvin), and
an account of Calvin's 1538 banishment from Geneva. Beza first makes
an appearance after thirty pages, if we follow the format of the *Histoire*
[...] *des trois principaux hérétiques* in its 1616 edition. Bolsec wants to
make the syndics see that their so-called holy minister is in fact a sexual
deviant given over to all sorts of depravity, and that his lifestyle is exactly
what might be expected of a so-called reformer. To achieve his aim,
Bolsec naturally makes the most of the *Poemata/Juvenilia* incident and
Beza's secret marriage. He portrays the reformer as 'the most lascivious,
detestable, shameless poet whose writings have ever come down to us.'[129]

As we know, Beza published his *Poemata* in 1548. Of the epigrams
contained in the volume, the ones that were to attract the most attention
were those addressed to Candida. Beza modelled them on Catullus' poems
to Lesbia, using the same metre and similar expressions. Although the
erotic component was slight, it was sufficiently prominent to be exploited
by Beza's adversaries, who published three pirate editions of the anthology
from 1550 onwards. Because one of the epigrams dealt with the classic
theme of friendship and love and compared Beza's feelings for his brother
Audebert (successor to his uncle Nicholas as prior of Saint-Éloi-lès-
Longjumeau) with his feelings for Candida, this naturally gave rise to
accusations of bisexuality from the late 1560s onwards.[130] Moreover,
Beza's adversaries were quick to misidentify Candida as Claudine Denosse,
despite the fact that Beza composed his epigrams some time before meeting
his future wife. As Dufour points out, the myth persisted well into the
nineteenth century, despite the fact that Beza himself did his best to refute
it in 1569,[131] and that, as we have seen, De la Faye in his *Life* of Beza was

---

[128]   Bolsec, *Beza* in Taillepied, *Histoire* (1616), fols 145v.–146r. According to Bolsec,
Calvin attempted to perform an exorcism on a possessed vineyard-owner, and was attacked,
badly beaten and scratched by the demon. This proves in Bolsec's view, 'qu'il n'estoit point
celuy lequel il vouloit donner à entendre d'estre, assauoir vray enfant et seruiteur de Dieu et
de nostre Seigneur Iesus Christ.'
[129]   Ibid., fol. 159r. For a full discussion of the polemic generated by Beza's *Poemata/*
Juuenilia, see Dufour, 'Théodore de Bèze', pp. 318–21. For recent research on the *Poemata*,
see Kirk Summers, 'The Classical Foundations of Beza's Thought', in Backus *et al.* (eds),
Théodore de Bèze, pp. 369–81, and literature cited ibid.
[130]   See Dufour, 'Théodore de Bèze', p. 319.
[131]   See ibid., p. 320.

very careful to describe the incident in such a way as to ensure its decline. As might be expected, Bolsec exploited it to the full. This is what he says:

> He debauched the wife of a Parisian tailor lodging in the Rue Calende and took her to your city [Geneva] and is still keeping her there now, to your very great disgrace and dishonour. And in case you did not know it, I can tell you that she is that very whore that he celebrates so in his Epigrams where he calls her Candide, even though her real name is Claude. The woman's unfortunate husband tried to seek reparation from Beza when the latter attended the Colloquy of Poissy, but because he and his companions were granted safe conduct, the aforesaid unfortunate husband was not allowed to institute legal proceedings.[132]

Not only does Bolsec ably perpetuate the confusion between Candida and Claudine Denosse, but he adds to it a version of the rumour initiated in the early 1550s by Antoine Catelan (an ex-Franciscan reconverted to Catholicism after a brief and unsuccessful stay at the Lausanne Academy). This rumour converts Beza's secret marriage into adultery. A cuckolded husband, shoemaker by trade, lodging in the Rue de la Harpe according to Catelan, or a tailor, domiciled in the Rue Calende according to Bolsec, thus comes into the picture.[133] Beza's depravity does not stop there. His biographer further tells us that, when in Lausanne, the reformer had a maid, curiously also called Claude, whom he got pregnant. So as not to incur the disapproval of the Bernese authorities, Beza, according to Bolsec, spread a rumour that the girl had the plague and got Pierre Viret to put up a cabin in his garden where she could be housed. At Beza's instigation, a young and inexperienced barber-surgeon was called to attend to her, who drew so much blood and administered such strong medicines to the girl that her child was still-born. In order to cover up his evil doings, Beza himself pretended to fall ill of the plague, and during that time he wrote his hymn thanking God, which was instantly published in Geneva and diffused everywhere.[134] The reference here is to the plague epidemic of 1548. Contrary to Bolsec's claims, Beza did actually catch the plague, and the hymn is none other than the *Ode au Seigneur par Th. de B. affligé d'une grave maladie.*

---

[132]   Bolsec, *Beza* in Taillepied, *Histoire* (1616), fols 162v.–163r.: '… c'est qu'il desbaucha la femme d'vn couturier de Paris logé en la rue de Calende et la mena en vostre ville et la tient encores à present à votre tres grand vitupere et deshonneur. Et si vous l'ignorez, ie vous declare que s'est ceste putain, laquelle il celebre si fort en ses Epygrammes, l'appellant Candide. Mais son vray nom est Claude. /163r./ Le pauure mary voulut demander iustice dudit Bèze, lors qu'il alla à la iournée et assemblée de Poissy, mais à cause du sauue-conduit qui luy auoit esté donné et à ses compagnons, il ne fut permis audit pauure mary d'intenter procez contre.'

[133]   See also Dufour, 'Théodore de Bèze', p. 339, and Paul-Frédéric Geisendorf, *Théodore de Bèze* (Geneva: Labor et Fides, 1949), pp. 28–30.

[134]   Bolsec, *Beza* in Taillepied, *Histoire* (1616), fols 167v.–168r.

Beza's sexual deviance naturally implies in Bolsec's view that not only he, but also the religious movement he stands for, is depraved, cruel, heterodox, and liable to any other form of wickedness the reader can think of. What of the consistory which earned the Genevan Reformation its reputation of a repressive dictatorship, an image which persists in some twentieth-century biographies of Calvin?[135] Bolsec obviously repeats a view commonly held when he asserts, even before embarking on Beza's *Life* (or, to be more exact, a catalogue of the reformer's depravities and crimes), that the consistory is far too soft and decadent an institution to stop the city of Geneva and its inhabitants from becoming a latter-day Sodom and Gomorrah. The abolition of private confession and the sacrament of penance mean that anything is allowed. As he puts it:

> For to do away with auricular confession and the sacrament of penance, which allow us to become aware of the sins we have committed, of their gravity so that we have a horror of them and hate them forever and reunite with God, – to do away with this sacrament is nothing other than to teach and encourage full licence to sin and to give oneself over totally to soiling our bodies and souls. You claim that your consistory watches over this, but it is too soft and too confined to one place to see clearly in hiding-places where secret and furtive sins are committed. When there is debauchery in your homes, when your male and female subjects soil themselves by adultery and other major sins, be it in deed or in thought and desire ... so long as they can do it in secret, they will never be uncovered by your consistory. If it gets wind of their misdeeds, they deny them while persisting in sin and continuing to do evil as long as they are not discovered. If they die in this state, they die in mortal sin, without either satisfaction or absolution ... So the doctrine of your ministers, that is to say, Calvin, Beza and others, serves to incite people to vice so long as they can do it without anyone knowing. For, given that men are inclined to abuse God's long-suffering patience, they will not abstain from vice once they have been told that they have no account to render to the clergy and the church of sins they have committed in secret.[136]

---

[135]   See, for example, Moura and Louvet, *Calvin*.

[136]   Bolsec, *Beza* in Taillepied, *Histoire* (1616), fols 132v.–134r: '... car oster la confession auriculaire et sacrement de penitence moyen de recognoistre les pechez qu'on a commis, la grauité d'iceux pour en auoir horreur, en conceuoir haine perpetuelle et de se reunir à Dieu. Quant oster, di-ie, ce sacrement, qu'est-ce autre chose sinon enseigner et donner cours à vne licence effrenee de pecher et s'adonner à toute souillure et de corps et d'ame? Vous alleguez l'œil de vostre Consistoire mais il est trop mouce et rebouché pour voir clair aux cachettes, où se commettent les pechez couuerts et cachez. Quand les paillardises se commettent en vos maisons, quand vos bourgeois et bourgeoises se souillent d'adulteres et d'autres pechez enormes, soit de fait ou d'ardent desir et affection (car la conuoitise est peché, combien que la /133r./ simple concupiscence, c'est à dire, la faculté de conuoiter ne le soit pas) quand, di-ie, ils se polluent en telles vilennies, autant qu'ils se peuuent couurir, vostre Consistoire n'y voit goutte. S'il sourd quelque doute de leurs faits, ils le nient, cependant demeurent tousiours en leur pechez et continuer tousiours de mal faire aussi long temps qu'ils ne sont point descouuerts. S'ils meurent en tel estat, ils meurent en péché mortel sans descouurir leur mal, sans satisfaction d'iceluy et sans obtenir absolution ... /133v./ ... La doctrine donc de vos ministres, soit Caluin, Beze ou autres et la discipline qu'ils vous ont prescripte, est pour

Thus the depraved lives of Calvin and Beza mirror their depraved doctrine, the licentious behaviour of their citizens, and the decadent and financially dilapidated state of the city. It is plain that Bolsec is not writing a biography in any sense of the word, ancient or modern, but rather a warning. He depicts Beza as symptomatic of the Genevan Reformation just as the Genevan Reformation is symptomatic of his and Calvin's depravity.

James Laing's Transposition of Bolsec's Life of Calvin into the Scottish Context

Laing produced a Latin version of Bolsec's *Life* of Calvin with very sizeable interpolations stressing mainly the devilish nature of the Genevan reformer and the movement in general. As noted already,[137] Laing incorporates into most of his biographies long excursus on various figures influential in the Scottish Reformation. We have seen that George Buchanan figured very prominently in his general preface to the work as the man who turned James away from the true religion of his ancestors.[138] In his adaptation of Taillepied's *Life* of Luther, he laid the blame on the Wittenberg reformer for female interference in Scottish church matters.[139] We also saw that he devoted some efforts in his *Life* of Vermigli to depicting David Fergusson in as sombre colours as possible.[140] It follows that Laing should incorporate into his adaptation of Bolsec libellous accounts of George Buchanan, Knox and other Scottish reformers. Laing's excursus on Buchanan takes up about half of Bolsec's text.

What is particularly interesting about the Buchanan episodes he inserts into the *Vita Calvini* is the way he rewrites Scottish history. He thus assimilates Buchanan to Marcion, collapses various stages of his early career into one, and makes no mention of the fact that Buchanan was appointed by James V as tutor to Lord James Stewart, which enables him to present James V as an unqualified foe of Buchanan:

> Thirdly, there was Ebion with his insane crowd who to this day contend that the observation of Jewish ceremonies is necessary for salvation and that it has something to do with the Gospel of Christ and this introduced very many contentions into the church. George Buchanan and many other heretics fell into this wretched heresy and ate the paschal lamb in time of Lent. When he was accused of heresy and considered a heretic some forty years ago, if I

---

apasteller les hommes à se veautrer aux vices, poureu que ce soit /134r./ secrettement. Car selon que les hommes sont enclins à abuser de la longue attente et patience de Dieu, ils ne se donnent pas peine de s'abstenir des vices quand on leur a persuadé qu'il ne faut poinct rendre compte à l'Église deuant les prestres de Dieu des pechez commis secretement.'

[137] See Chapters 1 and 2, pp. 34–45 and pp. 71–8.
[138] See Chapter 1, pp. 34–40.
[139] See Chapter 1, pp. 41–2.
[140] See Chapter 2, pp. 75–8.

am not mistaken, he was summoned by James V, the wisest and pious man and a staunch champion of the Roman Catholic and Apostolic Church, and questioned on this and asked how he had dared to attempt something like that against the tradition of the Catholic Church.[141]

Still according to Laing, Buchanan, when questioned about this practice by 'the most pious' James V, recommended that the king too should eat paschal lamb in Lent. The king consulted all the doctors of theology, including John Major. Predictably, they all found the practice applicable only under Jewish Law and so unchristian, whereupon James V had Buchanan thrown into prison. The latter, however, escaped and went to Portugal, where he was tried for heresy:

> During his trial he neither took his hat off nor showed any sign of piety, but stood motionless like a stone, while all around him shouted that he was a heretic and proclaimed him to be bad and damnable, a scourge to the commonweal, a plague to young people, one who should be stoned or burned alive or drowned in raging seas. I saw this wretched spectacle for I was there. And very many say that this total wretch, if you would pardon my language, had once defecated in a baptismal font.[142]

These short excerpts from Laing's account suffice to show that he adopted Bolsec's method for his biographical excursus on Buchanan, which he then inserted into Bolsec's *Life* of Calvin. Be that as it may, his attempt at converting the king in 1581 was not successful.

The situation had altered considerably between 1581 and 1585, the date of Laing's second expanded edition with a new preface addressed only to James VI. The year 1581 saw the death of Edmund Campion, commemorated by Laing in this second edition, which is further augmented by Laing's own Latin translation of Bolsec's *Life* of Beza, 'easily the chief heretic of our times.'[143] The year 1582 marked the death of George Buchanan. In 1583, the Throckmorton plot to free Mary from her incarceration and kill Elizabeth was discovered. A well-born Catholic Englishman, Throckmorton was given money and guidance by the duke of Guise. Guise wished to invade Scotland and England simultaneously, murder Elizabeth with the assistance of the English Catholics, and then place Mary on the throne. The plot was foiled, and Throckmorton was arrested and tortured on the rack before confessing everything. He was

---

[141] Laing (1585), fols 38v.–39r.

[142] Ibid., fols 39v.–40r.

[143] *De vita et moribus Theodori Bezae, omnium haereticorum nostri temporis facile principis et aliorum haereticorum breuis recitatio. Cui adiectus est libellus de morte patris Edmundi Campionis et aliorum quorumdam catholicorum qui in Anglia pro fide Catholica interfecti fuerunt primo die Decembris. Anno Domini 1581. Authore Iacobo Laingaeo doctore Sorbonico* (Paris apud Michaelem de Roigny, 1585 cum priuilegio). Laing did not add a separate preface to his Latin version.

executed at Tyburn on 10 July 1584. At the same time, James VI showed no signs of converting.[144] Under the weight of these events, Laing's preface to his second edition of the *Vitae* is brief, sober, and addressed to the Scottish monarch alone. Although the content of the *Life* of Calvin is the same as in the previous edition, including Laing's vituperative interpolations on Buchanan and others whose *Lives* blend into Calvin's own, the new preface makes no mention of James's former tutor. Nor is it an admonition, but more of a straightforward plea, making use of standard theological arguments. Laing argues that Protestantism cannot be considered a true religion because, unlike Catholicism, it is restricted to a few small corners of the world and represents several conflicting positions. He stresses particularly the conflict of opinions about the Eucharist. Whereas in 1581 he had acknowledged only Mary as the one true monarch, addressing James as the young prince whose duty it was to follow in his mother's footsteps,[145] he now recognises only James, whom he urges to return to the Catholic faith and defend it, the chief reason given being that he will find more loyal subjects among Catholics than among Protestants. In a vein similar to Ninian Winzet, who published an attack on Buchanan in 1582, linking Protestantism to political sedition,[146] Laing persists in using the Divine Right of Kings argument to persuade James. However, whereas, judging by its preface, his 1581 edition of the *Vitae* still expressed some hope of seeing Scotland return to the bosom of the Roman Catholic Church, by 1585 any real hope is gone.

Laing's collection thus represents an interesting case of a determined and unsuccessful attempt to use hostile *Lives* of the reformers to influence royalty. This entailed piling vast amounts of Bolsec-type scurrilous material onto Buchanan and other Scottish reformers so as to give the ex-Carmelite's *Life* of Calvin a local flavour.

François Bauduin as Source for Calvin's Biography. The Vita Calvini *of Jean-Papire Masson*

Although Bolsec nowadays is something of a household name in matters of biography hostile to Calvin, he was by no means the biographer who was taken the most seriously by the Catholic or Calvinist camps in the early seventeenth- and eighteenth centuries. Curiously, Jean-Papire Masson's Latin *Vita Calvini* has not been the object of study since Pierre Ronzy's

---

[144]   James was the object of solicitations from both Catholic and Calvinist theologians during his in-between period in the early 1580s. It was to him that Beza dedicated his *Icones* in 1580.

[145]   See Chapter 1, pp. 37–40.

[146]   On Winzet, see John H. Burns, 'Catholicism in Defeat: Ninian Winzet 1519–1592', *History Today*, 16 (1966): 788–95.

biography of Masson, which appeared in 1924.[147] Ronzy devotes just a few pages to Masson's *Vita Caluini*, emphasising the French historian's impartiality and his use of sources both written and oral, such as Calvin's works, his uncle Jacques Cauvin (blacksmith and son of Richard Cauvin, with whom Calvin stayed during his first sojourn in Paris in 1523[148]), and also François Bauduin and other people (unspecified) who knew Calvin personally. While there is no doubt that Masson's account is ahead of its time in its recourse to sources, it is by no means a modern biography as Ronzy would have it. Masson does not list his sources, and does not refer to them in the margins or anywhere else. Furthermore, his use of oral sources is more limited than Ronzy would prefer. If we go by explicit mentions in the text, he only consulted Jacques Cauvin for information about Calvin's first years in Paris. For the rest, he confined his enquiry to Calvin's works and to the testimony of François Bauduin, Calvin's former personal secretary, who became one of the reformer's religious adversaries.

Masson's *Vita* thus shows Bauduin in a new and unexplored light: an important source of information about Calvin's life, and a creator of a particular image of Calvin, which both rivalled and combined with that created by Bolsec in years to come.[149] In order to appreciate fully the significance and orientation of Masson's work on Calvin, a brief presentation of him and his relationship with Bauduin is necessary.

François Bauduin (1520–73) has been an object of studies in fairly recent years and is the better known of the two. He therefore requires the very minimum of introduction.[150] Son of a Flemish lawyer, he studied law at Louvain at the time when the *mos gallicus* was introduced. It is useful to remember here that the *mos gallicus*, which was first adopted in France in 1520 due to the influence of Andrea Alciato, consisted in interpreting Roman law as a system which was as such applicable only to the conditions and the historical context of imperial Rome. This meant that any sixteenth-century lawyer who took it upon himself to interpret it had to acquire some knowledge of Roman history, which would enable him to understand the original context and to see how it differed from the

---

[147]   Pierre Ronzy, *Un humaniste italianisant: Papire Masson (1544–1611)* (Paris: Édouard Champion, 1924). Hereafter : Ronzy.

[148]   Papire Masson talks of Jacques as the brother of Richard (*fratrique eius Jacobo*), which Théphile Dufour shows to have been impossible on grounds of chronology. See Dufour, 'Calviniana', pp. 1–6.

[149]   This escaped the attention of Bauduin's modern biographer: Michael Erbe, *François Bauduin (1520–1573). Biographie eines Humanisten* (Gütersloh: Mohn, 1978), and also of Ronzy, who devotes a whole chapter (Bk 1, Ch. 4, pp. 129–59) to relations between Masson and Bauduin.

[150]   Apart from Erbe's biography, see also Mario Turchetti, *Concordia o Toleranza? François Bauduin e i 'Moyenneurs'* (Geneva: Droz, 1984).

conditions and context of his own era. This entailed invariably relegating some (if not most of) Roman law to the status of an historical document. Until then, the commonly received system of Roman law interpretation was the *mos italicus* devised by Bartolomeo Sassoferrato, a fourteenth-century Perugian lawyer. According to the *mos italicus*, Roman law was applicable as such not just in its own time, but also in later centuries. This entailed no knowledge of history: various stratagems of logic and rhetoric were permissible to adapt it to the context in which it was interpreted.[151] Sometimes, the two *mores* blended together. The *mos italicus* was by its very nature flexible, and could accommodate even methods that contradicted its principles.[152] The success of the *mos gallicus* in France is well documented. Inevitably, it accentuated the national sentiment in considering Roman law as 'not ours'. However, it also influenced the study of history as a contextual discipline. Many lawyers, including Bauduin and Masson, were first and foremost historians.

After completing his studies, Bauduin settled in Paris in 1539, where he first came into contact with the theology of John Calvin. The earliest extant letter from him to the reformer dates from 20 July 1545.[153] Others followed. At first, he had nothing but admiration for his countryman. On his first visit to Geneva in 1546, he translated into Latin the *Excuse de noble Seigneur Iacques de Bourgoigne, S. de Fallez et Bredam*. Bauduin knew Jacques de Bourgogne personally. Michael Erbe voices the hypothesis that the seigneur's stand against the banishment of Bolsec in 1551 may have played a role in Bauduin's break with Calvin.[154] His second stay in Geneva took place over the summer and autumn of 1547,[155] and marked a high point in the relations between him and Calvin. It was during that time that Bauduin joined Calvin's household and worked as his secretary. This gave him ample opportunity to become acquainted with the reformer and his wife, and to gain access to Calvin's private papers.[156] Unlike many of Calvin's French disciples, however, Bauduin did not settle in Geneva, leaving for Lyon in the autumn of 1547 never to return. In 1548, he went to Bourges as professor of law and was to stay there until 1555, when he fell victim to quarrels between the *mos gallicus* and the *mos italicus* camps.

---

[151]   On this and on the success of the *mos gallicus* in France, see especially Donald Kelley, *Foundations of Modern Scholarship: Language, Law and History in the French Renaissance* (New York: Columbia University Press, 1970). On Bauduin's conception of history, see ibid., pp. 116–48.
[152]   See Ian McLean, *Interpretation and meaning in the Renaissance: The Case of Law* (Oxford: Oxford University Press, 1992), pp. 120–24.
[153]   See Erbe, p. 240, no. 4.
[154]   See ibid., pp. 49–50.
[155]   See ibid., pp. 53–4.
[156]   See Émile Doumergue, *Jean Calvin. Les hommes et les choses de son temps*, 7 vols (Lausanne-Neuilly: n.p., 1899–1927), vol. 2, pp. 762–5.

At the same time, he began to voice his irenicist views and to criticise Calvin's lack of tolerance for religious positions other than his own. He spent some time in Strasbourg, where he encountered among others Vermigli, Sleidan and Jean Sturm. He also had contacts with Caspar von Niedbrück and the authors of the *Magdeburg Centuries*.[157] It was here that he entered into conflict with François Le Douaren, a colleague at the Law Faculty,[158] the high point of which was marked by an open letter from the latter accusing Bauduin of incompetence and, more seriously, of being a religious turncoat, adjusting his faith to prevailing circumstances.

In 1556, Bauduin was appointed professor of law at Heidelberg, and it was during his years there (1556–61) that he produced his most important works on history, law and religious tolerance.[159] He left Heidelberg in 1561, when Elector Friedrich III officially went over to Calvinist faith, and by 30 May of that year was back in Paris. His conflict with Calvin broke out well and truly over the publication of Georg Cassander's *De officio pii viri*, a plea for the *via media* in religion.[160] Calvin wrongly suspected Bauduin of being its real author and responded (anonymously) with *Responsio ad versipellem quendam mediatorem*, an open allusion to Bauduin's defection from his own to the moderate camp. Bauduin replied by publishing his *Ad leges de famosis libellis et calumniatoribus commentarius*[161] on Roman imperial law forbidding the publication of libellous pamphlets, on pain of capital punishment for threat to public order. In the final part of the commentary, he showed that he was not the author of *De officio*, and pointed out that Calvin had harmed his (Bauduin's) reputation, thus laying himself open to the accusation of malevolent libel.[162]

Calvin responded with the *Responsio ad Balduini conuitia* in 1562. Apart from the *Responsio* itself, in which the reformer freely admits the rift between them, the work contains several early admiring letters from Bauduin, intended to show the latter's inconstancy, and also the 1555 open letter from Le Douaren accusing the Belgian lawyer of religious opportunism.

Bauduin replied by publishing his *Responsio altera*, in which he tries to show that it was not he but Calvin who has changed from what he was into a cruel tyrant. He cites diverse documents as proof, including an excerpt from Calvin's letter to Bucer in which he describes himself as a tyrant and

---

[157]   See Gregory B. Lyon, 'Bauduin, Flacius and the Plan for the Magdeburg Centuries', *Journal of the History of Ideas* (2003): 253–72.

[158]   For full details, see Erbe, pp. 78–92.

[159]   See ibid., pp. 103–22, 210–24.

[160]   See ibid., pp. 140–44.

[161]   Published in Paris by André Wechel, in 1562. See Erbe (bibliography), p. 218, no. 27.

[162]   Ibid., p. 141.

regrets that he is unable to control that aspect of his character.[163] Bauduin adds that others too consider Calvin a tyrant, particularly Melanchthon, who supposedly said this to Bauduin in so many words at the Colloquy of Worms. He compares the Reformed Church to the Donatists, and does not spare Calvin's associates, Beza and Hotman. He even cites excerpts from a letter of Sturm detailing Hotman's intrigues during his time in Strasbourg. In 1563, Bauduin returned to the bosom of the Roman Catholic Church.

After some time spent in Paris and in the Netherlands, he joined the University of Angers in 1569 as professor of law, having been offered the job by the chancellor of the duke of Anjou, Philippe Hurault de Cheverny, whom he had known for some time and who shared Bauduin's moderate views. It was here that he had Papire Masson among his students. He held the post until 1573, the year of his death.

If his relations with Calvin show that one would hardly expect him to be a source of information favourable to the reformer, this should be weighed off against his view of history, which would have influenced Papire Masson as much or more than the personal issue of his mentor's relations with the Genevan reformer. According to Lyon, Bauduin thought that it would not do in historical research to rely on the authority of testimonies to determine the fact. Rather, the fact itself had to be interrogated by the testimonies available. It was thus that an historian could establish the reliability of testimonies.[164] Bauduin was also a firm believer in the principle of the *similitudo temporum* – in other words, the capacity of historical situations –, if correctly analysed and studied in context, to yield a message that would make history instructive for the future. He thus saw the Age of Constantine as providing an answer to the religious conflict of his own era, and argued that Charles V should follow Constantine's example and convoke an ecumenical council. One would thus expect a disciple of Bauduin to pay close attention to sources as elucidating facts, and to espouse the *similitudo temporum* principle.

Masson was born in 1544, son of a merchant family in Forez. After a period of classical study in Lyon, he joined the Jesuit order and spent four years studying theology in Rome and Naples. On his return, he broke with the Jesuits and theology and took up a post teaching philosophy at the Collège du Plessis in Paris. Around that time, he acquired as patron Philippe Hurault de Cheverny, chancellor of the duke of Anjou, thanks to whom Bauduin was to be appointed professor of law at the University of Angers in 1569. According to Christophe de Thou's *Life* of Masson,[165] he and Bauduin got to know one another in Paris before the latter's

---

[163]   See Doumergue, *Calvin*, vol. 2, pp. 762–5, and Erbe, pp. 145–6 and ns. at pp. 125–6 ibid.

[164]   See Lyon, p. 265, and n. 43.

[165]   See Ronzy, p. 124, n. 1.

departure for Angers. They remained in correspondence during 1570 and 1571, when Masson could finally join Bauduin and become his student.[166] According to Ronzy and Erbe,[167] it was under Bauduin's influence that Masson finally gave his preference to history and began to aspire to combining his theological and historical knowledge and method with the study of law. Predictably, he took up law studies at the University of Angers, where his mentor was teaching. In June 1573, he was made *doctor vtriusque iuris* and entered the service of Hurault de Cheverny in Paris, becoming his librarian prior to being appointed *avocat au parlement de Paris* in 1576. He was Bauduin's literary executor after the latter's death in 1573, and wrote an *Elogium* of his former teacher which appeared in the same year. This presents Bauduin as a man who never really left the Roman Catholic Church and remained an irenicist all his life, wanting to put his historical and legal knowledge to the service of reconciling the Reformation schism.[168]

There are several indications that Bauduin's approach to history and biography influenced Masson, judging by the excerpts of their lost correspondence which he cites in his *Historia calamitatum Galliae*, written in 1600 but not published until 1636. Bauduin was especially concerned to draw his disciple's attention to the importance of weighing up sources in forming historical judgements, and to warn him expressly against works such as the three imperial Panegyrics of Sidonius Apollinaris, which he considered as suspect in matters of historical accuracy as funeral orations had been to Cicero.[169]

His extant literary production shows Masson to have been first and foremost a biographer[170] of antique and contemporary scholars, writers, philosophers, statesmen and so on. Among his best-known works are his *Elogia* of various figures, some of which were published singly prior to being anthologised posthumously by Jean-Baptiste Masson, the author's brother. However, Masson was probably the first early modern author to make a distinction between a biography (*Vita*) and an *Elogium* (posthumous praise in declamatory form). His *Vitae* tended to contain remarks (not necessarily on the hero) that would not do in an *Elogium*, a discourse sharply focused on the hero and composed of undiluted praise. A good example here is the contrast between his portrayal of Christophe de Thou in his *Elogium* and in the *Vita Caroli Molinaei*. In the former,

---

[166]   This correspondence is no longer extant. See ibid., pp. 124–5, n. 4. For a full bibliography of Masson's printed and MS works, see Ronzy, *Bibliographie critique des Œuvres imprimées et manuscrites de Papire Masson*, thèse complémentaire pour le doctorat (Paris: Edouard Champion, 1924).

[167]   Erbe, p. 129; Ronzy, pp. 124–5, n. 2.

[168]   Erbe, p. 197.

[169]   See Ronzy, p. 125, ns. 1–2. For Cicero on funeral orations, see *Or.* II, 84, 341.

[170]   See Ronzy, *Bibliographie*.

De Thou comes across as a model of kindness to his lawyers. In the *Vita Molinaei*, on the other hand, Masson mentions that De Thou, as president of the *parlement de Paris*, was prone to short-lasting and quickly regretted outbursts of bad temper.[171] His *Vita Caluini*, despite Ronzy's insistence to the contrary[172] and despite a fairly objective use of sources, is something of an odd man out, as it is his sole biographical work devoted to a religious adversary. Masson composed it in 1583, during his last years in Paris, after he had had ample opportunity to gather information on the reformer from the late Bauduin. However, it was not published until nine years after his death by his brother Jean-Baptiste Masson, who added some information on Calvin's year in Angoulême and a terse postface. The work is brief, numbering 34 small in-8° pages, and copies of it are scarce.[173] We do not know its original imprint, but we do know that this edition escaped the attention of most theologians and historians who took an interest in Calvin's life between 1620 and the end of the eighteenth century.[174] Jean-Baptiste Masson, as we shall see, was opposed to incorporating the *Vita* in the full edition of his brother's *Elogia* which he was planning. However, he never carried out his plan, and the *Elogia* did not come out as a collection until 1638. The edition was the work of the bibliophile Jean Balesdens. Balesdens did not distinguish, any more than Jean-Baptiste Masson had done, between *Elogium* and *Vita*, and collected both types of writing under the heading of *Elogia*. He was persuaded to include the *Vita Calvini* by Gui Patin (1601–72), the well-known physician and man of Letters of libertine persuasion, who was professor at the Collège Royal de France from 1655. The publisher (Sébastien Huré), who found himself under pressure from the Jesuits, put up an opposition, but Patin and Balesdens got their way. Given the situation, Jean-Baptiste Masson's postface was excised; only his appendix on Calvin's passage in Angoulême was maintained. In Balesdens's edition of *Elogia* of 1638, the *Vita* thus appeared with Masson's name, but without any hint of its ideological orientation. By 1656, Masson's authorship was put in doubt and the text was henceforth sometimes attributed to the Gallican Jacques Gillot, notably by Maimbourg.[175] Among seventeenth- and eighteenth-century

---

[171]   See also Ronzy, p. 312, n. 3.

[172]   Ibid., pp. 313–15.

[173]   I have used the copy held by the Bibliothèque de Sainte Geneviève in Paris (shelfmark: 4Q 897 (3) Inv. 358): *Vita Ioannis Calvini auctore Papirio Massono* (Lutetiae, 1620). Hereafter: Masson (1620)

[174]   See Ronzy, pp. 635–6.

[175]   Cl. viri Jo. Papirii Massonis, ... Elogiorum pars prima, quae imperatorum, regum, ducum, aliorumque insignium heroüm ... vitam complectitur Accessit ipsius P. Massonis vita, authore ... Jacobo Augusto Thuano ... Omnia haec ... e musaeo Joan. Balesdens, ... - *Cl. viri Jo. Papirii Massonis, ... Elogiorum pars secunda, quae vitam eorum complectitur qui ... dignitatum titulis vel eruditionis laude ... claruerunt. [Accesserunt Simonis Pietrei patris,*

historians, Pierre Bayle,[176] as we shall see, questioned this outright and attributed the *Vita* correctly on the basis of internal evidence. The reason for the misattribution was partly the seventeenth-century image (shared by Bayle) of Papire Masson as a conservative Catholic who could not possibly have written an impartial *Life* of Calvin. Without Jean-Baptiste's *caueat*, the text seemed to suggest that the editor of the *Traictez des droits de l'Eglise gallicane*, who was also co-author of the *Satire ménipée*, was a much more likely author. The misunderstanding was finally dispelled in 1913 by Théophile Dufour, who discovered a copy of the 1620 edition with Jean-Baptiste's postface.[177]

This is how the latter closes his brother's *Vita Calvini*:

> Having collected as many *Elogia* or *Vitae* of famous men and women written once upon a time by my brother, I would like to publish them shortly as a collection. However, I thought it most inappropriate to include in that collection his *Life* of Calvin in 19 chapters lest the pious and Catholic reader take offence at the unpleasant odour or rather stink that exudes from it. For this reason, I am sending it to Calvin's fellow-citizens and comrades who inhabit the region of the Lake Léman which the Swiss call the 'Genfer-See' so that the memory of him can drown and disappear in it. I shall add just a few facts about him which I learnt from several authoritative and very aged citizens of Angoulême when I served there as a canon.[178]

Jean-Baptiste Masson obviously does not fully understand his brother's distinction between *elogium* and *vita*. Secondly, he makes it quite clear that he did not publish the *Vita* either to praise or to blame the reformer, but to 'bury his reputation in the waters of Lake Léman.' There is no record of the 1620 edition making any impact on seventeenth-century Geneva, and, whatever the number of copies printed, it had disappeared from public view by 1638. However, Jean-Baptiste did not succeed in drowning or burying it for ever. In fact, as I shall show, once published as part of *Elogia*, it became as popular among Catholics as among Calvinists, and seems for a while to have enjoyed the status of the sole authoritative biography of the reformer. Those who cited it as such tended to attribute it to Masson without going into the finer points of the question of authorship. How

---

doctoris medici parisiensis, elogium, auctore G. Patin, et Vita Johannis Calvini, auctore J. Gillot.] Omnia haec e musaeo Joan. Balesdens, ... (Parisiis, apud S. Huré, 1656).

[176] See Pierre Bayle, *Dictionnaire historique et critique*, 5th edn, 5 vols (Amsterdam: Pierre Brunel, 1740), vol. 2, pp. 19–20, and Chapter 5, p. 214.

[177] See Dufour, 'Calviniana', p. 1, n. 1.

[178] Masson (1620), p. 33: 'Collectis quamplurimis illustrium virorum ac foeminarum vitis seu elogiis a fratre meo olim scriptis eas in lucem breui mittere cupio. Vitam autem Ioannis Caluini haeresiarchae 19 capita continentem operi miscendam minime duxi ne pius ac catholicus lector ingrato quodam odore aut foetore offendatur. Idcirco eam mitto ad conciues suos segreges lacum Lemanum inhabitantes quem Heluetii "Genfer Zee" vocant vt ibi demergatur pereatque memoria eius. De quo pauca referam quae dum canonicus essem ecclesiae Engolismensis a pluribus ciuibus, senioribus scilicet et doctis accepi.'

does the text differ from the standard hostile Calvin biographies of the period, and what does it tell us about the author's use of sources and Bauduin's possible role?

As Jean-Baptiste Masson says, the *Vita* is divided into nineteen short chapters. Jean-Papire did not append a preface worthy of the name, just one prefatory sentence:

> It is important to make the life of John Calvin publicly known so that posterity may know what sort of man was he who challenged the authority of the Roman Church and who came close to overturning ancestral faith in France.[179]

He subdivides the *Vita* into the following sections: Calvin's ancestry and home, his birth and childhood, his studies in the liberal disciplines, his departure from Paris, exile, his departure to Italy, Geneva and Germany, his activities in Germany, return to Geneva, his activities in Geneva, his writings, his adversaries, the harm he did to his native country, his death and burial, his will, his morality, his vices and reproaches made to him, some of his sayings, his virtues, conclusion. It would not be unfair to consider the *Vita* as a Plutarchan portrait of Calvin, in that it dwells on the hero's psychology at the expense of some of his deeds that made him famous. At the same time, however, its division into *loci communes* is reminiscent of Suetonius. Four other more important features, however, characterise the *Vita* and point to Bauduin as inspiration. One is Masson's very careful evaluation of his sources and unhesitating dismissal of some of them (Bolsec and other *authores plebeii*) as unreliable; another is his awareness of the usefulness of publishing Calvin's *Life* so that posterity can learn lessons from it according to the *similitudo temporum* principle; the third is the frequent mention of Bauduin as a source; and the fourth is Masson's portrayal of Calvin as a tyrannical, vindictive and bad-tempered despot, an image he would have inherited directly from his former teacher. Unlike a modern academic biographer, Masson does not cite his sources with any precision. He gives no specific references to documents consulted. In the case of the *Vita Calvini*, the issue is further obscured by the fact that he could not check the proofs, which means that it contains several mistakes, due no doubt to Jean-Baptiste's misreading or misinterpretation of the original. To give the most flagrant example of this, Papire Masson appears to say that he questioned personally (*a quibus haec didicimus*) Richard Cauvin, Gérard Cauvin's 'brother' and Richard's 'brother' Jacques, both blacksmiths in St Germain l'Auxerrois. However, appearances to the contrary, this passage[180] if taken literally turns out to contain multiple

---

[179]   Ibid., p. 3: 'Vitam Ioannis Caluni mandari literis publice interest vt posteri sciant a quo homine oppugnata Romanae ecclesiae dignitas ac pene euersa religio maiorum in Gallia fuit.'

[180]   Ibid., p. 6: 'Haec causa fuit cur pater eum quam doctissimum fieri cuperet mitteretque Lutetiam et Ricardo fratri commendaret, in vico D. Germani Altissiodorensis fabro ferrario

errors. As Théophile Dufour pointed out,[181] Richard Cauvin, John Calvin's
uncle who put him up in Paris in 1523, could not have still been alive in
1583. Similarly, Jacques Cauvin, who figures in the baptismal registers of St
Germain l'Auxerrois and Saint-Merry, would have been over one hundred
years old in 1583 had he really been Richard's brother. *Fratri* [brother] is
obviously an error for *filio* [son]. As for questioning the two 'brothers'
personally, it is obvious that the sentence contains a scribal anacoluthon
and that Masson would only have questioned Jacques, the son of Richard;
in other words, Calvin's (younger) cousin. The information the latter
provided, as Dufour points out, turned out to be neither extensive nor
particularly accurate, especially regarding other surviving members of the
Cauvin family either in Noyon itself or in Picardy.[182] However, copying
or proof errors notwithstanding, Masson constitutes an exception among
sixteenth-century biographers in having made the effort to discover a
potentially reliable source, which he names and uses to inform his readers
about Calvin's parentage and early years.

In general, however, he hardly names his sources at all. We are not
told where Masson obtained the very detailed and exact information
about Calvin's studies, any more than who informed him about Calvin's
movements until 1536 and his arrival in Geneva, or about his exile in
Strasbourg and the rest of his career. In fact, the only sources Masson
mentions *explicitly* are, firstly, Calvin's own works, of which he shows a very
thorough and impartial knowledge, which cannot be anything other than
first hand, and, secondly, François Bauduin, who is mentioned as a source
no fewer than eight times in what is a very short text. These references are
sufficiently detailed to throw light on Bauduin as Masson's main source.
They show that Masson did not just content himself with his mentor's
oral reminiscences, but that he had recourse to the acrimonious exchange
between him and Calvin prompted by the appearance of Cassander's *De
officio pii viri* in 1562/63. A detailed breakdown of references to Bauduin
illustrates this.

In the chapter on Calvin's activities in Germany:

> Therefore, when his [Calvin's] wife died in 1548 he refused to remarry not
> out of dislike of bigamy, but for the sake of his studies. He also had a stepson
> from her first marriage, judging by what Bauduin says in his *Responsio ad
> Caluinum*, he who was my teacher of civil law and before that Calvin's private

---

fratrique eius Iacobo qui nunc, anno scilicet supra 1500um 83o eandem artem Parisiis prope
sanctum Medericum via vulpis dicta exercet, viris quidem honestissimis, a quibus haec
didicimus, qui nunquam sectam secuti sunt, etsi Antonio fratre Caluini mercatore caligario
vt id facerent monente, quin ab eodem Iacobo narrante sciui nullum iam neque Nouioduni
neque in Belgica secunda sibi cognominem ac gentilem viuere. Ipse vero a Caluini naturali
nomine nunquam recessit.'
[181] See Dufour, 'Calviniana', pp. 1–6, esp. pp. 1–2.
[182] See ibid., p. 1, ns. 2–3.

secretary: 'when your stepson from your wife's first marriage was alive, you should have been more than a father to him and yet you brought him up in your own way of thinking. Were his mother still alive she would not deny this, as she often complained to me about this when I was at his home.'[183]

In the chapter on Calvin's adversaries:

When Calvin was already old, Bauduin, who had often called him his father and his teacher, put him to silence, this much to Calvin's grief.[184]

In the chapter on Calvin's will:

He slept very little and dictated many of his works at night from his bed to a personal secretary, a job which Bauduin, a Belgian by birth, admitted to having done once upon a time.[185]

In the chapter on Calvin's vices and reproaches made to him:

Sensation-seeking writers reproach him with worldly pleasures and debauchery. However, no one seems to have hated adultery more than he, even though his own family was not immune to it. For adultery was the reason why Antoine his brother took a second wife, even though his first wife, whom he divorced, was still alive and Calvin and his colleagues approved the divorce.[186] And Bauduin taxed Calvin with this.[187]

Although he appeared modest and disposed to expose his thoughts simply, this appearance concealed pride and self-love. This is a vice that all founders of sects are prone to, regardless of whether the sect is good or bad. Therefore Bauduin says quite rightly: 'your colleagues complain about your arrogance and unbelievable haughtiness.'[188]

---

[183]   Masson (1620), p. 14: 'Habuit et priuiginum; sic enim Balduinus praeceptor meus in Iure ciuili et olim familiaris et domesticus scriba eius: "vide cum priuiginus viuebat tuus, cui plus quam pater esse debuisti; eum quidem ex Anabaptista patre natum more tuo regenerasti, certe si eius mater viueret, credo non negaret quod domi eius saepe apud me conquesta est". Haec ille in Responsione ad Caluinum.' (Cf. Doumergue, vol. 2, pp. 762–5)

[184]   Ibid.: 'Ipsi silentium Balduinus Iurisconcultus imposuit seni, magno dolore Caluini quem ille patrem et praeceptorem saepenumero appellasset.'

[185]   Ibid., pp. 22–3: 'Somni erat breuissimi itaque magnam partem /23/ operum suorum noctu e lectulo dictauit domestico notario operam praebente, quo munere aliquandiu functum se esse Balduinus Attrebas non negabat.'

[186]   For a full account of the adultery case involving Calvin's sister-in-law, Anne Le Fert, see Robert Kingdon, *Adultery and Divorce in Calvin's Geneva* (Cambridge, MA: Harvard University Press, 1995), pp. 71–98.

[187]   Masson (1620), pp. 25–6: 'Antonius enim Caluini frater ob eam /26/ causam, viuente priore vxore quam repudiauit, alteram duxit, Caluino et collegis repudium probantibus. Quod ei Balduinus obiicit.'

[188]   Ibid., p. 26: 'Facie cum modesta videretur ad omnemque simplicis animi figuram compositus, tegebat latentem intus superbiam et filautian. Quo vitio sectarum auctores carere nequeunt, seu bonae seu malae sint. Itaque non immerito Balduinus ait: "colleagae tui conqueruntur de tua intolerabili arrogantia et incredibili fastu."' (Cf. *Calv. Opp.* 9, col. 57).

[Many writers reproach Calvin with having pretended to raise from the dead a man who was in fact alive.] I really wonder how he could have done this, seeing as he had already written what follows in the preface to his *Institutes*: 'they are wicked who demand miracles from us. For we are not forging a new Gospel but maintaining the very one whose authority rests on what was done by Christ and the Apostles.' As for the false miracle, whether there is any substance to it or not, it has turned into a standard anecdote so that both Lutherans and Catholics have held it against Calvin and his disciples. But Bauduin, who after all was hostile to Calvin, never accused him of this, and he certainly would not have omitted it, had he known for certain that Calvin had done such a thing.[189]

In the chapter on Calvin's virtues:

Calvin in his *Responsio* to Bauduin praises himself immoderately as the most eloquent of lawyers and dwells on his own virtues.[190]

[Concerning Calvin's self-congratulatory pronouncements.] Bauduin cites Calvin's own words on this, adding: 'he says all this and many other similar things about himself in a short work', but Bauduin does not refute any of it except to say: 'Calvin will pardon me I am sure if I do not give any credence to this vanity.'[191]

Masson's account shows that apart from Calvin's works, he had knowledge of all the hostile biographies and biographical notices on Calvin, as well as Beza's and Colladon's biographies, the most likely source for the summary he gives of Calvin's will and one or two other pieces of information. However, it is quite clearly Bauduin and, more particularly, Bauduin's controversy with Calvin, that he thinks the most reliable source against which to test other sources. Bauduin also constitutes his main source of information on Calvin's family life, his character and his working habits. Masson thus inevitably inherits Bauduin's perception of Calvin as a cruel, arrogant, tyrannical, hard-working insomniac, as we shall be showing in detail. At the same time, relying on Bauduin and his historiographical method means that Masson also does away with a large number of myths about Calvin much more authoritatively than Beza or Colladon in their

---

[189]   Ibid., pp. 27–8: 'Id quomodo ab eo factum sit miror, cum locum illum in praefatione Institutionis christianae pridem scripserit: "et quod miracula a nobis postulant improbe faciunt. Non enim recens aliquod /28/ Euangelium cudimus sed illud ipsum retinemus cuius confirmandae veritati seruiunt omnia quae umquam et Christus et Apostoli ediderunt." Illud tamen, siue verum est siue ab aliquo confictum versum est in fabulam, Lutheranique et Catholici id veluti gestum deinceps et Caluino et discipulis eius obiecere. Quod ne Balduinus quidem, Caluino infensus, vnquam obiecit, non obmissurus profecto si gestum scire potuisset.' (Cf. *Inst. Praef., Calv. Opp.* 2, col. 15).

[190]   Ibid., p. 29: 'Caluinus ipse in responsione ad Balduinum disertissimum iurisconsultum sese intemperanter laudat praedicatque virtutes suas.'

[191]   Ibid., p. 31: 'Haec quidem Balduinus de Caluino tradit iisdem verbis quibus ille vsus erat moxque subiicit: "haec et id genus alia de se profert multa in libello non magno", sed refutationis loco nihil adiicit propter hoc pauca: "Caluinus mihi veniam det si non possum credere vanitati."'

idealised accounts. At the same time, be it under Bauduin's influence or simply on the basis of his own reading, Masson does lavish a certain amount of approval on the reformer, as we are about to see. He concludes his account by saying, 'we have given this account of Calvin's life as neither his friend nor his foe. I will not be lying if I say that he was the ruin and destruction of France. If only he had died in childhood or had never been born! For he brought so many ills to his country that it is only just to hate and detest his origins.'[192] Although negative to say the least, once the reader has understood that the ills in question are the Wars of Religion, this judgement turns out to have nothing especially Roman Catholic about it, and could well express the opinion of Bauduin or any advocate of the *via media*.

The Profile of Masson's Vita Caluini

What, then, is the ideological profile of the *Vita Caluini*, and how does it differ from the standard Roman Catholic image of Calvin propagated by Bolsec? First and foremost, Masson ignores the myth of branding and substitutes for it the account of Calvin's brother Charles's unfortunate end, for which there was documentary support.[193] Masson does not exaggerate when he says that Charles, defrocked after refusing to take the Eucharist, was secretly buried under the public gibbet, so that the two benefices purchased by their father eventually devolved on John. He stresses that these benefices provided no more than modest revenue, and does not find the fact of John holding them scandalous in any way. Indeed, the buying and selling of two benefices so as to make sure they remained in the family was the biggest crime the Cauvins could be accused of, apart from the father's misuse of public funds for their purchase, which Masson does not seem to have known about.[194] On the other hand, he does devote attention to Calvin's Parisian period, and lavishes a certain amount of praise on the care the future reformer took to learn Greek, Latin and Hebrew. He considers as *elegantissimi* Calvin's comments on Seneca's *De clementia*

---

[192]   Ibid., pp. 31–2: 'Conclusio. Haec de vita Caluini scribimus neque amici neque inimici, quem si labem et perniciem Galliae dixero, nihil mentiar. Atque vtinam aut nunquam natus esset aut in pueritia mortuus /32/ Tantum enim malorum intulit in patriam vt cunabula eius merito detestari atque odisse debeas.'

[193]   Ibid., p. 5: 'Is patris concilio ecclesiastico ordini destinabatur vt Carolus eius frater et presbyter qui Nouioduni mortuus noctu et clam sepultus est et inter quatuor columnas furcae publicae quia eucharistiam sumere noluerat. Et duo sacerdotia quae habebat Ioanni Caluino affini suo et presbytero dari conferrique procurauit; parociam scilicet Pontis Episcopalis – sic enim Nouiomenses appellant vicinum vrbis suae oppidum ad Oesiam amnem situm – et capellam beatae Mariae Virginis de Partu, vulgo de la Gesine, in templo Virginis Maximo ad Leanam Ostii chori deseruiri solitam.'

[194]   The full account is given by Le Vasseur, *Annales*. See below, Chapter 5, notes 28–30.

published in 1532. Although he underlines the anti-Roman tone of the first
edition of the *Institutes*, he does not see it as impious or blasphemous, and,
in contrast with Bolsec, does not think that the endless revisions it was to
be subjected to suggest inconstancy in religious matters. On the contrary,
he notes that:

> In the *Institutes*, often augmented and published for a thousand times, he
> devotes 104 chapters to rejecting most of the teaching we receive from the
> Roman Church, but he also strikes a crucial blow against the errors of Servetus
> and his like, and refutes very astutely the impious baptismal teaching of the
> Anabaptists.[195]

Again in contrast with Bolsec, Masson does not see Calvin's first sojourn in
Geneva as a seditious attempt to overthrow civil powers. Although he does
describe him (not unjustly) as a 'self styled theologian', he attributes his and
Farel's expulsion simply to the desire of part of the community to restore
ancestral worship and rituals which had been abolished only recently.[196]

His description of Calvin's activity in Strasbourg is equally impartial. He
notes correctly that thanks to Bucer, 'the great defender of the Lutherans',
Calvin was given the freedom of the city, and his job was to look after
the French-speaking congregation. Masson is not averse to noting that at
that time Calvin's fame began to spread throughout 'Germany', especially
after the publication of his Commentary on Romans, which he dedicated
to Simon Grynaeus *eruditissimus Germanorum*. He is full of praise for
Calvin's conversion-work among the city's Anabaptists (*genus hominum
superstitionis nouae et maleficae* [a variety of men who believe in a new,
extremely harmful superstition]), including the first husband of Idelette de
Bure, the reformer's future wife.[197]

Equally sound and impartial is his account of Calvin's recall and return
to Geneva. He stresses that the instauration of ecclesiastical discipline was

---

[195]   Masson (1620), p. 11: 'Illa Institutione saepe aucta et millies excusa capitibus 104
magnam partem receptae a Romana et Catholica ecclesia doctrinae reiicit, obruit quoque
Seruetianos errores et Anabaptistarum impias de baptismo sententias acutissime refellit.'

[196]   Ibid., pp. 12–13 : 'Diu vero in Italia esse non potuit, ne forte agnitus ad supplicium
religionis causa raperetur etsi clericum sacerdoti inseruientem agebat. Igitur per Pennas
Alpes in Galliam reuersus Geneuae ad lacum Lemanum pedem fixit, precibus G'I Farelli qui
veteribus sacris muncipio illo fugatis, nouos ritus introducere coeperat.

Ibi Christiani theologi nomen adeptus, intermissum Catechismi vsum reuocauit, hac
ratione et facili methodo simul docens persuadensque elementa ac principia nascentis sectae.
At vero enata inter ciues discordia sententiis dictis, Farellus Caluinusque vrbe excedere
iubentur cupientibus quibusdam reuocare ritus et ceremonias maiorum, non multo ante
depulsas. Caluinus secundum exul Basileam, mox Argenti /13/ nam se contulit quae est
ciuitas Galliae ad Rhenum flumen.'

[197]   Ibid., pp. 13–14.

the reformer's primary concern, but he does not mention the Sadolet affair, presumably because he had no knowledge of it.[198]

Masson's judgement on Calvin's writings and his style is particularly interesting, as it is probably the only impartial literary judgement we have by a near-contemporary humanist and man of Letters who had good knowledge of Calvin's early education and considered his commentary on Seneca 'extremely elegant'. He does not criticise any of the reformer's literary production, while echoing Beza's judgement on Calvin's capacity for hard work:

> Practically not a day went by when he did not preach to the citizens. Three times a week, for as long as he lived, he lectured in theology. He was industrious and always active, writing or planning something. He used to re-read the works of Cicero once a year, although his style does not resemble that of Cicero in any way. Rather he seems to have imitated Tacitus and Seneca and the ancient theologians.[199]

A humanist such as Masson saw the Ciceronian ideal as very much something to strive for; his remark on the resemblance between Calvin's Latin and that of the later Roman writers has the merit of being correct, and should not be seen as a criticism. Indeed, as the following paragraph shows, Masson was fully aware of the strengths of Calvin's style:

> He wrote as much and as well as any secretary if we consider the quantity, the conciseness, the sting, the rhetorical stress, the vigour of expression. He published commentaries on nearly all the books of the Old and New Testament. However, out of all his books he particularly recommended his treatise on the Institutes of the Christian religion, and he also boasted that his Commentaries on the Minor Prophets would always be considered as good as any patristic commentary.[200]

In the chapter on Calvin's adversaries, he notes the reformer's outstanding polemical gifts. Under this heading, he mentions briefly Pighius, Sadolet and Bauduin (pointing out, as we have seen, that the latter, unlike all the other polemicists, managed to have the last word in his exchange with the reformer). More interesting to us are his remarks on Servetus, as they show

---

[198]   Ibid., pp. 15–16.

[199]   Ibid.: 'Nulla fere dies praeteriit, qua non ha/16/buerit concionem ad ciues de rebus sacris. Ter in octiduo quamdiu vixit theologiam professus est, operosus et semper aliquid scribens ac moliens Ciceronisque Opera quotannis relegens etsi stylus eius nihil minus quam Ciceronem sapuit. Tacitum enim et Senecam potius et veteres theologos imitari videtur.'

[200]   Ibid., pp. 16–17: 'Scripsit nec pauciora nec minus bene quam segregum quisquam, si numerum, si breuitatem, si aculeos, si emphasin, si argutias spectare volumus. Extant eius Commentarii ad omnes fere veteres ac Noui Testamenti libros. Caeterum ex omnibus scriptis Opus de Institutione christianae religionis praecipue commendabat et gloriabatur ad minores Prophetas quos ediderat Commentarios nullis /17/ patrum interpretationibus vnquam cessuros.'

that neither Masson nor, it is to be surmised, Bauduin disapproved of the
execution, although neither ever took up a spirited defence of it *à la* Beza:

> Another one of his adversaries was Michael Servetus, a Spaniard by race, who
> impiously compared the Trinity to Cerberus. When he came to Geneva, he was
> arrested and burnt at the stake. Calvin wrote a remarkable book on the errors
> of this individual of infinite viciousness and he includes a very brief summary
> of his observations on this in Book 1 of the *Institutes of the Christian religion*.
> Catholics taxed Calvin with this issue and affirmed that he, Calvin, was thus
> justly punished as enemy of the Gospel for having abandoned the religion of
> his forefathers.[201]

Masson does not use Servetus' execution to tax Calvin with cruelty,
despotism, arrogance, and so on, although as a matter of course, he is, as we
shall see, very liberal with examples of all these vices, relying on information
provided by Bauduin. More interestingly, he does not automatically
suppose, in contrast with most of his Catholic contemporaries, that the
Reformation entailed the rise of heresies such as Antitrinitarianism.

However, this absence of standard invective does not make Masson an
impartial, let alone a partisan, biographer. His chief aim, as we have said,
is to draw his countrymen's attention to all the ills that Calvin brought to
France. This is why an entire section is entitled *Caluinus quantum nocuit
patriae* [How much harm Calvin did to his fatherland]. According to
Masson, Calvin's harmfulness consisted initially in the persuasiveness of
his propaganda and his capacity to disseminate it. However, as might be
expected from a disciple of Bauduin, it is not the issue of corruption of
the innocent faithful or their damnation in large numbers that preoccupies
him. The real ill that Calvin brought to France is the Wars of Religion.

Masson notes that Calvin's works first began to circulate in France in
the reign of Henry II, despite a ban on them, for 'the greed of peddlers
was responsible for procuring them in large quantities.' That meant that
educated people read them, were converted, and in their turn influenced
the unlearned. Masson finds Calvin's errors infinitely greater and more
harmful than those of Berengarius, whose teaching in any case gained very
few disciples, unlike Calvin's doctrines. He sees the role of Antoine de
Navarre during the reign of Charles IX as very much a low point in this

---

[201]   Ibid., pp. 17–18: 'Horum plurimi quidem aduersus eum scripsere, nemo tamen pari
grauitate scribendi pondereque verborum et aculeis ad eius principia respondisse visus est. Pighium
ipse de libero arbitrio disserentem et Sadoletum pene terruit. Ipsi silentium Balduinus Iurisconcultus
imposuit seni, magno dolore Caluini quem ille patrem et praeceptorem saepenumero appellasset.
Aduersarium quoque habuit Michaelem Seruetum genere Hispanum. Hic Trinitatem cerbero
impie comparans, Geneuam cum venisset, comprehensus atque igni crematus est. De erroribus
tam scelerati hominis librum singularem /18/ scripsit Caluinus, idemque summam speculationum
eius breuissime complectitur lib. 1 de Institutione Christianae religionis. Hoc exemplum Catholici
Caluino obiecere vt assererent non iniuria punitum quasi hostem Euangelii qui defectionem a
veteribus sacris antea fecisset.'

process. Among other things, it resulted in the arrival in France of several of Calvin's ministers, especially Beza ('a poet turned theologian').[202] Although, according to Masson, Calvin himself decided not to come precisely because he wanted to avoid the burning of his ministers and his own death, things turned out otherwise:

> For an incredible number of people turned out to hear Beza and his associates, so that an armed defence of the sect was mounted and a civil war broke out, bloodier than any France had ever seen ….[203]

Masson, unlike all other biographers of the period, is not at all interested in whether Calvin's death was 'good' or 'bad', and he does not see his multiple illnesses, which he lists briefly but accurately, as symptomatic of either the reformer's depravity or his heretical opinions. What does interest him, however, are his character, virtues and vices, both real and those with which he was unjustly reproached. It is thus that Masson presents the reformer as a man rendered 'irascible by a fiery spirit and too much bile'; in other words, as a bad-tempered, unpleasant, overworked and arrogant despot. He naturally refers to the affair of Bucer's letter mentioned by Bauduin in his *Responsio*, and to Melanchthon's reproaches of *morositas*, which have the same source. Not unjustly, he notes that overwork, illness and lack of sleep were largely responsible for this.[204] He says that Genevans used to say that they would rather be in hell with Beza than in heaven with Calvin, an anecdote he obviously got from Bauduin, and draws the reader's attention to the reformer's biting wit and sarcasm. Although timid by nature, as he admitted himself, he was intrepid in the affairs of the state, as witnessed by his intervention in the quelling of the rebellion of the council, a piece of information which suggests that Masson, as well as relying on Bauduin, was familiar with Calvin's 1565 *Life* by Beza and

---

[202] He is referring to the period 1560–62 and the events which terminated in the outbreak of the first War of Religion in September 1562. On the role of Beza as councillor to the vacillating Protestant Antoine de Bourbon, king of Navarre; on the increase in numbers of Protestant parishes in France; and on the outbreak of the first War of Religion, see for example Dufour, 'Théodore de Bèze', pp. 359–77. See ibid., pp. 359–72 for analysis of 1561–62 as the period when Protestantism was a 'fashionable' religion in France.

[203] Masson (1620), pp. 19–20: 'Tamen accidit et valde praeter opinionem /20/ piorum hominum. Incredibili enim numero concursus factus ad audiendum Bezam et socios, parata arma ad defensionem sectae exortique motus ciuilis belli quo nullum vnquam funestius in Gallia fuit …'.

[204] Ibid., pp. 23–4: 'Ingenium ardens et multa bilis iracundium eum reddebat. Bucerus Lutheranae sectae acerrimus vindex etsi amicus familiari epistola eum castigaturus canem rabidum vocabat et scriptorem maledicendi studio infectum. Iudicare /24/ eum de hominibus prout amaret vel odisse prout liberet. Quod ei quoque a Balduino exprobratum est qui epistolam illam et signum Buceri viderat. Melanchthon praefractam eius vt ipse loquebatur, morositatem vituperabat. Sed morosum eum labores et vigiliae et morbi fecere.'

Colladon.[205] He categorically asserts that Calvin never sought personal advancement or financial gain, and echoes Beza's point that the reformer never sought rich patrons despite the fact that he was in touch with many heads of state. He is equally categorical in affirming (against Bolsec) that Calvin did not defect from the Roman Catholic Church because he wanted to constitute himself as head of his own church, but because he genuinely disagreed with the Roman religion over the number and nature of the sacraments, image-worship, rituals and biblical interpretation.[206]

We have already discussed Masson's perception of Calvin's real and imagined vices, for which he relies exclusively on Bauduin. One would expect an equally measured and well-balanced account of Calvin's virtues. However, although Masson apparently devotes a whole section to them, these turn out to be self-acclaimed. In other words, Calvin had no virtues, but a fair amount of vanity and self-love. Masson's *Vita* this could not be further removed from the model of an *elogium*.

Given the climate of the times and the circumstances surrounding its publication, Masson's *Life* had no chance of making an impact until the seventeenth century, as we shall see in the next chapter. It is not without significance that the first *Life* of the reformer, which avoided the main traps of a hagiography or an *elogium* on the one hand, and of a libellous caricature on the other, was so heavily marked by Bauduin's method and by his knowledge and perception of Calvin. With Masson, aided by Calvin's former secretary, Calvin's biography entered for the first time the realm of history-writing.

[205]   See above, pp. 133–5.
[206]   Masson (1620), pp. 24–5: 'Et timidum fuisse natura ipse non negat, intrepidum tamen sese exhibuit in magnis reipublicae negotiis ac bis terue in graui discordia ciuium per strictos enses nudus penetrans voce ac vultu seditiones sedauit. Deferebant ei collegae et discipuli vt doctori suo. Munera ipse publica neque ambiit neque aliis inuidit, contentus ea laude quam docendo /25/ scribendoque ad principes, ad reges consequi poterat. Scribebat enim vltro magnis principibus non expectata occasione scribendi nec responso quo illum raro honorarunt, neque defectionem tam a papa fecit vt alibi maior fieret, quam quod de numero reque sacramentorum, de imaginibus, ceremoniis, ritibus, interpretatione verbi Dei et similibus aliter sentiebat.'

Post-Masson Views of Calvin: Catholic and Protestant Images of Calvin in the Seventeenth Century, or the Birth of 'Calvinography'

Although the texts I shall be examining here do not fall within the literary genre of *vitae* or *elogia*, they are of some importance as they illustrate among other things the reception of Jean-Papire Masson's work in both Catholic and Protestant camps, and show it to be rather more complex than Ronzy's cut-and-dried distinction between its favourable reception by the Protestants and negative reception by the Catholics would have us believe. As the study of all seventeenth-century works of French history far exceeds the scope of this work, I have chosen some of the most distinctive authors from each camp, who best illustrate the seventeenth-century interest in 'Calvinography'.[1] This means that I shall consider Desmay, Le Vasseur and Richelieu for the Roman Catholic camp, and Drelincourt and Barckhausen for the Protestants. I have not included Florimond de Raemond's notice on Calvin in this enquiry, as it represents a part of a larger whole and a different orientation.[2]

Desmay

Little is known about Jacques Desmay. Vicar general to François de Harlay, archbishop of Rouen, dean of the collegiate Church of Notre Dame d'Escouys and doctor of theology of the Sorbonne, he authentified a miraculous healing in 1618 and sanctioned the publication of its account

---

[1]   This term was first used by Le Vasseur in his *Annales*, vol. 2, p. 1150 (where he entitles his pages on the reformer *la Calvinographie, c'est à dire la description de Calvin* [Calvinography, that is a description of Calvin]. The term is picked up by Charles Drelincourt in his *La Defense de Calvin contre l'outrage fait a sa mémoire dans vn Liure qui a pour tître 'Traitté qui contient la Methode la plus facile et la plus asseurée pour conuertir ceus qui se sont separez de l'Eglise. Par le Cardinal de Richelieu.'* (Par Charles Drelincourt, Geneva, Jean-Antoine and Samuel De Tournes, 1667 [first printing: 1666]). Hereafter: Drelincourt, *Defense* (1667), p. 192.

[2]   On Florimond de Raemond, cf. Barbara Sher Tinsley, *History and Polemics in the French Reformation. Florimond de Raemond defender of the Church* (Selinsgrove: Susquehanna University Press, 1992).

so as to stop the faithful from turning away from saint-worship.[3] In 1614, Charles de Balzac, bishop of Noyon and peer of the realm, invited him to preach there during the Advent of 1614 and Lent of 1615. During his time there, he conducted an extensive enquiry into Calvin's early years. In 1621, he published his *Remarques considérables sur la vie et moeurs de Jean Calvin, hérésiarque. Et ce qui s'est passé de plus mémorable en sa personne depuis le iour de sa naissance … iusq'au iour de son deceds … tirées des registres de Noyon par Jacques Desmay.*[4] Desmay gives a general description of his sources, but provides no detailed references or citations. He distinguishes carefully between the information in the *Registers* and information from oral sources, which are unnamed. Among his written sources, he singles out the records of the enquiry by M. de Mesle (to which Le Vasseur will also refer), as well as the Chapter Registers put at his disposal by the dean Philippe de Gourlay and the other canons. He apparently used five Chapter Registers in all. The first volume covered the years 1516–20; the second, the years 1522–24. Both were written by the notary Jean Quentin. The third volume began on 16 January 1525, and

---

[3]   *Miracle advenu à Andely la veille de la Pentecoste derniere, le second jour du mois de Juin, mil six cens dix-huict: Par l'intercession de saincte Clotilde Reyne de France, femme de Clovis, premier Roy Chrestien des François* (A Rouen, Chez Nicolas Le Prevost, près les Jésuites, [1618]).-8 p., in-12, p. 8: *Nous Jacques Desmay Prestre Docteur en Theologie, de la société de Sorbonne, Doyen de l'Eglise Collegialle de nostre Dame d'Escouys, & Vicaire general de mondit Seigneur, ayant examiné honorable homme Jean Grivet maistre de la maison du grand Dauphin parroisse de sainct Paul au fauxbourg de Martainville de Rouen, aagé de soixante et quinze ans ou environ, sur la subite santé par luy recouverte la veille de Pentecoste derniere: Et ayant recogneu par son examen de bouche, & deux autres tesmoings qui ont signé au procez verbal sur ce dressé, qu'apres huict ans de maladie & perclusion de ses membres il avoit fait vœu à saincte Clotilde, & l'avoit esté accomplir en sa Chappelle érigée dans l'enclos du Cimetiere de nostre Dame d'Andely, le second jour de ce present mois veille de Pentecoste, auquel jour il avoit entierement recouvert sa santé, la fonction naturelle de ses membres, & le mouvement progressif; ainsi que nous l'avons veu marcher. Nous de l'authorité que dessus pour ne point taire les merveilles de Dieu en ses Saincts, avons permis le narré du miracle estre imprimé, comme un tesmoignage evident que Dieu veut que le nom de ses Saincts et Sainctes soient honorables devant luy, & qu'ils soient reclamez, & invoquez par les hommes en leurs necessitez; en vertu dequoy nous avons signé à ces presentes ce vingtdeuxiéme de Juin mil six cens dix-huict. Signé J. Desmay Vicaire General, avec une paraphe.*

[4]   There do not seem to be any copies extant of the original edition. Drelincourt, who made extensive use of the text in his *Defense de Calvin*, had no knowledge of it and relied on the 1657 edition (Rouen, Richard Lallemant), which he thought wrongly to be the only one. Cf. *Defense* (1667), p. 155. Here I have used the reissue of the 1657 edition (which is almost as rare as the edition itself and unfortunately omits the first few pages, which deal with Calvin's ancestry, as well as Desmay's list of sources), published in *Archives curieuses de l'histoire de France, depuis Louis XI jusqu'à Louis XVIII … publiées d'après les textes conservés à la Bibliothèque Royale et accompagnées de notices et éclaircissements …,* par L. Cimber [pseudonym of L. Lefaist] et F. Danjou, 1ère série, tome 5e (Paris: Beauvais, membre de l'Institut historique, rue Saint-Thomas du Louvre no. 26, 1835), pp. 387–98. Hereafter: Desmay.

the fourth in 1530. These two volumes were the work partly of Quentin and partly of Trémon and Morlet, notaries under the two successive deans, M. Randoul and M. Antoine de Chermoluë. The fifth volume covered the years 1534–36, and was the work of Martin Morlet.[5]

Despite the extravagant claim made in the title of the work, Desmay turns out to have very scant knowledge of what happened to Calvin once he left Noyon. Indeed, his aim is not to produce a *Life* of Calvin in any sense, but an account of the reformer's youth and childhood. Of particular interest to Desmay is the issue of benefices Calvin is supposed to have held. He does not make a single reference to any document other than the Noyon Chapter Registers. They provide him with sufficient material to use Calvin as a warning of what happens to founders of heresies. Unlike Masson, he has no literary ambitions and gives no impression of ever having read any of Calvin's works. His *Remarques* mark a turn in Roman Catholic biographies of the Genevan reformer which will be accentuated by Le Vasseur a few years later with details corrected and added. Both aim to show that Calvin was never a good Catholic, and his dereliction of his clerical duties shows him to have set a very poor example to priests and holders of benefices generally. In other words, he provides an *exemplum horrendum* of a dissolute pre-Tridentine cleric to post-Tridentine clergy, as well as a warning to lay believers. At the same time, he and the other early seventeenth-century Catholic annalists and historians, Le Vasseur in particular, continue the trend set by Masson and dissociate themselves implicitly from the Bolsec image. They find it more important to condemn Calvin on the basis of what they consider to be sound evidence than to repeat or create myths. Desmay thus concentrates first and foremost on the evidence in the Registers which shows that Calvin in his youth compounded of all the vices of a bad pre-Tridentine cleric: plurality of benefices when far too young to be put in charge of a parish, absenteeism, simony and nepotism. In all this, young Calvin was aided and abetted by his father Gérard.

Thus Desmay records that Calvin obtained in 1521 the Chapel of Gésine, not from his brother Charles, as Le Vasseur was to assert, but from the vicars of Charles de Hengest, bishop of Noyon, following the resignation of one Michel Courtin, who had exchanged Gésine for Charles' Chapel of *La Madeleine*.[6] This evidence shows that Calvin was only twelve years

---

5   Desmay, cited by Drelincourt, *Defense* (1667), pp. 156–7.

6   Desmay, p. 388: 'Le 29 mai 1521, maistre Jacques Regnard, secretaire de révérend père en Dieu messire Charles d'Angestée, évesque de Noyon, rapporta en chapitre que les vicaires généraux de mondit seigneur avoient donné à Jean Calvin, fils de Gérard, aagé alors de 12 ans, vne portion de la chapelle de Gesine vacante par la pure et simple resignation du maistre Michel Courtin, suivant la procuration passée à vénérable homme, maistre Antoine d'Estrée, procureur fondé et nommé pour ceste fin. Alors lecture fut faicte par Jean Calvin des statuts et serment par luy presté suivant la coustume et fut mis en réelle possession de ladicte chappelle par celuy qui presidoit en chapitre. Le susdit Courtin avoit en ceste portion

old when he obtained this first living, something Desmay underlines with particular care. In 1523, according to Desmay (and Le Vasseur after him), Gérard Cauvin obtained leave for his son to flee the plague epidemic, following the example of the cathedral canons. Permission was granted 'until the next feast day of St Remigius' (*iusques à la feste de Saint-Remy suivant*).[7] It was at that point that young Jean Cauvin went to study in Paris, where, in Desmay's unsupported view, 'his mind, rather like his father's, was without any decorum, and was easily carried away by the licence of his youth.'[8] As Le Vasseur was to do a few years later, Desmay dwells on Calvin's conviction for absenteeism from his charge in January 1526:

> As there was absenteeism, it is easy to see that this young viper was already beginning to gnaw at the entrails of his mother the Holy Church who nurtured him; his libertinism was already making him forget the oath he had sworn on being received as chaplain.[9]

As if this were not enough, on Monday 6 May 1527 Calvin and his brother Charles were again condemned for absenteeism. However, continues our chronicler, Gérard persisted in seeking ecclesiastical advancement for his children, and would not rest until he obtained a presbytery for Jean.[10] It was thus on 27 September 1527 (Desmay cites folio 3, page 1 of the Registers) that Gérard appeared before the chapter to present a resignation from the presbytery of Saint-Martin de Martheville of one Jean Havart. Antoine Fauvel, the canon who was doing his turn presenting candidates to benefices, immediately presented Jean Calvin in absentia to the general approval of the canons. It was also Fauvel who was delegated by the chapter to present Calvin to the bishop or to the vicar general. Desmay finds this shocking, and says so:

---

de la chappelle de la Gésine par la permutation qu'il avoit faicte avec Charles Cauvin pour sa chappelle de la Magdelaine.'

[7]   Ibid.: 'En l'an 1523 une grande peste régnit en la ville de Noyon, qui fit abandonner la vie à plusieurs chanoines. Girard Cauvin, pour ce qu'il aimoit son fils Jean Cauvin pour ce qu'il le voyait de bon esprit, d'une prompte naturelle à concevoir et inventif en l'estude des lettres humaines, luy procura un congé de s'absenter et sortir de la ville, tel qu'on avoit accordé en chapitre aux chanoines, ainsi que nous voyons au chapitre tenu le 5 d'aoust auquel requeste se voit presentée par Girard, à ce que son fils Jean Cauvin obtint congé d'aller où bon luy sembleroit durant la peste, sans perdre ses distributions; ce qui luy fut accordé iusques à la feste de Sainct-Remy suivants.Ce fut alors que Calvin s'en alla à Paris estudier dans l'Université, aagé seulement de 14 ans, où son esprit sans conduite et retenue, semblable à celuy de son père, se porta facilement à la liberté de jeunesse.'

[8]   See preceding note.

[9]   Desmay, p. 389: 'Puisqu'il y a de la contumace, il est facile à juger que desjà ce petit vipereau commençoit à ronger le ventre de sa mère saincte église, de laquelle il recevoit sa nourriture; ses libertez luy faisoient desjà oublier le serment qu'il auoit faict le iour de sa réception au nombre de chapelains.'

[10]   Ibid.

The same man that they condemned for absenteeism in two of their chapters meetings, they now receive as one able to take care of souls without asking him to make amends for his past – and he not even a full clergyman, a simple tonsured clerk not yet of age, a mere eighteen-year-old, full of the folly and libertinism of youth![11]

Desmay makes no mention of sodomy or any punishment for it, but, unlike Le Vasseur after him, he does hint that Calvin was the subject of a condemnation, the nature of which he does not reveal, but which, he implies, could well have been for an act of a sexual nature. According to the Registers, says Desmay, Jean before his consecration was convoked twice before the chapter at the bidding of Jean de la Ruë, canon of Rheims. However, he adds, the Registers, as he saw them, make no mention of what was at issue, although he did hear the eldest canons say that they had seen a blank sheet inserted into the Registers with just the heading *Condemnatio Ioannis Calvini*, 'which gave many people occasion to guess the nature of the offence.'[12] Desmay does not extrapolate from the missing page, and is very careful to distinguish the case involving the reformer from the 1550 case involving another Jean Calvin and his keeping of 'a woman of ill repute' at his home.[13] This latter case was to be treated more fully in Le Vasseur's *Annales*, expressly with a view to contradicting Bolsec's myth of sodomy and branding.

Desmay explains Calvin's chopping and changing of benefices by his restless spirit's forever seeking change and novelty.[14] This is also why the future reformer made it a habit to travel from one university to another, and why he visited several cities in France and Italy, including Rome and Venice. While Desmay's information about Calvin's post-Noyon days is

---

[11]   Ibid., pp. 389–90: 'Le vendredy 27 septembre 1527 ainsi qu'il est enregistré au feuillet 130, page 1, Girard se présenta en chapitre, porteur d'une procuration ad resignandum de maistre Iean Havart, curé de l'église paroissiale de Sainct-Martin de Marteville, diocèse de Noyon, par laquelle ledit Havart résignoit purement et simplement entre les mains du chapitre sa cure de Marteville. Alors maistre Antoine Fauvelae, chanoine, qui estoit en tour ad praesentandum, présenta à la dicte cure Iean Calvin, laquelle présentation fut acceptée de messieurs de chapitre. On voit par là que c'est d'un corps à plusieurs testes. Celuy qu'ils avoient condamné de contumace en deux divers chapi-/390/tres, ils le recoivent à prendre charge des ames sans correction du passé, n'estant promeu à aucun ordre sacré, n'ayant que simple tonsure et en un aage incompétent, n'ayant encore que dix-huict ans, remplis de follies et libertez de jeunesse. Le mesme Fauvel fut député en ce chapitre pour présenter Jean Calvin à monsieur l'evesque ou à son grand vicaire.'

[12]   Ibid., p. 390: 'J'ay bien ouy dire a aucuns chanoines des plus anciens, qu'ils ont veu autrefois un feuillet blanc dans les registres, où en teste y avoit escrit: *Condemnatio Iohannis Calvini* et n'y avoit rien d'escrit d'autre en toute la page, ains demeuroit en blanc; cela a donné à deviner à beaucoup ce que ce pouvoit estre.'

[13]   Ibid., pp. 390–91.

[14]   Ibid., p. 391: 'Par autres divers moyens et plusieurs conférences que i'ay recherché avec gens notables et spécialement avec personnes d'aage, tant ecclesiastiques que laiques, i'ay apprins que Iean Calvin estoit d'vn esprit qui aimoit le change et nouueauté.'

extremely vague, he is the only biographer to make the point about Calvin's general restlessness in preference to insisting on the change of name from Cauvin to Calvin, of which he manifests no knowledge. Furthermore, unlike Le Vasseur, he does not seek to make the reformer's transactions with benefices to be anything other than what they were: fairly small-time, but no less despicable for it – another sign of a restless and shiftless nature. Desmay notes the transfer by Calvin of the Gésine Chapel to his brother Antoine on 30 April 1529, and Jean's recovery of it on 26 February 1531 on the occasion of his final stay in Noyon.[15] In the meantime, on 5 July 1529, he is supposed to have resigned the presbytery of Saint-Martin de Marteville in favour of Jean de Bray[16] 'because he wished to settle in Pont-l'Evesque, the birth and deathplace of his ancestors.' At this point, the chronicler inserts a pious note, showing that Calvin's lineage (with the exception of Gérard) was anything but suspect, and that Jean constitutes an aberration in an otherwise respectable and right-thinking line:

> Please God, if only he had been able to settle there [in Pont-l'Evesque], without looking for a road other than his ancestors had opened up for him, for all his grandfathers died good Catholics (according to M. de Mesle's enquiry).[17]

Shortly afterwards (Desmay does not specify the date), Calvin was presented as De Bray's successor in the parish of Pont-l'Evesque by Claude d'Hengest, prior of St Eligius' monastery, to whom Calvin was to dedicate his *De clementia*. However, he was no more resident there than in any of his other livings, as he went to Orléans to study law, where he was turned away from his faith by a 'Dominican of German origins with whom he lodged' (an allusion to Melchior Volmar). Desmay further adverts to Calvin's purported theft of a silver cup belonging to the Picard Nation at the university in order to finance his travels. He also has knowledge of the future reformer's escape out of a window of the Collège le Moyne in order to avoid being arrested for spreading the teaching of the Reformation.[18] Returning to Noyon, he recovered Gésine from his brother but continued to be absent from it. Still according to Desmay, on 7 January 1533, his stand-in at the chapel, one Aubin Ploquin, complained to the chapter that Calvin owed him money for fifteen months of service-saying Masses. Charles was asked to appear in Jean's place, and agreed that all the profits from the living for that period should revert to Ploquin. Finally, on 4 May

---

[15]   Ibid., pp. 391, 394.

[16]   Ibid., p. 392.

[17]   Ibid.: 'Pleust à Dieu qu'il eut sceu y demeurer stable, sans cercher autre chemin que celuy que ses majeurs luy avoient frayé, car tous ses grandspères sont morts bons Catholiques (dit lenqueste de M. de Mesle).'

[18]   Ibid., p. 393.

1534, Calvin signed the chapel over to Antoine de Marlière. At about the same time, he gave Pont-l'Evesque to one Caïm.

Portraying Calvin as a wolf, a dissolute cleric, a thief and a follower of the 'new sects' does not prevent Desmay from also depicting him as a lost soul, who left it too late to return to the bosom of the church. Thus, he cites the dean of Noyon Cathedral as saying that Calvin's nephew (who apparently died during Desmay's visit) once visited his uncle in Geneva and asked him whether he thought that Catholics were damned. To this, the reformer is supposed to have replied, 'No'. What is more, he apparently never put pressure on his nephew to convert to Protestantism. Indeed – here Desmay cites another aged canon of the Noyon Cathedral as his source –, Calvin wanted to return to the bosom of the Roman Church, but, faced with the same canon's attempt to reconvert him, he simply replied that it was too late. Moreover, according to the dean of the cathedral, who had known the reformer's valet, Calvin nearly reconverted on his deathbed and asked the valet to bring him the Book of Hours of our Lady as used in Noyon.[19]

Desmay's Calvin is very fragmentary. However, he does show certain distinctive traits that do not feature in any of the other biographies. First and foremost, he emerges as a restless youth, forever seeking change and novelty. This, so Desmay implies, is the immediate cause of his straying from the straight and narrow, regardless of whether it takes the form of pluralism, absenteeism, and nepotism or 'joining the new sects'. At the same time, as already noted, Calvin with his traffic of benefices, his supposed stealing and his absenteeism serves as a model of how not to behave to any young clergyman. In another register, far from being the 'devil's disciple', he is shown as one regretting his departure from the Roman Church, although he finds that it is too late to return. While the parts of Desmay's account that adhere strictly to the Noyon Registers are obviously reliable, given that they resurface with some corrections in Le Vasseur's *Annales*, the parts based on (mainly second-hand) verbal testimony contain a fair amount of fiction and fulfil above all a rhetorical end.

Le Vasseur

Jacques Le Vasseur was born in 1570, in Wismes, not far from Abbeville, and became archdeacon at Noyon. He also taught at Orléans and Paris, whence he fled in 1608 because of the plague. As well as compiling the *Annals* of Noyon Cathedral, he is known as the author of *Le Bocage de Jossigny. Où est compris le Verger des Vierges, & autres plusieurs pièces sainctes, tant en vers qu'en prose. / Antitheses ou Contrepointes du Ciel*

---

[19]   Ibid., pp. 396–7.

et de la Terre. This collection of religious poetry was printed by P. Fleury Bourriquant, in 1608. He composed it while seeking refuge from the plague at Jossigny (Brie). He also wrote, among other things, *Antithèses* or *Contrepointes*, a work of 111 quatrains of reflexions on God, the fight between the flesh and the spirit, and other devotional topics. His *Annales* show him to have been particularly devoted to propagating the image of Noyon as a city quite unscathed by Calvin's heresy.

Indeed, it was a source of great pride to the French Catholics in general, and to the civil and ecclesiastical powers of Noyon in particular, that, despite having given birth to a heretic of Calvin's calibre, the city itself remained resolutely loyal to Rome. Already by 1570, the controversialist Antoine de Mouchy, one of the canons of Noyon Cathedral, had addressed the city's inhabitants in these glowing terms in the preface to his *De veritate Christi*:

> For at no point (although you knew Calvin from childhood and although many of you knew his mother and father) did you take him seriously enough to believe rashly what he wrote and did, which would have meant deserting your own faith; nor did you follow his example and abjure the true God, the Catholic religion and the Christian teaching of the holy fathers. On the contrary, when you first sensed that he had defected from our true religion, you shrank from him as if he were worse than a dog or a serpent and you wisely averted your eyes from his writings (as one would from the stare of a basilisk), when they were first forced upon you against your will, lest your very eyes be contaminated by the sight. And you were afraid to pollute your clean hands by letting them come into contact with his works.[20]

However, since Bolsec's time, rumour was about that Noyon was just as much a seat of iniquity as Geneva, or any other place connected with Calvin. It was with this in mind that Jacques Le Vasseur, when he was writing his *Annales*, searched the Noyon Cathedral Registers for mentions of the reformer, intending to sharply distinguish once and for all between him and the city that gave him birth.[21] He fully acknowledged that he was

---

[20] Preface cited by Jacques Le Vasseur, *Annales*, vol. 2, p. 1179: 'Non anim aliquando tanti fecistis Caluinum quem a teneris annis, sicut patrem et matrem eius plerique vestrum cognouistis, vt statim dictis, scriptis suis ac actis temere crederetis, deserta fidei receptae pietate aut huius instar Deum verum, catholicam religionem et christianam sanctorum patrum institutionem perfide abiuraretis. Sed contra, vbi primum hunc a nostra et vera defecisse religione subolfecistis, vt cane et angue peiorem abhorruistis et a librorum suorum quos vobis nihil minus cogitantibus gratis obtrudebant lectione, velut a basilisco, ne visu inficerentur, oculos sapienter auertististis, sicut et horum tactu puras manus vestras pollui caute timuistis.'

[21] Ibid., vol. 2, p. 1162: 'Noyon n'est pourtant ce qu'aucuns l'ont fait estre à son suiet: vne Paneropole, vne carriere venimeuse et la sœur des cinq villes comprises sous le nom de Pentapole. Ce sont les tiltres que quelques estrangers luy donnent, escriuans de Caluin et en haine de luy, comme ci ce n'estoit assez de le rendre immonde, si on ne faisait quant et quant de Noyon, ville innocente, vne cloaque publique et sentine generale de toutes ordures,

not the first historian to attempt a portrait of Calvin on the basis of the evidence provided by the Registers. Indeed, Le Vasseur had read Desmay's *petit liure* [booklet] on the reformer's life, and refers to it several times in the text of the *Annales*.[22] However, it would be mistaken to suppose that he copies Desmay. Although, as we have mentioned, he does echo his account on several points, on other occasions he passes it over in silence, adds to it or diverges from it. He is also infinitely more damning than Desmay, who confined himself to the minimum of comment over and above what he had read in the Registers or heard from what he called reliable witnesses. Le Vasseur also admits to having consulted extensively the *Vita* of Jean-Papire Masson, to which he refers as another highly reliable source, while correcting it occasionally when it is contradicted by local evidence.[23] On the a whole, Le Vasseur's account is far more comprehensive than Desmay's digest of the Cathedral Registers and of the local, oral tradition surrounding the reformer. Thus while Le Vasseur's portrait of Calvin emerges as extremely hostile, it has the merit of citing sources and distinguishing between sources and commentary. Le Vasseur also carefully compares printed sources, especially Masson's *Vita*, with the manuscript evidence available.

---

au prejudice de sa bonne renommée, du Royaum et de la Chrestienté. C'est ce qu'ont fait plusieurs de temps en temps.'

[22]   See ibid.: 'Maistre Iacques Desmay <maistre Iacques Desmay en son petit liure de la vie de Caluin, imprimé à Rouen, chez Richard l'Allement 1621 auec priuilege du Roy et approbation des docteurs> docteur en theologie mentionne cy-dessus, qui preschant Aduent et Caresme à Noyon en 1614 et 1615 y fit tres-exacte recherche des vies et vices de ce decrédité, n'a rien découuert dauantage.'

[23]   Ibid., vol. 2, p. 1152: 'La seconde fille de Gerard suiuit son frere Iean à Genèue où il l'attira par ses inductions. Papire Masson en sa Vie de Caluin en nomme d'autres de ceste race [Cauvin]. Car apres auoir fait mention des deux benefices que Gerard procura à Iean son fils, fait suiure ces mots: "Haec causa fuit cur pater eum quam doctissimum fieri caperet mitteretque Lutetiam et Ricardo fratri commendaret in vico diui Germani Altissiodorensis, fabro ferario fratrique eius Iacobo, qui nunc anno 1583 eandem artem Parisiis prope sanctum Medericum, via Vulpis dicta exercet etc." S'en informe qui voudra, en voilà les enseignes.' (Evidently the Noyon Registers did not contain any information on Gérard's brother Richard and his children. Otherwise Le Vasseur would have spotted the anachronism and corrected *fratri* [brother] to *filio* [son], as Théophile Dufour was to do some three hundred years later. Cf. Chapter 4, p. 178). Ibid., vol. 2, p. 1161: 'Le lundy 4 iour de May 1534 il resigna la chappelle susdite à maistre Antoine de la Marlière et sa cure du Pont-l'Evesque à Caïm. Et de là, après quelques courses se retira à Genèue, où il fut suiui de son frère Antoine. Tout ce que dessus auéré par l'information de feu M. Antoine de Mesle, docteur es droit, thrésorier et chanoine de l'Eglise de Noyon, iuge ordinaire en l'audience episcopale du lieu, mon tres honoré deuancier et par le tesmoigange de Papire Masson, duquel entr'autres sont ces mots: *Duo illa supra memorata modici prouentus beneficia vendidit, Antonio Marlero vnum, alterum Gulielmo Bosio, presbyteris Nouiomensis ecclesiae. Antonius religionis causa exsul postea ad venditorem Geneuae se contulit.* Mais le Masson prend Bosius (ou du Bois) pour Caïm.'

Nowadays, the value of the *Annales* thus consists in their listing of all the documentary evidence about John Calvin and his family, which was available in the Noyon Registers before they burnt down later in the seventeenth century. Just as importantly, perhaps, Le Vasseur's work shows that the method of comparing sources advocated by Bauduin and, in his wake, Masson, found fruitful ground among French Catholic clergy and theologians; and that, from the early seventeenth century onwards, those who wrote about Calvin no longer wanted to portray him as a scourge unless they could back up their assertions with documentary evidence. Religious biography, even hostile religious biography, thus entered the sphere of history, but without fully inhabiting it. Le Vasseur achieves his end of portraying the reformer as a stain on Noyon's orthodoxy not by falsifying or by inventing facts, but by letting his commentary do the dirty work. The pages he devotes to Calvin's ancestry and early years are especially interesting in this respect, providing a large amount of solid information which is invariably presented as 'another nail in Calvin's coffin'.

He corrects Masson's information that Calvin's grandfather was a sailor, and notes that it is considered in Noyon that he was a cooper. The grandfather, however, escapes censure, as nothing is known about him or his ancestors except that they came from Pont l'Evesque and that they died in the Catholic faith.[24] Although there is no record of Calvin's parents, Gérard and Jeanne, ever having flirted with the Reformation, information about them is much fuller and therefore easier to interpret in the worst possible light. Gérard died excommunicated for embezzling church funds. Apparently gifted with money, he was made, according to the Registers, apostolic notary, tax collector, clerk in the ecclesiastical court and diocesan secretary. Le Vasseur naturally presents Gérard's penchant for plurality of offices as a sign of greed and dishonesty, which led to his ultimate downfall:

> For being of a keen mind and extremely well-versed in the fine art and algebra of judicial procedures, he managed to inveigle himself everywhere and to seek as much business as possible, which sought him in return and made him worse. For everyone wanted the services of a man of such fancy footwork, who was hard-working as well as inventive. He thus became apostolic notary, tax officer for the county, clerk of the ecclesiastical court, diocesan secretary and chapter representative at various meetings and other occasions. In a word, he took on so much that he came unstuck and became destitute, hoisting himself on his own petard, as we are about to see.[25]

24   Ibid., vol. 2, p. 1151: 'Papirius Massonus en la Vie de Calvin escrit que son pere grand fut marinier, en latin nauicularius. On tient à Noyon qu'il fut tonnelier, natif et habitant du Pont l'Euesque, bourg distant d'un quart de lieue dudit Noyon, sans qu'il soit autre memoire de luy ny de ses deuanciers sinon qu'ils furent et sont morts Catholiques.'
25   Ibid.: 'Car estant d'vn esprit ardent et de mieux entendu en la plus fine pratique et algebre des procez il se fourra par tout et brigua grandement les affaires, lesquelles le chercherent et changerent en la fin, chacun desirant se seruir d'vn homme si luré en telle escrime, qui ne manquoit de diligence non plus que d'innouation. Il devint donc notaire

As for his first wife, Jeanne Le Franc, she was apparently the daughter of an innkeeper originally of Cambray who settled in Noyon. It was she who bore Gérard's six children: four boys (one of whom died in infancy, leaving Charles, Jean and Antoine) and two girls. Two of Jean's siblings – Antoine, his younger brother, and one of the sisters – were to follow him to Geneva.[26] Again, there seems to be nothing much with which to reproach Calvin's maternal origins. All Le Vasseur can accuse Jeanne of is her apparently 'bad reputation', for which he does not cite any sources.

Father, descendant of a cooper who spent his time in (dubious) financial dealings and who remarried after Jeanne's death; mother, daughter of an innkeeper, and of poor reputation despite or because of her beauty[27] – Le Vasseur does his utmost with the little evidence he has at his disposal to present Calvin's lineage as the diametrical opposite of the standard biographical lineage of the time. The hero of an *elogium* or of a funeral oration had to have an irreproachable lineage, preferably noble, but above all pious, honest and honourable. Calvin's family (while not exactly the bunch of criminals Le Vasseur would have liked them to be) apparently possessed none of these characteristics. The first black mark that he can find against the reformer, even before his coming into the world, are his low origins, or, as Le Vasseur puts it, *l'obscurité de son extraction* or *vilité de sa descente*, which, he is keen to point out, Calvin himself is constrained to deplore in his preface (addressed to Claude de Hengest, prior of the monastery of St Eligius, in Noyon) to *De clementia*.[28] To the disgrace of not just humble but obscure origins, is added the ultimate black mark of the opprobrium he suffered on seeing his father die excommunicated.

---

apostolique, procureur fiscal du comté, scribe en cour d'Eglise, secretaire de l'eueschè et promoteur de chapitre en diuers temps et rencontres; bref, il en embrassa tant qu'il s'embarrassa pour toute sa vie, sans ressources, s'estant pris à sa glus, à laquelle il vouloit prendre les autres, ainsi que nous ferons voir incontinent.'

[26]   Antoine was to be the beneficiary of Calvin's Will. As regards his sister, cf. ibid., vol. 2, p. 1152: 'La seconde fille de Gerard suiuit son frère Iean à Genèue où il attira par ses inductions.'

[27]   See ibid.: '… belle femme mais d'assez mauuais bruit.'

[28]   See ibid., vol. 2, pp. 1152–3: 'Voilà sommairement ce que ie trouue des pere et mere de Iean Caluin et de la qualité de son extraction, l'obscurité de laquelle il /1153/ ne peut luy-mesme dissimuler en l'adresse qu'il fait de son commentaire sur le De clementia de Seneque à Messire Claude de Hengest, abbé du monastère de S. Eloy de Noyon où il confesse qu'il n'est qu'vn petit compagnon de la populace *vnus de plebe homuncio*. Ce sont les tiltres qu'il se donne luy-mesme; la noblesse dont il se vante et qu'il va poursuiuant par ceste autre tirade: *Haec quidem ignobilitatis meae conscientia fecerat vt abstinerem publico* – le ressentiment que i'ay de la bassesse du lieu d'où ie viens, m'a iusques ici rebuté du public. Pleust à Dieu qu'il eust aduancé telles paroles plutost par l'humilité que forcé par sa conscience qui en ce passage a donné la torture a son humeur altiere et luy a faict à contrecoeur aduouer la verité ne la pouvant pallier en vne ville où sa race n'estoit que trop cognue et mesestimée. C'est le louange que le sieur Demochares donne au clergé et peuple de Noyon, de n'auoir donné plus de poids aux paroles, actions et escrits de Caluin que luy et ses parens n'ont valu.'

Le Vasseur's sources for this are the Registers of the Dean and Chapter for 27 June 1526, which mention explicitly Gérard Cauvin's condemnation for failing to render account of two Wills of which he was executor. Convicted of embezzlement, he was promptly excommunicated. According to Le Vasseur, he purchased benefices for his sons with his ill-gotten gains, a standing example to all parents of what not to do.[29]

A mother of dubious reputation and an embezzler father, both of humble social origins, added to which is the disgrace of the reformer's elder brother Charles, buried under the gibbet for refusing to take the sacrament – it is only inevitable, in Le Vasseur's view, that the reformer himself should have died a *hérésiarche et banqueroutier à la foy*.[30] Small wonder that the eldest women of the village have heard it told to their mothers that a swarm of flies flew out of Jeanne Le Franc's womb on Jean's birth![31] Le Vasseur does not invent written sources where none exist, and does not pretend that myths such as the 'fly myth' are the product of anything other than oral tradition. He works with the facts that he can document either from his reading of other biographies (especially Masson and Desmay), or from the Noyon Cathedral records, or from hearsay. He interprets the facts as unfavourably to Calvin as he possibly can without falsifying the evidence. Significantly, he does not pick up Desmay's myth of Calvin's deathbed attempt at reconversion. It is even more significant, however, that he says nothing about the supposed sodomy or branding. That was not Calvin's crime. What, then, was it in Le Vasseur's view, given

---

[29]   Ibid., pp. 1153, 1155: 'Caluin donc a eu subject de regretter non seulement la vilité de sa descente mais aussi l'opprobre paternel, ayant veu son pere lié de censures ecclésiastiques dès l'année 1526 et mourir en icelles en l'année 1531 pour n'auoir satisfaict à la reddition de deux comptes, d'autant d'executions testamentaires dont il estoit chargé. Car comme ce praticien (ie dis Gerard) preuoist par tout, aussi entreprenoit-il facilement tout sans preuoir par où la sortie. Il entreprit premierement auec maistre Iean Baloche chanoine de Noyon, l'execution du testament de feu maistre Nicolas Obry chappellain dudit lieu et la gera seul. Pourquoy estant poursuiuy auec ledit Baloche pour la reddition du compte, il fit ceste dette sienne et promit de la nettoyer de son chef. Il en passa condamnation. "Recepit condemnationem et nunc prout ex tunc (dit la Conclusion) <Conclusion capit. Du 27 iuin 1526> *casu quo non reddiderit*." [LeVasseur cites two other similar cases involving Gerard Cauvin and stresses that he died excommunicated 1528(?)] ... /1155/ Voilà la farce du pere iouée, iuge, lecteur, de la façon qu'il a ioué son rolle et s'il a atteint son but qui ne fut autre que d'aduancer par toute voye ... Icy donc est la fin du scribe, du notaire apostolique, du secretaire, du procureur fiscal, du promoteur, bref du praticien à cinq parties, ietté hors de l'Église par le glaiue de l'anathème, par faute d'auoir satisfait du bien d'autruy; qui sçait si ce ne fust par vne iuste punition, pour y auoir introduit ses trois mauuais garnemens d'enfans, malgré le Saint-Esprit? Pour instruction aux parens de ne pourchasser auec tant d'ardeur et de soin les benefices pour leurs enfans, lesquels n'y estans appelllez les tournent bien souuent en malefices et scandales, greuans par trop celle qu'ils deuoient entierement soulager, ie dis l'Église ...'.

[30]   'Heresiarch and a bankrupt in faith.' See ibid., vol. 2, p. 1156.

[31]   Ibid., vol. 2, p. 1157.

that he was in no position to comment (nor had any interest in doing so) on Calvin's activities in Geneva?

The obvious charge was one of plurality of benefices, which had the advantage of serving as a parallel with Gérard's plurality of offices, thus sustaining the 'like father, like son' assumption which Le Vasseur's entire account was intended to illustrate. The other, very similar, but less serious, charge was Calvin's penchant for pseudonyms, proof of a deceitful nature.[32] Added to these Le Vasseur cites Bauduin's judgement that Calvin, in view of his liking for *accusing* his comrades, had not learned his Latin declensions beyond the *accusative* case.[33]

The most interesting of these three charges to us is that of plurality of benefices, which also caught Desmay's attention. Not only is it the most serious of the three, it is grounded in fact and, more importantly, it implies that Calvin, far from reforming the church, as he claimed, gave in to its most flagrant abuses. Le Vasseur's summary of the Registers echoes Desmay's, barring a few omissions, corrections and additions. According to it, Calvin inherited from his elder brother Charles the chapel of la Gésine de la Vierge on 29 May 1521, when he was only eleven years old. On 5 August 1523, the chapter, upon his father's request, authorised him to absent himself because of the plague epidemic until the feast day of St Rémi. The Registers make no further mention of him until 16 January 1526, when the chapter convoked him for absenteeism. Calvin did not respond, and was condemned in absence. As Le Vasseur points out, he was absent for study in Paris, but should have sent a letter from the rector of the university. The chapter condemned him again on 6 May 1527. On 24 July of that year, his father represented him in a legal dispute against Jean le Vic, canon of the cathedral. The outcome of the dispute is not known.

Le Vasseur does not pick up on Desmay's hint of a sexual offence, and makes no mention of a blank page in the Registers. Moreover, he transforms Desmay's Jean de la Ruë into Jean le Vic. These and similar divergences between the two accounts would suggest that Le Vasseur did in fact work primarily from the Registers and was not content just to repeat Desmay's version of them. As the two accounts are by and large in agreement about the basic facts, we can take their picture of Calvin's youth to be reliable.

On 27 September 1527, Calvin, according to Le Vasseur and Desmay before him, compounded absenteeism by pluralism when he was made rector of the parish of St Martin de Marteville at the age of eighteen. Two years later, he exchanged it for Pont- l'Evesque with one Jean de Bray. At the same time, he ceded the cathedral chapel of *Gésine de la Vierge* to his brother Antoine. At some time, he also acquired a small chapel

---

[32]   Ibid., vol. 2, pp. 1157–8.
[33]   Ibid., vol. 2, p. 1158.

of St Jean de Bayencourt. What Le Vasseur does not say is that Calvin never held more than two very modest benefices at once, just enough to finance his studies. On 26 February 1531, Jean was back as incumbent at Gésine, his younger brother having returned it to him. Finally, on 4 May 1534, he handed over the chapel to Antoine de Marlière and the parish of Pont l'Evesque to a relative called Caïm. Shortly afterwards, he left Noyon. In accordance with his chosen method, Le Vasseur has compared several sources for this information. He did not confine his searches to the Registers, but also had his findings verified by 'the late M. Antoine de Mesle [who had also been Desmay's source], doctor of law, treasurer and canon of the Noyon Cathedral, judge in the episcopal court of the same, and my highly respected predecessor and by the testimony of Jean-Papire Masson who writes: "he [John] sold the two benefices which had provided him with a modest revenue, one to Antoine de Marlière, the other two Guillaume du Bois, priests of the Noyon Church. Antoine, subsequently religious exile, went to dwell with the seller in Geneva."'[34] He takes this opportunity to correct Masson's error in the name of the second buyer: it was not Du Bois, but Caïm.

Although containing more than their fair share of invective as well as fanciful information about the circumstances of Calvin's birth based on hearsay, the *Annales* put to rest all the myths put about by Bolsec. Le Vasseur carefully compares his sources so as to stay within the realm of fact. Although Calvin comes off very badly as the stain on the good name of the city that bore him, he is not credited with any misdeeds which are not documented in some way by either the Cathedral Registers or another reliable source. This leaves our annalist in something of a predicament, as evidence of the reformer's misdeeds in Noyon is very scant. However, he has the precedent of Desmay, who says in his 'little book on Calvin' that despite very careful researches he conducted in Noyon, he could find nothing explicit against the reformer with the exception of the record of the court case that opposed him to Jean le Vic. In the light of this, Desmay declares that he had not set out to go beyond such records of Calvin's birth and conversion as he could find and to leave it at that. His chief aim was to dissociate Noyon from Calvin, not to present a fictitious, hostile portrait of the reformer.[35]

---

[34]   Ibid., vol. 2, p. 1161: 'Tout ce que dessus auéré par l'information de feu M. Antoine de Mesle, docteur es droit, thrésorier et chanoine de l'Eglise de Noyon, iuge ordinaire en l'audience episcopale du lieu, mon tres honoré deuancier et par le tesmoigange de Papire Masson, duquel entr'autres sont ces mots: Duo illa supra memorata modici prouentus beneficia vendidit, Antonio Marlero vnum, alterum Gulielmo Bosio, presbyteris Nouiomensis ecclesiae. Antonius religionis causa exsul postea ad venditorem Geneuae se contulit. Mais le Masson prend Bosius (ou du Bois) pour Caïm.' [Cf. Masson (1620), pp. 7–8.]

[35]   Ibid., vol. 2, p. 1162: 'Permets-moy mon cher lecteur de ne point nommer ses crimes, mais de les abhorrer et de ne les point rechercher mais de les fuir et sois content si ie te donne

The Masson/Bauduin approach of showing 'the real man' by comparing sources, and by carefully distinguishing between rumour, hearsay and fact, thus prevailed temporarily over the Bolsec method of creating hostile myths. Admittedly, neither Desmay nor Le Vasseur shared Masson's well-balanced judgement on Calvin, which caused him to underline the reformer's good as well as his bad sides.

Thus, alongside the Bolsec image, new images of Calvin, unbranded and innocent of sexual crimes, but above all source-based and historically founded, were taking shape in accounts of his life that his adversaries devoted to him in the early seventeenth century. This recourse to documentary evidence did not mean that Calvin's Catholic reception was more favourable. The degenerate of Bolsec's account was replaced by a mixture of a bad-tempered tyrannical heresiarch of dubious origins, a rash youth precipitated into heresy by his taste for novelty and unable to extricate himself from it subsequently, and a villain tinged with the stigma of Beelzebub at birth. Masson's favourable judgement on his sincerity, his undoubted intellectual gifts, his capacity for hard work, and his stand on Anabaptists and Servetus found no posterity in the Catholic tradition. The Protestants for their part rested content with Beza's *Discours* and, to a lesser extent, the two other Beza/Colladon *Lives* of Calvin, at least until mid-seventeenth century. This was going to change in 1651, with the publication of Richelieu's *Traitté*.

The Influence of Richelieu on Calvin Biography

The posthumous publication of Richelieu's *Traitté qui contient la méthode la plus facile et la plus asseurée pour conuertir ceux qui se sont séparés de l'Église* in 1651 marked a return to the mythical Calvin and led eventually to a re-evaluation of Masson and other Catholic 'Calvinographers'[36] by

---

ce que i'en apprens sur les lieux sans curiosité d'en plus sçauoir. Maistre Iacques Desmay <maistre Iacques Desmay en son petit liure de la vie de Caluin, imprimé à Rouen, chez Richard l'Allement 1621 auec priuilege du Roy et approbation des docteurs> docteur en theologie mentionne cy-dessus, qui preschant Aduent et Caresme à Noyon en 1614 et 1615 y fit tres-exacte recherche des vies et vices de ce decrédité, n'a rien découuert dauantage. "Ie n'ay sceu descouurir autre chose dans lesdits registres (ce dit-il parlant de Caluin) que les plaintes et approches cy-dessus <Il appelle approches la cause deux fois appellée en chapitre entre luy [Caluin] et M. Iean de Vic, rapportée cy-dessus>. C'est pourquoy ie n'en dirai rien plus expres, n'ayans entrepris d'escrire que ce que j'ay appris sur les lieux de sa natiuité et conuersion premiere". Aussi qui dit Heresiarque, dit le comble de tous les crimes; non que Caluin demeure iustifié pour cela de tous les autres par luy commis où que ce soit, dont ie m'informe, mais qu'il soit ce qu'il est et ce qu'il a esté.'

[36]   I have consulted the copy held by the Bibliothèque Sainte Geneviève in Paris. Shelfmark: FOL D551 INV 621 RES: *Traitté qui contient la méthode la plus facile et la plus asseurée pour conuertir ceux qui se sont séparés de l'Eglise*. Par le Cardinal Richelieu (Paris, Sebastien

Protestant writers. Now, Richelieu's three-volume treatise was obviously not a biography of Calvin. Its aim was to expose every single aspect of Protestant belief and practice as wicked. Only one chapter, Chapter 10 in Book 2, touched on biographies of reformers. The cardinal's aim was to show in twelve brief pages that the 'debauched lives of the first instigators of the so-called Reformation make it clear to us that the church they founded cannot be the true Church of Jesus Christ.'[37] He contrasts the sinful and wicked lives of the reformers with the holy lives of Christ and the Apostles, and notes that God who first founded the church by the agency of 'very holy people' could not possibly have had recourse to depraved individuals to restore it. Calvin is not the sole object of his attack. He runs through Luther, Zwingli, Calvin and Beza, showing each to have been of loose morals and therefore heterodox. His knowledge of their lives is scant to say the least, and he relies on excerpts from their writings to show the symmetry between loose morals and wicked convictions. Calvin constitutes an exception, however. Richelieu does not append extracts from his writings or say much about his teaching. He concentrates entirely on the reformer's sexual degeneracy, his taciturnity, and his tyrannical nature. The printed *marginalia* or shoulder-notes show that he was familiar with both the Bolsec and Masson image and biographies of Calvin. It is uncertain whether he had also read either Desmay's or Le Vasseur's account of Calvin's youth based on the Noyon Registers. If he did, he certainly does not share their view that a biographer's job is to remain as close as possible to his sources. He does, however, show knowledge of Bauduin's *Responsiones* (possibly via Masson's *Vita Calvini*), and of Edmund Campion's controversy with Whittaker.[38] The result is, as we are about to see, an amalgam of all the negative remarks any of Calvin's adversaries had ever made about the reformer, combining the most pejorative of the Bolsec and the Bauduin/Masson tradition.[39]

The cardinal devotes only three of the twelve pages to Calvin. However, the three pages were to raise a veritable storm of controversy, and therefore deserve to be examined in detail. Basing himself very loosely on Masson, he notes that Calvin was born in Noyon in 1509, and that he held benefices of Martheville which he exchanged for Pont l'Evesque as well as

---

et Gabriel Cramoissy, 1651). Hereafter: Richelieu (1651). There exists a modern edition by Stéphane-Marie Morgain and Françoise Hildesheimer (Paris: H. Champion, 2005).

[37]   Richelieu (1651), p. 282: 'Que la vie déréglée des premiers autheurs de la pretendue reforme nous fait connoistre que l'Eglise qu'ils ont fondée ne peut estre la vraye Eglise de Jesus Christ.'

[38]   On this, see Peter Lake and Michael Questier, 'Puritans, Papists and the Public Sphere in Early Modern England: The Edmund Campion Affair in Context', *The Journal of Modern History*, 72 (2000): 587–627, and literature cited ibid.

[39]   Richelieu shows no direct knowledge of Laing, who would have served his purpose admirably.

a chapel in Noyon. He also stresses that Calvin was barely eighteen years old when he obtained his first living (eleven, according to Le Vasseur!). More significantly, he seems to conflate Jean with his father Gérard, as he tells his readers that:

> While he held these benefices, he was reprimanded several times for his bad debts and for his depraved morals, but having been finally condemned for his debauchery, which pushed him to the outer reaches of vice, he moved away from the region of Noyon and at the same time from the Roman Church.[40]

As further evidence for Calvin's dissolute morals, he refers to the dispute between Edmund Campion and William Whitaker, in which Campion accused the Protestants among other excesses of having had a leader (Calvin) who was a fugitive branded with a *fleur-de-lys*, to which Whitaker replied that St Paul was also branded.[41]

Indeed, about a half of the short notice is devoted to Calvin's purported branding, which was obviously something of a *locus classicus* to Richelieu. The best proof of its authenticity, according to the cardinal, was that the Genevans never denied it, not even when Philibert Berthelier brought back with him a document signed by the most prominent men in Noyon attesting to it. It is this document, according to Richelieu, which stated that the capital punishment normally incurred for sodomy was commuted to branding by Calvin's bishop. 'And the Genevan Church, adds Richelieu, does not belie this information about Calvin's life and it would certainly have done so, had it thought that this would be possible without bending the truth.'[42] What is more, he concludes, Berthelier himself never denied

---

[40]   Richelieu (1651), livre 2, chap. 10, p. 291: '<Il naquit en la ville de Noyon en 1509. Il eut vne chapelle dans Peronne et vne dans Noyon. La premiere cure estoit celle de Martheville et la seconde celle du Pont l'Evesque; à 25 ans il se défit de la cure et de la chapelle> Calvin fut nourry dès son bas âge pour estre ecclésiastique. N'ayant encore que 18 ans, par la licence du siecle il fut dès lors pourveu d'vne cure, laquelle deux ans apres il permuta auec vne austre. Pendant qu'il possedoit ces beefices il fut plusieurs fois repris et de la liberté de sa créance et de la deprauation de ses mœurs mais ayans esté enfin condamné pour ses incontinences qui le porterent mesmes jusqu'aux dernieres extremitez du vice, il se retira et des enuirons de Noyon et de l'Eglise romaine tout ensemble.'

[41]   Ibid.: 'Campianus qui mourut en Angleterre sous le regne de la royne Elisabeth <en 1581> reprochant à nos aduersaires la vie infame de Caluin et vsant de ces termes: "que leur chef auoit esté fleurdelisé et fugitif", Witaker en sa Reponse n'en a point d'austre que celle-ci: "Caluin a esté stigmatisé mais S. Paul l'a esté, d'autres l'ont esté aussi." A quoi Duraeus repartant en la replique qu'il fait pour Campianus dit: "que c'est vne chose impie de comparer Caluin marqué par ses crimes à S. Paul marqué pour la confession de Iesus-Christ."'

[42]   Ibid., livre 2, chap. 10, pp. 291–2: '... depuis qu'il a esté chargé de ceste accusation l'Eglise de Genèue non seulement n'a pas justifié le contraire mais mesmes n'a pas nié l'information que Berthelier enuoyé par ceux de la mesme ville fit à Noyon. Cette information estoit signée des plus apparens de la ville de /292/ Noyon et auoit esté faicte auec toutes les formes ordinaires de la iustice. Et dans la mesme information on void que cet Heresiarque aynas esté conuaincu d'vn peché abominable que l'on ne punit que par le feu, la peine qu'il

this information, and he had the opportunity to do so as he was still alive
when Bolsec's *Life* of Calvin appeared.[43]

It is in fact Bolsec's *Life* of Calvin that constitutes Richelieu's sole
source for this. It is well known that Philibert Berthelier, exiled after being
excommunicated, never occupied the position of the city clerk or secretary
that Bolsec attributes to him, and that he was never sent by the council to
Noyon to seek out any documents about Calvin's early misdemeanours.
(This invention by Bolsec, immortalised by Richelieu, was to prompt a
full-scale enquiry into Genevan Council records a few years later to check
on the documentary evidence. None was found.)

To this image of Calvin as worse than a common criminal, the cardinal
adds the strictures passed on the reformer's character by Jean-Papire
Masson, whose account he had read with some care, carefully extracting
what he considered as the most damaging information while omitting
anything that did not contribute to tarnishing the reformer's reputation.
Stressing the objectiveness of Masson's account, he quotes extensively and
out of context Masson's account of Calvin's choleric temperament, his
vindictiveness, his arrogance, his chronic bad temper, his dislike of being
contradicted and his invincible superiority complex. Completely ignoring
Masson's remarks on Calvin's sincerity, he points out:

> This is what Papirius says, quite rightly in my opinion, about Calvin's vices,
> which were all the more detestable as their starting-point was the greatest vice
> of all, and that is pride, ambition and the wish to be considered intellectually
> superior to all other men, all faults leading to contempt of God, Jesus Christ
> and his church.[44]

Richelieu was not interested in Calvin's life, but only in portraying the
reformer as a thoroughly wicked, debauched and unpleasant megalomaniac,
who passed himself off as a religious leader. The *Traitté* was after all meant
to convert first and foremost. He was fully aware of his goal and of the
best means to achieve it, and made selections from Bolsec, Masson and
one or two other authors quite deliberately. The result was a thoroughly
libellous portrayal of the reformer's morals and character, without even
a symbolic homage being paid to search for the truth about him. The

---

auoit meritée fut, à la prière de son euesque modérée à la fleur de lys. Et l'Eglise de Geneue
qui ne desauoue pas cette information touchant à la vie de Caluin, n'eut pas manqué de la
déauouer, si elle eut cru le pouuoir faire sans blesser la vérité.'

[43]   Ibid., livre 2, chap. 10, p. 292. On Philibert Berthelier and his excommunication, see
Christian Grosse, *L'excommunication de Philibert Berthelier: histoire d'un conflit d'identité
aux premiers temps de la Réforme genevoise (1547–1555)* (Genève: Société d'histoire et
d'archéologie de Genève, 1995).

[44]   Richelieu (1651), livre 2, chap. 10, p. 293: 'C'est ce qu'écrit Papyrius, judicieusement à
mon avis, touchant les vices de Caluin, qui ont été d'autant plus détestables qu'ils ont eu pour
origine le plus grand de tous, qui est l'orgueil et l'ambition d'exceller sur les autres hommes
dans les auantages de l'esprit jusqu'au mépris de Dieu, de Jésus-Christ et de son Eglise.'

Genevan authorities were initially not keen to refute it. Authors such as Charles Drelincourt, who did refute it, referred to it as a treatise 'published under the name of Cardinal Richelieu', as we shall see below.

Seventeenth-Century Genevan Reprint of the Beza/Colladon *Life of Calvin*

Thus contrary to any modern historian's expectations, the 1656 reprint of the Beza/Colladon *Life* of Calvin, although situated in the wake of the publication of Richelieu's *Traitté*, turns out to be a reaction not to Richelieu, but to the controversy between the Jesuit Pietra-Santa and André Rivet.[45] Richelieu is not mentioned.

As already noted, Colladon's *Life* was reprinted five times in all in the course of the seventeenth century, with the express purpose of defending the reformer's reputation. Of particular interest is the Pierre Chouet Geneva reprint of 1656 and 1663: *L'Histoire de la Vie et mort de feu Mr. Iean Calvin, fidele serviteur de Iesus Christ par Theodore de Bèze augmentée de diuerses pièces considerables et sur tout de plusieurs tesmoignages authentiques de ses aduersaires qui seruent à sa justification.*[46] The 'sundry important documents' [*diverses pièces*] all serve to confirm Calvin's excellent morals and provide supporting evidence for some of the information in the text of the *Life*. Interestingly enough, this reissue of *Histoire de la vie et mort* of 1565 is the first biographical work to cite *in extenso* Calvin's autobiographical remarks in his preface to the Psalms Commentary, treating them as historical testimony. Among other

---

[45]   Silvestro di Pietra-Santa (1590–1647), a Roman Jesuit who stayed for some time in Germany as confessor to the papal nuntius Carafa, took in his sights Du Moulin's *Lettre à M. de Balzac* (Geneva, 1633) with its attacks on the Roman Church. (The Balzac in question was the author Jean-Louis Guez de Balzac [1595–1654]). His treatise is entitled *Silvestri Petrasanctae ... Notae in epistolam Petri Molinaei ad Balzacum, cum responsione ad haereses, errores et calumnias ejus ...*, Antwerpiae, ex officina Plantiniana, 1634. The disputed passages are quoted in French in the margin. In Chapter 9, for example, he refutes Du Moulin's statement that the Jesuits do not forbid regicide; in Chapter 10, he turns the tables on Du Moulin, showing that it is the Calvinists who permit regicide, with quotations from Zwingli, Calvin, Goodman, Knox and Buchanan. Chapter 11 contains one of Beza's purportedly lascivious epigrams with some sharp criticism of it, and other notes. The treatise naturally takes up Bolsec's and others' attacks on Calvin's morals. Rivet took up the battle for Du Moulin with his *Andreae Riveti Jesuita vapulans. Siue Castigatio notarum S. Petraesanctae in Episolam Molinaei ad Balzacum* (Lugduni Batuorum, 1635), but Du Moulin was able enough to defend himself with his *Hyperaspistes* (Geneva, 1636). Chouet printed a new edition of *Jesuita vapulans* in 1644, with some of Rivet's other works and some of Grotius' opuscules: *Andreae Riveti Pictavi Catholicus orthodoxus, oppositus Catholico Papistae: In quatuor partes seu tractatus distinctus ... Accesserunt huic editioni Jesuita Vapulans Silvestrum Petra Sancta et opuscula adversaria Hugonis Grotii.* Edito nova (Geneva, Iacobi Chouet, 1644).
[46]   Cf. Gardy (1960), nos. 192 and 194, pp. 114–16 (text identical in both printings).

documents we find the reformer's letter to Farel of 30 May 1540, in which Calvin complains about his poor health and envisages prematurely a succession to Farel and himself, as well as his letter to Viret expressing pleasure that rumours of Viret's death turned out to be false. The hostile testimonies cited include Florimond de Raemond, Jean-Papire Masson, Christophe de Thou, Etienne Pasquier, the results of an enquiry into the Calvin family conducted in Noyon as reported by André Rivet, and a digest of Le Vasseur's account. Admittedly, the two letters from Calvin to Farel and Viret respectively are only intended as blank page fillers.[47] The same cannot be said, however, of the excerpt from the reformer's preface to the Psalms[48] and the other pieces. The extract from Calvin's preface to his Psalms Commentary is presented as a complement to the Beza/Colladon *Life* with no further comment.[49] The other pieces are intended as further corroboration, with the anonymous compiler (Chouet himself, perhaps) arguing that 'to shut even more firmly the mouth of calumny, we wanted to add the testimonies of several of our adversaries who had no choice but to testify truly in this matter after conducting an exhaustive enquiry and to proclaim loudly and clearly that all the so-called crimes of which Calvin has been accused are imaginary and have no basis in fact.'[50]

The compiler presents hostile testimonies very carefully, selecting only those passages that serve his cause. Citing the testimony of Florimond de Raemond, he omits the famous extract from the latter's *post mortem* horoscope of Calvin meant to show that Calvin was predestined by the stars to be a heresiarch along with Luther and Melanchthon.[51] He does, however, draw the reader's attention to another passage from the Jesuit's text, which stresses Calvin's distaste for carnal pleasures, his poor health and his capacity for hard work.[52] The compiler's comments show very

---

[47]   I am referring to the 1663 imprint. Hereafter: *L'Histoire de la Vie et mort* (1663). See ibid., p. 166 [! = 176]: 'afin que quelques pages ne demeurassent blanches, nous auons ici aiousté deux lettres familieres du seruiteur de Dieu, à ses deux grands amis M. Guillaume Farel et Pierre Viret.'

[48]   Ibid., pp. 179–92.

[49]   *L'Histoire de la Vie et mort* (1663), p. 179: 'Parce que ce fidele seruiteur de Dieu dont la vie a esté descrite ci dessus, en a remarqué lui mesmes beaucoup de circonstances bien considerables dans sa preface sur les Pseaumes, qui pourront donner de la lumière à ce qui en a desia esté representé, l'on a retrouvé à propos d'y ioindre l'extrait suiuant.'

[50]   Ibid., p. 193.

[51]   See Florimond de Raemond, *L'Histoire de la naissance, progrez et decadence de l'heresie de ce siecle, diuisee en huict liures* (Rouen, Estienne Vereul, 1622), livre 8, chap. 8, p. 900 [! = p. 880]. For recent treatment of Calvin's horoscope cast by Florimond de Raemond, see Max Engammare, 'Les horoscopes de Calvin, Mélanchthon et Luther: une forme inattendue de polémique catholique post-tridentine', in Zinguer and Yardeni (eds), *Les deux réformes chrétiennes*, pp. 172–203.

[52]   See *L'Histoire de la Vie et mort* (1663), p. 194.

clearly that his work is to be situated in the context of the Rivet–Pietrasanta controversy, and in the context of Jesuit attacks on Calvin generally.

> The first testimony is that of Florimond de Raemond ... who despite being Calvin's adversary speaks of him in terms likely to make the Jesuits blush with shame, had they not lost all sense of shame some time ago, especially if what Pierre Matthieu says in his *Histoire de la paix* is true, that is that the Jesuit Richeome had used Florimond's name to defend the Antichrist[53] [that is, the papacy].

His second testimony is drawn from the *Life* of Jean-Papire Masson, which he significantly places among Masson's *Eloges des hommes célèbres*, having no knowledge of Jean-Baptiste Masson's postface, which, as we have seen, sharply distinguished his brother's *Vita Caluini* from the *elogium* genre. The printer of the 1638 edition of Masson's *Elogia* obviously had not intended to play into the hands of Calvin supporters when he included the *Vita Caluini* in his volume. That, however, was the overall result. The compiler of the 1656 appendices to the Beza/Colladon *Vie et mort* notes:

> Papire Masson, a man of great reputation in whose praise the president de Thou erected a glorious monument, wrote Elogia of many famous men, among which he included the Elogium of Calvin. In it he clears the reformer of all the main charges, which other writers held against him in an attempt to besmirch his reputation ....[54]

These testimonies, together with those of De Thou and Etienne Pasquier,[55] serve to counter the Bolsec myth, which was exploited by the Jesuit writers in the seventeenth century. Issues of confessional propaganda apart, what strikes the modern reader in the 1656 *Vie et mort* is the importance that historical accuracy has come to assume in Protestant apologies of Calvin. The compiler of the testimonies (perhaps Chouet himself) is not content to present a refutation of the Bolsec myth by insisting on Calvin's moral and other qualities in such a way as to construct an alternative hagiography. Under the influence of Masson particularly, he is far more concerned with the historical accuracy of documents cited. However, there is still a strong rhetorical component to his defence. In his view, the fact that the authors he adduces are Calvin's adversaries makes them all the more reliable, the argument being that had they been able to find any corroboration of the crimes of which Calvin was accused, they would have produced it. Calvin's hostile biographers, such as Florimond de Raemond, Masson, De Thou, and so on, thus become, in the compiler's view, 'good

---

[53]   Ibid. He is referring to: Pierre Matthieu, *Histoire de France et des choses mémorables advenues aux provinces estrangères durant sept années de paix du règne de Henri IIII* [...] (Paris, Jamet Metayer, 1605).

[54]   *L'Histoire de la Vie et mort* (1663), p. 195.

[55]   Ibid., pp. 195–8.

historians'. Their testimony is to be valued instead of curtly dismissed for its confessional orientation.[56] This argument obviously does not hold in cases where the Catholic accounts of Calvin contain errors. One of the Noyon enquires provides a good example of the historiographical fallacy underlying his main argument. Chouet is not familiar with Desmay's work. He does, however, have knowledge of the results of an enquiry made by a notary public in Noyon, a document, which, he notes, 'M. Rivet, in his book *Jesuita vapulans*,[57] certifies having seen in the hands of Monsieur Wandermyle, who obtained it, while staying in Noyon, from the very notary who conducted it.'[58] The document as cited is succinct, to say the least, and amounts to basic data about Calvin's parents' names and origin, details of the number and names of his brothers and sisters, and his life and travels prior to settling in Geneva.

Chouet can only use it as negative evidence and is aware of the document's limitations when he says:

> This account has been translated word for word from the registers of this notary public. Admittedly, they contain various pieces of information, particularly with regard to Calvin's travels, which are not true. Nonetheless, it is a fact that this information emanates from Noyon, from those who were hardly favourable to Calvin, and who therefore would have taken care not to dissimulate the accusations of crimes that were made against him, had there been the slightest suspicion of them.[59]

The fallacy is obvious: there is no reason to assume that an historical document which contains errors in its account of Calvin's travels can be relied upon for conveying accurate information on the falsity of crimes that the reformer was accused of by Bolsec and others. This is obviously of some subliminal concern to our compiler, as he goes on to say:

> The second document is even more authentic. It is the testimony of Jacques Le Vasseur, dean of Noyon, in his *Annals* of the Cathedral of Noyon, which he published in Paris in 1633. This author, who testifies having detested to the utmost Calvin and all of his family, brought to light all that could be found in the Archives and Registers of the Chapter of Noyon and in the records of the Noyon notaries. But after conducting all these searches, he could find nothing to reproach him with, excepting the exchange or handing over of a few benefices while he studied in Paris, and could reside neither in Noyon, where he held a chapel in the cathedral, nor in Pont-l'Evesque, where he also held a living.[60]

---

56   See ibid., p. 196 notice on De Thou: 'D'où nous pouuons recueillir vn argument bien fort pour l'innocence de Caluin, car s'il eust eu quelque verité dans tout ce qu'on lui a reproché, il ne faut pas douter que Monsieur le President de Thou, qui avoit eu des memoires tres particulieres et tres fideles de toutes choses...'
57   See note 45 above.
58   *L'Histoire de la Vie et mort* (1663), pp 194–5.
59   Ibid., p. 202.
60   Ibid., pp. 202–3.

Chouet considers Le Vasseur 'even more authentic' (*encor plus autentique*) for a mixture of historical and dogmatic reasons. Judging by the summary he gives,[61] he was obviously able to read Le Vasseur's account with its full references to the original documents, as opposed to reading it in a hostile work such as Rivet's *Jesuita vapulans*. He thus considers it as 'even more authentic' because it is historically sounder, and not slanted by any intermediate source and therefore illustrative of his argument, 'had there been any sexual crimes, his adversaries would not have concealed their existence.'

By and large, the 1656 reprint of the second *Life* of Calvin shows that Protestant views on Calvin biographies had undergone a subtle transformation. Now obviously, as will become clear from our examination of Drelincourt's account, the notion of Protestant hagiography had not disappeared, and a *Life* written nearly a century before still retained its interest. Nor had it become less important to clear the reformer of false rumours spread notably by Bolsec, but also by Du Préau and Van der Linden.[62] What changed between the end of the sixteenth- and the mid-seventeenth century was the appreciation of historical sources, which meant in turn that the use of Catholic material became not just permissible but desirable if the material was perceived as sound. This entailed a modification in the Protestant view of Calvin. Whereas Colladon or Beza would have found it inconceivable to mention Calvin's exchange of benefices or his absenteeism, Chouet, or whoever the 1656 compiler was, found it perfectly acceptable and not to be disputed on historical grounds, Catholic sources being reliable on this point. As he puts it:

> It is indeed remarkable that these people who had so little liking for Calvin conducted such a painstaking enquiry in the city of Noyon itself, where they had easy access to all the public and private records, and that they could find nothing to reproach him with other than the exchange and the handing-over of benefices conducted at a time when, being absent, he could not take on his pastoral duties.[63]

Chouet thus hoped to put to death the Bolsec myth of Calvin's sexual crimes.[64] However, his reply did not suffice, as Calvin's misdemeanours had meanwhile gained a new lease of life with the appearance of Richelieu's *Traitté* in 1651.

---

[61] Ibid., pp. 203–5.

[62] Ibid., p. 206.

[63] Ibid., pp. 205–6.

[64] Ibid., p. 206: 'Apres cela ie me persuade que s'il se rencontre encore quelque personne assez impudente et malicieuse pour ietter de nouueau contre la mémoire de ce saint personnage les infames calomnies qv'vn Bolsec, vn Campian, vn Prateolus et semblables bouches d'enfer ont vomi autresfois contre lui et qui ont esté si souuent refutées, ie me persuade dis-ie que tous ceux qui en voudront iuger sans passion en reconnoistront aisément la fausseté et ne s'estonneront pas si les fideles seruiteurs de Dieu reçoiuent vn si mauuais traitement, puis que leur Seigneur et leur Maistre n'en a pas receu vn meilleur.'

Drelincourt and his *Defense* of Calvin

Charles Drelincourt (d. 1669), the fiery preacher of the Church of
Charenton and author of numerous treatises of Catechetics, consolation
and so on, many of which became prescribed reading in the Genevan
Church,[65] published his *La Defense de Calvin* in 1667 as a reaction to
Richelieu's *Traitté*.[66] The work is not a biography any more than the *Traitté*.
However, being roughly twenty times the length of Richelieu's chapter
on the personalities and lives of the reformers, it constitutes a digest of
biographies, particularly Catholic biographies, of Calvin. Drelincourt read
them all and noticed, like Chouet before him, that the scabrous 'Bolsecian'
image of the reformer was revised and corrected by subsequent Roman
Catholic writers. In his view, Richelieu thus represents an anomaly all the
more regrettable because it is a throwback to the 'bad old days' of the
Roman Catholic reception of Calvin. As he puts it in the preface dedicated
to *messieurs les pasteurs et les professeurs de l'Église et de l'Académie de
Genève* [the ministers and professors of the Genevan Church and Genevan
Academy],

> We thought that the black and stinking calumnies, which threatened to denigrate
> one of the finest and the most holy lives ever known, were locked up forever in
> the abyss and that no honourable person felt anything other than ashamed of
> them. But seeing that all these hellish calumnies were being once again put on
> display ... I thought that they were likely to bedazzle people and to shock those
> who are simple and do not know the hidden depths of Satan.[67]

However, this does not explain why he waited fifteen years before
publishing his reply to the cardinal. We must bear in mind here that, in
the 1660s, Geneva was being steadily undermined by Victor Emmanuel II,
who wanted to cut down on the privileges granted to the city by the Treaty
of St Julien of 1603.[68] At the same time, the Protestant churches in France
were under increasing pressure, as more and more concerted attempts
were made to convert the Huguenots to Catholicism, and as freedom to
celebrate Protestant worship became restricted. The morale was low, and a
work of edification evoking former glories was much needed. Drelincourt
thus had recourse to the time-honoured device of evoking the example of

---

[65]   On Drelincourt, see E. Haag and E. Haag (eds), *La France protestante*, second edn,
rev. by H. Bordier, vol. 5 (Paris: Fischbacher, 1886), cols 485–95. For most recent work
on him, see Jane McKee, 'The Life and Times of a Paris Clergyman: The Correspondence
of Charles Drelincourt', *Proceedings of the Third International Huguenot Conference*, in
Bulletin of the Historical Society of South Africa, 39 (2002): 173–82.

[66]   See note 1 above.

[67]   Drelincourt, *Defense* (1667), fol. ¶3r.

[68]   See Anne-Marie Piuz, *Affaires et politique: recherches sur le commerce de Genève au
17ᵉ siècle* (Geneva: A. Julien, 1964); Gabriel Pérouse, *Les relations de la Savoie avec Genève
du 16ᵉ au 18ᵉ siècle* (Belley: Chaduc, 1932).

an historical, saintly figure while replying to attacks on that same saint's reputation. Teissier, as we have seen, attempted something similar, albeit in a different spirit, with his French translations of Beza's 1575 *Life* of Calvin and De la Faye's 1606 *Life* of Beza in 1681.

Drelincourt's *Defense* thus revives the image of Calvin as saint, and gives it new emphasis without referring to the sixteenth-century *Lives* of Colladon and Beza. He states that his aim is to provide inspiration in difficult times, and addresses the Genevans thus:

> If you did not have all the love and passion that you have for the glory of God and for the honour of those who are entrusted to you, I believe that the thought of Calvin's burning zeal and his indefatigable labours would be most likely to inspire you with heavenly ardour and to make you work in the cause of our Lord with holy zeal.[69]

At the same time, Drelincourt was fully aware of the usefulness of seventeenth-century Catholic historical writings when it came to clearing Calvin's reputation, and so exploited them more extensively than Chouet. He too cites Masson, Florimond de Raemond, Etienne Pasquier, 'the enquiry of M. Wandermyle' as cited by Rivet, and the *Annales* of Le Vasseur. Moreover, in contrast with Chouet, he shows excellent knowledge of Desmay's account, which he apparently read in the 1657 edition.[70] He uses all these works to show Catholic authors, Richelieu in particular, that the scabrous image of Calvin had been shown to be false by their own side. This stratagem allows him not to enter into open conflict with the Catholic hierarchy, as he would have done had he overtly attacked Richelieu. As it is, Drelincourt is member of a tolerated religious minority fully aware that it would be highly counterproductive to take polemics against Richelieu as far as he would like. Thus, although writing some twenty-five years after the cardinal's death (1642), he still refers to the *Traitté* as 'published under the name of Cardinal Richelieu', and as causing offence to 'such an excellent intellect and to such a great statesman.'[71] At the same time, he accuses the late cardinal of having seen the Noyon Registers in 1640 when he stayed near Noyon with Louis XII shortly before the Siege of Arras, and of having made no use of them deliberately because they contained nothing incriminating.[72]

He shows no knowledge of the 1656 Genevan publication, and in his efforts to clear the reformer's reputation he even has recourse to Baronius' *Annales ecclesiastici* to show that Calvin's holding of a chapel at the age of twelve, and of two benefices at the age of eighteen (Richelieu's reproaches

---

[69] Delincourt, *Defense* (1667), fol. ¶4v.
[70] Ibid., p. 155.
[71] Ibid., pp. 57, 71, 155.
[72] Ibid., p. 8.

notwithstanding), was not an abuse but common practice in the medieval church. Referring to Baronius, he cites among many other examples Agapetus II, who was made pope at the age of eighteen in 946, and Benedict IX, who became pope aged ten in 1032. He notes that Baronius himself deplores this premature elevation to papacy as a symptom of the 'plague-like sickness of simony', and asks which is more abnormal: Calvin's acceding to one miserable chapel aged twelve, or Benedict IX's elevation to the supreme headship of the church aged ten?[73] Drelincourt then turns against Richelieu the debate between Edmund Campion and William Whittaker, which the cardinal cites[74] as proof that Calvin was branded:

> To cut a long story short, Whittaker would have been absolutely right to compare Calvin's stigmata with those of St Paul. For, if by the phrase *perfuga stigmaticus* [the phrase used by Campion] we mean a Roman soldier who, after receiving the insignia of his service, abandons it without leave and goes over to the enemy, the name befits St Paul, who abandoned not just Judaism, but the religion of the Pharisees, having been not only a Jew, but also a Pharisee and the son of a Pharisee. In the same way, Calvin was not just born into the Roman Church, but was a priest and one in charge of two livings at that.[75]

Calvin was indeed stigmatised, he continues, not in the sense that Richelieu means, however, of being branded with a *fleur-de-lys*, but in the sense of being tortured and bearing marks of it, which were spiritual, not physical, in contrast to those borne by St Paul.[76] Drelincourt thus very carefully constructs the image of holy Calvin, and, to drive his point home, refers to the reformer as *bienheureux* [blessed].[77] All that is missing is the martyrdom. Drelincourt naturally cannot invent one, as to do so would imply recourse to legend, which he seeks to avoid at all costs, keeping to historical documents as closely as possible and citing them at some length. However, he can legitimately consider Calvin a Roman imperial martyr in the figurative sense of the distortions suffered not by his body, but by his teaching. He establishes the parallel very clearly:

> Just as in former times martyrs were dressed in animal skins so that they could be all the better torn apart by dogs, so all sorts of infamous and abominable

---

[73]   Ibid., pp. 13–16 (esp. p. 16).
[74]   Richelieu (1651), p. 291: 'Campianus qui mourut martyr en Angleterre [marg.: 1581 – sous le regne de la royne Elisabeth reprochant à nos aduersaires la vie infame de Caluin et vsant de ces termes: "que leur chef auoit esté fleurdelisé et fugitif," Witaker en sa Reponse n'en a point d'austre que celle-ci: "Caluin a esté stigmatisé mais S. Paul l'a esté, d'autres l'ont esté aussi." A quoi Duraeus repartant en la replique qu'il fait pour Campianus dit: "que c'est vne chose impie de comparer Caluin marqué par ses crimes à S. Paul marqué pour la confession de Iesus-Christ." Witaker en sa replique se taist sur cet article et ce qui doit passer pour vne conuiction indubitable des crimes imputez à Caluin.']
[75]   Drelincourt, *Defense* (1667), pp. 63–4.
[76]   Ibid., pp. 64–5.
[77]   Ibid., p. 64.

teachings have been attributed to this faithful servant of the Lord so that scurrilous, hellish tongues could tear him apart all the more easily.[78]

As well as portraying Calvin as a martyr with respect to his doctrine, Drelincourt's *Defense* constitutes a veritable arsenal of extracts from sixteenth- and seventeenth-century Catholic accounts of the reformer, from Masson to Richelieu. This suggests that, despite the dedication to the Genevan Church and Academy, Drelincourt intends the work for the use of French ministers in a difficult situation, a collection of material to help them refute any accusations against Calvin's reputation that they might encounter from the Catholic side. Drelincourt is no more objective than Richelieu, and his judgement on Calvin's absenteeism and pluralism cannot be called balanced. However, his *Defense* adds new features to the Protestant image of the Genevan reformer. Calvin is still portrayed as a model of selflessness and piety, but with the added ingredient of intellectual martyrdom. At the same time, Drelincourt's extremely detailed use of Catholic testimonies to refute Bolsec-type criticisms shows a lack of interest in producing a new biography based on new evidence, which characterises seventeenth-century 'Calvinography'. While Drelincourt and his fellow Calvinists still find the sixteenth-century Beza/Colladon image of Calvin to be authoritative, they submit his *reputation* not just to apologetics, but also to scholarly enquiry.

Drelincourt's *Defense* placed the Genevan authorities in something of a quandary. Although neither the council nor the Company of Pastors raised any resistance to giving permission to print the work, and although the work was intended for the French rather than the Genevan context, the Company of Pastors still had to explain why the most detailed defence of the Genevan reformer had France and not Geneva as its land of origin. Thus we read in the *approbation* of the work by the pastoral corps, which is printed directly after Drelincourt's preface:

> We cannot but grant that this our church (which has so many obligations to the memory of this faithful minister of Christ and which is the beneficiary to this day of the fruits of his incomparable labours that bring great solace) would not have failed to render unto him what is his in this particular instance, by refuting all these infamous calumnies, had it not sincerely believed that, being so gross and so far removed from the truth, they would refute themselves and so deserved nothing but contempt ... But seeing as the enemy's zeal will not be quenched unless the same calumnies are repeated ... and that they have no shame to vomit up yet again all that the blackest malice could invent against the memory of this blessed [*bienheureux*] servant of God, we praise God all the more for having given to our brother the saintly idea of working on such an important subject.[79]

---

[78] Ibid., p. 65.
[79] Ibid., fols ¶2v.–3r.

The publication of Drelincourt's work thus sealed the fate of Calvin biographies. The Calvinist churches in Geneva and France were from then on guided by a dual purpose so far as Calvin biography was concerned. They wanted to cherish and preserve the reformer's saintly memory on the one hand, and on the other, they insisted on a *scholarly* examination of sources, especially hostile sources, to clear his reputation. No new Calvin biographies were produced until Doumergue's seven-volume work *Jean Calvin: les homes et les choses de son temps*, published between 1899 and 1917, which, despite being far more exhaustive than all the previous biographies, still chiefly aimed to clear Calvin's reputation via scholarly enquiry into sixteenth- and seventeenth-century biographies of the reformer.

Pierre Bayle

Along with clearing Calvin's reputation via scholarly enquiry, another concern made itself manifest in the late seventeenth- and early eighteenth century: interest in scholarly enquiry as such, never completely devoid of controversial questions, but never completely overshadowed by them either. This latter approach crystallised in the Calvin notice in Pierre Bayle's *Dictionnaire historique et critique*. In the twelve-page notice that Bayle devotes to the reformer,[80] the quantity of notes far outweighs the text, which deals only with selected episodes from Calvin's life, mainly his early life, while the notes are concerned with confronting and refuting biographical errors. Naturally, Bayle does not view Calvin in the devotional light characteristic of Beza, Colladon, Chouet, Drelincourt or Teissier. He does, nonetheless, single him out as one of the most important *réformés*, and therefore significant enough to have multiple errors about him corrected. Bayle read all the notices and *Lives* of Calvin from Beza onwards. He shows great familiarity with hostile accounts, and goes to great lengths to refute particularly those emanating from the pens of Jesuits: Florimond de Raemond, Varillas, Maimbourg and many others. Papire Masson does not escape his critical attention, although he comes off very well compared to other authors. Bayle considers the misattribution of Masson's work to Gillot as just one of the many errors of writers such as Maimbourg. As regards early biographies of Calvin, Bayle had read the three sixteenth-century *Lives* by Beza and Colladon (all three of which he attributes to Beza only). He is of the opinion that if anything accurate is to be known about any particular feature of Calvin's *Life*, Beza's text is the most reliable. He also treats Drelincourt as totally sound, and confronts his account with

---

[80]   Bayle, *Dictionnaire historique et critique*, vol. 2, pp. 13–24.

those of the Jesuits – Florimond de Raemond,[81] Varillas and Maimbourg –, which he finds to be full of mistakes and anachronisms. Bayle's notice is not part of the present enquiry, and I do not propose to devote a detailed analysis to it, but simply to show that it is not a defence of, less still an attack on Calvin, but a series of minute corrections of details of his life and career (such as, for example, Varillas' misapprehension that Calvin's Commentary on Seneca's *De constantia* was in fact a book entitled *De constantia*, a sort of religious manifesto urging the persecuted Protestants to remain firm in their convictions in the face of persecution). Bayle's refutation of Maimbourg's and Varillas' attribution to Gillot of Jean-Papire Masson's *Vita* provides an excellent example of his method, and of his polemical and historical concerns. Thus we see that he had access to at least some of the correspondence of Gui Patin, the physician who persuaded the printer Sébastien Huré to include Masson's *Vita Caluini* in Balesdens' edition of *Eloges des hommes illustres* of 1638. Bayle cites one of Patin's letters:

> As for Papire Masson [Patin writes], 'he wrote a *Life* of Calvin, which the author's brother [Jean-Baptiste Masson], who was a canon, gave me in 1619. But since that time, as the collection of Masson's *Elogia* was being printed here, with great difficulty I got the publisher to include the *Life*. The publisher asked permission from the Jesuits, who forbade him to publish it. However, I managed to convince him that including the *Life* would increase the book's selling potential.'[82]

Bayle confronts this evidence with Varillas' assertion in his preface to Volume I of the *Histoire de l'hérésie*, which he finds to be manifestly false. He gives the full text of the passage from Varillas' work:

> 'Balesdens published the *Elogia* of Papire Masson and included Calvin's *Life* among them because he found it among Masson's papers and imagined him to be its author. His blindness on this matter is all the more intolerable as the way the *Life* is written is so different from Masson's other works that very scant knowledge of Latin is enough to see that he cannot be its author ... I learnt from M. Dupuys that it was written by the famous Jacques Gillot, *conseiller clerc* at the *Grande Chambre* of the *Parlement de Paris* ... and indeed it seems worthy to me of such a great man. It is a masterpiece of its kind and although longer *Lives* of Calvin exist, we have none that is more carefully crafted and revised with greater care. However, I have not been able to make much use of it as it concerns itself more with refuting what Bauduin and Westphal said about Calvin than with relating his actions.'[83]

---

[81]   His judgement of Florimond de Raemond is unqequivocal in *Dictionnaire*, vol. 2, p. 21: 'Un semblable historien doit être traité comme ces marchands insolvables, qui ont perdu tout crédit ...'.

[82]   Ibid., vol. 2, p. 19.

[83]   Ibid.

Bayle's refutation of Varillas shows that his aim is to revive an interest in scholarship and put an end to errors of the kind Calvin biography has suffered from.[84] This does not make his notice dispassionate; he uses accurate scholarship as another tool in his controversy with the Jesuits. Referring to Patin's letter, he points out that Balesdens, the editor, did not find the *Vita* among Papire Masson's papers, but was given it by Patin, who had obtained it from Jean-Baptiste Masson. After Masson himself, Bayle is the first author to show awareness of the difference between a *Vita* and an *Elogium*, which, he points out, accounts for the difference of tone between Masson's *Vita Caluini* and most of the other pieces in the volume, which fall under the category of *Elogia*. According to Bayle, Varillas had only to study Masson's *Vitae* of Charles IX, Dante or Boccaccio to see that they are composed on the same model as the *Vita Calvini*. Moreover, he notes, the author of the *Vita Caluini* is known to have studied Law under Bauduin, information which corresponds to Masson's career and not to Gillot's. Finally, he points out rightly that the object of Masson's *Vita* was not to refute Bauduin or Westphal: on the contrary, Masson used Bauduin as a source.[85] Interestingly enough, Bayle had no knowledge of the separate publication of the *Vita* by Jean-Baptiste and the latter's damning postface. Nor was he particularly impressed by the objectivity and the accuracy of the *Vita*, although he did not include scurrilous rumours of the sort perpetuated by Varillas and Maimbourg.

In all, Bayle is the first modern historian to undertake not so much a biography of Calvin as a critical investigation of sources of false information about the reformer. Accordingly, he does not aim to convey any specific religious image of Calvin. He devotes no attention to his doctrine or his role as the Genevan religious leader at a particular time. He is fighting historiographical errors, and at the same time settling his own accounts with the Jesuits and other Roman Catholic writers who propagate myths and legends. Even so, Bayle's sympathy for Calvin is quite evident, especially for his moral, intellectual and literary qualities. As he puts it:

> He was a man whom God had endowed with many great talents, a lot of intelligence, excellent judgement, good memory and the ability to write articulately, eloquently without tiring, and with great zest for the truth.[86]

---

[84]   As he says himself (ibid., vol. 2, p. 21): 'Il est quelquefois très mal-aisé d'ôter la vie éternelle à des erreurs en les réfutant solidement. Que sera-ce donc si on les laisse en repos?'

[85]   Ibid., vol. 2, pp. 19–20.

[86]   Ibid., vol. 2, p. 17: 'C'étoit un homme à qui Dieu avoit conféré de grands talens, beaucoup d'esprit, une iugemen exquis, une fidelle mémoire, une plume solide, éloquente, infatigable, un grand savoir, un grand zèle pour la vérité.'

Barckhausen, His Edition of Jean-Papire Masson, and the Controversy Surrounding It

Konrad Heinrich Barckhausen or Barckhusen (1677–1732), son of a lawyer from Detmold, was a reformed theologian who taught in Berlin, first at the Calvinist Gymnasium or High School of Joachimsthal, and then at the Friedrich Werder Gymnasium, of which he became rector in 1715. He is chiefly known nowadays because of his involvement in the controversy over universal grace, which sparked off much passion in Germany and especially in the Calvinist churches of Brandenburg in the early eighteenth century. The problem originated with the *Confessio Sigismundi* of 1614, which had followed the *Augsburg Confession* in putting forward a view of grace which was not just universalist, but synergistic. In other words, it taught both the absolute election of every believer and universal grace. The need of making concessions to the Lutherans led to some modifications, as witnessed by the *Colloquium Lipsiense* of 1631, the *Declaratio Thoruniensis* of 1645, and other documents.[87] The Brandenburg Church thus separated from orthodox Calvinism, while still remaining Calvinist in its general orientation, given that a large number of French congregations bound to Calvin's *Confessio Gallicana* were settled in the country.

The Barckhausen–Volkmann controversy began with the publication (Cologne, 1712) of the *Theses theologicæ syntagmatis* of Paul Volkmann (under the pseudonym of L. Crocius), who was a colleague of Barckhausen and rector of the Joachimsthal Gymnasium in Berlin. He intended the work, which argued for universal grace and conditional election, to serve as a new textbook replacing Johann Wolleb's *Compendium theologiae christianae* of 1626, with its defence of the Dort doctrine of twin decrees of salvation and condemnation, grace being limited to those predestined to be saved. Konrad Heinrich Barckhausen hotly contested Volkmann's views, and postulated the double decree or the particularist doctrine of grace. Under the pseudonym *Pacificus Verinus*, he thus published in 1712 an *Amica collatio doctrinæ de gratia*, and followed it the next year with a highly polemical treatise in German: *Mauritii Neodorpii Calvinus orthodoxus, d. i. sin kurzes Gespräch ... worin bescheiden untersucht wird ob und wie weit die Lehre der Universalisten mit der Lehre der ersten reformirten*

---

[87] Cf. *Corpus constitutionum Marchicarum, oder Königl. Preussis. und Churfürstl. Brandenburgische in der Chur und Marck Brandenburg, auch incorporirten Landen publicirte und ergangene Ordnungen, Edicta, Mandata, Rescripta &c. Von Zeiten Friedrich Wilhelms ... ad annum 1736 ... colligiert und ans Licht gegeben von Christian Otto Mylius...*, ed. C. O. Mylius, 6 vols (Berlin and Halle: n. p., 1737–51), vol. 1, pp. 382 ff. On the controversy, see also Daniel Heinrich Hering, *Beiträge zur Geschichte der evangelisch-reformierten Kirche in den Preuss. Brandenburgischen Ländern*, 2 vols (Breslau: Meyer, 1784–85), vol. 1, p. 57 ff., and Alexander Schweizer, *Die protestantischen Centraldogmen in ihrer Entwicklung innerhalb der reformierten Kirche* (Zürich: Orell Füssli, 1856), p. 816 ff.

Lehrer welche in Berlin vor 100 Jahren gelehrt übereinkommen. A Berlin preacher, Stercki by name, took up the discussion on Volkmann's side, and Philippe Naudé replied for the orthodox side. The controversy got so heated that the Prussian king, Frederick William I, issued an edict in 1719 putting both sides to silence. Thus Volkmann was ordered to reintroduce Wolleb's *Compendium* as the official textbook, and Barckhausen's *Calvinus orthodoxus* was banned from sales.

Barckhausen is far less well known as a biographer of Calvin,[88] or as editor of Masson's *Vita Calvini*, without Jean-Baptiste Masson's additions or postface, which he annotated.[89] His own biography of Calvin, entitled *Historica Narratio de Johanne Calvino*, was published in 1721. It was followed by his edition of Masson's *Vita Caluini* the same year. The publication sparked off a response in 1727 from an anonymous correspondent calling himself Pythalethes, who pointed out a number of errors. Barckhausen supplied brief replies to Pythalethes' objections.[90] Thereupon appeared another pamphlet entitled *Crantzii a Fluuio Erklaerung an Pythalethen auf Herrn Conradi Henrici Barckhusen's Beantwortung des Critischen Brief-Wechsels betreffend*, together with Barckhausen's supplements and replies. The latter work was printed in Prentzlau by Christian Ragoczy, also in 1727.[91]

The preface to Barckhausen's *Historica Narratio*, as well as the full title of the work, reveals the circumstances behind the publication. The Prussian Calvinist sets out to defend Calvin's reputation against Roman Catholic rumours, as might be expected, but also against Hugo Grotius' portrayal of the Calvin–Servetus affair, which accentuated Calvin's reputation as a cruel tyrant and apostle of intolerance among the Remonstrants. Grotius

---

[88] C. H. Barckhausen, *Historica Narratio de Johanne Calvino. Historische Nachricht von Johanne Calvino. Dessen Eltern, Geburt, Ersten Jugend, Lebens-Art usw. Sampt einer unmbstandlicher Erzehlung von Serveto und dessen greulichen Lehren, aus Serveti eigenen Schriften dargethan. Von Conr. Henr. Barckhusen, Dethmoldia-Lippiaco* (Berlin, Johann Grynaeus, 1721). Herafter: Barckhausen, *Historica Narratio*.

[89] *Johannis Papirii Massonis Foresii in senatu Parisiensi et regia aduocati Vita Johannis Caluini quam animaduersionibus historicis illustrauit Conradus Henricus Barckhusen, Dettmoldia-Lippiacus*, ed C. H. Barckhausen (Berlin: Johannes Grynaeus, 1722). Hereafter: Barckhausen, *Massonis Vita Calvini*.

[90] *Conradi Barckhusen kurze Beantwortung des Critischen Brief-wechsels betreffend Calvini Leben* (Berlin, the widow of Gotthard Schlechtiger, 1727). Hereafter: Barckhausen, *Beantwortung*.

[91] Hereafter: *Crantzii Erklaerung*. On the choronology of these works, see Barckhausen, *Beantwortung*, p. 5 (replying to 'Herr Censor's' remark that he had misspelt Calvin's mother's name in the *Historica Narratio* as *Joanna Franea* instead of *Jeanne le Franc*): 'Es sind weit mehr Druckfehler in der Lebensbeschreibung Calvini zu finden also specificiert worden. Ich kann meinen gelehrten Hn. Censori versichern, das ich in mehr also hundert Exemplarien, welche in gelehrte Leute Handen sind, diesen Druckfehler mit eigener Hand corrigiert ... Ich habe diesen Lebens-Lauf Calvini Anno 1721 drucken lassen, dass folgende Jahr habe ich Papirii Massonis *Vitam Caluini* lateinisch mit historischen Anmerckungen heraus gegeben ...'.

had been dead since 1645, and the virulence of Barckhausen's preface, an invective against Grotius' ignorance of the full iniquity of Servetus' doctrines, might seem surprising. However, the real aim of his invective is not Grotius, but the heterodox Pietist physician Johann Konrad Dippel (1673–1734), whose views would have been intolerable to an orthodox Calvinist such as Barckhausen.[92] In 1712, Dippel had published a defence of Servetus under the pseudonym 'Dr Ernst Christian Kleinmann'.[93] Barckhausen's *Historica Narratio* is a reaction to Dippel's work, as he himself points out in the closing phrases of his preface:

> Among the new Servetus apologists, Herr Dippel, writing under the name Kleinmann, has particularly distinguished himself. What the Calvinists object to in Herr Dippel's story, the impartial reader [*unparthayische Leser*] will find for himself in this book.[94]

The mention of the impartial reader is an ironic allusion to titles of some of Dippel's works, and to his being a disciple of Gottfried Arnold, whose views on tolerance and high respect for Servetus and Castellio as its apostles were well known. As for the *Historica Narratio* itself, although it does contain allusions to Dippel's work, quoting passages from it,[95] it is mainly a refutation of all the Catholic errors in Calvin biography, spanning not just a few columns, like the notice in Bayle's *Dictionnaire*, but over one hundred pages. Like Bayle (whose work Barckhausen knew, and whose notice on Calvin he mentions in his notes), he read all the biographies and notices on Calvin: Beza, Bolsec, Laing, Florimond de Raemond, Drelincourt, Teissier, Varillas, Maimbourg – all those that Bayle had read, and more. Like Bayle, too, he goes to some trouble to point up the extent of their errors. However, in contrast with Bayle, Barckhausen is not so much

---

[92]   For Dippel, see Wilhelm Bender, *Johann Konrad Dippel, der Freigeist aus dem Pietismus: ein Beitrag zur Entstehungsgeschichte der Aufklärung* (Bonn: Weber, 1882); Johannes Wallmann, *Der Pietismus* (Göttingen: Vandenhoeck & Ruprecht, 2005).

[93]   *Ernst Christian Kleinmanns Medicinae Doctoris und Kirchen-Raths, Ausführliche und Freywillige Replic an die Tit: Herren Consistoriales und sämtliches Ministerium der Evangelisch-Reformirten Gemeinde zu Wesel in Sachen Hn. Ernst Christoph Hochmanns de Hochenau. Warhaffte Historie von Johanne Calvino, Wie er mit Michael Serveto und andern verfahren, In einem Gespraeche zwischen Simeon und Obadiah* (Amsterdam: n.p., 1712).

[94]   Barckhausen, *Historica Narratio*, fol. I 3v.

[95]   See, for example, ibid., p. 68: 'Herr Dippel wil aus Castellione einen sonderlich frommen Menschen machen. Seine Worte lauten also: "Dass aber dieser Castellio ein sowol Gottseeligkeit als Gelehrsamkeit fürtrefflicher Mann gewesen, kan man Sonnen-klar sehen an dem schönen Epitaphio, so ihm gemacht worden, als er Anno 1563 in dem Herrn zu Basel entschlieff, und in die grosse Kirche daselbst beygesetzt wurde, so dann an dem herrlichen Zeugniss, welches ihme so viel wackere Männer ertheilet, und fürnemblich an dem, dass die Universitaet zu Basel sowol seinet zum allerbesten gedacht, als auch dass sie biss an das Ende seines Lebens ohne Regardirung aller Laesterungen Calvini in seinem Professorat ruhig zu lassen kein Bedencken getragen, und also hiemit das Siegel auf dieses Mannes Unschuld, und zugleich auf seine Unpartheiligkeit im Schreiben gedrucket hat."'

concerned with stopping the proliferation of error which Bayle considered a wickedness in itself (regardless of whom it affected) as he is with clearing Calvin's reputation not just over the matter of Servetus' condemnation, but in general. Also unlike Bayle, Barckhausen singles out Papire Masson as the one Catholic writer who was not only truthful and objective about the reformer, but who actually did much to clear his reputation. He is cited as 'the learned Papist who goes so far as to admit that Calvin frightened Sadolet.'[96] He also cites Masson's testimony of Calvin's theological gifts as demonstrated at the Colloquy of Worms, which earned him the cognomen *theologus* from theologians as venerable as Melanchthon. If only other Catholics got this open admission of Calvin's merits by Masson into their heads, notes Barckhausen.[97] In his very brief preface to his edition of Masson's *Vita Caluini*, he adds:

> There have always been many writers in the Papist Church who busied themselves with writing about Calvin's life, for instance, Bolsec, Laing, Beyerlingius, Lessius, Gualterius, Maimbourg, Varillas and many others. However, as regards historical reliability, Papirius Masson leaves all the others far behind. And this in my view is why the Jesuits devoted every effort to stop the publication of his *Vita Caluini*. However, Patin got the upper hand, for it was on his say-so that the *Vita* was printed together with Masson's *Elogia*. The venerable Jesuit fathers had good reason to feel as they did. For if what they say is true and the recently dead General of the Order, Gonzaletius Thyrsius, was extremely angry with Maimbourg for treating as fable the question of Calvin's sodomy and his punishment for it, what do you think would have happened had the same General seen this account or rather this apology of Calvin by Papire Masson? And the table that follows will show the fair-minded reader that Masson did write an apology of Calvin, not in every respect but in most.[98]

Barckhausen is the first Calvinist writer to go as far as calling Masson's *Vita* an apology of Calvin, although he does grant that the sixteenth-century biographer has erred in some respects, and that he, Barckhausen, has corrected such errors as he found. Among his corrections we might note Masson's statement about Calvin's arrogance based on Bauduin's testimony, which was contradicted by Beza and Drelincourt, and Masson's affirmation that Calvin and Farel had to leave the city because there was a movement to return to the Roman Catholic Church.[99] The confessional issue being his uppermost concern, he feels that Calvin has to be correctly presented according to the criteria established by Beza and Drelincourt, which is why he is so careful about glossing any negative statement in the

---

[96]   Ibid., p. 36. He indicates in a footnote that the *gelehrte Papiste* is 'Papyrius, *Vita Calvini*'.

[97]   Ibid., p. 39: 'Diese offenhertzige Bekandtnis Papyrii wil anderen Papisten nicht in den Kopff.'

[98]   Barckhausen, *Massonis Vita Caluini*, fol. A2v.

[99]   Ibid., p. 15.

Vita. At the same time, the very fact that he faithfully reproduces Masson's text, minus only the postface of Jean-Baptiste (which he did not know), shows that, partly in the wake of Bayle, the objective truth and falsehood of who said what about Calvin, and issues such as the chronology of the publication of the *Institutes* (which we are about to examine), were becoming almost as important as any questions to do with the reformer's spiritual image or the preservation of his memory.

The age of Calvin hagiography and Calvin slander was over, and the age of partial but minute enquiry into historical detail, partly for the purposes of historical enquiry and partly for those of controversy, was well and truly underway. This interest in historical detail, combined with the continued need to defend Calvin, as we have already noted, put a stop to new biographical approaches to Calvin until the twentieth century.

This hounding-down of minutiae is the most striking feature of the controversy, which is the object of the other two texts, both published in 1727. The first of these, as noted above, is a letter from Pythalethes to Barckhausen. We do not know who Pythalethes ('he who persuades of the truth') was. It is highly probable, however, judging by his frequent references to Bayle, that we are dealing with a Dippel-supporter. The debate, however, is very largely of a purely historical nature and centres on details of Calvin's life such as the name of his mother or the completeness of information provided about *De clementia*, all points to which Barckhausen replies in his *Beantwortung*.[100]

The Problem of the Chronology of Editions of the Institutes

The issue of the chronology of the editions of the *Institutes* is rather complex, and was finally settled only with the appearance of the Baum–

---

[100] See Barckhausen, *Beantwortung*, p. 7: Pythalethes notes: 'was das Buch de Clementia betrifft, dessen der Autor allhier gedencket, wünschte ich, er hätte mögen belieben nachzuschlagen, was Mr. Baile davon sagt, so würde er bey demselben sonder Zweiffel angetroffen haben, was den begierigen Leser etwas völliger vergnügen könnte.' The remark refers to *Historica Narratio*, p. 5, where Barckhausen states very briefly that Varillas was completely wrong in saying '[Calvin] habe ein Buch drucken lassen von der Standhaftkeit.' In fact, says Barckhausen, 'Dieses ist falsch, es war Senecae Buch *De clementia*.' And furthermore, again citing Varillas: '[Calvin] habe in demselbigen Buche die seinigen encouragiret, Tod vor die neue Lehre zu leiden.' To this, he replies: 'Nicht ein einziges Wort stehet davon in dem gantzen Commentario. Varillas hat wie es scheint, das Buch niemals gelesen.' It is worth noting here that Bayle's account (*Dictionnaire*, vol. 2, p. 14) goes into Varillas' errors in some detail over roughly a column of text. He agrees with Varillas that Calvin confused the chronology of the two Senecas, but does not consider the matter serious. Faced with Pythalethes reproach that he should have cited Bayle at greater length, as giving a more nuanced appraisal, Barckhausen replies in his *Beantwortung*, p. 7: 'Baile habe ich gelesen. Was ich vermeinet, das von diesem Buche zu wissen nöthig sey, stehet so wohl hier, als in Massonis *Vita Caluini*, p. 11 & 12.'

Cunitz–Reuss edition in 1863 in the *Corpus Reformatorum*. The problem lay in dates. Baum, Cunitz and Reuss established beyond the shadow of a doubt that the first edition of the *Institutes* with Latin text, divided into six chapters, was printed in Basel by Thomas Platter and Balthasar Lasius, and came out in March of 1536.[101] However, they did so only after resolving various questions of dating. In the first edition, Calvin's dedicatory epistle to François I of France is dated from 23 August, without the year. However, all the subsequent Latin editions date the same letter from 1 August 1536. The first French edition of 1541 (which is in fact a translation of the 1539 edition made by Calvin himself) gives 23 August 1535 and the subsequent French editions 1 August of the same year. This led some historians to think that Calvin initially published the first edition of the *Institutes* in French in 1535, and that the Latin edition of 1536 was chronologically the second. Baum, Cunitz and Reuss, however, conclude quite rightly that 23 August 1535 in the first French, and 23 August without the year in the first Latin edition, refer to the same date – that is, the date when Calvin finished the prefatory epistle to François I in the first Latin edition, which then appeared only in March of 1536. There was no first French edition of the *Institutes* in 1535. Baum, Cunitz and Reuss mention the names of several nineteenth-century historians who made the mistake of thinking the contrary.[102] They also quote the view of Jules Bonnet, among others, who was struck by the length of time elapsed between Calvin finishing the epistle to François I and the actual publication of the work.[103] Bonnet's hypothesis was that Platter and Lasius were too quick to date the work, which they did not expect to produce until 1536, but which in fact appeared in time for the Frankfurt Bookfair of the autumn of 1535. The chronology of publication of the early editions of the *Institutes*, however, was not a purely nineteenth-century problem; it went back to sixteenth- and seventeenth-century biographies of Calvin.

As we have seen, Bolsec argued quite simply that the very number of revised editions of the work guaranteed that it was full of lies. Papire Masson, on the other hand, expressed his great admiration of the book's refutation of Servetus and the Anabaptists, and placed its first edition in Basel in 1536, considering it to have already been divided into four books. Varillas among others perpetuated the error. Masson was fully aware that

---

[101]   See *Calv. Opp.*, vol. 1, pp. xxiii–xxxii. Cf. Rodolphe Peter and Jean-François Gilmont, *Bibliotheca calviniana*, 3 vols (Geneva: Droz, 1991–2000), vol. 1, pp. 35–9. The work was supposed to come out in time for the Frankfurt Bookfair of September 1535, but its publication was delayed until the Spring Bookfair of 1536.

[102]   *Calv. Opp.*, vol. 1, pp.xxvii–xxviii.

[103]   Ibid., pp. xxviii–xxix.

it then underwent multiple revisions in successive editions, but did not consider this in any way an indication of its untruthfulness.[104]

As for other biographers and historians, Maimbourg thought that the first edition appeared in French. Moreri, who obviously saw only the 1539 edition, thought that the first *Institutes* came out under the name of Alcuin. Opinions varied as to the year of the publication, Masson notwithstanding. Moreri thought 1534; others, 1535; others still, 1536.[105] Bayle, having never seen a complete 1536 edition himself,[106] also disputed the dating, and argued that the work was first published in 1535 in Latin.[107] Despite this, he presumed correctly, following partly Cornelius Schultingius (author of the *Bibliotheca catholica*, a systematic refutation of Calvin's *Institutes* published in 1602[108]), that the second edition came out in 1539 (under the anagram 'Alcuin'), and the third in 1543.[109] In his *Historica Narratio*, Barckhausen listed all the errors that had been made until 1721 regarding the date of the first edition, and was in fact the first Calvin biographer not just to date it correctly (which Masson had done already), but also to attribute the correct language of composition to it and to give an accurate summary of its contents. The only curious

---

[104] Masson (1620), pp. 10–11: 'Abiit in exilium ad Heluetios et Basileae anno 1536 publicauit de *Institutione christianae religionis libros* 4 ad Franciscum Francorum regem christianissimum, principem suum vt tanti regis magnitudine ad decipiendos subditos eius abuteretur. In praefatione quaesitur nullum sanae doctrinae in Gallia locum esse, eam carcere, exilio, praescriptione, incendio mulctari, seditionis et maleficii praeter meritum insimulari ac mendacibus apud regem calumniis traduci, quod illa non aliorsum spectaret aduersariorum sententia (aiebat ipse) nisi vt regibus sua spectra /11/ manibus extorqueat, tribunalia iudiciumque omnia praecipitet, subuertat ordines omnes et politias, pacem et quietem populi perturbet, leges omnes abroget, dominia et passiones dissipet, omnia denique sursum deorsum voluat. Quae etsi vera erant, vt euentus postea docuit, negat in cogitationem piorum cadere, pios appellans qui traditam libris illis doctrinam amplectebantur. Illa *Institutione* saepe aucta et millies excusa capitibus 104 magnam partem receptae a Romana et Catholica ecclesia doctrinae reiicit, obruit quoque Seruetianos errores et Anabaptistarum impias de baptismo sententias acutissime refellit.'

[105] For a summary of the various misapprehensions, see Barckhausen, *Historica Narratio*, pp. 16–17.

[106] Bayle, *Dictionnaire*, vol. 4, p. 171.

[107] Ibid., vol. 2, p. 15: 'Au reste si l'edition de Bâle per Thomam Platterum et Balthasarem Lasium mense Martio Ao. 1536 est la premiere, il faut dire que l'auteur data son ouvrage avant que le donner aux imprimeurs.'

[108] For Cornelius Schultingius (*c.* 1540–1604), see for example J. Höfer and K. Rahner (eds), *Lexikon für Theologie und Kirche*, 2nd edn, 11 vols (Freiburg i. Br: Herder, 1957–67), vol. 9, pp. 354 and 517. His *Bibliothecae catholicae et orthodoxae contra summam totius theologiae Calvinianistae in Institutionibus Ioannis Calvini et Locis communibus Petri Martyris breviter comprehensae, vel potius variarum lectionum et contra I. (II.) librum Institutionum Ioannis Calvini tomus I. (II.)* appeared in Köln in 1602. See Bayle, *Dictionnaire*, vol. 4, pp. 170–71. Schultingius also thought that the 1536 Basel edition was the *editio princeps*.

[109] Bayle, *Dictionnaire*, vol. 2, p. 15. Schultingius thought that the second edition was that of 1539, and the third that of 1545. See ibid., vol. 4, pp. 170–71.

feature of his correction of the various errors is his misspelling of Alcuin as 'Acurinus' when he refutes Moreri. He does not go into the details of later editions, but gives a very careful summary of the 1536 Latin *editio princeps*.[110] In his edition of Masson's *Vita*, he confines himself to a brief note pointing out that Masson's statement about the text division of the first edition is wrong.[111]

Thus far, it would seem that the seventeenth century saw the beginnings of the erudite debate which was carried on through the eighteenth- and nineteenth century. However, Barckausen's reply to Pythalethes, or, as he calls him in the *Kurze Beantwortung*, 'Herr Censor', shows the full importance of controversy in the seventeenth- and eighteenth-century debate, which demarcates it sharply from the later period. Barckhausen refutes one by one all of Bayle's suppositions regarding the chronology and the dating of the first three editions. He is particularly concerned to disown the edition of 1539, which came out under the anagram 'Alcuin', and passes off Moreri's observation as one of many *papistische Einfaelle* about Calvin's supposed penchant for pseudonyms, indicative of his duplicity. Indeed, the first (1536) edition did appear under Calvin's own name.[112] However, 'Herr Censor' was quick enough to notice the apparently deliberate misspelling of Alcuin as 'Acurinus' in the *Historica Narratio*, and pointed out that Alcuin was in fact the anagram of Calvin.[113] Barckhausen replies sharply that it is a printing error and that, as he says on the same page, other papists had other imaginings (*andere Papisten haben andere Einfaelle*). However, he does not propose to waste any time over this.[114] Obviously, the pseudonym Alcuin adopted by Calvin solely for reasons of personal safety still proved to be a sore point for his disciples.

For Barckhausen, the issue was apparently sensitive enough to make him go to some lengths to pass over in silence the existence of the 1539 edition and to criticise Bayle's chronology. This is what he says:

> Bayle is quite wrong when he writes that the edition of 1539 is the second edition. I own an edition of 1535 and this is the second edition. This seems indeed paradoxical, but it is really so. He who wants to know how this comes

---

[110] Barckhausen, *Historica Narratio*, pp. 16–24, esp. pp. 16–17: 'Ob diese erste Edition vier Buecher und 104 capitel gehabt? Dieses sagt Varillas.'

[111] Barckhausen, *Massonis Vita Caluini*, p. 13: 'Falsum, prima editio continet vnum librum sex capitibus distinctum. Secunda editio Argentorati per Wendelinum Rihelium continet vnum librum et 21 capita.' The latter statement is wrong. The second edition dates from 1539 (also Strasbourg, Wendelin Rihel), and contains seventeen chapters. The third dates from 1543 (Strasbourg, Rihel), and contains twenty-one chapters.

[112] See Barckhausen, *Historica Narratio*, p. 17.

[113] See Barckhausen, *Kurze Beantwortung*, p. 12: 'Pag. 17. lin. Penult. Findet sich ein Versehen, welches gut gwesen, so es unter den Erratis wäre marquiert worden. Man lieset alda. "Acurinus" vor "Alcuinus", welches das Anagramma ist von Calvinus.'

[114] Ibid., p. 13: 'Allein ich will mich hierbey nicht aufhalten.'

about, will not find anything in the editions that Bayle cites. When, however, he looks at a later edition, he will be enlightened straightaway. The learned Herr Censor can try it and see if he can solve this particular conundrum.[115]

Barckhausen is referring to one of the French editions which dates the epistle to François I to 1535, as we have seen. He continues:

> Bayle is wrong when he says that the 1543 edition published by Wendelin Rihel is the most complete. I took the trouble to collate the first chapter *De cognitione Dei* as printed in the 1535 edition with the edition of 1543 that Bayle cites. And in the 1535 edition it contains one whole quire more than in the 1543 Strasbourg edition.[116]

His opponent's reply[117] shows that he was not convinced. After expressing a hope that he would one day be able to obtain the documents that were obviously in Barckhausen's hands, showing that the French edition of the *Institutes* followed the first Latin edition rather than preceding it, he added that he himself found the latter hypothesis more probable for historical reasons: Calvin wanted to evangelise France first and foremost, and he dedicated his edition to the king of France. There was no reason to publish the work in Latin.

As it happens, all the protagonists were wrong. Bayle, as we have seen, was mistaken about the date of the Latin *editio princeps*, thinking it to be 1535. 'Herr Censor' made the error of presuming that the *editio princeps* was in French, and that it came out in 1535. Barckhausen, on the other hand, although correct in identifying the Basel, Latin edition of 1536 as the first, was misled by the dating of the letter to François I into thinking that the French edition he saw was the second. It is not unlikely that what he saw was in fact a fairly late French edition, which would explain the additions he found in relation to the Latin of 1543. By arguing against Bayle, he did manage to obscure the issue of the pseudonymous 1539 edition, which obviously still rankled. Be that as it may, it is clear that none of our historians saw more than one or two editions of the *Institutes*, and that the various historical assumptions and hypotheses which arose in the context of seventeenth- and eighteenth-century confessional debates were to occupy Calvin scholarship until the mid-nineteenth century and beyond. What Calvin wrote and when had become an issue as important as who Calvin was and what he did. It is also at this stage that the

---

[115]   Ibid., p. 19: 'Irret Baile gar sehr, wann er schreibt die Edition de anno 1539 sey die zweyte. Ich habe eine Edition in Quarto von anno 1535, das ist die zweyte edition. Dieses scheint nun zwar ein Paradoxum zu seyn, und ist doch in der Tat also: Wer wissen will, wie dieses zugehe, der wird in allen denen Editionibus, welche Bayle anfuhret nichts finden. Wann er aber eine weit jungere Edition zu Huelffe nimt, so kan er sich leicht helfen. Der gclehrte Hr. Censor kan es probiren, und sehen, ob er disen Knoten aufloesen koenne.'

[116]   Ibid., p. 19.

[117]   *Crantzii Erklaerung*, pp. 19–20.

Institutes emerge as Calvin's key work, overshadowing the rest of his corpus. Beza did not assign them a particularly prominent place in the catalogue of Calvin's treatises that he appended to the 1564 *Discours*, and put biblical commentaries at the head of the list. It was Bolsec who drew public attention to the *Institutes* by insisting on the number of times that Calvin revised the work, this constituting in Bolsec's view a proof of the falsehood of its teaching, as we said. However, it was Masson who first drew attention to the doctrinal importance of the *Institutes*. This view, together with the fact that the *Institutes* were difficult to obtain and that none of Calvin's later biographers could examine a significant number of their editions, meant that the work slowly came to assume a very special place within the Calvin corpus, not just in the eyes of his disciples, but also in the eyes of his religious opponents.

Conclusions

Although the seventeenth century was generally considered as something of a golden era of biography,[118] and although this was also true of France, if we go just by the number of biographical dictionaries produced during that time, when it came to Calvin biographies, time had more or less stopped in the sixteenth century. No new Calvin *Lives* and no biographies of Calvin were produced until the nineteenth century. Efforts made by Desmay or Le Vasseur to discover Calvin material in the Noyon Cathedral Registers represent the sole attempts to discover archival material likely to throw new light on the reformer. The other writers contented themselves with analysing and correcting details in the existing biographical accounts, or, like Richelieu and Drelincourt respectively, with attacking or defending Calvin on the basis of details in existing biographical accounts. Reasons for this were not difficult to see. The Genevan authorities preferred not to encourage any further biographies after the unfortunate experience with Beza's *Life* by De la Faye, partly for religious and partly for diplomatic reasons. It was significant that such reprints or translations of Calvin's and Beza's *Lives* as did appear, appeared in France and were the work of French Protestant authors, such as Teissier, who used them to defend causes very far removed from the original purpose for which these writings were intended. Similarly, the only responses to Richelieu's attack on Calvin emanated from France.

As regards the hostile *Lives* of Calvin, Bolsec's work became something of a household name, and was used even as part of an attempt by Laing to convert James VI of Scotland to Catholicism. As we have seen, it

---

[118]   For England during that period, see Allan Pritchard, *English Biography in the Seventeenth Century: A Critical Survey* (Toronto: Toronto University Press, 2005).

marked the reformer's image for several centuries to come. Masson's *Vita Caluini* was the object of a more discreet reception by both Catholics and Protestants, although both sides were quick to spot its usefulness when it came to correcting historical details of Calvin's life and context. Much more extraordinary was the eighteenth-century recovery of Masson by Protestants such as Barckhausen, who used it against Dippel as proof of the justice of Servetus' execution.

Concluding Remarks

As stated from the outset, this work was not intended as an exhaustive survey of *Lives* written during the Reformation period, but as an analysis of the role and function of selected *Lives* of the more important reformers. We refer the reader to the final paragraph of each chapter for detailed conclusions. The purpose of these general remarks is really to underline the importance of early biographies as religious and historical documents. While historians of the Reformation in the recent past have devoted much fruitful effort to the study and edition of documents such as church ordinances, consistory records, records of synods, correspondence, works of history and historiography, biblical commentaries and sermons, contemporary or near-contemporary biographies of reformers, major or minor, have tended to be neglected. By unearthing at least some of them, I hope to have shown that they do have a considerable amount to teach us, not so much about the reformers' personal lives as about the nature, status and context of the various Reformations. In other words, they constitute an integral part of the intellectual and cultural history of the period, serving as an important source of information about the changes in religious climate, the reputation and image of different reformers, the obstacles they encountered, and their relations with civil authorities.

The *Lives* of Luther examined here show the peculiar nature of Luther's national appeal and his value as symbol of unified Lutheranism. They are to be situated in the context of nascent nationalism. They also corroborate the importance of eschatology and Luther's function as prophet of the last days. Furthermore, they show that his life, and therefore any biographical account of it, was tantamount to his teaching, and that his teaching was his life. As we have seen, to his biographers Luther was directly inspired by the Holy Spirit, which meant that any official document containing his teaching was also thus inspired. Lutheran *Lives* of Luther were not biographies, and the person of the reformer was not essential to their composition. What was essential was his role in the history of salvation and his value as purveyor of the right teaching, which united all the German factions and was divinely inspired. This conception of biography explains why Luther's *Lives* often took the form of sermons or theology lectures. This is also why Luther, as viewed by his biographers, never moved very far away from the medieval ideal of sainthood. Given that Luther's *Lives* were intended for a very wide public, or rather for a variety of publics, they provide a bridge between theological and popular literature, and show how the basic doctrines of the Lutheran Reformation were being sold to students, civil authorities and the 'common man' at various crucial stages. While the public that partisan *Lives* of Luther were meant to reach was national, the public that his hostile biographers had in their sights was international. The biographical accounts of Luther by Cochlaeus, Fontaine, Surius, Taillepied and others distinguished themselves from those of their Lutheran counterparts by their international appeal. Cochlaeus, whose work was a history of the Reformation as well as an extremely negative biography of Luther, served as the basic source for all the later hostile biographers. These accounts did not lay stress on doctrine, but on the reformer's person, without worrying too much about historical accuracy. Of diabolical origin, wicked, lascivious and self-interested, Luther could not but preach wicked doctrines regardless of their nature.

Swiss *Lives* of the reformers in general and Zurich *Lives* in particular stand in sharp contrast with biographical accounts of Luther in many respects; the one point they share is nascent nationalism or patriotism. No one person stands out from what was obviously conceived as collected *Lives* intended to federate the faithful along the model of the Roman Imperial *Lives*, which was transformed to fit the Christian context. From our examination of these texts, we see that while Zwingli was treated as a patriotic saint complete with miracles, and while Bullinger received no fewer than three *Lives* in the year immediately following his death, each of them intended for a slightly different public and each stressing his unique role as head of Reformed Christendom, all the other reformers who had *Lives* devoted to them were treated on the same level. Their *Lives* were meant to take the reader back to the roots of the Zurich Reformation. By their lineage as well as by their convictions, these reformers instantiated a set of values that all faithful should imitate. The *Lives* of men like Stucki, Lavater or Simler provide a lesson in civic responsibilities, family values and solid learning of the sort that befits a good Protestant. They are depicted as good sons of good citizens, and faithful servants of the state. In Zurich biographies of the period, mothers provide models of how to bring up a family in difficult circumstances, sons respect their parents, fathers are solid and decent, and even though some cannot be portrayed as Protestant due to problems of chronology, they are at the very least portrayed as Protestant *avant la lettre*. The Zurich *Lives* provide advice on the perfect style and length of sermons, and on the right educational curriculum, including the advisability and the timing of study abroad. Some, such as Simler's *Life* of Gesner, even act as school manuals. Even though they are not a mirror of Zurich life of the time, they provide a very accurate picture of what it was supposed to be. They provide an excellent source for local historians of Zurich and family history specialists. They tell us much about the role of women. Above all, they show that the glories of the Zurich Reformation were underlined and brought to life via the *Lives* of the main actors. At the same time, these writings were viewed as a means of reforming popular culture. All the *Lives*, as we have seen, were highly stylised, and the implicit rules for writing a biography forbade the inclusion of any details that were likely to compromise the glory of the Reformation. This is shown particularly clearly by Lavater's edition of Pellikan's autobiography, with its careful excision of confessional ambiguities such as the mention of the advisability of wearing a monk's habit when travelling through hostile territory, or the reference to the sexual transgressions of an uncle who was also a priest. It is all the more surprising, therefore, that Zurich *Lives* were never the object of an anthology on the model of Plutarch or Suetonius, despite the fact that antique models were frequently invoked and referred to in the text. Obviously, it was felt that a collection would be too reminiscent of *Lives* of the saints, which is why these texts remained somewhat confidential and did not receive as wide a distribution as other types of edifying literature. Moreover, despite being written for the most part in Latin, they were intended primarily for the local public, which somewhat limited their interest. However, their importance as a tool of propaganda and a testimony to how the Zurich Reformation portrayed itself via its main actors remains unquestionable.

The Genevan Reformation, by contrast, did not have recourse to biography to propagate itself and its image. The situation, as we have seen, was too risky, and the fear of establishing a new form of hagiography was omnipresent. Admittedly, Zurich *Lives* were not free from it, hence their steady and constant insistence on antique models, and their emphasis on civic as well as religious values that the Reformation represented and improved upon. However, Genevan *Lives* of Calvin and Beza were not intended for the local market. The function of the *Lives* of Calvin especially was to convey a particular image of the reformer and his undertaking to the French public, in the hope of converting some, and consoling and edifying those who had converted already. The embarrassment of Beza, Calvin's main biographer, was evident. In fact, the successive editions of his *Life* of Calvin show that, aided by Colladon, he kept trying to find a distinctive voice and identity for Calvinist biography in general and for biography of Calvin in particular. His efforts were to prove only partly successful. While his later *Icones* (1580), composed on the model of Varro, found a wide echo, probably because of their collective status and inclusion of illustrations, his monograph-length *Lives* of Calvin seem to have done more harm than good when it came to conveying an image of the reformer that was both distinct and positive. The hagiographic *Discours* of 1564, which, paradoxically, was to prove the most popular of Beza's three attempts at a biography, was quickly discarded in favour of a chronological *Life* of 1565, embellished by Colladon with intimate anecdotes calculated to make Calvin seem more human. This resulted in accusations of a Calvin cult, which came from both within and without the Protestant camp. Beza could hardly attempt another *Life* straightaway, as this would have only reinforced the accusations. It was not until ten years later that he produced another *Life*, this time in Latin only, which he appended as a preface to a folio-sized volume of Calvin's letters, which guaranteed its being read by the learned only. It was there for the first time that Beza first allowed himself some methodological remarks about what a Calvinist *Life* should and should not be. These reflexions were to be taken up and elaborated by Antoine de la Faye in his *Life* of Beza, which, as we have seen, was censured by the authorities for reasons of decorum on the one hand, and falsification of certain facts deemed crucial for the future of the Genevan Church on the other.

Given the general uncertainty about what a Protestant *Life* of Calvin should be, it was very easy for Bolsec, who was very probably acting under instructions from one or two eminent representatives of the League, to produce an anti-*Life* of Calvin, replying almost word for word to Beza's hagiographic *Discours* of 1564. Its success was out of all proportion to the fairly limited success encountered by the *Discours* itself. Bolsec's *Life* of Calvin was to influence adversely the image of the reformer until well into the twentieth century and beyond. Its impact in France, Germany, Italy and Scotland was unquestionable. It was used, as we have seen, for a wide variety of purposes, including attempts to reconvert James VI of Scotland to Catholicism.

By the 1580s, there were thus two competing *Lives* of Calvin on the market: Beza's *Discours*, with its very strong hagiographic overtones, and Bolsec's *Life*, portraying Calvin as the impostor, the agent provocateur inciting the people to rebellion, the local lecher and the heretic, who spent his entire life writing and rewriting the same mendacious and evil book. Beza's and Colladon's *Lives* of 1565 and 1575 had fallen into oblivion. Against this background, the Catholic disciple of François Bauduin, Jean-Papire Masson, wrote the first-ever objective and historical *Life* of Calvin, which was never to equal Bolsec in popularity, although it influenced considerably the French and German 'Calvinography' of the seventeenth- and eighteenth centuries, as we have seen.

The early *Lives* of Calvin show that the sharply contrasted image that we have to this day of the reformer as either a saint or a cruel, depraved tyrant goes back to the sixteenth century. Despite recent attempts by Bouwsma and Crouzet[1] to get away from it, the image persists to this day

---

[1]   William J. Bouwsma, *John Calvin: A Sixteenth Century Portrait* (New York and Oxford: Oxford University Press, 1988); Denis Crouzet, *Jean Calvin: Vies parallèles* (Paris: Fayard, 2000). For nineteenth- and twentieth-century works defending Calvin, see Doumergue, *Jean Calvin*; R. Stauffer, *L'humanité de Calvin* (Neuchâtel: Delachaux & Niestlé, 1964); A. Perrot, *Le visage humain de Jean Calvin* (Geneva: Labor et Fides, 1986); Bernard Cottret, *Calvin: A Biography* [trans. by M. Wallace-McDonald from the French edition of 1998: *Calvin: une biographie*, Paris: Payot & Rivages] (Grand Rapids: Eerdmans, 1998). Among modern works

and is very likely to be with us for some time to come. Similarly, we could say that the prophetic image of Luther and Lutheranism, and Luther's image as the spokesman of the German nation, takes its origins in the sixteenth century, and is not a modern fabrication.[2] Finally, the *Lives* of the main actors of the Zurich Reformation corroborate the modern views of the specificity of the Reformation in the cities and the delicate balance between the civil and church authorities, which implied close coexistence of civic and civil virtues on the one hand, and reformed piety on the other hand. At the same time, they give a new and detailed insight into the exact nature of the Zurich Reformation's attempt to transform popular culture as to make it conform to the Reformation ideal.[3]

Were the reformers the saints of the Reformation? As we have seen, the question did not arise for the *Lives* of Luther, who had before his death written a preface to the expurgated version of the *Vitaspatrum* in Georg Major's edition. The ideal of sainthood did exist in Wittenberg after the Reformation in a skilfully adapted form. This, however, did not hold for either Zurich or Geneva. After Myconius' portrayal of Zwingli as the saint complete with miracles, efforts were made to avoid this particular trap, which is probably what partly explains the Zurich biographers' constant appeal to civic as well as religious values incarnated by the reformers. Geneva, and more particularly the *Life*-writing of Calvin, proved to be the most open to the accusation of hagiography, not unjustly so if we go by Beza's *Discours* of 1564. In general, however, the very existence of the *Lives* we have examined shows that the rejection of early and medieval *Lives* of the saints had left a gap, which needed filling with other saintly *Lives*, those of the actors of the Reformation. These *Lives* took many shapes and forms, and were as diverse in scope and purpose as the biographical literary *genre* itself. As well as rendering their authors vulnerable to accusations of idol worship, they also had the potential of constituting a threat to Catholicism; otherwise, the need for hostile *Lives* and biographical notices would not have made itself felt to the extent that it did.

---

attacking Calvin, Stefan Zweig's *Castellio gegen Calvin. Ein Gewissen gegen die Gewalt* (Vienna: Reichner, 1936), recently translated into French (*Castellion contre Calvin* [Bègles: Le Castor astral, 1997]), deserves a special mention, although it is not strictly a biography. Other recent or fairly recent anti-Calvin biographies include: Moura and Louvet, *Calvin*; André Favre-Dorsaz, *Calvin et Loyola. Deux Réformes* (Paris: Editions universitaires, 1951).

   [2]   See on this, Bernhard Lohse, *Martin Luther. Eine Einführung in sein Leben und sein Werk* (München: C. H. Beck, 1997), and literature cited ibid. Lohse does not make this point, but takes it for granted that Luther was both a prophet and the force uniting the German nation.

   [3]   The latest work on this is Gordon, *Swiss Reformation*. See also literature cited ibid.

Bibliography

Printed Primary Sources

A famous and godly history contayning the Lyves and Actes of three renowned reformers of the Christian churche, Martin Luther, John Oecolampadius and Huldericke Zwinglius, Newly Englished by Henry Bennet (London, John Awdley, 1561).

Adam, Melchior, *Dignorum laude virorum quos musa vetat mori immortalitas seu Vitae theologorum, iureconsultorum et politicorum, medicorum atque philosophorum, maximam partem Germanorum, nonnullam quoque exterorum*, 3rd edn (Frankfurt, n.p., 1705). [Initially published in Frankfurt as separate volumes between 1611 and 1620.]

Barckhausen, Conrad Heinrich, *Conradi Barckhusen kurze Beantwortung des Critischen Brief-wechsels betreffend Calvini Leben* (Berlin, the widow of Gotthard Schlechtiger, 1727).

_____, *Crantzii a Fluuio Erklaerung an Pythalethen auf Herrn Conradi Henrici Barckhusen's Beantwortung des Critischen Brief-Wechsels betreffend* (Prentzlau, Christian Ragoczy, 1727).

_____, *Historica Narratio de Johanne Calvino. Historische Nachricht von Johanne Calvino. Dessen Eltern, Geburt, Ersten Jugend, Lebens-Art usw. Sampt einer unmbstandlicher Erzehlung von Serveto und dessen greulichen Lehren, aus Serveti eigenen Schriften dargethan. Von Conr. Henr. Barckhusen, Dethmoldia-Lippiaco* (Berlin, Johann Grynaeus, 1721).

_____, *Johannis Papirii Massonis Foresii in senatu Parisiensi et regia aduocati Vita Johannis Caluini quam animaduersionibus historicis illustrauit Conradus Henricus Barckhusen, Dettmoldia-Lippiacus*, ed C. H. Barckhausen (Berlin: Johannes Grynaeus, 1722).

Bauduin, François, *Ad leges de famosis libellis et calumniatoribus commentarius* (Paris, André Wechel, 1562).

Bayle, Pierre, *Dictionnaire historique et critique*, 5th edn, 5 vols (Amsterdam: Pierre Brunel, 1740).

Beza, Theodore, *Correspondance de Théodore de Bèze*, eds Hippolyte Aubert, Alain Dufour, Henri Meylan et al., 29 vols (Geneva: Droz, 1960– [continuing]).

_____, *Discours de M. Théodore de Besze, contenant en bref l'histoire de la vie et mort de Maistre Iean Caluin avec le Testament et derniere volonté dudict Calvin. Et le catalogue des liures par luy compose* (n.p., n.l., 1564).

_____, *Icones id est verae imagines virorum doctrina simul et pietate illustrium, quorum praecipue ministerio partim bonarum litterarum studia sunt restituta, partim vera religio in variis orbis Christiani regionibus nostra patrumque memoria fuit instaurata, additis eorundem vitae et operae descriptionibus, quibus adiectae sunt nonnullae picturae quas Emblemata vocant* (Geneva, Jean de Laon, 1580).

_____, *Les vrais pourtraits des hommes illustres en piete et doctrine, du travail desquels Dieu s'est servi en ces derniers temps pour remettre sus la vraye Religion en divers pays de la Chrestienté. Avec les descriptions de leur vie et de leurs faits plus memorables. Plus quarante quatre emblemes chrestiens* (Geneva, Jean de Laon, 1581).

_____, and Nicolas Colladon, *L'Histoire de la Vie et mort de feu Mr. Iean Calvin, fidele serviteur de Iesus Christ par Theodore de Bèze augmentée de diuerses pièces considerables et sur tout de plusieurs tesmoignages authentiques de ses aduersaires qui seruent à sa justification* (Geneve, Pierre Chouet, 1663).

Bolsec, *see also* Taillepied *below.*

Bolsec, Jérôme, *De Ioannis Caluini magni quondam Geneuensium ministri vita, moribus, rebus gestis ac denique morte. Historia ad reuerendissimum archiepiscopum et comitem Lugdunensem per Hieronymum Bolsecum medicum Lugdunensem conscripta et nunc ex gallico eius Parisiis impresso exemplari Latine reddita.* (Coloniae, apud Ludouicum Alectorium et haeredes Iacobi Soteris, anno 1580).

_____, *Histoire de la vie, mœurs, actes, doctrine, constance et mort de Jean Calvin ..., recueilly par M. Hierosme Hermes Bolsec* (Paris, G. Mallot, 1577). [Another imprint: Lyon, Jean Patrasson, 1577.]

_____, *Histoire de la vie, mœurs, actes, doctrines et deportements de Theodore de Beze, iadis archiministre de Geneue. Aux magnifiques et honorez seigneurs sindicques et assistans du petit et grand conseil de la ville de Geneue, desire, salut, sapience et assistance du S. Esprit, Hierosme Hermes Bolsec, theologien et medecin, leur bon et sincere amy...* (Paris, chez Guillaume Chaudière, 1582).

Breuis narratio exponens quo fine vitam in terris suam clauserit reuerendus vir D. Philippus Melanchthon vna cum praecedentium proxime dierum et totius morbi, quo confectus est breui descriptione. Conscripta a professoribus Academiae Witebergensis qui omnibus quae exponuntur interfuerunt (Wittebergae: n.p., 1560).

Calvin, Jean, *Commentaires de M. Iean Calvin svr le liure de Iosué. Auec une Preface de Theodore de Besze, contenant en brief l'histoire de la vie et mort d'iceluy: augmentee depuis la premiere edition deduite selon l'ordre du temps, quasi d'an en an...* (A Geneve, De l'imprimerie de François Perrin, 1565).

_____, *Ioannis Caluini opera quae supersunt omnia* [*Calv. Opp.*], eds G. Baum, E. Cunitz and E. Reuss, 59 vols (Braunschweig: Schwetschke etc., 1863–1900).

_____, and Theodore Beza, *Ioannis Caluini Epistolae et responsa. Eiusdem I. Caluini Vita a Theodoro Beza Geneuensis ecclesiae ministro accurate descripta... Omnia nunc primum in lucem edita* (Geneva, Pierre Saint-André, 1575).

Camerarius the Elder, Joachim, *De Philippi Melanchthonis ortu, totius vitae curriculo et morte, implicata rerum memorabilium temporis illius hominumque mentione atque indicio cum expositionis serie cohaerentium narratio diligens et accurata Joachimi, Camerarii Pabergensis* (Leipzig, E. Voegelin, 1566).

Capito, Wolfgang, *see also below*: Oecolampadius, Johannes and Zwingli, Ulrich, *Monumentum instaurati patrum memoria...*

Cochlaeus, Johannes, and Philip Melanchthon, *Two contemporary accounts of Martin Luther*, eds, trans. and ann. Elizabeth Vandiver, Ralph Keen and Thomas D. Frazel (Manchester and New York: Manchester University Press, 2002).

Corpus constitutionum Marchicarum, oder Königl. Preussis. und Churfürstl. Brandenburgische in der Chur und Marck Brandenburg, auch incorporirten Landen publicirte und ergangene Ordnungen, Edicta, Mandata, Rescripta &c. Von Zeiten Friedrich Wilhelms ... ad annum 1736 ... colligiert und ans Licht gegeben von Christian Otto Mylius..., ed. C. O. Mylius, 6 vols (Berlin and Halle: n.p., 1737–51).

Correspondance des réformateurs dans les pays de langue française, ed. A. L. Herminjard, 9 vols (Geneva: H. Georg, and Paris: G. Fischbacher, 1866–97).

De la Faye, Antoine, *Brief Discours de la vie et mort de M. Theodore de Beze de Vezelay, personnage très renommé. Pasteur et professeur des sainctes lettres à Geneve. Avec le catalogue des livres qu'il a composez* (Genève, Jean Cartel, 1610).

_____, *De vita et obitu clariss. viri, D. Theodori Bezae Vezelii, Ecclesiastae et Sacrarum literarum Professoris, Genevae, 'hypomnêmation' autore Antonio Fayo* (Geneuae, apud Jacobum Chouet, 1606).

De Raemond, Florimond, *L'Histoire de la naissance, progrez et decadence de l'heresie de ce siecle, diuisee en huict liures* (Rouen, Estienne Vereul, 1622).

Dempster, Thomas, *Thomae Dempsteri Historia ecclesiastica gentis Scotorum, sive, De scriptoribus Scotis*, ed. D. Irving, rev. edn, 2 vols (Edinburgh: Bannatyne Club, 1829).

Desmay, Jacques, *Miracle advenu à Andely la veille de la Pentecoste derniere, le second jour du mois de Juin, mil six cens dix-huict: Par l'intercession de saincte Clotilde Reyne de France, femme de Clovis, premier Roy Chrestien des François* (Rouen, Chez Nicolas Le Prevost, près les Jésuites, [1618]).

_____, *Remarques considérables sur la vie et moeurs de Jean Calvin, hérésiarque. Et ce qui s'est passé de plus mémorable en sa personne depuis le iour de sa naissance ... iusq'au iour de son deceds ... tirées des registres de Noyon par Jacques Desmay*, in L. Cimber [pseudonym of L. Lefaist] and F. Danjou (eds), *Archives curieuses de l'histoire de France, depuis Louis XI jusqu'à Louis XVIII ... publiées d'après les textes conservés à la Bibliothèque Royale et accompagnées de notices et éclaircissements...*, 1st ser., Book 5 (Paris: Beauvais, membre de l'Institut historique, rue Saint-Thomas du Louvre no. 26, 1835), pp. 387–98.

Die Bekenntnisschriften der evangelisch-lutherischen Kirche herausgegeben im Gedenkjahr der Augsburgischen Konfession 1930, ed. Deutscher evangelischer Kirchenausschuss, 10th edn (Göttingen: Vandenhoeck & Ruprecht, 1986).

Dippel, *see* Kleinmann *below*.

Drelincourt, Charles, *La Defense de Calvin contre l'outrage fait a sa mémoire dans vn Liure qui a pour tître 'Traitté qui contient la Methode la plus facile et la plus asseurée pour conuertir ceus qui se sont separez de l'Eglise. Par le Cardinal de Richelieu.' Par Charles Drelincourt* (Geneva, Jean-Antoine and Samuel De Tournes, 1667).

Epiphanii episcopi Cypri De prophetarum vita & interitu commentarius graecus, una cum interpretatione e regione Latina, Albano Torino interprete. Sophronii graece & Hieronymi latine libellus de vita Evangelistarum, cum scholijs Eras. Rot. Parabolae & miracula, quae a singulis Evangelistis narrantur, graecis versibus a Gregorio Nazianzeno conscripta, addita interpretatione latina. D. Hieronymi Scriptorum ecclesiasticorum vitae, per Sophronium e Latina lingua in graecam translatae, & scholijs per Eras. Rot. illustratae. Gennadii illustrium virorum catalogus, ob historiae cognitionem lectu non indignus (Basileae, Andreas Cratander, 1529).

Epître de S. Clément aux Corinthiens, trans. Antoine Teissier (Avignon, 1685).

Fergusson, David, *An answer to one Epistle written by Renat Benedict, the French doctor, professor of Gods worde (as the translator of this Epistle calleth him) to John Knox and the rest of his brethren ministers of the word of God, made by David Fergussone minister of the same word at this present in Dunfermiling* (Edinburgh, n.p., 1563).

Fichard, Johannes, *Virorum qui superiori nostroque seculo eruditione et doctrina illustres atque memorabiles fuerunt Vitae iamprimum in hoc volumen collectae* (Frankfurt, Christian Egenolph, 1536).

Fontaine, Simon, *Histoire catholique de nostre temps, touchant l'estat de la religion chrestienne contre l'histoire de Iean Sleydan composee par S. Fontaine, docteur en Theologie* (Anvers, Iean Steelsius, 1558).

Histoire des vies et faits de quatre excellens personnages... (n.p., n.l., 1564). [The three *Lives* as in entry below, with the addition of Beza's *Discours* on the life of Calvin.]

Histoire des vies et faits de trois excellens personnages, premiers restaurateurs de l'Evangile en ces derniers tems (Geneva, n.p., 1555). [Luther's *Life* by Melanchthon, Zwingli's *Life* by Myconius, Oecolampadius' *Life* by Capito.]

Hubertius, Conradus (ed.), *Historia vera de vita, obitu, sepultura, accusatione haereseos, condemnatione, exhumatione, combustione honorificaque tandem restitutione beatorum atque doctissimorum theologorum D. Martini Buceri et Pauli Fagii quae intra annos XII in Angliae regno accidit. Item Historia Catharinae Vermiliae, D. Petri Martyris Vermilii castissimae atque piissimae coniugis, exhumatae eiusdemque ad honestam sepulturam restitutae* (Argentinae, apud Paulum Machaeropoeum, sumptibus Iohannis Oporini, 1562).

Humfrey, Laurence, *Ioannis Iuelli Angli episcopi Sarisburensis vita et mors, eiusque verae doctrinae defensio cum refutatione quorundam obiectorum, Thomae Hardingi, Nicolae Sanderi, Alani Copi, Hieronymi Osorii Lusitani, Pintaei Burdegalensis, Laurentio Humfredo, S. theologiae apud Oxonienses professore Regio* (Londini, apud Johannem Dayum, 1573).

Kerquifinen, Claude, *Dialogue des deux natures du Christ* (Lyon, à la Salemandre, 1565). [French translation of Vermigli's *Dialogus de vtraque natura*.]

Kessler, Johannes, *Joachimi Vadiani Vita per Joannem Kesslerum conscripta. E codice autographo Historicis Helueticis D. D. D. historicorum et amatorum historiae Sangallensium coetus nonis Septembribus anno 1865* (St Gallen: Zollikofer, 1865).

———, *Sabbata. St. Gallen Reformationschronik 1523–1539*, ed. Traugott Schiess, in *Schriften des Vereins für Reformationsgeschichte*, nos. 103/104 (Leipzig: Rudolf Haupt, 1911), pp. 1–113.

Kleinmann, Ernst Christian, *Ernst Christian Kleinmanns Medicinae Doctoris und Kirchen-Raths, Ausführliche und Freywillige Replic an die Tit: Herren Consistoriales und sämtliches Ministerium der Evangelisch-Reformirten Gemeinde zu Wesel in Sachen Hn. Ernst Christoph Hochmanns de Hochenau. Warhaffte Historie von Johanne Calvino, Wie er mit Michael Serveto und andern verfahren, In einem Gespraeche zwischen Simeon und Obadiah* (Amsterdam: n.p., 1712).

Laing, James, *De vita et moribus atque rebus gestis haereticorum nostri temporis etc. Traductis ex sermone Gallico in Latinum quibus multa addita sunt quae in priori editione quorumdam negligentia omissa fuere, Authore Iacobo Laingaeo Scoto, doctore Sorbonico* (Parisiis apud Michaelem de Roigny, via Iacobea sub signo 4 elementorum, 1581).

_____, *De vita et moribus Theodori Bezae, omnium haereticorum nostri temporis facile principis et aliorum haereticorum breuis recitatio. Cui adiectus est libellus de morte patris Edmundi Campionis et aliorum quorundam catholicorum qui in Anglia pro fide catholica interfecti fuerunt primo die Decembris. Anno domini. 1581. Authore Iacobo Laingaeo doctore Sorbonico* (Parisiis apud Michaelem de Roigny, 1585 cum priuilegio).

_____, *Summarische Historia Vnd Warhafftig Geschicht Von dem Leben, Lehr, Bekantnuss vnd Ableyben Martin Luthers vnd Joann Caluini, auch etlich andrer jhrer Mitgrhülffen vnd Diener dess Newoffenbarten Euangelii, Erstlich auss Frantzösischer Sprach durch Iacobum Laingaeum Scotum, der H. Schrifft Doctorem Sorbonicum zu Paris, ins Latein gebracht: An jetzo aber Zu guthertziger Warnung, vnd notwendiger Erinnerung, was von solchen Lehrern vnd anderen Newen Concordisten zu halten, auch wie sie aus Jhren Früchten zu erkennen seyn, trewlich verteuscht. Mit einer ernstlichen vnd sehr nützlichen Vorred obgemeltes Doctoris Laingaei*, trans. Johann Engerd (Ingolstadt, n.p., 1582).

Lavater, Ludwig, *Nehemias. Liber Nehemiae qui et secundus Ezrae dicitur* (Zürich, Froschouer, 1586).

_____, *Vom leben und tod dess Eerwirdigen unnd Hochgeleerten Herren Heinrychen Bullingers, dieners der Kyrchen ze Zürich* (Zürich, Froschouer, 1576).

_____, *Von Gespänsten / unghüren / fallen / u. anderen wunderbaren dingen / so merteils wenn die menschen sterben söllend / oder wenn sunst gross sachen unnd enderungen vorhanden sind / beschähend / kuirtzer und einfaltiger bericht* (Zürich, Froschouer, 1569).

Le Vasseur, Jacques, *Annales de l'Eglise de Noyon jadis dite de Vermand, ou le troisiesme liure des Antiquitez, Chroniques ou plustost Histoire de la Cathedrale de Noyon. Par M. Iacques le Vasseur, docteur en theologie de la Faculté de Paris, doyen et chanoine deladite Eglise*, 2 vols (Paris: Sara, 1633).

_____, *Le Bocage de Jossigny. Où est compris le Verger des Vierges, & autres plusieurs pièces sainctes, tant en vers qu'en prose. / Antitheses ou Contrepointes du Ciel et de la Terre* (Paris, P. Fleury Bourriquant, 1608).

Les Vies des électeurs de Brandenbourg, trans. Antoine Teissier (Berlin, 1707).

Lettres choisies de Calvin, trans. Antoine Teissier (Berlin, 1702).

Lindanus, Wilhelm, *De fugiendis nostri saeculi idolis nouisque ad vnum omnibus istorum euangelicorum dogmatibus nefariisque irreligiosorum quorundam moribus religiosa piaque ad omnes vbique Christianos piosque inprimis concionatores admonitio. Auctore Wilhelmo Damasi*

Lindano, ecclesiae Ruremundensis episcopo. Cui auctarii loco attexta est popularis Apologia qua ecclesia Christi Catholica defenditur ... (Coloniae, apud Maternum Cholinum, 1580).

————, *Discours en forme de dialogue ou histoire tragique* (Paris, G. Chaudière, 1566).

Masson, Jean-Papire, *Cl. viri Jo. Papirii Massonis, ... Elogiorum pars prima, quae imperatorum, regum, ducum, aliorumque insignium heroüm ... vitam complectitur. Accessit ipsius P. Massonis vita, authore ... Jacobo Augusto Thuano ... Omnia haec ... e musaeo Joan. Balesdens, ... – Cl. viri Jo. Papirii Massonis, ... Elogiorum pars secunda, quae vitam eorum complectitur qui ... dignitatum titulis vel eruditionis laude ... claruerunt. [Accesserunt Simonis Pietrei patris, doctoris medici parisiensis, elogium, auctore G. Patin, et Vita Johannis Calvini, auctore J. Gillot.] Omnia haec ... e musaeo Joan. Balesdens, ...* (Parisiis, apud S. Huré, 1656).

————, *Vita Ioannis Calvini auctore Papirio Massono* (Lutetiae, n.p., 1620).

Mathesius, Johann, *Historien von dem Leben und den Schicksalen des grossen Reformators Doctor Martin Luther im Jahr 1565 in 17 Predigten beschrieben von Johann Mathesius, vormals Pfarrer zu Wittenberg* (Leipzig: bey Salomo Lincke, 1806; reprint of the 1566 edn).

Meier, Georg, *Vitae patrum in vsum ministrorum Verbi quo ad eius fieri potuit repurgatae. Per Georgium Maiorem cum praefatione D. Martini Lutheri* (Wittembergae, apud Seitzium, 1544).

Melanchthon, Philip, *Histoire de la vie et faitz de venerable homme M. Martin Luther, pur et entier Docteur de Theologie, fidèlement redigée par escrit par M. Philippe Melanchthon* (Geneve, chez Iean Girard, 1549).

Migne, J.-P. (ed.), *Patrologiae cursus completus*, 217 vols (Paris: Migne, 1844–55).

Myconius, Oswald, *Vom Leben und Sterben Huldrych Zwinglis. Das älteste Lebensbild Zwinglis*, ed. E. G. Rüsch (St Gallen: Fehr'sche Buchhandlung, 1979).

Oecolampadius, Johannes, and Ulrich Zwingli, *Ioannis Oecolampadii et Huldrichi Zwinglii epistolarum libri IV... Vtriusque vita et obitus, Simone Grynaeo, Wolfgango Capitone et Oswaldo Myconio autoribus* (Basel: Thomas Platter and Balthasar Lasius, 1536).

————, *Monumentum instaurati patrum memoria per Heluetiam regni Christi et renascentis Euangelii, id est Epistolarum d. Iohannis Oecolampadii et Huldrichi Zwinglii aliorumque eximiorum Iesu Christi seruorum libri IIII... Operi autem praefixa est apologia de istorum tων hegoumenων pia doctrina et historia de praeclarae illorum conuersationis praeclaro exitu* (Basilaeae: per Sebastianum Henricpetri, 1592).

Pellikan, Konrad, *Das Chronicon des Konrad Pellikan*, ed. Bernard Riggenbach (Basel: Banheimer, 1877).

_____, and Ludwig Lavater, *In Pentateuchum siue quinque libros Mosis, nempe Genesim, Exodum, Leuiticum, Numeros, Deuteronomium, Conradi Pellikani sacrarum literarum in schola Tigurina Professoris commentarii. His accessit narratio de ortu, vita et obitu eiusdem, opera Ludouici Lauateri Tigurini, iam primum in lucem edita...* (Tiguri: excudebat Christophorus Froschouerus, Anno 1582).

Pietra Sancta, Silvestro di, *Silvestri Petrasanctae... Notae in epistolam Petri Molinaei ad Balzacum, cum responsione ad haereses, errores et calumnias ejus...* (Antwerpiae, ex officina Plantiniana, 1634).

Plutarch, *Selected Lives*, trans. Thomas North, selected and with an introduction by Judith Mossman (Ware: Wordsworth Editions, 1998).

Registres de la Compagnie des Pasteurs de Genève [RCP], ed. R. Kingdon, J. F. Bergier *et al.* (Geneva: Droz, 1962– [continuing]).

Richelieu, Armand Jean du Plessis, *Traitté qui contient la méthode la plus facile et la plus asseurée pour conuertir ceux qui se sont séparés de l'Eglise. Par le Cardinal Richelieu* (Paris, Sebastien et Gabriel Cramoissy, 1651).

_____, *Traitté qui contient la méthode la plus facile et la plus assurée pour convertir ceux qui se sont séparés de l'Eglise. Par le Cardinal Richelieu*, eds Stéphane-Marie Morgain and Françoise Hildesheimer (Paris: H. Champion, 2005).

Rivet, André, *Andreae Riveti Jesuita vapulans. Siue Castigatio notarum S. Petraesanctae in Epistolam Molinaei ad Balzacum* (Antwerpiae, 1634).

_____, *Andreae Riveti Pictavi Catholicus orthodoxus, oppositus Catholico Papistae: In quatuor partes seu tractatus distinctus... Accesserunt huic editioni Jesuita Vapulans Silvestrum Petra Sancta et opuscula adversaria Hugonis Grotii*, new edn (Geneva, Iacobi Chouet, 1644).

Rosweyde, H. (ed.), *Vitae patrum. Historiae eremiticae libri decem* (Antwerp, 1615).

Schultingius, Cornelius, *Bibliothecae catholicae et orthodoxae contra summam totius theologiae Calvinianistae in Instutionibus Ioannis Calvini et Locis communibus Petri Martyris breviter comprehensae, vel potius variarum lectionum et contra I. (II.) librum Institutionum Ioannis Calvini tomus I. (II.)* (Coloniae Agrippinae, n.p., 1602).

Selnecker, Nikolaus, *Historica oratio vom Leben und Wandel des Ehrwirdigen Herrn und thewren Mannes Gottes D. Martini Lutheri. Auch von einhelliger und bestendiger Eintrechtigkeit Herrn Lutheri und Philippi* (Fürth/Bay.: Flacius-Verlag, 1992; reprint of the 1576 edn).

_____, *Nicolai Selnecceri D. Historica narratio et oratio de D. D. Martino Luthero, postremae aetatis Elia et initiis, causis et progressu Confessionis Augustanae atque Lutheri ac Philippi homonoia sancat [sic], Lipsiae publice habita et recitata, mensis novembris die XXII. ante enarrationem eiusdem Confessionis propter Historiam et alias utilitates studiosae Iuuentuti perquam necessaria. Anno salutis abundantis 1574* (Lipsiae, apud haeredes Iacobi Berualdi, 1575).

_____, *Symbolorum, Apostolici, Niceni et Athanasiani Exegesis fideliter repetens doctrinam perpetuam Ecclesiae Dei... scripta et edita Autore Nicolao Selneccero D. electorali professore in Academia Lipsica...* (Lipsiae, Joannes Rhamba, 1575).

Simler, Josiah, *Oratio de vita et obitu viri optimi, praestantissimi theologi D. Petri Martyris Vermilii, Sacrarum litterarum in Schola Tigurina professoris* (Zurich, Froschouer, 1563).

_____, *The Life, Early Letters and Eucharistic Writings of Peter Martyr*, eds J. C. Mclelland and G. Duffield (Sutton Courtenay: Sutton Courtenay Press, 1989). [The volume contains the English sixteenth-century translation by Edward Marten of Simler's *Oratio de vita et obitu ... Vermilii*, first published in 1563.]

_____, *Vita clarissimi philosophi et medici excellentissimi Conradi Gesneri Tigurini conscripta a Josia Simlero Tigurino. Item Epistola Gesneri de libris a se editis. Et carmina complura in obitum eius conscripta. His accessit Caspari Wolphii Tigurini medici et philosophi Hyposchesis, siue de Conr. Gesneri Stirpium historia ad Ioan. Cratonem S. Caes. Maiest. Medicum excellentis. pollicitatio* (Tiguri excudebat Froschouerus, 1566).

_____, and Johann Wilhelm Stucki, *Narratio de ortu, vita et obitu Reuerendi viri, d. Henrici Bullingeri, Tigurinae ecclesiae pastoris, inserta mentione praecipuarum rerum quae in ecclesiis Heluetiae contigerunt et appendice addita qua postrema responsio Iacobi Andreae confutatur auctore Iosia Simlero Tigurino. Item Oratio funebris auctore D. Ioanne Gulielmo Stukio Sacrarum litterarum professore in Schola Tigurina* (Zurich, Froschouer, 1575).

Stucki, Johann Wilhelm, *Vita clarissimi viri D. Iosiae Simleri Tigurini S. Theologiae in Schola Tigurina professoris fidelissimi a Ioanne Gulielmo Stuckio Tigurino descripta. Doctorum item virorum quaedam in eiusdem obitum Carmina* (Tiguri excudebat Frosch. Anno 1577).

Sturm, Kaspar, *Ain kurtze anzaygung und beschreybung Römischer Kaiserlicher Maiestät einreyten // Erstlich von Innspruck gen Schwatz, volgendt zu München, vñ zu letst gen Augspurg auf // den Rychstag, vnd was sich mittler // zeyt daselbst täglich verlauffen // und zugetragen hatt, // Anno 1530* (n.l., n.p.).

Surius, Laurentius, *Commentarius breuis rerum gestarum ab anno salutis 1500 vsque in annum 1567 ex optimis quibusque scriptoribus congestus et nunc recens multis locis non parum auctus et locupletatus per F. Laurentium Surium Carthusianum* (Cologne, Geruinus Calenius et haer. Joh. Quentel, 1567).

Taillepied, Noel, *Histoire de l'Estat et Republique des Druides, Eubages, Sarronides, Bardes, Vacies, Anciens Français, gouuerneurs des païs de la Gaule depuis le deluge universel iusques à la venue de Iesus-Christ en ce monde* (Paris, Jean Parant, 1585).

_____, *Les antiquités et singularités de la ville de Pontoise. Réimpression de l'ouvrage de F. Noël Taillepied, lecteur en théologie des Cordeliers de cette ville. Edition revue et annotée sur les manuscrits des Archives de Pontoise et collationnée sur l'imprimé de 1587 par A. François. Précédée d'une notice biographique et bibliographique sur l'auteur par Henri Le Charpentier* (Pontoise et Paris: H. Champion, 1876).

_____, and Jerôme Bolsec, *Histoire des actes, doctrine et mort de quatre Heretiques de nostre temps a savoir Martin Luther, André Carlostadt, Pierre Martyr et Iean Caluin iadis ministre à Genève. Recueillie par F. Noel Talepied C. [apucin] de Pontoise et M. Hierosme Hermes Bolsec docteur medecin a Lyon. Le tout faict pour aduertir et diuertir les Catholiques de ne se laisser abuser par leurs doctrines mortiferes. Dédié au M. Archeueque, conte de l'Eglise de Lyon et primat de France* (Paris, Iean Parant, [1577]).

_____, *Histoire des vies, meurs, doctrine et mort des trois principaux heretiques de nostre tems à sçavoir Martin Luther, Jean Calvin et Théodore de Bèze jadis archiministre de Geneve. Recueillie par F. Noel Taillepied C. de Pontoise et Hierosme Bolsec...* (Douay, Jean Bogard, 1616).

Teissier, Antoine, *Abrégé de la vie de divers princes illustres avec des refléxions historiques sur leurs actions* (Amsterdam, 1710).

_____, *Catalogus auctorum qui librorum catalogos, indices, bibliothecas, virorum litteratorum elogia, vitas aut orationes funebres scriptis consignarunt* (Geneva, 1686).

_____, *Les Vies de Jean Calvin et de Théodore de Bèze mises en françois* (Geneve, Jean Herman Widerhold, 1681).

_____, *Traité de la concorde ecclésiastique des Protestants dans lequel on fait voir que la différence des sentimens qu'il peut y avoir entre eux ne doit point empêcher leur réunion* (Amsterdam [Geneva], 1687).

Vadian, Joachim, *Orthodoxa et erudita D. I. V., viri clariss., epistola, qua hanc explicat quaestionem, An corpus Christi propter coniunctionem cum verbo inseparabilem, alienas a corpore conditiones sibi sumat, nostro saeculo perquam utilis et necessaria. Accesserunt huic D. Vigilii martyris et episcopi Tridentini libri V pii et elegantes, quos ille ante mille annos contra Eutychen et alios haereticos, parum pie de naturarum Christi proprietate et personae unitate sentientes, conscripsit* (Zürich, Froschouer, 1539).

_____, *Pro veritate carnis triumphantis Christi, quod ea ipsa, quia facta est et manet in gloria, creatura, hoc est nostra caro, esse non desierit ...*

recapitulatio. Ad clarissimum virum D. D. Ioannem Zviccium, urbis Constantiensis ecclesiasten (Zürich, [Froschouer], 1541).

Vermigli, Peter Martyr: *see also* Kerquifinen *above*

Vermigli, Peter Martyr, *Dialogus de vtraque in Christo natura* (Zurich, Chr. Froschouer, 1561).

_____, *Petri Martyris Vermilii Florentini, praestantissimi nostra aetate theologi Loci communes, ex variis ipsius authoris scriptis in vnum librum collecti et in quator Classes distributi* (Londinii, ex typographia Ioannis Kyngstoni, 1576).

_____, *The Common Places of the most famous and renowned Divine Doctor Peter Martyr, diuided into four principall parts, with a large addition of manie theologicall and necessarie discourses, some neuer extant before. Translated and partlie gathered by Anthonie Marten one of the Sewers of hir Maiesties most honourable Chamber* (London, Henry Denham, 1583).

Vie de Galéas Caracciol, mise en françois et Hist. de la mort horrible de François Spierre, trans. Antoine Teissier (Lyon, 1681). [Published under the pen-name of Sieur de Lestan.]

Vitae quatuor Reformatorum. Lutheri a Melanchthone, Melanchthonis a Camerario, Zwinglii a Myconio, Caluini a Theod. Beza conscriptae. Nunc iunctim editae, ed. A. F. Neander (Berlin: G. Eichler, 1841).

Vite dei Santi, ed. Christine Mohrmann, vol. 3: *Vita di Cipriano, Vita di Ambrogio, Vita di Agostino*, ed. A. A. R. Bastiaensen, trans. into Italian by L. Canali and C. Catena (Milan: Mondadori, 1997).

Wolf, Johannes, and Johann Wilhelm Stucki, *In Esdrae librum primum de reditu populi Iudaei e captiuitate Babylonica in patriam et templi... Item de vita et obitu eius narratio scripta a clarissimo viro D. Io. Gulielmio Stuckio sacrae theologiae professore* (Tiguri, Frosch., 1584).

Secondary Sources

Aigrain, René, *Hagiographie, ses sources, ses méthodes, son histoire* (Brussels: Société des Bollandistes, 2000).

Arbenz, Emil, *Joachim Vadians Wirksamkeit von der Schlacht zu Kappel bis zu seinem Tode* (St Gallen: Zollikofer, 1910).

Armogathe, Jean-Robert, 'Les vies de Calvin aux XVIe et XVIIe siècles', in Philippe Joutard (ed.), *Historiographie de la Réforme* (Paris: Delachaux & Niestlé, 1977), pp. 45–59.

Attolini, M., R. S, Cecchini, M. Galli and T. Nanni, 'Solar Activity Variations in Historical Aurorae Records and Tree Radiocarbons', in W. Schroeder (ed.), *Advances in Geosciences* (Bremen: Interdivisional Commission on History of the International Association of Geomagnetism, 1990), pp. 28–35.

Bächtold, Hans Ulrich (ed.), *Schola Tigurina und ihre Gelehrten um 1550* (Zürich & Freiburg/Br.: Pano, 1999).

Backus, Irena, 'Bullinger and Humanism', in E. Campi and P. Opitz (eds), *Heinrich Bullinger. Life–Thought–Influence, Zurich, Aug. 25–29, 2004. International Congress Heinrich Bullinger (1504–1575)*, 2 vols (Zurich: TVZ, 2007), vol. 2, pp. 637–59.

———, 'Connaître le diable. Évolution du savoir relatif au diable d'Augustin à Martin del Rio', in Frédéric Gabriel and Pascale Hummel (ed.), *La mesure du savoir* (Paris: Philologicum, 2007), pp. 33–54.

———, *Historical Method and Confessional Identity in the Era of the Reformation (1378–ca. 1615)* (Leiden: Brill, 2003).

———, 'Le Tertullien de Lambert Daneau dans le contexte religieux du 16ᵉ siècle', in Maria Rosa Cortesi (ed.), *Atti del convegno 'I Padri sotto il torchio', le edizioni dell'antichità cristiana nei secoli 15–16* (Florence: SISMEL, 2002), pp. 33–52.

———, *Reformation Readings of the Apocalypse: Geneva, Zurich and Wittenberg* (Oxford and New York: Oxford University Press, 2000).

———, 'Roman Catholic Lives of Calvin from Bolsec to Richelieu. Why the interest?', in Randall Zachman (ed.), *John Calvin and Roman Catholicism* (forthcoming).

———, 'The Beast. Interpretations of Daniel 7.2–9 and Apocalypse 13.1–4, 11–12 in Lutheran, Zwinglian and Calvinist Circles in the Late Sixteenth Century', *Reformation and Renaissance Review*, 3 (2000): 59–77.

———, 'What prayers for the dead in the Tridentine period? Pseudo-John of Damascus' *De his qui in fide dormierunt* and its "Protestant" translation by Johannes Oecolampadius', *Zwingliana*, 19/2 (1992): 13–24.

———, *et al.* (eds), *Théodore de Bèze (1519–1605). Actes du colloque de Genève (septembre 2005)* (Geneva: Droz, 2007).

Bangerter, Olivier, *La pensée militaire de Zwingli* (Berne: Peter Lang, 2003).

Barnes, Robin, *Prophecy and Gnosis: Apocalypticism in the Wake of the Lutheran Reformation* (Stanford, CA: Stanford University Press, 1988).

Bender, Wilhelm, *Johann Konrad Dippel, der Freigeist aus dem Pietismus: ein Beitrag zur Entstehungsgeschichte der Aufklärung* (Bonn: Weber, 1882).

Boesch, Paul, 'Julius Terentianus, Factotum des Petrus Martyr Vermilius und Korrektor der Offizin Froschauer', *Zwingliana*, 8/10 (1948): 587–601.

Bouwsma, William J., *John Calvin: A Sixteenth Century Portrait* (New York and Oxford: Oxford University Press, 1988).

Brown, H., and H. di Lorena, 'The Assassination of the Guises as described by the Venetian Ambassador', *The English Historical Review*, 10 (1895): 304–32.

Burns, John H., 'Catholicism in Defeat: Ninian Winzet 1519–1592', *History Today*, 16 (1966): 788–95.

Büsser, Fritz, *Heinrich Bullinger: Leben, Werk und Wirkung*, 2 vols (Zurich: Theologischer Verlag, 2003, 2005).

Calinich, H. J. R., *Kampf und Untergang des Melanchthonismus in Kursachsen in den Jahren 1570 bis 1574 und die Schicksale seiner vornehmsten Häupter* (Leipzig: n.p., 1866).

Carbonnier-Burkard, Marianne, 'Une *Histoire d'excellens personnages*', in Ilona Zinguer and Myriam Yardeni (eds), *Les deux Réformes chrétiennes. Propagande et diffusion* (Leiden: Brill, 2004), pp. 43–59.

Chazalon, Christophe, 'Les *Icones* de Théodore de Bèze (1580), entre mémoire et propagande', *Bibliothèque d'Humanisme et Renaissance*, 66/2 (2004): 359–76.

———, 'Théodore de Bèze et les ateliers de Laon', in Irena Backus *et al.* (eds), *Théodore de Bèze (1519–1605). Actes du colloque de Genève (septembre 2005)* (Geneva: Droz, 2007), pp. 69–87.

Cottret, B., *Calvin. A Biography* [trans. by M. Wallace-McDonald from the French edn of 1998: *Calvin: une biographie* (Paris: Payot & Rivages)] (Grand Rapids: Eerdmans, 1998).

Crouzet, Denis, *Jean Calvin. Vies parallèles* (Paris: Fayard, 2000).

Dingel, Irene, *Concordia controuersa. Die öffentlichen Diskussionen um das lutherische Konkordienwerk am Ende des 16. Jhdts.* (Gütersloh: Gütersloher Verlagshaus, 1996).

Döring, Detlef, *Pufendorf-Studien: Beiträge zur Biographie Samuel von Pufendorfs und seine Entwicklung als Historiker und theologischer Schriftsteller* (Berlin: Duncker & Humblot, 1992).

Donaldson, Gordon, *All the Queen's Men: Power and Politics in Mary Stewart's Scotland* (New York: St Martin's Press, 1983).

———, *The Scottish Reformation* (Cambridge: Cambridge University Press, 1960).

Doumergue, E., *Calomnies antiprotestantes*, vol. 1: *Calvin* (Paris: Foi et Vie, 1912).

———, *Jean Calvin. Les hommes et les choses de son temps*, 7 vols (Lausanne-Neuilly: n.p., 1899–1927).

Dubois, Claude-Gilbert, *Celtes et Gaulois au XVIe siècle. Le développement littéraire d'un myth nationaliste. Avec l'édition critique d'un traité inédit de Guillaume Postel 'De ce qui est premier pour réformer le monde'* (Paris: Vrin, 1972).

Dubois, Jacques and Jean-Loup Lemaître, *Sources et méthodes de l'hagiographie médiévale* (Paris: Cerf, 1993).

Duff, J., *Plutarch's Lives: Exploring Virtues and Vice* (Oxford: Clarendon Press, 1999).

Dufour, Alain, 'Théodore de Bèze', in Académie des inscriptions et Belles-Lettres (ed.), *Histoire littéraire de la France, vol. 42* (Paris: De Boccard, 2002), pp. 315–470.

Dufour, Théophile, 'Calviniana', in [no editor], *Mélanges offerts à M. Émile Picot, membre de l'Institut, par ses amis et élèves* (Paris: Librairie Damascène Morgand, 1913), pp. 1–16.

Ebel, Jobst, 'Die Herkunft des Konzeptes der Konkordienformel', *Zeitschrift für Kirchengeschichte*, 91 (1980): 237–82.

Engammare, Max, 'Les horoscopes de Calvin, Mélanchthon et Luther: une forme inattendue de polémique catholique post-tridentine', in Ilona Zinguer and Myriam Yardeni (eds), *Les deux réformes chrétiennes. Propagande et diffusion* (Leiden: Brill, 2004), pp. 172–203.

Erbe, Michael, *François Bauduin (1520–1573). Biographie eines Humanisten* (Gütersloh: Mohn, 1978).

Fatio, Olivier and Louise Martin, 'L'Église de Genève et la Révocation de l'Édit de Nantes', in Société d'Histoire et d'Archéologie de Genève (ed.), *Genève au temps de la Révocation de l'Édit de Nantes 1680–1705 (Mémoires et documents publiés par la Société d'Histoire et d'Archéologie de Genève)* (Geneva: Droz; and Paris: Champion, 1985), vol. 50, pp. 164–91.

Favre-Dorsaz, André, *Calvin et Loyola. Deux Réformes* (Paris: Editions universitaires, 1951).

Ford, Philip J., 'Georges Buchanan et ses paraphrases des Psaumes', in J. C. Margolin (ed.), *Acta Conventus neo-Latini Turonensis*, 2 vols (Paris: Vrin, 1980), vol. 2, pp. 947–57.

_____, *George Buchanan, Prince of Poets* (with *Miscellanaeorum liber*, eds Ford and W. S. Watt) (Aberdeen: Aberdeen University Press, 1982).

La France protestante, eds Eugène Haag and Émile Haag, 10 vols (Paris: Joël Cherbuliez, 1846–59).

La France protestante, eds Eugène Haag and Émile Haag, 2nd edn, rev. by H. Bordier, 6 vols (Paris: Fischbacher, 1877–88).

Gamper, Rudolf (ed.), *Vadian als Geschichtsschreiber* (St Gallen: Sabon-Verlag, 2006).

Gardy, Frédéric, *Bibliographie des œuvres de Théodore de Bèze* (Geneva: Droz, 1960).

Geisendorf, Paul-Frédric, *Théodore de Bèze* (Geneva: Labor et Fides, 1949).

Gordon, Bruce, 'Peter Martyr Vermigli in Scotland. A sixteenth century Reformer in a seventeenth century Quarrel', in E. Campi, Frank A. James III and Peter Opitz (eds), *Peter Martyr Vermigli. Humanism, Republicanism, Reformation* (Geneva: Droz, 2002), pp. 275–94.

_____, *The Swiss Reformation* (Manchester: Manchester University Press, 2002).

Grosse, Christian, *L'excommunication de Philibert Berthelier: histoire d'un conflit d'identité aux premiers temps de la Réforme genevoise (1547–1555)* (Geneva: Société d'histoire et d'archéologie de Genève, 1995).

Halbach, Silke, *Argula von Grumbach als Verfasserin reformatorischer Flugschriften* (Frankfurt/M., Berlin: Peter Lang, 1992).

Hasse, Hans-Peter, 'Die Lutherbiographie von Nikolaus Selnecker. Selneckers Berufung auf die Autorität Luthers im Normenstreit der Konfessionalisierung in Kursachsen', *Archiv für Reformationsgeschichte*, 86 (1995): 91–123.

Hering, Daniel Heinrich, *Beiträge zur Geschichte der evangelisch-reformierten Kirche in den Preuss. Brandenburgischen Ländern*, 2 vols (Breslau: Meyer, 1784–85).

Herte, Adolf, *Das katholische Lutherbild im Bann der Lutherkommentare des Cochläus*, 3 vols (Münster/W.: Aschendorff, 1943).

_____, *Die Lutherkommentare des Johannes Cochläus. Kritische Studie zur Geschichtsschreibung im Zeitalter des Glaubensspaltung* (*Reformationsgeschichtliche Studien und Texte*, vol. 33) (Münster/W.: Aschendorff, 1935).

Hillerbrand, Hans (ed.), *Oxford Encyclopedia of the Reformation*, 6 vols (Oxford and New York: Oxford University Press, 1996).

Höfer, J. and K. Rahner (eds), *Lexikon für Theologie und Kirche*, 2nd edn, 11 vols (Freiburg i. Br: Herder, 1957–67).

Holtrop, Philip, *The Bolsec Controversy on Predestination from 1551 until 1555* (Lewiston, ID, and Lampeter, UK: Edwin Mellen Press, 1993).

Jahnke, G., *Autobiographie als soziale Praxis. Beziehungskonzepte in Selbstzeugnissen des 15. und 16. Jhdt in deutschsprachigem Raum* (Cologne: Böhlau, 2002).

Jostock, Ingeborg, *La censure négociée: le contrôle du livre à Genève, 1560–1620* (Geneva: Droz, 2007).

Kelley, Donald, *Foundations of Modern Scholarship: Language, Law and History in the French Renaissance* (New York: Columbia University Press, 1970).(4.71)

Kingdon, R., *Adultery and Divorce in Calvin's Geneva* (Cambridge, MA: Harvard University Press, 1995).

_____, and P. Donnelly, *Bibliography of the Works of Peter Martyr Vermigli* (Kirksville, MO: The Sixteenth Century Journal Publishers, 1990).

Kirchhofer, Melchior, *Oswald Myconius. Antistes der Baslerischen Kirche* (Zurich: n.p., 1813).

Koch, Ernst, 'Der kursachsische Philippismus und seine Krise in den 1560er und 1570er Jahren', in Heinz Schilling (ed.), *Die reformierte*

Konfessionalisierung in Deutschland – Das Problem der 'zweiten Reformation' (Gütersloh: Gütersloher Verlagshaus, 1986), pp. 60–77.

Kolb, Robert, 'Umgestaltung und theologische Bedeutung des Lutherbildes im späten 16. Jahrhundert', in Hans Christoph Rublack (ed.), *Die lutherische Konfessionalisierung in Deutschland. Wissenschaftliches Symposion des Vereins für Reformationsgeschichte 1988* (Gütersloh: Gütersloher Verlag, 1992), pp. 202–31.

Lake, Peter and Michael Questier, 'Puritans, Papists and the Public Sphere in Early Modern England: The Edmund Campion Affair in Context', *The Journal of Modern History*, 72 (2000): 587–627.

Le Charpentier: *see* Taillepied *in* Primary Printed Sources *above*

Leu, Urs, *Konrad Gesner als Theologe* (Berne: P. Lang, 1990).

Lohse, Bernard, *Martin Luther. Eine Einführung in sein Leben und sein Werk* (München: C. H. Beck, 1997).

Lyon, Gregory B., 'Bauduin, Flacius and the Plan for the Magdeburg Centuries', *Journal of the History of Ideas*, 64 (2003): 253–72.(4.72)

MacDonald, Alan R., *The Jacobean Kirk, 1567–1625: Sovereignty, Polity and Liturgy* (Aldershot: Ashgate, 1998).

McFarlane, I. D., *Buchanan* (London: Duckworth, 1981).

McKee, Jane, 'The Life and Times of a Paris Clergyman: The Correspondence of Charles Drelincourt', *Proceedings of the Third International Huguenot Conference*, in *Bulletin of the Historical Society of South Africa*, 39 (2002): 173–82.

McLean, Ian, *Interpretation and meaning in the Renaissance: The Case of Law* (Oxford: Oxford University Press, 1992).

Matheson, Peter, *Argula von Grumbach: A Woman's Voice in the Reformation* (Edinburgh: T & T Clark, 1995).

Ménager, Daniel, 'Théodore de Bèze, biographe de Calvin', *Bibliothèque d'Humanisme et Renaissance*, 45 (1983): 231–55.

Momigliano, Arnaldo, *The Development of Greek Biography* (Cambridge, MA: Harvard University Press, 1971).

Moura, Jean and Paul Louvet, *Calvin* (Paris: Bernard Grasset, 1931).

Mühling, Andreas, 'Vermigli, Bullinger und das Religionsgespräch von Poissy', in E. Campi, Frank A. James III and Peter Opitz (eds), *Peter Martyr Vermigli. Humanism, Republicanism, Reformation* (Geneva: Droz, 2002), pp. 241–9.

Pelling, C. B. R., 'Biography, Greek and Roman', in Simon Hornblower and Anthony Spawforth (eds), *The Oxford Companion to Classical Civilization* (Oxford and New York: Oxford University Press, 2004), pp. 116–18.

Pérouse, Gabriel, *Les relations de la Savoie avec Genève du 16ᵉ au 18ᵉ siècle* (Belley: Chaduc, 1932).

Perrot, A., *Le visage humain de Jean Calvin* (Geneva: Labor et Fides, 1986).

Peter, Rodolphe and Jean-François Gilmont, *Bibliotheca calviniana*, 3 vols (Geneva: Droz, 1991–2000).

Pfeilschifter, Frank, *Das Calvinbild bei Bolsec und sein Fortwirken im französischen Katholizismus* (Augsburg: FDL, 1983).

Piuz, Anne- Marie, *Affaires et politique: recherches sur le commerce de Genève au 17ᵉ siècle* (Geneva: A. Julien, 1964).

Pressel, T., *Joachim Vadian nach handschriftlichen und gleichzeitigen Quellen* (Elberfeld, n.p., 1861).

Pritchard, Allan, *English Biography in the Seventeenth Century: A Critical Survey* (Toronto: Toronto University Press, 2005).

Ronzy, Pierre, *Bibliographie critique des Œuvres imprimées et manuscrites de Papire Masson*, thèse complémentaire pour le doctorat (Paris: Edouard Champion, 1924).

———, *Un humaniste italianisant: Papire Masson (1544–1611)* (Paris: Édouard Champion, 1924).

Rüetschi, Kurt Jakob, 'Gwalther, Wolf und Simler als Herausgeber von Vermigli-Werken', in Emidio Campi, Frank A. James III and Peter Opitz (eds), *Peter Martyr Vermigli. Humanism, Republicanism, Reformation* (Geneva: Droz, 2002), pp. 251–74.

Schwarte, Wiebke, *Nordlichter. Ihre Darstellung in der Wickiana* (Münster: Waxmann, 1999).

Schweizer, Alexander, *Die protestantischen Centraldogmen in ihrer Entwicklung innerhalb der reformierten Kirche* (Zürich: Orell Füssli, 1856).

Seidel, Robert, 'Melchior Adams Vitæ (1615–1620) und die Tradition frühneuzeitlicher Gelehrtenbiographik', in Gerhard von Kosselek (ed.), *Oberschlesische Dichter und Gelehrte vom Humanismus bis zum Barock* (Bielefeld: Aisthesis, 2000), pp. 179–204.

Spiegel, Gabrielle, *The Chronicle Tradition of Saint-Denis. A Survey* (Brookline, MA, and Leiden: Classical Folia Editions, 1978).

Staehelin, Ernst, *Oekolampad-Bibliographie* (Nieuwkoop: B. De Graaf, 1963; repr. of 1917 edn).

Stauffer, R., *L'humanité de Calvin* (Neuchâtel: Delachaux & Niestlé, 1964).

Stintzing, R. von, art. 'Fichard', in *Allgemeine Deutsche Biographie*, vol. 6 (Leipzig: Duncker & Humblot 1961), pp. 757–9.

Summers, Kirk, 'The Classical Foundations of Beza's Thought' in Irena Backus *et al.* (eds), *Théodore de Bèze (1519–1605). Actes du Colloque de Genève (septembre 2005)* (Geneva: Droz, 2007), pp. 369–81.

Tinsley, Barbara Sher, *History and Polemics in the French Reformation. Florimond de Raemond, defender of the Church* (Selinsgrove: Susquehanna University Press, 1992).

Turchetti, Mario, *Concordia o Toleranza? François Bauduin e i 'Moyenneurs'* (Geneva: Droz, 1984).

Van Veen, Mirjam, *'In excelso honoris gradu.* Johannes Calvin und Jacques de Falais', *Zwingliana*, 32 (2005): 5–22.

Vischer, Manfred, *Bibliographie der Zürcher Druckschriften des 15. und 16. Jahrhunderts erarbeitet in der Zentralbibliothek Zürich* (Baden-Baden: V. Körner, 1991).

Volz, Hans, *Die Lutherpredigten des Johannes Mathesius: Kritische Untersuchungen zur Geschichtsschreibung im Zeitalter der Reformation* (*Quellen und Forschungen zur Reformationsgschichte*, vol. 12) (New York: Johnson Reprint Corporation, 1971; reprint of Leipzig, 1930 edn).

Von Greyerz, K., H. Medick and P. Veit (eds.), *Von der dargestelleten Person zum erinnerten Ich. Europäische Zelbstzeugnisse als historische Quelle (1500–1800)* (Cologne: Böhlau, 2001).

Wallmann, Johannes, *Der Pietismus* (Göttingen: Vandenhoeck & Ruprecht, 2005).

Wengert, Timothy, 'With Friends Like This … The Biography of Philip Melanchthon by Joachim Camerarius', in Thomas F. Mayer and D. R. Woolf (eds), *The Rhetorics of Life-Writing in Early Modern Europe: Forms of Biography from Cassandra Fedele to Louis XIV* (Ann Arbor, MI: University of Michigan Press, 1995), pp. 115–31.

Wolgast, Eike, 'Biographie als Autoritätsstiftung: Die ersten evangelischen Lutherbiographien', in Walter Berschin (ed.), *Biographie zwischen Renaissance und Barock* (Heidelberg: Mattes Verlag, 1993), pp. 41–72.

Zürcher, Christoph, *Konrad Pellikans Wirken in Zürich, 1526–1556* (Zürich: P. Laing, 1975).

Zweig Stefan, *Castellio gegen Calvin. Ein Gewissen gegen die Gewalt* (Vienna: Reichner, 1936).

_____, *Castellion contre Calvin* (Bègles: Le Castor astral, 1997).

Index

Dupréau, Gabriel, xxi, 28, 154, 209
Dupuys, M. de, 215

Ebion, 158
Eck, Johannes, 121 n.
Egenolph, Christian, xxv
Elizabeth I, 36, 168, 212 n.
Engerd, Johannes, 33–4
Epiphanius, xv, 28, 102
Erasmus, xvi, 6, 10, 47, 55, 63, 69, 117
Erasmus of Limburg, xxiv n.
Espinac, Pierre d', 27–8, 155 n., 157,
    162 f.

Fabri, Johann, 121 n.
Fagius, Paul, xxi, xxv, xxix–xxxiii, 3,
    135, 136
Falais, Jacques de, 161, 171
Farel, Guillaume, 88 f., 206, 220
Fauvel, Antoine, 190 f.
Fergusson, David, 41, 72–8
Ferdinand I of Bohemia, 21 f.
Fichard, Johannes, xxiv–xxix
Fisher, John, 42
Flavius Josephus, 138
Fontaine, Simon, 16, 23–5, 30–34, 46,
    230
François I, 222, 223 n., 225
Frederick William I of Prussia, 218
Frideswide, St., 70
Friedrich III, 172
Froschouer, Christoph, 121 f.

Gaius Fannius, x
Gallus, Jodocus, 118 ff.
Gansfort, Wessel, xxvi ff.
Geiler of Kaisersberg, Johann, 9
Gennep, Kaspar von, 16
Georg of Saxony, 22
Gerson, Jean, 55
Gesner, Conrad, xxiv n, 80, 97–101,
    106, 109, 123 f., 125, 230
Gibier, Éloi, 126 ff.
Gillot, Jacques, vii n., 176, 214, 215
Girard, Jean, 7 n.
Glareanus, Henricus, 48
Goulart, Simon, xviii n.
Gourlay, Philippe de, 188
Grebel, Conrad, 58

Grebel, Martha, 58, 61
Gregory the Great, 28,
Gregory of Nazianzus, xii, 67
Gregory of Tours, xvi
Grotius, Hugo, 218–19
Grumbach, Argula von, 41–2
Grynaeus, Simon, xx n, 47, 52–7, 106,
    134 n., 182
Gualterius, J., 220
Gwalther, Rudolf, the Elder, xxiv n, 66 f.
Gwalther, Rudolf, the Younger, xxiv n.

Haller, Berthold, 87 n.
Haller, Berthold, 87n.
Havart, Jean, 190
Heerbrand, Jacob, xxiv n.
Hegner, Regula, 110
Heidenreich, Isaiah, 14
Hengest, Charles de, 189 n.
Hengest, Claude de, 192, 197 n.
Henry II of France, 89, 185
Henry III of France, 155 n, 157
Henry IV of France, 152 f.
Henry VIII, 41
Henry I, duke of Guise, 169
Hesiod, 50
Hesshusen, Tillemann, 130
Heusler, Paul, 13–20
Hibernicus, Mauritius, 57
Hildouin, 26
Homer, viii, 50
Honoratus, xiv
Hosius, Stanislaw, 29
Hotman, François, 173
Hubert, Conrad, xxix n, xxxi
Huebert, Christoph, 34
Humfrey, Lawrence, 115 n.
Hurault de Cheverny, Philippe, 173, 174
Huré, Sebastian, 175, 215
Hutten, Ulrich von, 63
Hyginus, x

Iacobus Papiensis, cardinal, xxvi ff.
Illyricus, Flacius, 42, 89, 90
Ion of Chios, ix
Isocrates, ix

James V of Scotland, 37, 167–8

'Practical Divinity': The Works and Life of Revd Richard Greenham
Kenneth L. Parker and Eric J. Carlson

Belief and Practice in Reformation England: A
Tribute to Patrick Collinson by his Students
Edited by Susan Wabuda and Caroline Litzenberger

Frontiers of the Reformation: Dissidence and
Orthodoxy in Sixteenth-Century Europe
Auke Jelsma

The Jacobean Kirk, 1567–1625: Sovereignty, Polity and Liturgy
Alan R. MacDonald

John Knox and the British Reformations
Edited by Roger A. Mason

The Education of a Christian Society: Humanism and
the Reformation in Britain and the Netherlands
Edited by N. Scott Amos, Andrew Pettegree and Henk van Nierop

Tudor Histories of the English Reformations, 1530–83
Thomas Betteridge

Poor Relief and Protestantism: The Evolution of
Social Welfare in Sixteenth-Century Emden
Timothy G. Fehler

Radical Reformation Studies:
Essays presented to James M. Stayer
Edited by Werner O. Packull and Geoffrey L. Dipple

Clerical Marriage and the English Reformation:
Precedent Policy and Practice
Helen L. Parish

Penitence in the Age of Reformations
Edited by Katharine Jackson Lualdi and Anne T. Thayer

The Faith and Fortunes of France's Huguenots, 1600–85
Philip Benedict

Christianity and Community in the West:Essays for John Bossy
Edited by Simon Ditchfield

Penitence, Preaching and the Coming of the Reformation
Anne T. Thayer

Huguenot Heartland:
Montauban and Southern French Calvinism
during the French Wars of Religion
Philip Conner

Charity and Lay Piety in Reformation London, 1500–1620
Claire S. Schen

The British Union: A Critical Edition and Translation of
David Hume of Godscroft's De Unione Insulae Britannicae
Edited by Paul J. McGinnis and Arthur H. Williamson

Reforming the Scottish Church:
John Winram (c. 1492–1582) and the Example of Fife
Linda J. Dunbar

Cultures of Communication from Reformation to Enlightenment:
Constructing Publics in the Early Modern German Lands
James Van Horn Melton

Sebastian Castellio, 1515-1563:
Humanist and Defender of Religious Toleration in a Confessional Age
Hans R. Guggisberg translated and edited by Bruce Gordon

The Front-Runner of the Catholic Reformation:
The Life and Works of Johann von Staupitz
Franz Posset

The Correspondence of Reginald Pole:
Volume 2. A Calendar, 1547–1554: A Power in Rome
Thomas F. Mayer

William of Orange and the Revolt of the Netherlands, 1572–1584
K.W. Swart, translated J.C. Grayson

The Italian Reformers and the Zurich Church, c.1540–1620
Mark Taplin

William Cecil and Episcopacy, 1559–1577
Brett Usher

The Correspondence of Reginald Pole
Volume 4 A Biographical Companion: The British Isles
Thomas F. Mayer and Courtney B. Walters